STUDY GUIDE TO ACCOMPANY SCHILLER

THE MACRO ECONOMY TODAY

STUDY GUIDE TO ACCOMPANY SCHILLER

THE MACRO ECONOMY TODAY

SIXTH EDITION

PREPARED BY

Michael M. Tansey

ROCKHURST COLLEGE

AND

Lawrence F. Ziegler

UNIVERSITY OF TEXAS

AT ARLINGTON

McGRAW-HILL, INC.

NEW YORK   ST. LOUIS   SAN FRANCISCO   AUCKLAND   BOGOTÁ   CARACAS

LISBON   LONDON   MADRID   MEXICO CITY   MILAN   MONTREAL   NEW DELHI

SAN JUAN   SINGAPORE   SYDNEY   TOKYO   TORONTO

STUDY GUIDE TO ACCOMPANY SCHILLER: THE MACROECONOMY TODAY

2 3 4 5 6 7 8 9 0 MAL MAL 9 0 9 8 7 6 5 4

ISBN 0–07–056304–7

The editors were James A. Bittker and Elaine Rosenberg;
the production supervisor was Richard A. Ausburn.
The cover designer was Hermann Strohbach

Contents

To the Instructor

This *Study Guide* is an important part of the complete and fully integrated textbook package called *The Economy Today*. Students who use this *Study Guide* on a continuous basis should be able to remember what they have read in their textbook and heard in your lecture. It should enable them to apply to examinations the principles they learn and, more importantly, should help them recognize the same principles at work in their daily experiences. Each section of each chapter has a particular objective, which is described in the following paragraphs.

The *Quick Review* and *Learning Objectives* sections provide summaries of the basic contents of the corresponding text chapters and outline the important areas of the *Study Guide*. Each learning objective is keyed to specific pages in the text and to specific questions and problems that follow. Look at page 2 for examples.

Economic terminology is often an obstacle to new students in economics. Thus the *Key-Term Review* and *Crossword Puzzle* sections of the *Study Guide* provide practice in the use of terminology. Both sections help the students to link economic terms to the appropriate economic concepts. The *Study Guide* reinforces the terminology by repetition. However, we have taken pains not to make the repetition burdensome. The crossword puzzles we have introduced in some of the chapters, for example, help to make the repetition fun.

The *True or False* and *Multiple Choice* sections help students advance from memorizing terminology to applying economic principles in a familiar problem-solving setting. This will help greatly in their preparation for exams.

The *Problems and Applications* sections let the students discover economic principles for themselves. Students not only learn the techniques that economists use, but they also discover the basis for the economic principles they have learned. In each chapter, a media application shows the students how to recognize the economic principles of the chapter in an In the News or World View media article from the text. If an instructor uses a media exercise from the Instructors' Manual for homework, the students can refer to one of the last applications in this *Problems and Applications* section to see how to do it. The final problem and application for many of the chapters is a data exercise in which students find data (usually from the front cover of the book), graph them, and make generalizations based on the data.

The section called *Common Errors* was introduced in the first edition of this book in 1980, and at that time it was unique to this *Study Guide*. Since then a number of competing books have begun including similar sections, a strong indicator of its usefulness to students and its popularity with instructors. It is our feeling that, semester after semester, students have difficulty with the same concepts and make the same mistakes; hence the name *Common Errors*. We've tried to draw attention to some of these problem areas and provide explanations using the appropriate economic principles. You may wish to add to those we have provided.

Another unique feature of this *Study Guide* is what we call the "media exercise." The media exercises are contained in the *Problems and Applications* section of each chapter. Each one directs the students to reread a certain newspaper, magazine, or other media article from among those interspersed throughout the text. The students then answer a series of questions based on the article, using the economic principles they have learned in the chapter. The media exercises should help the students see economic principles at work in the world around them, and make them aware of how to get the "economics" out of a critical reading of the "news" long after they leave the economics classroom.

To the Student

This *Study Guide* is designed to be used with *The Macro Economy Today*, Sixth Edition, by Bradley R. Schiller. Working through the *Study Guide* should reinforce what you have learned in the textbook and help you to recognize economic principles in your daily experiences.

Note the following points in the various sections of each of the chapters:

- The *Quick Review* provides a brief summary of the concepts in the corresponding text chapter. If you are not comfortable with the terminology and concepts in this review, you should reread the appropriate sections of the text chapter.

- The *Learning Objectives* focus on the basic information in each text chapter and provide outlines for material to be covered in the *Study Guide*. The learning objectives are keyed to questions and problems that follow and to pages in the text. If you have difficulty with a particular idea, you can quickly find the text material and review it.

- The *Key-Term Review* and *Crossword Puzzles* give you practice in the use of terminology in the specific chapters. As a learning aid, you are encouraged to write out the definitions of the key economic terms.

- The *True or False* and *Multiple Choice* questions test your understanding of the basic economic principles discussed in the text chapter.

- The *Problems and Applications* section contains one or more real-world problems, which allow you to work out in a practical way the economic principles that you have been studying.

- Nearly all chapters contain a "media exercise" that refers you to specific newspaper, magazine, or other articles reprinted in the text. These exercises will assist you in developing your critical thinking skills.

- The *Common Errors* section identifies some of the errors that students often make and explains the correct principles. This is a very effective way to help you discover and correct your mistakes.

- *Answers* to *all* problems, exercises, and questions are provided at the end of each chapter of the *Study Guide*, so you can quickly check your answers and go back and review where necessary.

Aknowledgments

This is the sixth edition of the *Study Guide to Accompany the Economy Today*, and over the years, we have accumulated debts to many individuals for their help. We continue to thank the students who endured our testing of the first edition exercises. Their patience, creativity, and critical thinking prompted many of the improvements from which current students still benefit. Some even contributed their own crossword puzzles. They include Sidi Habi, Patricia Eason, Margaret Gatchell, Louise Oller, and Robin Burdette. Richard Bayer originated two excellent exercises in the macroeconomics section. These contributions have all been retained in every edition.

Bryce Jones, professor emeritus of economics, and Robert Clark, Dean of the School of Management at Rockhurst College, provided commentary and support, respectively, for the *Study Guide*, and we are grateful to them both. Raphael Arinaitwe was invaluable in organizing, preparing, and criticizing the material for this edition.

We acknowledge the support of the McGraw-Hill staff. They are terrific. We especially thank Jim Bittker, economics editor, for being responsive to our requests and for the calm and friendly manner in which he dispatched his responsibilities. Elaine Rosenberg, editing supervisor, is a real professional. We thank her for her no-nonsense approach and for her skillful management of a difficult project. Our thanks go also to Alice Jaggard who provided superb copy editing.

Finally, we remember the late Mary Griffin, who was the project editor for the first edition. She was a relentless taskmaster who set high standards for two first-time authors. The typists for the first three editions—Nancy Bloodgood Sproba, Mildred Simms, and Cyndy Carver—were superb in the days before word processing made the task much easier. Mehrdad Setayesh, Linda Wilson, and Chandra Kalyanaraman provided assistance of a superior quality on a timely basis. Their efforts added greatly to the quality of the final product. Brett Stilwell helped with computer work and word processing on this edition. We thank Joshua Howard and Emmanuel Reyes of the Collegiate Communications Group, who provided superior production and artistic talents to this camera ready manuscript.

We continue to value the friendship of Paul Shensa, who got us started with Random House over fifteen years ago.

Michael M. Tansey
Lawrence F. Ziegler

CHAPTER 1

An Overview

Quick Review

Over 200 years ago, Adam Smith laid the foundations for the theory of market-based economies. As an alternative, Karl Marx later developed the rationale for centrally planned economies. The twentieth century has pitted these two concepts against each other. The fall of communist states and the adoption of market-based strategies in the nineties seems to have weighed in favor of capitalism.

The collapse of communism in the Soviet Union and Eastern Europe focused great attention on economics, the science concerned with how societies allocate their scarce resources to competing uses. The emerging consensus indicated that the market mechanism relied on in the United States and elsewhere is vastly superior to the central-planning mechanism which characterized the communist world. This result leads us to focus on two central questions?

- What forces determine economic outcomes?
- What can we do to improve economic outcomes?

To begin the study of economics, we note that the U.S. economy produces an output of over $6 trillion per year. In the process it must allocate its land, labor, capital, and entrepreneurship to competing uses. Resources are considered scarce, even when they seem abundant, because there are not enough of them to satisfy all of society's wants. Thus, every society confronts the problem of scarcity and must somehow answer these basic questions:

- WHAT is to be produced?
- HOW should it be produced?
- FOR WHOM should the output be produced?

Because of the imbalance between society's wants and resources, choosing to produce one thing means choosing not to produce something else. Economists illustrate these choices by drawing a production-possibilities curve. This curve shows the combinations of goods and services a society could produce if it were operating efficiently and all of its resources were fully employed. The production-possibilities curve appears bowed out from the origin because of the law of increasing opportunity costs. To the economist, cost is measured by the best alternative opportunity forgone when choosing a course of action.

In the United States, our choices are determined by the market mechanism. Through the "invisible hand" of the market mechanism the production and consumption decisions of individuals directly affect the allocation of resources. Changes in relative prices (called price signals) are what make the system go. The individual decisions of households and firms are supplemented with generous doses of public-sector activity. When the market mechanism fails to provide goods and services efficiently and equitably -- a situation called "market failure" -- the public sector must provide assistance. For example, market systems do not automatically generate pollution-control mechanisms which assure us of clean air and water. Such market imperfections must be overcome by government activity. In some economies the market mechanism has not been allowed to work. Planned (or command) economies, like that of the old Soviet Union, are good examples of this. But even in mixed economies "government failure" can make things worse.

In the study of the economy, it is useful to break economics into two categories: microeconomics and macroeconomics. Microeconomics focuses on a specific individual, firm, industry, or government agency; macroeconomics focuses on the entire economy. It should be noted that economics is not a settled body of doctrine. There is much controversy over how the economy works. That is what makes it so interesting.

Learning Objectives

After reading Chapter 1 and doing the following exercises, you should:	True or false	Multiple choice	Problems and applications	Common errors	Pages in the text
1. Understand that economics is the study of how to allocate society's scarce resources – land, labor, capital, and entrepreneurship.	1	1-3, 4, 6, 19		1	1-6
2. Know that scarcity results because resources are not sufficient to satisfy all of society's wants.	3, 4	4, 5, 7		4	6-10
3. Be able to define and illustrate opportunity costs using a production-possibilities curve.	2, 5	5, 7-10, 14	1, 2	4	10-12
4. Understand the law of increasing opportunity costs.	12, 17	14-16	1		12-13
5. Be able to demonstrate efficiency, growth, unemployment, and underemployment using a production-possibilities curve.	12-15, 21	11, 12	1		13-15
6. Know why every economy must answer the same basic questions – WHAT, HOW, FOR WHOM.	10	13			15-16
7. Be able to distinguish macroeconomic issues from microeconomic issues.	16	17, 18, 23			19-20
8. Be able to describe how the market mechanism seeks to allocate society's resources to their highest valued uses.	7-10	6			16-18
9. Be aware that there is much serious debate and controversy over how the economy works.	11-16			1-3	20-21
10. Be able to discuss the tradeoffs inherent in the "peace dividend."			2, 3		21-24
11. Understand the role of venture capitalists.		22, 24, 25			7, 14
12. Be able to describe the mixed economy and distinguish market failure from government failure.	6, 19, 20	20-22			17-18

Key-Term Review

Review the following terms; if you are not sure of the meaning of any term, write out the definition and check it against the Glossary in the text.

capital
ceteris paribus
economic growth
economics
efficiency
entrepreneurship
factors of production
government failure
laissez faire

macroeconomics
market failure
market mechanism
microeconomics
mixed economy
opportunity cost
production-possibilities
scarcity

Fill in the blank following each of the statements below with the appropriate term from the list above.

1. A Latin phrase meaning "all other things being equal" is _____ .

   1. _____

2. The branch of economics that focuses on the activities of individual decision-making units is _____ .

   2. _____

3. When economists say that to have more schools we must give up houses, they are illustrating the principle of _____ .

   3. _____

4. When market prices signal what goods and services should be produced, the allocation of resources is being accomplished by the _____ .

   4. _____

5. Those things that are transformed into final goods and services desired by society are _____ .

   5. _____

6. The branch of economics that focuses on the behavior of the entire economy is _____ .

   6. _____

7. A curve showing the various combinations of goods and services that a society can produce with its scarce resources is a _____ curve.

   7. _____

8. _____ is a factor of production that is produced using society's scarce resources.

   8. _____

9. Opportunity costs arise in every society because of the problem of _____ .

   9. _____

10. The science that studies how societies allocate scarce resources is _____ .

    10. _____

11. Some resource allocation in the United States is done through the public sector, indicating that we have a _____ .

11. _____

12. Where there is an increase in real output, there is _____ .

12. _____

13. Society's pollution problem is an example of _____ .

13. _____

14. Public-sector intervention that fails to improve economic outcomes is an example of _____ .

14. _____

15. The factor of production that is most concerned with risk taking is called _____ .

15. _____

16. For Adam Smith's *invisible hand* to work most effectively requires a _____ attitude on the part of society.

16. _____

17. "Getting the most from what you've got" represents the idea of _____ .

17. _____

True or False: *Circle your choice.*

T   F   1.   Karl Marx developed the economic rationale for market-driven economies in *Das Kapital*.

T   F   2.   Students do not pay tuition in elementary school, so in this case education is a free good from society's point of view.

T   F   3.   Goods are scarce because society's desire for them exceeds society's ability to produce them.

T   F   4.   If a commodity has a market price that is greater than zero, it must be scarce.

T   F   5.   A production-possibilities curve can be drawn only if a scarce resource prevents production of as much as we want of a commodity.

T   F   6.   The market-directed or price-directed economy is capable of solving the problems created by pollution without intervention by government.

T   F   7.   The U.S. economy is referred to as a mixed economy because a large fraction of our resources are allocated by the public sector (government).

T   F   8.   When a factory pollutes the air we breathe, this situation is known in economics as market failure.

T   F   9.   In the U.S. market system, the government gives the signals for deciding how to use resources.

T   F   10.   Prices signal the answer to the WHAT, HOW, and FOR WHOM decisions in a laissez faire economy.

4

T F 11. The task of economic theory is to explain and predict the economic behavior of economic resources.

T F 12. One reason that the production-possibilities curve is bowed out is that more production means the economy is less efficient in producing output.

T F 13. If the economy is fully and efficiently employing its resources, then the only way to acquire more of one good is to accept less of something else.

T F 14. If the economy is inside the production-possibilities curve, then more can be produced from the same amount of resources.

T F 15. Technological advance shifts the production-possibilities curve inward.

T F 16. When the economy experiences reduced resource availability, then the production-possibilities curve shifts inward.

T F 17. Microeconomics focuses on the economy as a whole.

T F 18. The opportunity cost of a good can be measured as the absolute value of the slope of a production-possibilities curve for the good.

T F 19. Pollution is a government failure, not a market failure.

T F 20. Pollution is an example of a market failure.

T F 21. An inequitable distribution of income can result from either market failure or government failure.

T F 22. The economy achieves the greatest efficiency when it is inside the production possibilities curve.

Multiple Choice: *Select the correct answer.*

_____ 1. Adam Smith wrote:
   (a) *The Wealth of Nations*, which provided the rationale for centrally planned economies.
   (b) *The Wealth of Nations*, which described the virtues of market-based economies.
   (c) *Das Kapital*, which provided the rationale for centrally planned economies.
   (d) *Das Kapital*, which described the virtues of market-based economies.

_____ 2. Which of the following best describes the subject matter included in principles of economics?
   (a) How the economy allocates its scarce resources.
   (b) How households make decisions.
   (c) How governments make choices about resources.
   (d) How society purchases resources.

3. Which of the following best describes the term "resource allocation"?
   (a) Which goods and services society will produce with available factors of production.
   (b) How society spends the income of individuals based on resource availability.
   (c) How society purchases resources, given its macroeconomic goals.
   (d) How individual market participants decide what to produce given fixed resource constraints.

4. The best description of the focus of economic studies is:
   (a) For whom resources are allocated to increase efficiency.
   (b) How society spends the income of individuals.
   (c) How resources are allocated to fulfill society's goals.
   (d) What resources are used to produce goods and services.

5. In economics, what does scarcity mean?
   (a) When there is a shortage of a particular good, the price will fall.
   (b) A production-possibilities curve cannot accurately represent the tradeoff between two goods.
   (c) Society's desires exceed the want-satisfying capability of the resources available to satisfy those desires.
   (d) None of the above.

6. Which of the following *best* describes the most important way that resources are allocated in the U.S. economy?
   (a) By tradition.
   (b) By command.
   (c) By markets.
   (d) By government.

7. Which of the following are considered scarce in the U.S. economy?
   (a) Hamburgers.
   (b) Automobiles.
   (c) Petroleum products.
   (d) All of the above.

8. I plan on going to a $5 movie this evening instead of studying for an exam. The total opportunity cost of the movie:
   (a) Depends on how I score on the exam.
   (b) Is $5.
   (c) Is what I could have purchased with the $5 plus the study time I forgo.
   (d) Is the forgone studying I could have done in the same time.

9. The opportunity cost of installing a traffic light at a dangerous intersection is:
   (a) Negative, since it will reduce accidents.
   (b) The cost of the stoplight plus the cost savings from a reduction in the number of accidents.
   (c) The time lost by drivers who approach the intersection when the light is red.
   (d) The best possible alternative bundle of other goods or services that must be forgone in order to build and install the traffic light.

10. The frequently used phrase "time is money" is a way of stating:
    (a) The idea of opportunity cost.
    (b) Everyone has a price.
    (c) People work for free.
    (d) Money is an economic goal.

_____ 11. Which of the following events would cause the production-possibilities curve to shift *inward?*
(a) The labor supply grows.
(b) New factories are built.
(c) A technological breakthrough occurs.
(d) None of the above.

_____ 12. Which of the following events would cause the production-possibilities curve to shift *outward?*
(a) The economy grows.
(b) A new, strong plastic is developed for use in building houses.
(c) More women enter the labor force.
(d) All of the above.

_____ 13. The market mechanism in the United States generates a distribution of income that is viewed as:
(a) Equal, since everyone gets the same income.
(b) Equitable, since public policy does not tamper with it.
(c) Both equal and equitable, since they mean the same thing.
(d) Inequitable, apparently, since we change it through the activities of the public sector.

_____ 14. The *slope* of the production-possibilities curve provides information about:
(a) The growth of the economy.
(b) Technological change in the economy.
(c) Opportunity costs in the economy.
(d) All of the above.

_____ 15. The bowed-out shape of the production-possibilities curve indicates:
(a) Increasing opportunity costs.
(b) Pollution.
(c) Market imperfections.
(d) A mixed economy.

_____ 16. The law of increasing opportunity cost explains:
(a) How everything becomes more expensive as the economy grows.
(b) The shape of the production-possibilities curve.
(c) Inflation.
(d) All of the above.

_____ 17. Which of the following are major macroeconomic goals of the economy?
(a) Full employment.
(b) Control of inflation.
(c) An equitable distribution of income.
(d) All of the above.

_____ 18. Macroeconomics focuses on the performance of:
(a) Individual consumers.
(b) Firms.
(c) Government agencies.
(d) None of the above.

_____ 19. The most likely source of the failure of communism in the Soviet Union was the problem of:
  (a)   Inadequate land, labor, and capital.
  (b)   Centralization of decision making.
  (c)   Devastation from World War II.
  (d)   The focus on too few social goals.

_____ 20. The collapse of communism is evidence of:
  (a)   Government failure.
  (b)   Market failure.
  (c)   The failure of a mixed economy.
  (d)   *Ceteris paribus.*

_____ 21. Which of the following is a government failure?
  (a)   Bureaucratic delays.
  (b)   Shortages.
  (c)   Inefficient incentives.
  (d)   All of the above.

_____ 22. Which of the factors of production are centrally planned, command economies most likely to underestimate or ignore?
  (a)   Capital.
  (b)   Labor.
  (c)   Land.
  (d)   Entrepreneurship.

_____ 23. Which of the following groupings contains a term which does not belong?
  (a)   Unemployment, unfair income distribution, pollution.
  (b)   Public laws (regulation), taxes, centralized government planning.
  (c)   Macroeconomics, microeconomics, mixed economies.
  (d)   Bureaucratic delays, shortages, inefficient incentives.

_____ 24. Reread the World View article "Free Enterprise Blooms in Wenzhou,China, Out of the Party's Sight." The article best illustrates:
  (a)   The success of Karl Marx's view of market-based economies.
  (b)   Market failure.
  (c)   The concepts described in *The Wealth of Nations*.
  (d)   None of the above.

_____ 25. Reread the In the News article "The Peace Dividend." Implicitly, the article is suggesting the opportunity cost of one person's nursing home care in terms of Phoenix air-to-air missiles is:
  (a)   1/35.
  (b)   35.
  (c) $1 million.
  (d)   None of the above.

Problems and Applications

Exercise 1

This exercise is similar to the problem at the end of Chapter 1 in the text. It provides practice in drawing and interpreting a production-possibilities curve and demonstrating shifts of such a curve.

1. A production-possibilities schedule showing the production alternatives between corn and lumber is presented in Table 1.1. Graph combination A in Figure 1.1 and label it. Do the same for combination B. In going from combination A to combination B, the economy has sacrificed _____ billion board feet of lumber production per year and has transferred the land resources to production of _____ billion bushels of corn per year. The opportunity cost of corn in terms of lumber is _____ board feet per bushel.

Table 1.1

Combination	Quantity of corn (billions of bushels per year)	Quantity of lumber (billions of board feet per year)
A	0	50
B	1	48
C	2	44
D	3	38
E	4	30
F	5	20
G	6	0

2. In answering Question 1 you determined the opportunity cost of corn when the economy is initially producing no corn (combination A). Using the information in Table 1.1, graph the rest of the production-possibilities combinations in Figure 1.1 and label each of the points with the appropriate letter.

Figure 1.1

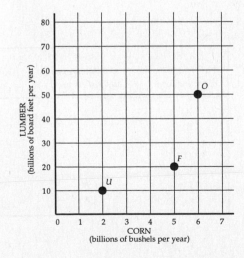

3. When Table 1.2 is completed, it should show the opportunity cost of corn at each possible combination of lumber and corn production in the economy. Opposite "1st billion bushels" insert the number of board feet per year of lumber sacrificed when the economy shifts from combination A to combination B. Complete the table for each of the remaining combinations.

Table 1.2

Corn production (billions of bushels per year)	Opportunity cost of corn in terms of lumber (billions of board feet per year)
1st billion bushels	_____
2nd billion bushels	_____
3rd billion bushels	_____
4th billion bushels	_____
5th billion bushels	_____
6th billion bushels	_____

4 In Table 1.2, as more corn is produced (as the economy moves from combination A toward combination G), the opportunity cost of corn (falls, rises, remains the same), which illustrates the law of _____ .

5. Suppose that lumber companies begin to clear-cut forest areas instead of cutting them selectively. Clear-cutting improves the economy's ability to produce lumber but not corn. Table 1.3 describes such a situation. Using the information in Table 1.3, sketch the new production-possibilities curve in Figure 1.1 as you did the initial production-possibilities curve based on Table 1.1. For which combination does the use of clear-cutting fail to change the amount of corn and lumber produced? _____

Table 1.3

Combination	Corn (billions of bushels per year)	Lumber (billions of board feet per year)
A'	0	75
B'	1	72
C'	2	66
D'	3	57
E'	4	45
F'	5	30
G'	6	0

6. After the introduction of clear-cutting the new production-possibilities curve is (outside, inside, the same as) the earlier curve. The opportunity cost of corn has (increased, decreased) as a result of clear-cutting.

7. Study your original production-possibilities curve in Figure 1.1 and decide which of the combinations shown (U, F¹, O) demonstrates each of the following. (*Hint:* Check the answers at the end of the chapter to make sure you have diagramed the production-possibility curve in Figure 1.1 correctly.)
    (a) Society is producing at its maximum potential. Combination _____
    (b) Society has some unemployed or underemployed resources. Combination

    _____
    (c) Society cannot produce this combination. Combination _____
    (d) Society might be able to produce this combination if technology improved but cannot produce it with current technology. Combination _____
    (e) If society produces this combination, some of society's wants will go unsatisfied unnecessarily. Combination _____

Exercise 2

The following exercise shows how to recognize and infer the concept of production possibilities from statements made by public officials.

In a speech before the American Society of Newspaper Editors on April 16, 1953, President Eisenhower stated:

> Every gun that is made, every warship launched, every rocket fired signifies, in the final sense, a theft from those who hunger and are not fed, those who are cold and not clothed. This world in arms is not spending money alone. It is spending the sweat of its laborers, the genius of its scientists, the hopes of its children... This is not a way of life at all in any true sense. Under the cloud of threatening war, it is humanity hanging from a cross of iron.

Answer the following questions on the basis of the preceding quotation:

1. What factors of production did Eisenhower point to as the resources that limit our production possibilities?
    (a) Guns, warships, rockets.
    (b) Food, clothes.
    (c) Money.
    (d) Laborers, scientists, and the hopes of our children.

2. What are the final goods and services that society desires?
    (a) Guns.
    (b) Warships.
    (c) Clothes.
    (d) All of the above.

3. What would be placed on one of the axes of the production-possibilities curve that Eisenhower has implicitly described?
    (a) Guns, warships, rockets, and other armaments.
    (b) Laborers, scientists, and other labor.
    (c) Money.
    (d) None of the above.

4. Which of the following is the opportunity cost of armaments (guns, warships, and rockets)?
    (a)   The amount of clothing or food given up to produce a given quantity of armaments.
    (b)   The dollar value of armaments absorbed in providing national defense.
    (c)   The amount of money that Congress appropriates for purchasing armaments.
    (d)   None of the above.

5. Implicitly, President Eisenhower recommended that there be greater:
    (a)   Expenditure on armaments relative to clothing.
    (b)   Expenditure on clothing and on food relative to armaments.
    (c)   Development of labor, genius, and hopes to make more armaments, food, and clothing possible.
    (d)   Expenditure of money for all of society's needs.

6. If Eisenhower's speech achieved a cutback in production of armaments and greater production of food and clothing, then, assuming the law of increasing opportunity costs applies, the opportunity cost of:
    (a)   Both armaments and clothing-food should rise.
    (b)   Both armaments and clothing-food should fall.
    (c)   Armaments should fall while the opportunity cost of food-clothing should rise.
    (d)   Armaments should rise while the opportunity cost of food-clothing should fall.

Exercise 3

Newspapers contain a great deal of information about the tradeoffs involved in producing different combinations of goods and services. To describe tradeoffs, the articles should provide certain information. By using one of the articles in the text, this exercise will show the kind of information to look for. If your professor makes a newspaper assignment from the *Instructor's Manual*, this exercise will provide an example of how to do it.

Reread the In the News selection on page 9 in Chapter 1 of the text entitled "The Peace Dividend."

1. How many pairs of goods are matched to illustrate the tradeoff between the goals of the defense buildup and the nondefense buildup?

2. What "resources" do the tradeoff examples suggest are in limited supply?

3. List all of the quotations that explicitly refer to this resource.

4. What passages in the article indicate a possible shift of the production-possibilities curve or a movement along it? The shift or movement may have occurred already, may be occurring now, or may occur in the future.

5. Pick one of the tradeoffs in Question 1. Assume the tradeoff between the two goods did not exhibit increasing opportunity cost. Carefully and neatly draw a production-possibilities curve for the two goods. Don't use any numbers. However, be careful to label both of your axes, and draw the production-possibilities curve with a shape consistent with the assumption that the law of increasing opportunity cost *does not* apply.

Figure 1.2

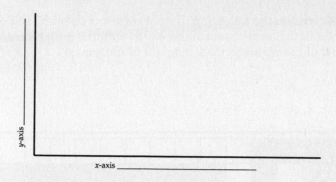

6. In what direction in your diagram of a production-possibilities curve would there be a movement along the production-possibilities curve or in what direction would the curve shift based on the passage in Question 4 above? Draw an arrow in your diagram to indicate the direction of the movement or shift.

Crossword Puzzle

Select the economic term in the following list that corresponds with each of the defintions and descriptions below. Then fit the term or one of the words within it into the crossword puzzle at the number indicated. Some of the words in the list do not fit the puzzle.

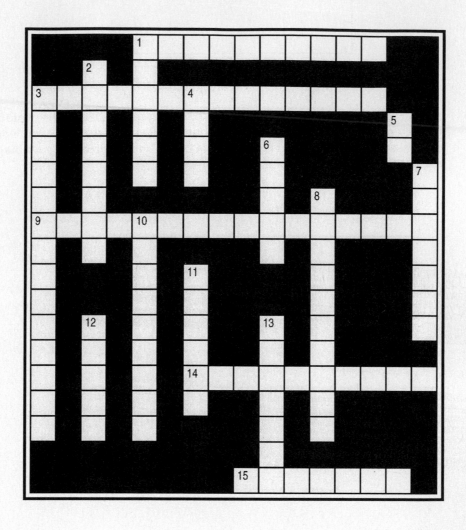

capital	macroeconomics
ceteris paribus	market failure
economic growth	market mechanism
economics	microeconomics
efficiency	mixed economy
entrepreneurship	opportunity cost
factors of production	production possibilities
government failure	scarcity
laissez faire	

Across

1. The former Soviet Union serves as a monumental example of _____ ; the government failed to improve upon laissez faire in controlling markets.

3. From the point of view of the overall economy, which is studied in the area of _____ , there was slow economic growth.

9. The republics from the former Soviet Union now are trying to sponsor _____ , in which private interests rather than the state assemble resources.

14. Private property should provide entrepreneurs the incentive to increase _____ , which would raise the output the Russians can achieve from their resources.

15. Because it is not possible for the assumption of _____ to be met, some historians are unwilling to say that the breakup of the Soviet Union was due solely to communism because it is not possible to hold constant the effects of other events that changed the twentieth century.

Down

1. _____ of the former Soviet Union was believed to be as much as 20 percent per year by Western intelligence organizations because there was not accurate data on the GDP.

2. While certain sectors of the former Soviet Union, such as defense, thrived, there was _____ of consumer and agricultural goods

3. which appeared in many studies of _____ in which the individual behavior of households and Soviet organizations was examined in detail.

4. The _____ of government control could be measured in the goods that were foregone by not having a

5. _____ were wasted or misunderstood, particularly the role of entrepreneurship in organizing those resources.

6. _____ , in which some economic tasks could be handled by the private sector while others were handled by the state.

7. _____ was kept as long as it worked, even if it was inefficient

8. and resulted in production that was well below _____ that the Soviet Union potentially could have achieved.

10. _____ , which is the study of how to meet goals within the given resources that are available,

11. has also undergone change within the former Soviet republics as they send students to study the _____ in which prices are allowed to signal the allocation of resources.

12. As the governments of Russia and other republics learn to exercise a _____ policy which eliminates their role in directing resources

13. they are experiencing the new problems of _____ which prevent optimal outcomes from being achieved.

Common Errors

The first statement in each "common error" below is incorrect. Each incorrect statement is followed by a corrected version and an explanation.

1. Words mean the same thing in economics that they do in our everyday conversation. WRONG!

   Words used in everyday conversation *very often* have different meanings when they are used in economics. RIGHT!

   You'll have to be very careful here. Words are used with precision in economics. You'll have difficulty if you confuse their everyday meanings with their economic meanings. For example, the term "capital" in economics means simply "man-made instruments of production." In everyday usage it may mean money, machines, a loan, or even the British response to the question "How are you feeling?"

2. Economic models are abstractions from the real world and are therefore useless in predicting and explaining economic behavior. WRONG!

   Economic models are abstractions from the real world and *as a result* are useful in predicting and explaining economic behavior. RIGHT!

   You have to be willing to deal with abstractions if you want to get anything accomplished in economics. By using economic models based on specific assumptions, we can make reasonable judgments about what's going on around us. We try not to disregard any useful information. However, to try to include everything (such as what cereal we like for breakfast) would be fruitless. For example, the production-possibilities frontier is an abstraction. No economist would argue that it is an economy! But it certainly is useful in focusing on public-policy choices, such as the choice between guns and butter.

3. Because economics is a "science," all economists should come up with the same answer to any given question. WRONG!

   Economics is a science, but there is often room for disagreement in trying to answer a given question. RIGHT!

   Economics is a social science, and the entire society and economy represent the economist's laboratory. Economists cannot run the kind of experiments that are done by physical scientists. As a result, two economists may attack a given problem or question in different ways using different models. They may come up with different answers, but since there is no answer book, you cannot say which is right. The solution is, then, to do more testing, refine our models, compare results, and so on. By the way, the recent space probes have given physicists cause to reevaluate much of their theory concerning the solar system, and there is much controversy concerning what the new evidence means. But physics is still a science, as is economics!

4. Increasing opportunity cost results from increasing inefficiency. WRONG!

   Increasing opportunity cost occurs even when resources are being used at their peak efficiency. RIGHT!

Increasing opportunity cost and inefficiency are confused because both result in a lower amount of output per unit of input. However, inefficiency results from poor utilization or underemployment of resources, while increasing opportunity results from the increasing difficulty of adapting resources to production as more of a good is produced. Inefficiency can be represented as a movement inward from the production-possibilities curve, while increasing opportunity cost can be measured in movements along the production-possibilities curve. Specifically, opportunity cost is measured by the absolute value of the slope of the production-possibility curve. As the slope becomes steeper in movements down the production possibility curve, the good on the x-axis experiences increasing opportunity cost (a steeper slope). Similarly, a movement up along the production-possibilities curve represents a higher opportunity cost for the good on the y-axis – this time in the form of a flatter slope as more of the good on the y-axis is produced.

•ANSWERS•

Key-Term Review

1. *ceteris paribus*
2. microeconomics
3. opportunity cost
4. market mechanism
5. factors of production
6. macroeconomics
7. production possibilities
8. capital
9. scarcity
10. economics
11. mixed economy
12. economic growth
13. market failure
14. government failure
15. entrepreneurship
16. laissez faire
17. efficiency

True or False

1.	F	5.	T	9.	F	13.	T	17.	F	20.	T
2.	F	6.	F	10.	T	14.	T	18.	T	21.	T
3.	T	7.	T	11.	F	15.	F	19.	F	22.	F
4.	T	8.	T	12.	F	16.	T				

Multiple Choice

1.	b	5.	c	9.	d	13.	d	17.	d	20.	a
2.	a	6.	c	10.	a	14.	c	18.	d	21.	d
3.	a	7.	d	11.	d	15.	a	19.	b	22.	d
4.	c	8.	c	12.	d	16.	b				

23. c   Mixed economies are not an area of economic theory. Related terms for other groupings: (a) market imperfections, (b) government interventions to correct market failures, and (d) government failure.

24. c   25. a

Problems and Applications

Exercise 1

1. 2, 1, 2

2. **Figure 1.1 Answer**

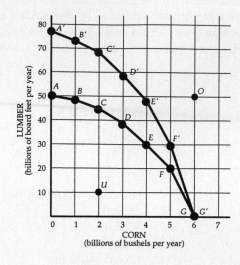

3. **Table 1.2 Answer**

Corn production (billions of bushels per year)	Opportunity cost of corn in terms of lumber (billions of board feet per year)
1st billion bushels	2
2nd billion bushels	4
3rd billion bushels	6
4th billion bushels	8
5th billion bushels	10
6th billion bushels	20

4. rises; increasing opportunity costs

5. See Figure 1.1 Answer; combination G

6. outside, increased

7. (a) F^1
   (b) U
   (c) O
   (d) O
   (e) U

Exercise 2

1. d   2. d   3. a   4. a   5. b   6. c

Exercise 3

1. seven

2. The article focuses on the budget limitation. The budget limitation, in turn, reflects the economy's limited resources.

3. "cutbacks," "peace dividend," "$120 billion," "$40 billion," "$25 billion," "$5 billion," "$532 million," "$2.6 million," and "$1 million"

4. "Could be cut $120 billion" suggests reduced military spending. The quotation "A `peace dividend' of additional nonmilitary goods" suggests greater nonmilitary spending. These two changes suggest a movement along the production-possibilities curve.

5. and 6. **Figure 1.2 Answer**

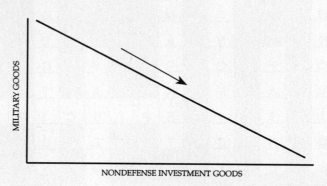

19

Crossword Puzzle Answer

Across   *governmen*t failure
3. *macroeconomics*
9. *entrepreneurship*
14. *efficiency*
15. *ceteris* paribus

Down
1. economic *growth*
2. *scarcity*
3. *microeconomics*
4. opportunity *cost*
5. factors *of* production
6. *mixed* economy
7. *capital*
8. *production* possibilities
10. *economics*
11. *market* mechanism
12. laissez *faire*
13. market *failure*

CHAPTER 2

The American Economy

Quick Review

To understand what the American economy is, we must look to the answers it generates to the following questions:

- WHAT goods and services does the United States produce?
- HOW is that output distributed?
- FOR WHOM is the output produced?

The WHAT question is answered by a summary measure called gross domestic product (GDP). GDP is the total dollar value of all final goods and services produced *in a country* during a given time period. Although there are several ways to break up the GDP, a frequently used technique is to classify the *output which is produced* by the groups which purchase it: consumer goods by households, investment goods by business, and output taken by government at the federal, state, and local levels. In addition we must account for goods and services produced here and sold abroad (exports) and those which are produced abroad and sold here (imports).

The HOW question is answered by entrepreneurs and government officials who make decisions about how the nation's factors of production (which vary in quantity, quality, and mobility) will be allocated.

The economy never stands still, and we have observed in this century both the decline of agriculture and manufacturing and the rise of the service sector in the U.S economy. The relative importance (both in size and numbers) of various forms of business organization – proprietorships, partnerships and corporations – has undergone substantial revision as well.

The FOR WHOM question is answered by the nation's income distribution, where those at the upper end of the distribution receive incomes which are disproportionate to their numbers.

In the future we can expect new answers to the WHAT, HOW and FOR WHOM questions as different market signals and changing government directives render the old answers obsolete.

Learning Objectives

After reading Chapter 2 and doing the following exercises, you should:	True or false	Multiple choice	Problems and applications	Common errors	Pages in the text
1. Be able to define GDP and explain its components.	1-4, 6-8, 10, 14	1, 3, 4, 6-8, 10, 14	1, 2, 4	1, 3, 4	32-39
2. Understand that factors of production differ in quantity, quality, and mobility in the United States and elsewhere.	4, 5, 9, 11, 18	5, 6, 9, 11, 12, 18		2	39-40
3. Be able to trace the broad changes in industry structure in the United States from 1900 to the present.	11-13	13			41-43
4. Know the basic types and relative importance of business organizations in the United States.	14	15, 16			43-44
5. Understand that the economy's answer to the FOR WHOM question lies in the income distribution.	2, 3, 7, 15-17, 19	2, 17	2, 3	1	44-47
6. Expect that new market signals and government directives will change the answers to the WHAT, HOW, and FOR WHOM questions.	19	2, 10, 17, 19-22			47-50

Key-Term Review

Review the following terms; if you are not sure of the meaning of any term, write out the definition and check it against the Glossary in the text.

capital intensive	income quintile
economic growth	income transfers
exports	investments
factors of production	net exports
gross domestic product (GDP)	per capita GDP
imports	productivity

Fill in the blank following each of the statements below with the appropriate term from the list above.

1. The most often used measure of the economy's total output is the _____ .

1. _____

2. The economy's _____ are allocated so as to produce a diverse output of goods and services.

2. _____

3. This output includes both consumer goods purchased by households and _____ goods purchased by businesses.

3. _____

4. Some of the goods and services produced in the United States are shipped abroad as _____ , while some of the things purchased by Americans are _____ , which means they were produced abroad.

4. _____
   _____

5. To calculate the GDP, subtract the dollar value of imports from the dollar value of exports to get _____ .

5. _____

6. When the economy experiences _____ that is faster than population growth, _____ must increase.

6. _____
   _____

7. Those industries which are _____ tend also to be those where worker _____ is high.

7. _____
   _____

8. Because the highest _____ receives a disproportionate share of income in the United States, _____ are used to improve the answer to the FOR WHOM question.

8. _____
   _____

True or False: *Circle your choice.*

T F 1. The United States produces about 25 percent of the world's output and accounts for roughly 25 percent of world trade.

T F 2. Per capita GDP indicates the mix of output that has actually been distributed evenly to the population.

T F 3. If the economic growth rate exceeds the population growth rate, per capita GDP will decline.

T F 4. Investment requires saving.

T F 5. Saving is a way to limit consumption so that factors of production may be channeled toward investment.

T F 6. Federal government purchases of goods and services make up approximately 20 percent of GDP.

T F 7. Food stamps, public housing, and Head Start classes are counted as government services in the GDP.

T F 8. Since the United States is the world's largest exporter and importer, its net exports are positive.

T F 9. Comparisons of production methods used in industrialized countries with those used in poor countries indicate that the former tend to use the more capital-intensive methods of production.

T F 10. The GDP is the sum of the value of the factors of production used to produce output in a country.

T F 11. The decline in the number of workers employed in American agriculture has been accompanied by an increase in productivity for the remaining workers.

T F 12. Although the relative share of total U.S. output produced in the manufacturing sector has declined, total manufacturing output has increased.

T F 13. The decline in the manufacturing sector's relative share of the GDP means that the dollar value of manufacturing output has gone down.

T F 14. The import ratio can rise even though the value of imports falls.

T F 15. The corporation is the dominant form of business organization in the United States in terms of numbers, assets, and sales.

T F 16. In-kind transfers include cash payments such as a welfare check.

T F 17. In developed countries the richest quintile of the population gets a much larger proportion of total income than that quintile receives in poor, developing nations.

T F 18. The answer to the HOW question is determined largely by businesses which are responding to market forces.

T F 19. In-kind transfers are government provision of goods and services which are intended to alter the answer to the FOR WHOM question.

Multiple Choice: *Select the correct answer.*

_____ 1. The economic growth rate of the economy is best measured by:
(a) The percentage change in the GDP between two points in time.
(b) The percentage change in per capita GDP between two points in time.
(c) The sum of the value of the factors of production used to produce output in a country.
(d) A measure of output divided by a measure of population.

_____ 2. The standard of living will decline:
(a) Whenever the GDP falls.
(b) If the percentage change in per capita GDP rises.
(c) If the rate of population growth exceeds the rate of economic growth.
(d) If factor growth exceeds economic growth.

_____ 3. The GDP is the sum of:
(a) The value of consumer goods, investment goods, government services, and net exports produced over a given period of time.
(b) The dollar values of all final goods and services produced in a country during a given time period.
(c) The dollar value of the payments earned by the factors of production used to produce output in a country.
(d) All of the above.

4. Suppose that during the course of a year, an economy produces $4.8 trillion consumer goods, $1.2 trillion investment goods, $1.4 trillion government services, $0.6 trillion exports, and $0.8 trillion imports. For that economy, GDP would be:
   (a) $8,000 billion.
   (b) $7,000 billion.
   (c) $10,000 billion.
   (d) None of the above.

5. Investment goods:
   (a) Both maintain and expand production possibilities.
   (b) Maintain production possibilities but do not expand them.
   (c) Expand production possibilities but do not maintain them.
   (d) Include consumption goods.

6. Which of the following is an example of the economic meaning of investment?
   (a) The purchase of a delivery van by IBM.
   (b) The purchase of IBM stock by a mutual fund manager.
   (c) The purchase of land by a real estate developer.
   (d) The purchase of a U.S. government savings bond by a commercial bank.

7. Federal government purchases of goods and services account for:
   (a) A smaller percentage of GDP than net exports.
   (b) A greater percentage of GDP than state and local government purchases.
   (c) A greater percentage of GDP than investment goods.
   (d) None of the above.

8. The percentage of the GDP contributed by federal government purchases, state and local government purchases, investment goods, and exports, respectively, is:
   (a) 8 percent, 12 percent, 14 percent, and 11 percent.
   (b) 14 percent, 12 percent, 8 percent, and 11 percent.
   (c) 14 percent, 12 percent, 11 percent, and 8 percent.
   (d) 12 percent, 14 percent, 8 percent, and 11 percent.

9. If federal government purchases are 8 percent, state and local government purchases are 12 percent, investment goods are 15 percent, and net exports are negative at 2 percent in terms of the GDP of a country, then consumption goods would constitute:
   (a) 67 percent of GDP.
   (b) 65 percent of GDP.
   (c) 63 percent of GDP.
   (d) None of the above.

10. Which of the following are included in the GDP?
    (a) Social security benefits.
    (b) Food stamps.
    (c) Imports.
    (d) Net exports.

11. Which of the following definitely means productivity has increased?
    (a) More output from fewer workers.
    (b) More output from more workers.
    (c) Less output from fewer workers.
    (d) Less output from more workers.

_____ 12. Which of the following explains the low productivity of workers in poor, developing countries?
(a) Labor intensity of their production processes.
(b) The low factor mobility.
(c) The low quality of labor as a result of poor education.
(d) All of the above.

_____ 13. Since 1900 the change in the relative importance of different sectors in the U.S. economy is best characterized as:
(a) Relative growth in farm output.
(b) Relative growth in manufacturing output.
(c) Relative growth in service output.
(d) None of the above.

_____ 14. The U.S. import ratio:
(a) Is the value of imports divided by value of exports.
(b) Has grown from 5 percent in 1920 to 12 percent today.
(c) Is over 25 percent today.
(d) None of the above.

_____ 15. The primary way to distinguish among corporations, partnerships, and proprietorships is through:
(a) Their ownership characteristics.
(b) The size of firms.
(c) The market share of leading firms.
(d) The number of firms in each classification.

_____ 16. Corporations tend to be larger than partnerships or proprietorships because:
(a) They can be more easily directed with a single owner than can other types of businesses which have many owners.
(b) Most firms are corporations, which means legal services, government services and others are better adapted to this type of business, making it easier to expand.
(c) They are the only type of organization that can have operations in many different countries.
(d) They limit the liability of the owners for the firm's debt.

_____ 17. Food stamps, public housing, and Head Start classes are:
(a) Not included as government services in the GDP.
(b) Income transfers.
(c) In-kind benefits.
(d) All of the above.

_____ 18. The HOW question within a country can best be measured using data about which of the following?
(a) The GDP.
(b) Per capita GDP.
(c) Productivity.
(d) Income quintiles.

_____ 19. Which of the following would government change most directly by making income transfers?
(a) The mix of output.
(b) The factors of production.
(c) Income distribution.
(d) Industry structure.

_____ 20. Market signals:
  (a)   Are sent by consumer purchases.
  (b)   Provide incentives for improving efficiency.
  (c)   Are answered by resource reallocations.
  (d)   All of the above.

_____ 21. Which of the following is a market signal?
  (a)   The Clean Air Act of 1970.
  (b)   Federal minimum wage laws.
  (c)   The Americans with Disabilities Act.
  (d)   None of the above.

_____ 22. One World View article in the text reports: "Communist leaders in Beijing are wringing their hands over how to revive rotting Soviet-style state factories." This quotation suggests that communism failed to answer:
  (a)   The FOR WHOM question with market signals.
  (b)   The FOR WHOM question with government directives.
  (c)   The WHAT question with market signals.
  (d)   The HOW question with government directives.

Problems and Applications

Exercise 1

The following problem sorts out the different ways in which the gross domestic product can be used to calculate indicators of the standard of living and the rate of economic growth in an economy.

1. Using the data provided in the textbook and the data in Table 2.1, complete the first five rows of Table 2.1 (Use the "Real Gross Domestic Product," not the "Nominal Gross Domestic Product," from the tables in the text.)

Table 2.1
Gross Domestic Product and Economic Growth

Row	1970	1990	Percentage change
(1) U.S. GDP (billions of dollars)	_____	_____	_____
(2) U.S. population (thousands)	205,052	249,924	_____
(3) U.S. per capita GDP (dollars per person)	_____	_____	_____
(4) World population (thousands)	_____	_____	_____
(5) U.S. Share of World Population	_____	_____	_____
(6) World GDP if the world at U.S. per Capita GDP (billions)	_____	_____	_____

2. Compute the world's GDP in the last row of Table 2.1 assuming that per capita GDP is at the U.S. level.

3. T   F   World economic growth would have had to increase nearly 100 percent to keep pace with the growth rate of the U.S. per capita GDP. (*Note:* See the percentage change calculated in the last column and row of Table 2.1.)

4. Why must the world economic growth be greater than the U.S. economic growth to maintain the same standard of living? _____

_____

Exercise 2

After comparing economic growth rates for different countries, you will be able to predict the future share of world output for different continents.

1. Table 2.2 shows data on five-year average percentage changes in GDP. Circle all of the five year periods for each of the countries (or country groups) in which the economic growth rate exceeds that of the United States over the same period of time.

Table 2.2
Growth Rates (average annual percentage change)

	1971-75	1976-80	1981-85	1986-90
United States	2.4	3.2	2.6	2.6
Canada	5.2	4.0	2.9	2.9
Japan	4.5	4.6	3.8	4.6
European Community	2.9	3.2	1.4	3.2
(Former) USSR	3.0	1.8	1.7	1.1
China	5.5	6.2	10.0	7.7
Africa	4.0	2.7	.9	3.7

Source: The Economic Report of the President, 1993 (Table B-108, p. 471)

Answer the following questions on the basis of your analysis of this information. Circle your choice.

2. Which of the following areas appears to be experiencing the fastest rate of growth?
   North America   Europe   Former USSR   Asia   Africa

3. Which of the following areas appears to be experiencing the slowest rate of growth?
   North America   Europe   Former USSR   Asia   Africa

4. Which of the following areas appears generally to be experiencing an acceleration in growth rates (rising growth rates)?
   North America   Europe   Former USSR   Asia   Africa

5. Which of the following areas appears generally to be experiencing a deceleration in growth rates (falling growth rates)?
   North America   Europe   Former USSR   Asia   Africa

6. Which of the following areas appears generally to be experiencing constant growth rates)?
   North America   Europe   Former USSR   Asia   Africa

7. By the twenty-first century, which of the following would you predict will be growing faster than the United States?
   North America   Europe   Former USSR   Asia   Africa

8. Predict what will happen to the share of total output that will be produced by each of the areas by the twenty-first century (circle one response for each continent):

North America	smaller	larger	unchanged
Europe	smaller	larger	unchanged
Former USSR	smaller	larger	unchanged
Asia	smaller	larger	unchanged
Africa	smaller	larger	unchanged

Exercise 3

This exercise provides practice in using the tools to measure and analyze the distribution of both income and wealth.

Inequality applies not only to income- what people earn each year – but also to wealth – what people own at any given point in time. The Federal Reserve Board conducts a survey of consumer finances every three years. It measures household wealth by computing each household's "net worth." In 1983, the richest 1 percent of American households owned 31 percent of the wealth. By 1989, the richest 834,000 households, which constituted 1 percent of total U.S. households, had $5.74 trillion of the $15.5 trillion of total wealth, while the poorest 90 percent of the households had only $4.8 trillion.

1. What percentage of total wealth was owned by the richest 1 percent of the households in 1989? _____

2. T F From 1983 to 1989 the rich got richer.

3. What was the percentage of total wealth owned by the poorest 90 percent of the households in 1989? _____

4. How many households are there in all? _____

5. Suppose we define the "next richest group" as the number of households who are not in the poorest 90 percent, nor in the richest 1 percent, of all households. Determine the following about this "next richest group":
   (a) How many households are in this group? _____
   (b) How much wealth (in dollars) is owned by this group? _____
   (c) What is the average wealth per household in this group? _____

6. The same report showed that of all the income received in the year, the top 1 percent of households received 10 percent, the next 9 percent received 20 percent, and the poorest 90 percent received 70 percent. Assuming this data are consistent and comparable with the income groups in Table 2.1 of the text on page 46, compute the percentage of income earned by the:
   (a) Richest 10 percent of households _____
   (b) Next richest 10 percent of households _____

7. Inequality in the distribution of wealth is (greater than, less than, the same as) the distribution of income. How do you know? _____
   _____

Exercise 4

This is an excecise in critical thinking. It is designed to give you practice in reaching conclusions from graphs of data through time. It also provides insight into U.S. trade patterns and international policy problems facing the United States.

1. Graph both exports and imports (see the data on the inside cover of the text) on the same axis in Figure 2.1. Be sure to use real exports and real imports.

Figure 2.1

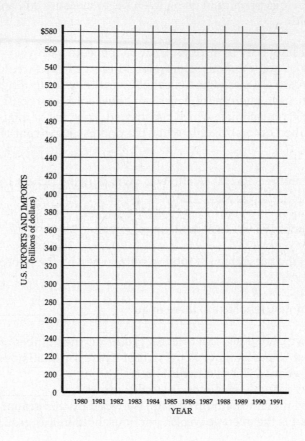

2. In which years are exports greater than imports? _____

3. During the period 1982-86 the amount by which exports exceeded imports generally became (circle one): more positive, less positive, more negative, less negative

4. During the period 1986-90, the amount by which exports exceeded imports generally became:
    more postive   less positive   more negative   less negative

5. The amount by which imports exceeds exports is a measure of which of the Terms to Remember on page 51 of Chapter 2? _____.

Crossword Puzzle

Select the economic term in the following list that corresponds with each of the defintions and descriptions below. Then fit the term or one of the words within it into the crossword puzzle at the number indicated. Some of the words in the list do not fit the puzzle.

capital intensive
economic growth
exports
factors of production
gross domestic product (GDP)
imports

income
income transfers
investments
net exports
Per capita (GDP)
productivity

Across

4. The description of a production process which uses large amounts of capital relative to labor.

7. As more capital becomes available, workers produce more output per hour of their work, which means _____ is improved.

10. Subtracting imports from exports is the measure of _____ , which may be a significant part of a country's GDP.

11. Sales of goods and services to foreign consumers.

12. A measure of the total output that is produced in a country over a given period of time.

Down

1. Like capital and land, people also are _____ in whom a country must invest.

2. A measure of a country's standard of living, which is computed by dividing a measure of output by total population.

3. A country's _____ can be measured by the percentage change in GDP between two points in time.

5. A country must save to allow _____ which adds to its capital.

6. To help the people in the lowest _____

8. developed countries have generally instituted government payments, called _____ .

9. Sales of foreign goods and services to consumers within a country.

Common Errors

1. A higher GDP means an increase in the standard of living. WRONG!

    A high per capita GDP is an imperfect measure of the standard of living. RIGHT!

    Many developing countries experience a rise in GDP, but their population grows faster. This means that there is actually less income per person and the standard of living falls! The growth in population must be taken into account in measuring the standard of living, which is the reason that the per capita GDP, not just the GDP, is used. However, even the per capita GDP measure fails to take into account the distribution of income. In Chapter 7, as we examine the mix of output more closely, we find that many goods and services that add to the standard of living are not even included in the GDP. Furthermore, the mix of output changes from one country to another, making international comparisons of the standard of living questionable.

2. Investors make an economic investment when they invest in the stock market. WRONG!

    Economic investment occurs only with the *tangible* creation or maintenance of capital goods. RIGHT!

    A distinction must be made between financial investment and economic investment. Common usage usually refers to financial investment in which individuals purchase a financial security backed by a financial institution. Such an activity is called saving, which is the alternative to immediate consumption. Such saving may eventually be used by financial corporations to make loans that will eventually lead to economic investment. But economists have found that there are a lot of things that can happen to saving before it turns into tangible production of capital goods. Therefore economists analyze saving and investment separately.

3. As the United States imports more, consumption rises and therefore so does the GDP. WRONG!

Imports replace consumption of goods produced in the United States and lower the GDP. RIGHT!

The GDP is the sum of consumption, investment, government purchases and *net exports*. Net exports are computed by *subtracting* imports from exports. So, let's look at the GDP as an equation:

GDP = consumption + investment + government purchases + exports - imports

Greater imports mean a lower GDP *ceteris paribus*! Consumption of foreign goods is not the concept of U.S. consumption used by economists. Economists focus on the output that is actually produced *in the United States* to satisfy U.S. consumers, not all of the expenditures that consumers make.

4. Export goods are not included in the GDP because they are not consumed by Americans. WRONG!

Export goods are produced in the United States and therefore are included in the GDP. RIGHT!

The GDP is the sum of consumption, investment, government purchases and *net exports*. Once again the equation appears as follows:

GDP = consumption + investment + governmnet pruchases + exports - imports

Larger exports mean a higher GDP! The GDP focuses on the output of the economy and our use of resources to produce that output, regardless of who consumes it.

•ANSWERS•

Key-Term Review

1. gross domestic product (GDP)
2. factors of production
3. investment
4. exports
   imports
5. net exports

6. economic growth
   per capita GDP
7. capital intensive
   productivity
8. income quintile
   income transfers

True or False

1. T	5. T	8. F	11. T	14. T	17. F
2. F	6. F	9. T	12. T	15. F	18. T
3. F	7. F	10. T	13. F	16. F	19. T
4. T					

Multiple Choice

1. a	5. a	9. a	13. c	17. d	20. d
2. c	6. b	10. b	14. b	18. c	21. d
3. d	7. c	11. a	15. a	19. c	22. b
4. d	8. a	12. d	16. d		

Problems and Applications

Exercise 1

Table 2.1 Answer

(Row)	1970	1990	Percentage change
(1) U.S. GDP (billions of dollars)	2,873.9	4,877.5	69.7%
(2) U.S. Population (thousands)	205,052	249,924	21.9%
(3) U.S. per capita GDP (dollars per person)	14,013	19,513	39.2%
(4) World population (thousands)	3,722,000	5,329,000	43.2%
(5) U.S. share of world population	5.5%	4.7%	*******
(6) World GDP if the world at U.S. per capita GDP (billions of dollars)	52,164	104,000	99.4%

3. T
4. Since the world population growth rate is faster than that of the United States, it takes a higher economic growth to maintain the same standard of living.

Exercise 2

Table 2.2

	1971-75	1976-80	1981-85	1986-90
United States	2.4	3.2	2.6	2.6
Canada	*5.2	*4.0	*2.9	*2.9
Japan	*4.5	*4.6	*3.8	*4.6
European Community	*2.9	*3.2	1.4	*3.2
(Former) USSR	*3.0	1.8	1.7	1.1
China	*5.5	*6.2	*10.0	*7.7
Africa	*4.0	2.7	.9	*3.7

* Starred entries indicate a higher growth rate that of the United States.

2. Asia
3. Former USSR
4. Asia
5. Africa and the former USSR
6. North America and Europe.
7. Canada, Europe, Asia, and possibly Africa
8. North America: smaller
   Europe: larger
   Former USSR: smaller
   Asia: larger
   Africa: unchanged or smaller

Exercise 3

1. 37% (= 5.74/15.5)

2. T

3. 31% (= 4.8/15.5)

34

4. If 1 percent of the households includes 834,000 households, then the total number of households must be 100 times that, or 83,400,000 households.

5. (a) Middle-class households are 9 percent (= 100% - 90% - 1%) of the total number of households (83,400,000), which is 7,506,000

    (b) $4.96 trillion (= $15.5 - $5.74 - $4.8 trillion)

    (c) $660,000 per household

6. (a) Since the highest 1 percent receive 10 percent of the income and the next 9 percent receive 20 percent of the income, the richest 10 percent of households receive 30 percent of the income.
    (b) Since the richest 10 percent receive 30 percent of the income, and the richest 20 percent receive 46.5 percent of the income (according to Table 2.1 in the text), the second richest 10 percent earns the difference, 16.5 percent (= 46.5% - 30%)

7. greater than. The richest 1% of households has a much larger percentage (37%) of the wealth than the richest 1% have of the income (10%).

Exercise 4

1. **Figure 2.1 Answer**
    Exports and Imports, 1980-1991

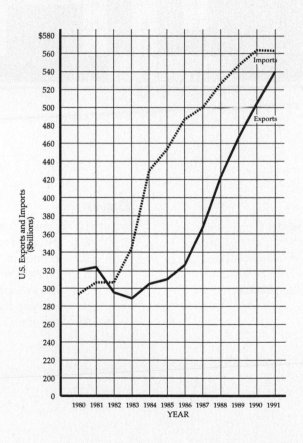

2. 1980 and 1981
3. more negative
4. less negative
5. net exports

Crossword Puzzle Answer

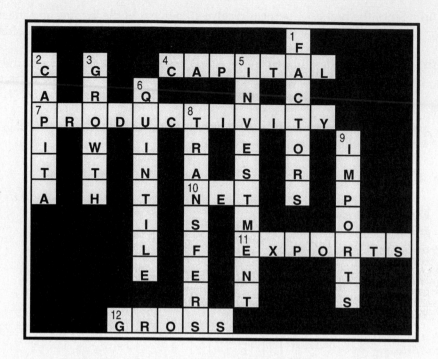

Across

4. *capital* intensive
7. *productivity*
10. *net* exports
11. *exports*
12. *gross* domestic product

Down

1. capital *factors*
2. per *capita* GDP
3. economic *growth*
5. *investment*
6. income *quintile*
8. income *transfers*
9. *imports*

CHAPTER 3

Supply and Demand

Quick Review

Nations around the world have abandoned central planning as a means of answering the WHAT, HOW, and FOR WHOM questions and are hastily turning to free markets for solutions instead. To understand how a market economy solves these same questions requires an understanding of the essential features of market-directed activity—demand and supply. To focus our discussion, we take up the following questions:

- What determines the price of a good or service?
- How does the price of a product affect its production or consumption?
- Why do prices and production levels often change?

All market participants share a common characteristic. They try to maximize some goal subject to one or more constraints. They do so by fully participating in markets.

Let's look at some market participants and see how they interact. Households and firms exchange factors of production in factor markets and goods and services in product markets. The quantity supplied of factors or products in a market is the quantity that sellers are willing and able to sell at a particular price. Market prices are likely to affect the quantity supplied. Economists represent the relationship between price and the quantity supplied in a supply schedule or supply curve. Supply represents the ability and willingness to sell specific quantities of a good at alternative prices in a given time period, *ceteris paribus*.

The quantity demanded of factors or products in a market is the quantity that buyers are willing and able to buy at a particular price. When prices fall, people tend to buy more. Economists represent the relationship between price and the quantity purchased in the form of a demand schedule or demand curve. Demand is the ability and willingness to buy specific quantities of a good at alternative prices in a given time period, *ceteris paribus*. Demand and supply do not determine what is actually exchanged, nor do they tell why an exchange occurs.

Market supply and market demand curves can be used to find the equilibrium price and rate of production in a market. A market supply curve is the sum of the supply curves of the sellers in the market. Similarly, a market demand curve is the sum of the individual demand curves of buyers in the market. When the market demand curve intersects the market supply curve, the market is in equilibrium. The market mechanism moves price toward the equilibrium price level as follows:

1. If the market price is above the equilibrium price, surpluses appear. To get rid of the surplus, sellers lower prices and production rates. Buyers buy more at lower prices.
2. If the market price is below equilibrium price, shortages occur. Buyers bid up the price of the commodity and sellers raise production rates in response to the increased price.

In both cases price and production rates change until the market reaches the equilibrium price and equilibrium production rate - the price and production rate that clears the market. The market mechanism is not perfect and may fail if there are externalities, and it may not allocate income in a desirable way, but it does answer the questions WHAT to produce, HOW to produce, and FOR WHOM to produce.

Market demand and market supply curves shift for a variety of reasons. Changes in the price or availability of other goods, tastes, income, expectations, and the number of buyers can alter market demands. Changes in resource prices, in technology, in expectations, in taxes, and in the number of sellers can alter market supply. With each shift the market finds its way through trial and error back to equilibrium. Governments sometimes feel compelled to interfere with the market mechanism by establishing maximum prices (price ceilings) for certain things. No matter how laudable the goals of the program for which they are instituted, price ceilings result in intractable shortages. In some cases the results have been so perverse that public-sector intervention moves society away from, rather than toward, preferred economic outcomes. Participants in the market for rent-controlled apartments in New York and Moscow can attest to this.

Learning Objectives

After reading Chapter 3 and doing the following exercises, you should:	True or false	Multiple choice	Problems and applications	Common errors	Pages in the text
1. Know the basic questions in economics and how the U.S. economy answers the questions.	1, 2, 3	20, 21	5		52, 70-72
2. Be able to describe the different types of markets and the motivations of participants in those markets.		1-4			52-56
3. Understand how a demand schedule represents demand and how a supply schedule represents supply.	4-6, 10, 11	4-7, 12, 15		1	56-59, 63-65
4. Be able to define and graph supply and demand curves.		6	1		57, 64
5. Know why supply and demand curves shift.	5-7, 12	13, 22	2, 4		58-59, 65
6. Know what causes movements along demand and supply curves.	6, 7, 14	15		5-7	60-61, 63-64
7. Know the difference between individual demand and market demand and between individual supply and market supply.	8, 9, 13, 14	8-11, 14	1, 3		61-64
8. Be able to explain shortages and surpluses and the effects of price ceilings and price floors.	16-18, 20, 21	16, 17	4	2-4	66-70
9. Be able to describe how and why markets move toward equilibrium.	15, 16, 19, 22	18, 19	5		72-75

Key-Term Review

Review the following terms; if you are not sure of the meaning of any term, write out the definition and check it against the Glossary in the text.

ceteris paribus   market mechanism
demand   market shortage
demand curve   market supply
demand schedule   market surplus
equilibrium price   opportunity cost
factor market   price ceiling
law of demand   product market
law of supply   shift in demand
market demand   supply

Fill in the blank following each of the statements below with the appropriate term from the list above.

1. The sum of the quantities demanded by all of the individual buyers in a market at every price is called _____ .

    1. _____

2. The relationship between prices and the quantity a buyer is willing and able to purchase at those prices is shown in tabular form as a _____ .

    2. _____

3. The value of the next most desirable use of resources is called the _____ .

    3. _____

4. By adding together all the quantities that individual suppliers are willing and able to sell at different prices, you can find _____ .

    4. _____

5. The quantities a buyer is willing and able to buy at various prices per unit of time, *ceteris paribus* is called _____ .

    5. _____

6. The quantities a seller is willing and able to sell at various prices per unit of time, *ceteris paribus* is called _____ .

    6. _____

7. When quantity demanded equals quantity supplied, this correspondence establishes the _____ .

    7. _____

8. Changes in tastes, income, or prices of other goods may cause a _____ .

    8. _____

9. The quantities that buyers are willing and able to buy at various prices are shown graphically as a _____ .

    9. _____

10. When prices are determined by buyers and sellers in a market, the economy is using the _____ to allocate resources.

10. _____

11. A decline in market price below the market equilibrium level causes a _____ .

11. _____

12. Finished goods are exchanged in a _____ .

12. _____

13. A rise in market price above the market-equilibrium price level causes a _____ .

13. _____

14. Resources are exchanged for money in a _____ .

14. _____

15. A Latin phrase meaning "all other things remaining equal" is _____ .

15. _____

16. The idea that quantity demanded increases as price falls, *ceteris paribus*, is known as the _____ .

16. _____

17. The idea that quantity supplied increases when price increases, *ceteris paribus*, is known as the _____ .

17. _____

18. Attempts by government to hold certain prices down with a _____ lead to shortages.

18. _____

True or False: *Circle your choice.*

T   F   1.   In all markets there is an exchange of money for goods and services.

T   F   2.   People who are producers at work may be consumers when they go to the store to buy groceries.

T   F   3.   When a buyer will buy as much as possible of a good at a given price, there is a high opportunity cost for a good.

T   F   4.   The demand curve shows how much of a good a buyer will actually buy at a given price.

T   F   5.   When a buyer purchases a good, the demand curve shifts to the left.

T   F   6.   A change in price changes the demand for goods purchased by consumers.

T   F   7.   A change in the price of a good always causes a movement along the demand curve for the good.

T   F   8.   A market demand curve can always be found by adding, horizontally, the demand curves of all the buyers in a given market.

T   F   9.   When individual demand curves shift, the market demand curve shifts because it is the horizontal sum of the individual demand curves.

T F 10. Supply curves reflect the potential behavior only of the sellers or producers of a good or service, not of the buyers.

T F 11. The law of supply explains the negative slope of the supply curve.

T F 12. When a seller sells a good, the supply curve shifts to the right.

T F 13. When the number of suppliers in a market changes, the market supply curve for goods and services also changes, even if the individual supply curves of original suppliers do not shift.

T F 14. When the supply curve for a good shifts downward, the supply of the good is reduced.

T F 15. Surpluses and shortages are determinants of demand and supply.

T F 16. At the equilibrium price, sellers receive signals to increase production rates while buyers receive signals to increase purchases in a given time period.

T F 17. The equilibrium price occurs at the price where the market supply and market demand curves intersect.

T F 18. The equilibrium price can be determined through the process of trial and error by both the buyers and the sellers in a market.

T F 19. There are never shortages or surpluses when the price in a market is equal to the equilibrium price for the market.

T F 20. When the quantity actually bought in a market equals the quantity actually sold, the market is in equilibrium.

T F 21. In a market economy, prices are determined by the consumer; in a planned or command economy, prices are determined by the seller.

T F 22. To be effective, price ceilings should be set above equilibrium prices.

Multiple Choice: *Select the correct answer.*

_____ 1. The principal actors in an economy are all constrained from achieving their goals:
  (a) Consumers by income, businesses by profits, and government by taxes.
  (b) Consumers by available goods and services, businesses by scarce resources, government by resources not used in businesses.
  (c) Consumers by the satisfaction derived from purchasing goods and services, businesses by profits, and government by the general welfare.
  (d) Consumers by available goods and services, businesses by scarce resources, and government by the general welfare.

_____ 2. The goods and services sold in a factor market are:
  (a) Utility, profits, and general welfare of society.
  (b) Rent, wages, profit, and interest.
  (c) Land, labor, capital, and entrepreneurship.
  (d) Resource constraints, budget constraints, legal constraints, and social constraints.

_____ 3. The incentives for economic interaction among market participants include:
   (a) Limited ability to produce what we need.
   (b) Constraints on time, energy, and resources.
   (c) The gains possible from specialization.
   (d) All of the above.

_____ 4. When one firm offers to buy out and merge with another firm, it is offering to make:
   (a) A sale in its product market.
   (b) A purchase in its product market.
   (c) A sale in the factor markets.
   (d) A purchase in the factor markets.

_____ 5. In which of the following cases may the opportunity cost be extremely high to a consumer for a good?
   (a) The demand curve is vertical.
   (b) The supply curve is horizontal.
   (c) Buyers will buy as much of the good as possible at a given price.
   (d) Buyers are willing to pay no more than one price, regardless of how much of a good is offered.

_____ 6. Which of the following must be held constant according to the _ceteris paribus_ assumption in defining a demand schedule?
   (a) Prices of the good itself.
   (b) Expectations of sellers.
   (c) Income.
   (d) All of the above.

_____ 7. The law of demand states that:
   (a) As price falls, quantity demanded falls, _ceteris paribus_.
   (b) As price falls, quantity demanded increases, _ceteris paribus_.
   (c) As price falls, demand increases.
   (d) As price falls, demand increases, _ceteris paribus_.

_____ 8. When the number of buyers in a market changes, _ceteris paribus_:
   (a) Both individual demand curves and market demand curves shift.
   (b) Individual demand curves change, but the market demand curve remains unchanged.
   (c) Individual demand curves remain unchanged but the market demand curve shifts.
   (d) There are no changes to either type of curve.

_____ 9. When a seller sells a good, _ceteris paribus_:
   (a) There is no change in supply or the quantity supplied.
   (b) The supply curve shifts to the left, but quantity supplied remains the same.
   (c) The quantity supplied of the good falls, but supply remains unchanged.
   (d) The supply curve shifts to the left, and the quantity supplied falls.

_____ 10. Market supply and demand curves both have determinants which depend on:
   (a) Opportunity costs.
   (b) Expectations.
   (c) Number of market participants.
   (d) All of the above.

_____ 11. Market supply and market demand curves are similar in that both:
   (a) Involve the willingness and ability of a supplier to sell a product or service.
   (b) Can be derived by adding horizontally all of the supply and demand curves of the individuals in the market.
   (c) Are affected by income.
   (d) Have price on the x-axis and production rate (quantity) on the y-axis.

_____ 12. A supply schedule matches, _ceteris paribus_:
   (a) Price and the quantity supplied of a good by an individual.
   (b) Price and the quantity supplied of a good by the sellers in a market.
   (c) What sellers are willing and able to provide at different prices.
   (d) All of the above.

_____ 13. A downward shift in a demand curve and a leftward shift in a supply curve both result in a:
   (a) Lower equilibrium price.
   (b) Higher equilibrium price.
   (c) Lower equilibrium quantity.
   (d) Higher equilibrium quantity.

_____ 14. Market supply represents:
   (a) The total quantity of a good that sellers are willing and able to sell at alternative prices in a given time period, _ceteris paribus_.
   (b) The horizontal sum of individual supply curves.
   (c) The combined willingness and ability of market suppliers to sell goods and services at various prices, in a given time period, _ceteris paribus_.
   (d) All of the above.

_____ 15. The emphasis on "willingness and ability" in the definitions of supply and demand warns us that supply and demand do not necessarily tell us:
   (a) The actual quantities produced and bought in a market.
   (b) The reasons that a particular quantity is demanded or supplied.
   (c) Who actually produces or receives the quantity demanded or supplied.
   (d) All of the above.

_____ 16. By definition, the equilibrium price in a market:
   (a) Occurs when the supply and demand curves are the same, _ceteris paribus_.
   (b) Is the price at which the quantity of a good or service demanded in a given time period equals the quantity supplied.
   (c) Is the market price.
   (d) All of the above.

_____ 17. Equilibrium prices include:
   (a) List prices that firms post on their products or in catalogs to inform the buyer of the price that is being offered.
   (b) Bid prices of buyers to inform the seller of the highest price that a buyer is willing and able to pay for a product.
   (c) Transaction prices that leave no shortages or surpluses at the end of the transaction period.
   (d) Prices at which there is excess supply.

_____ 18. A market surplus is:
- (a) The amount by which the quantity supplied exceeds the quantity demanded.
- (b) Excess supply.
- (c) A situation in which market price does not equal equilibrium price so that producers are not able to sell all of the goods and services they are willing and able to produce at that price.
- (d) All of the above.

_____ 19. When effective price ceilings are set for a market:
- (a) Quantity supplied will be less than the equilibrium quantity, and price will be less than the equilibrium price.
- (b) Quantity supplied will be less than the equilibrium quantity, and price will be greater than the equilibrium price.
- (c) Quantity supplied will be greater than the equilibrium quantity, and price will be less than the equilibrium price.
- (d) Quantity supplied will be greater than the equilibrium quantity, and price will be greater than the equilibrium price.

_____ 20. Which of the following groupings contains a word which does not belong?
- (a) Central planning, command economy, decentralized markets.
- (b) Laissez faire, market economy, invisible hand.
- (c) Technology, factor prices, number of sellers.
- (d) Tastes, income, expectations.

_____ 21. One World View article about Poland reports: "The price of electricity, natural gas and central heating went up by as much as 70 percent on New Year's Day as part of Poland's program to eliminate communist-era subsidies." From this quotation it can be concluded that:
- (a) The market equilibrium for natural gas was below the prices charged during the communist era.
- (b) The higher prices indicate that shortages are becoming larger.
- (c) The electricity market is in transition from central planning to the market mechanism.
- (d) All of the above.

_____ 22. One World View article described the difficulty faced by consumers of electricity who were already "severely pinched by . . . the new, real-world prices for food, rents, and other services." The determinant that is shifting electricity market demand on the basis of this quotation is:
- (a) The price of electricity.
- (b) The price of other goods.
- (c) Seller expectations.
- (d) Income.

Problems and Applications

Exercise 1

This exercise provides practice in graphing demand and supply curves for individual buyers and sellers as well as graphing market demand and market supply curves.

1. Suppose you are willing and able to buy 20 gallons of gasoline per week if the price is $1 per gallon, but if the price is $3 per gallon you are willing and able to buy only the bare minimum of 10 gallons. Complete the demand schedule in Table 3.1.

Table 3.1
Your demand schedule for gasoline

Price (dollars per gallon)	Quantity (gallons per week)
$1	_____
3	_____

2. Use your demand schedule for gasoline in Table 3.1 to diagram the demand curve in Figure 3.1. Assume your demand curve is a straight line.

Figure 3.1
Your demand curve for gasoline

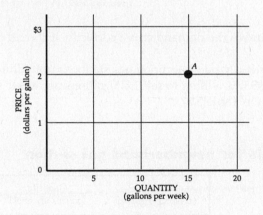

If you have drawn your demand curve correctly, it should go through point *A*.

3. Suppose that 999 other people in your town have demand curves for gasoline that are just like yours in Figure 3.1. Fill out the town's market-demand schedule in Table 3.2 at each price. (Remember to include your own quantity demanded along with everyone else's at each price.)

Table 3.2
Market-demand schedule for gasoline in your town

Price (dollars per gallon)	Quantity (gallons per week)
$1	_____
3	_____

4. Using the market-demand schedule in Table 3.2, draw the market-demand curve for gasoline for your town in Figure 3.2. Assume that the curve is a straight line, and label it D.

Figure 3.2
Market supply and demand curves for gasoline in your town

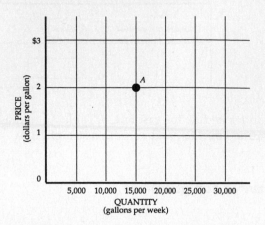

If you have drawn the demand curve correctly, it should pass through point A.

5. Suppose the friendly neighborhood gas station is not willing to sell anything at $1 per gallon, but at $3 it is willing to sell 1,500 gallons per week. Fill in the supply schedule for this gas station in Table 3.3.

Table 3.3
Supply schedule for neighborhood gas station

Price (dollars per gallon)	Quantity (gallons per week)
$1	_____
3	_____

6. Graph the supply curve for the gas station in Figure 3.3 using the information in Table 3.3. Assume that the supply curve is a straight line and label it S.

Figure 3.3
Supply curve for neighborhood gas station

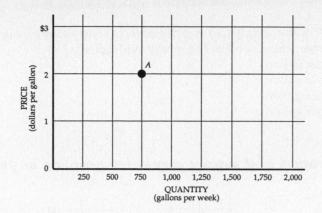

If you have drawn the supply curve correctly, it should pass through point *A*.

7. Suppose that nineteen other gas stations in your town have the same supply schedule as your neighborhood gas station (Table 3.3). Fill out the market-supply schedule for gasoline of the twenty gas stations in your town in Table 3.4.

Table 3.4
Market supply schedule for gasoline in your town

Price (dollars per gallon)	Quantity (gallons per week)
$1	_____
3	_____

8. Using the market supply schedule in Table 3.4, draw the market supply curve for gasoline for your town in Figure 3.2. Assume that the market supply curve is a straight line. If you have drawn the curve correctly, it should pass through point *A*. Label the supply curve *S*.

9. The equilibrium price for gasoline for your town's twenty gas stations and 1,000 buyers of gasoline (see Figure 3.2) is:
    (a) Above $2.
    (b) Exactly $2.
    (c) Below $2.

10. At the equilibrium price there are:
    (a) Shortages.
    (b) Surpluses.
    (c) Excess inventories.
    (d) None of the above.

Exercise 2

This exercise shows the market mechanics at work in shifting market demand curves.

1. In Figure 3.4, the supply (S_1) and demand (D_1) curves for gasoline as they might appear in your town are presented. The equilibrium price is:
    (a) $3 per gallon.
    (b) $2 per gallon.
    (c) $1 per gallon.
    (d) $0 per gallon.

Figure 3.4
Market demand and supply curves for gasoline in your town

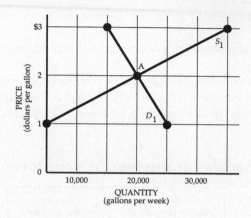

2. Assume that one-half of the people in your town move away. Because of this, suppose that the remaining buyers are willing and able to buy only half as much gasoline at each price as was bought before. Draw the new demand curve in Figure 3.4 and label it D_2.

3. T   F   When the number of buyers in a market changes, the market demand curve for goods and services shifts.

4. When half of the buyers move from your town, the equilibrium price:
    (a)   Rises above the old equilibrium price.
    (b)   Equals the old equilibrium price.
    (c)   Falls below the old equilibrium price.

    (*Hint:* See the second demand curve, D_2, in Figure 3.4.)

5. If the old market price ($2) does not change to the new equilibrium price, there will be:
    (a)   A larger quantity demanded than would be supplied at the new equilibrium price.
    (b)   A smaller quantity demanded than would be supplied at the new equilibrium price.

6. If the market price does not adjust to the new equilibrium price after the potential buyers leave, there will be:
    (a)   A market shortage.
    (b)   A market surplus.
    (c)   Neither shortage nor surplus.

7. When there is a surplus in a market, prices are likely to fall:
   (a) Because buyers do not wish to buy as much as sellers want to sell.
   (b) Because sellers are likely to offer discounts to eliminate expensive excess inventories.
   (c) Because buyers who cannot buy commodities at the current market price are likely to make offers to buy at lower prices that sellers will accept.
   (d) For all of the above reasons.

8. Whenever there is a leftward shift of the market demand curve, market forces should push:
   (a) Market prices upward and market quantity downward.
   (b) Market prices upward and market quantity upward.
   (c) Market prices downward and market quantity upward.
   (d) Market prices downward and market quantity downward.

9. Whenever there is a rightward shift of the market demand curve, market forces should push:
   (a) Market prices upward and market quantity downward.
   (b) Market prices upward and market quantity upward.
   (c) Market prices downward and market quantity upward.
   (d) Market prices downward and market quantity downward.

Exercise 3

This exercise gives practice in computing market demand and market supply curves using the demand and supply curves of individuals in a market. It is similar to the problem at the end of Chapter 3 in the text.

1. Table 3.5 shows the weekly demand and supply schedules for various individuals. Fill in the total market quantity that these individuals demand and supply.

Table 3.5
Individual demand and supply schedules

	Price			
	$4	$3	$2	$1
Buyers				
Al's quantity demanded	2	3	5	6
Betsy's quantity demanded	2	2	2	3
Casey's quantity demanded	1	2.5	3	3.5
Total market quantity demanded	___	___	___	___
Sellers				
Alice's quantity supplied	8	3	2	0
Butch's quantity supplied	7	5	4	0
Connie's quantity supplied	9	7	3	0
Ellen's quantity supplied	6	5	1	0
Total market quantity supplied	___	___	___	___

Use the data in Table 3.5 to answer Questions 2-4.

2. Construct and label market supply and market demand curves in Figure 3.5.

3. Identify the equilibrium price and label it *EQ* in Figure 3.5.

4. What is the amount of shortage (surplus) that would exist at a price of $1?

Figure 3.5
Market supply and market demand curves for buyers and sellers

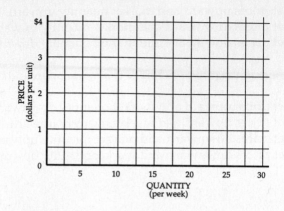

Exercise 4

This exercise provides examples of events that would shift demand or supply curves. It is similar to the exercise at the end of Chapter 3 in the text.

Choose the letter of the appropriate diagram in Figure 3.6 that best describes the type of shift that would occur in each of the following situations. The shifts are viewed as occurring in the market for U.S. defense goods. (*Hint:* Ask yourself if the change occurs initially through the buyers or the sellers. Then look for the determinant that is changing. Finally, ask yourself how the quantity or price should change as a result of the hypothesized event. Use common sense. With these three pieces of information it should be possible to determine the shift that occurs. The nonprice determinants of demand are tastes and preferences, incomes, buyer expectations, prices and availability of other goods, and number of buyers. The nonprice determinants of supply are technology, price and availability of resources, expectations, taxes, and number of suppliers.)

Figure 3.6
Shifts of curves

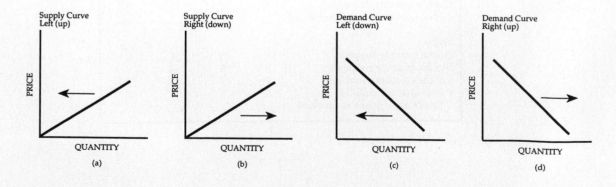

_____ 1. The economies of belligerent developing countries experience rapid growth in income and obtain more dollars with which to make purchases.

_____ 2. Because of increased protectionism for steel, steel producers are able to raise the price of specialty steel, which is a key resource in the production of defense goods.

_____ 3. Preparations for war begin among previous noncombatants in the Middle East.

_____ 4. The president is successful in getting Congress to increase the Defense Department's budget.

_____ 5. A new superior engineering design is developed that reduces the amount of materials needed to produce nuclear submarines.

_____ 6. New firms enter the market to produce defense goods.

_____ 7. A large firm in the defense industry goes into liquidation when it loses a defense contract and becomes bankrupt.

_____ 8. Consumers expect gun-control legislation to be enacted that will make it more difficult to purchase handguns in the future.

9. When you know what is shifting, you should be able to tell how equilibrium price and quantity will change. Fill in the blanks in Table 3.6 with "Rises" or "Falls."

Table 3.6
Response of equilibrium price and quantity to shifts in market supply and demand

Type of shift (ceteris paribus)	Equilibrium price	Equilibrium quantity
Market supply shifts leftward	_____	_____
Market supply shifts rightward	_____	_____
Market demand shifts leftward	_____	_____
Market demand shifts rightward	_____	_____

Exercise 5

The media often provide information about supply and demand shifts. This excercies uses one of the articles in the text to show the kind of information to look for. If your professor makes a newspaper assignment from the *Instructor's Manual*, this exercise will provide an example of how to do it.

Reread the In the News article from the *Washington Post* on page 75 in Chapter 3 entitled "Poles Strike Against Economic Reforms." Then answer the following questions:

1. Which of the four diagrams in Figure 3.6 in the previous exercise best represents the shift in the energy market (electricity, natural gas, and central heating) caused by the increased unemployment in Poland?   a   b   c   d   (circle one)

2. Determine whether the energy market is effectively an international, national, regional, or local market. What phrase gives you the answer.

3. What single word describes the change in the determinant of demand or supply that has caused the shift you chose in Figure 3.6?

4. Is it the buyer or the seller of energy who is initially affected by the change? How do you know?

5. What phrase indicates the change in price or quantity that results from the unemployment?

Crossword Puzzle

Select the economic term in the following list that corresponds with each of the definitions and descriptions below. Then fit the term or one of the words within it into the crossword puzzle at the numbers indicated. Some of the words in the list do not fit the puzzle.

ceteris paribus	government failure	market surplus
command economy	invisible hand	opportunity cost
demand	laissez faire	price ceiling
demand curve	market demand	product market
demand schedule	market mechanism	shift in demand
equilibrium price	market shortage	shift in supply
factor market	market supply	supply

Across

1. What occurs when market price is above the market-equilibrium price level.

3. Where resources are exchanged for money.

5. A French way of saying "let alone."

6. The total quantity that all sellers in a market are willing and able to make available at various prices.

10. A table that shows the relationship between prices and the quantities a buyer is willing and able to buy at various prices.

11. What occurs when market price is below the market-equilibrium price level.

13. Changes in tastes, incomes, or opportunity costs cause this to happen.

14. What guides market prices if the government does not interfere.

15. Intervention that does not improve market outcomes.

16. The total quantity demanded by all of the individual buyers in a market at every price.

17. The quantities a seller is willing and able to sell at various prices.

Down

2. A Latin term meaning "all other things being equal."

4. A graph representing the quantities that buyers are willing to buy at various prices, *ceteris paribus*.

6. When prices are determined by buyers and sellers in a market, the economy is using this.

7. When quantity demanded equals quantity supplied, this is established.

8. The value of the best alternative that must be forgone as a result of the decision to use resources in a particular way.

9. What a buyer is willing and able to buy at various prices.

12. A government limitation on prices set below the market equilibrium price.

Common Errors

The first statement in each "common error" below is incorrect. Each incorrect statement is followed by a corrected version and an explanation.

1. If a large number of people petition the government in order to get something, then there is a large demand for that item. WRONG!

   If a large number of people desire a commodity *and have the ability to pay for it*, then there is a large demand for that commodity in a particular time period. RIGHT!

   People want something, but there is no "demand" for it unless they are able to pay for it. Economists use the word "demand" in a way that is quite different from normal usage. People who want (desire; have preferences, a taste, or liking for) a commodity are seen as going to a market to purchase the commodity with money or through bartering. As economists use the word, "demand" has no connotation of stridency or imperiously claiming the right to something when a person hasn't the ability to buy it.

2. Market price is the same thing as equilibrium price. WRONG!

   The market price moves by trial and error (via the market mechanism) toward the equilibrium price. RIGHT!

   When demand and supply curves shift, the market is temporarily out of equilibrium. The price may move along a demand or supply curve toward the new equilibrium.

3. Since the quantity bought must equal the quantity sold, every market is always in equilibrium by definition. WRONG!

   Although quantity bought equals quantity sold, there may be shortages or surpluses. RIGHT!

   Although the quantity *actually* bought does equal the quantity *actually* sold, there may still be buyers who *are willing and able* to buy more of the good at the market price (market shortages exist) or sellers who are willing and able to sell more of the good at the market price (market surpluses exist). If the market price is above the equilibrium price, there will be queues of goods (inventories). Prices will be lowered by sellers toward the equilibrium price. If the market price is below the equilibrium price, there will be queues of buyers (shortages). Prices will be bid up by buyers toward the equilibrium price.

4. The intersection of supply and demand curves determines how much of a good or service will actually be exchanged and the actual price of the exchange. WRONG!

   The intersection of supply and demand curves shows only where buyers and sellers *intend* and have the *ability* to exchange the same amount of a commodity. RIGHT!

   Many institutional interferences may prevent the market from ever reaching the equilibrium point, where supply and demand curves intersect. All that can be said is that, given a free market, prices and production will tend to move toward equilibrium levels.

5. A change in price changes the demand for goods by consumers. WRONG!

A change in price changes the quantity demanded by consumers in a given time period. RIGHT!

Economists differentiate between the terms "quantity demanded" and "demand." A change in the quantity demanded usually refers to a movement along the demand curve as a result of a change in price or production rate. A change in demand refers to a shift of the demand curve as a result of a change in incomes, tastes, prices or variability of other goods, or expectations.

6. A change in price changes the supply of goods produced by a firm. WRONG!

A change in price changes the quantity of a good supplied by a firm in a given time period. RIGHT!

Economists differentiate between the terms "quantity supplied" and "supply." A change in the quantity supplied usually refers to a movement along a supply curve as a result of a change in price or production rate. A change in supply refers to a shift of the supply curve as a result of a change in technology, prices of resources, number of sellers, other goods, expectations, or taxes.

7. A rise in the supply curve is the same as an increase in supply. WRONG!

An upward shift in the supply curve implies a decrease in supply. RIGHT!

In Figure 3.7 the *rise* of the supply curve from S_1 to S_2 will result in a fall in quantity from Q_1 to Q_2 at any price, p^*. Supply is *lower*. A fall in the supply curve means an increase in supply.

Figure 3.7

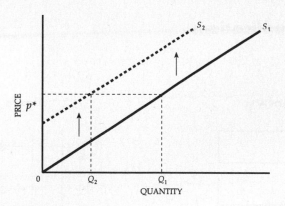

Be careful: When a shift in the supply curve is mentioned, it may help to think of the shift as a movement to the left or right, not up or down.

•ANSWERS•

Key-Term Review

1. market demand
2. demand schedule
3. opportunity cost
4. market supply
5. demand
6. supply
7. equilibrium price
8. shift in demand
9. demand curve
10. market mechanism
11. market shortage
12. product market
13. market surplus
14. factor market
15. *ceteris paribus*
16. law of demand
17. law of supply
18. price ceiling

True or False

1. F	5. F	9. T	13. T	17. T	20. F
2. T	6. F	10. T	14. F	18. T	21. F
3. F	7. T	11. F	15. F	19. T	22. F
4. F	8. T	12. F	16. F		

Multiple Choice

1. b	5. a	9. a	13. c	17. c	20. c
2. c	6. c	10. d	14. d	18. d	21. c
3. d	7. b	11. b	15. d	19. a	22. b
4. d	8. c	12. d	16. b		

Problems and Applications

Exercise 1

1. **Table 3.1 Answer**

p	q
$1	20
3	10

2. **Figure 3.1 Answer**

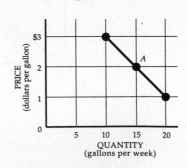

3. **Table 3.2 Answer**

p	q
$1	20,000
3	10,000

4. **Figure 3.2 Answer**

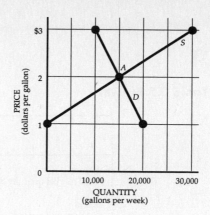

5. **Table 3.3 Answer**

p	q
$1	0
3	1,500

6. **Figure 3.3 Answer**

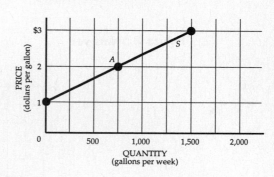

7. **Table 3.4 Answer**

p	q
$1	0
3	30,000

8. See Figure 3.2 Answer.

9. b
10. d

Exercise 2

1. b

2. **Figure 3.4 Answer**

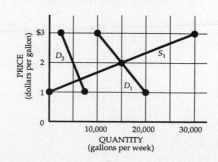

3. T

4. c   5. b   6. b   7. d   8. d   9. b

Exercise 3

1. **Table 3.5 Answer**

		Price		
	$4	$3	$2	$1
Buyers Total market quantity demanded	5	7.5	10	12.5
Sellers Total market quantity supplied	30	20	10	0

2. **Figure 3.5 Answer**

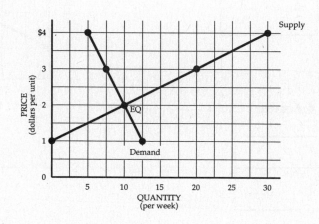

3. See point *EQ* in Figure 3.5 Answer.

4. Since the quantity supplied is zero at a price of $1, the *shortage* is the same as the quantity demanded (12.5 units).

Exercise 4

1. d   A rise in income shifts the demand curve upward (to the right).

2. a   An increase in the price of a resource shifts the supply curve upward (to the left).

3. d   An increase in the number of buyers shifts the demand curve upward (to the right).

4. d   A larger budget (income) for defense shifts the demand curve upward (to the right).

5. b   An improvement in technology shifts the supply curve downward (to the right.)

6. b An increase in the number of suppliers shifts the supply curve downward (to the right).

7. a A decrease in the number of suppliers shifts the supply curve to the left.

8. d Buyers' expectations that guns will be more difficult to obtain in the future shift the demand curve upward (to the right) today.

9. **Table 3.6 Answer**

Type of shift (ceteris paribus)	Equilibrium price	Equilibrium quantity
Market supply shifts leftward	Rises	Falls
Market supply shifts rightward	Falls	Rises
Market demand shifts leftward	Falls	Falls
Market demand shifts rightward	Rises	Rises

Exercise 5

1. c Increased unemployment results in lower incomes and fewer potential buyers.

2. "real world prices" indicate an international market. Even though energy can be bought from all around the world, the supply of energy has been carefully controlled by the government, indicating the retail market for energy has effectively been made a national market. The consumers being discussed are the Poles, providing further evidence of a national market.

3. The key word is in the fourth paragraph of the article, ("unemployment.")

4. Unemployment affects the buyers of energy. They are the ones who are "severely pinched."

5. The article at first appears confusing because a leftward shift of demand should result in lower prices. However, the article is talking about higher energy prices! As in most articles in the press, it is very important to focus on one shift at a time. The higher prices result from a shift in the supply curve owing to the government's action. However, the words "severely pinched" suggest much more careful purchasing by consumers, which should result in lower quantity demanded.

Crossword Puzzle Answer

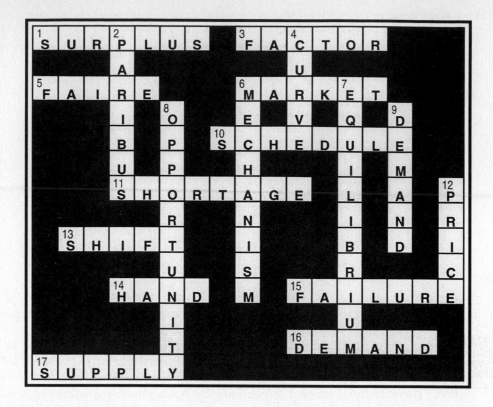

Across

1. market *surplus*
3. *factor* market
5. laissez *faire*
6. *market* supply
10. demand *schedule*
11. market *shortage*
13. *shift* in demand
14. invisible *hand*
15. government *failure*
16. market *demand*
17. *supply*

Down

2. ceteris *paribus*
4. demand *curve*
6. market *mechanism*
7. *equilibrium* price
8. *opportunity* cost
9. *demand*
12. *price* ceiling

CHAPTER 4

The Business Cycle

Quick Review

The Great Depression of the 1930s was a worldwide phenomenon. No market economy seemed to avoid it. High unemployment and low production for a decade led to despair nearly everywhere. They also caused a major rethinking of our views on the U.S. economy. Serious questions were raised, including:

- How stable is a market-driven economy?
- What forces cause instability?
- What, if anything, can the government do to promote steady economic growth?

The basic purpose of macroeconomics is to answer these questions—that is, to explain the alternating periods of expansion and contraction in gross domestic product (GDP) known as the business cycle. If we can develop a macro theory to explain such changes, perhaps we can develop macro policies to control them.

The Classical school of thought, which was largely in vogue prior to the 1930s, stressed the self-adjusting nature of the economy. Automatic adjustment mechanisms—such as flexible wages and prices, falling interest rates, and the like—were thought to ensure that any downswing would be short if the economy was left alone, that is, if a laissez faire attitude prevailed.

The Great Depression lasted a long time, and economists and politicians everywhere began to question Classical theory. The great British economist John Maynard Keynes developed an alternative theory that took issue with the self-adjusting view of Classical economics. Keynes asserted that the economy was, in fact, inherently *unstable*. To leave the economy alone was poor policy. Instead, he prescribed increased government spending, income transfers, and lower interest rates to get the economy moving again. The arguments about business cycles are still not settled, but we have learned a great deal and agree to measure the cycle from peak to trough by watching the fluctuation in real GDP. Two consecutive quarters of decline in real GDP is considered a recession. Growth for a period below the 3 percent long-run trend of the economy is called a "growth recession." The statistics presented in this chapter make it clear that business cycles vary greatly in length, frequency, and intensity.

Today economists focus on aggregate demand and aggregate supply to explain how the economy works. These concepts are the macroeconomic counterparts to demand and supply in individual markets. The aggregate demand curve slopes downward and to the right when plotted against the price level. The aggregate supply curve slopes upward and to the right in the short run, but is likely to be vertical in the long run. The macro equilibrium that is defined by their intersection may or may not be the employment level we desire. Even if the macro equilibrium is at the output, employment, and price levels we desire, it may not last for long. The forces lying behind the equilibrium can change. Shifts in aggregate demand and/or aggregate supply can lead to unemployment, inflation, or, worse yet, stagflation—a combination of the two.

The aggregate-demand and aggregate-supply framework provides a convenient way to compare various theories about how the economy works. The theories can be classified as demand-side, supply-side, or eclectic, which draws on both. The three policy levers used to discuss and demonstrate the several theories are:

1. Fiscal policy—changes in taxes and government spending to alter economic outcomes.
2. Monetary policy—the use of money and credit to control economic outcomes.
3. Supply-side policies—those that favor tax cuts and other policies to increase incentives for producers.

Much of what follows in the next several chapters is devoted to explaining the theory of macroeconomic behavior introduced here.

Learning Objectives

After reading Chapter 4 and doing the following exercises, you should:	True or false	Multiple choice	Problems and applications	Common errors	Pages in the text
1. Understand the dimensions of the business cycle.	1, 4-6, 8, 11, 14, 21	3, 4, 6, 7	3, 4	1, 2	81-83
2. Have in mind a historical perspective on the business cycle from the Great Depression to the present.	7-11	5	3	1	83-89
3. Be able to distinguish the Keynesian and Classical positions on how the macro economy works.	2, 3	1, 2, 27, 28	2		83-89
4. Understand the definitions of aggregate demand and aggregate supply and the implications of macroeconomic equilibrium.	15-20	8-14, 16, 18-20, 22	3	2	89-96
5. Be aware that there are several explanations of the business cycle—demand-side, supply-side, and eclectic.	22-23	15-17, 20, 23, 26-29	1, 2		96-100
6. Be able to differentiate the policy levers advocated in the various business cycle theories.	12, 13	20, 24-27, 30			100-102

Key-Term Review

Review the following terms; if you are not sure of the meaning of any term, write out the definition and check it against the Glossary in the text.

aggregate demand
aggregate supply
business cycle
equilibrium (macro)
fiscal policy
growth recession
inflation

laissez faire
law of demand
macroeconomics
monetary policy
real GDP
recession
Say's Law
supply-side policy

Fill in the blank following each of the statements below with the appropriate term from the list above.

1. The idea that "supply creates its own demand" is known as _____ .

    1. _____

2. The idea that greater quantities will be demanded at lower prices, *ceteris paribus*, is the _____ .

    2. _____

3. When GDP grows, but at a rate less than the long-term trend, this is called a _____ .

    3. _____

4. A _____ is said to occur when real GDP declines for two consecutive quarters.

    4. _____

5. The price level at which _____ and _____ intersect determines macroeconomic equilibrium.

    5. _____
    _____

6. _____ is the use of money and credit controls to influence macroeconomic activity.

    6. _____

7. _____ is the use of government taxes and spending to influence macroeconomic activity.

    7. _____

8. The first Reagan administration emphasized tax cuts as a _____ .

    8. _____

9. The observed pattern of economic growth and contraction is known as the _____ .

    9. _____

10. The branch of economics that focuses on the behavior of the entire economy is _____ .

    10. _____

11. GDP adjusted for inflation is called the _____ .

    11. _____

12. _____ is the combination of price level and real output where aggregate demand and aggregate supply intersect.

12. _____

13. When the average level of prices increases continuously, the process is known as _____ .

13. _____

14. The classical view that the economy would self-adjust relied on a _____ philosophy for the macroeconomy.

14. _____

True or False: *Circle your choice.*

T   F   1. The Great Depression is important in the study of macroeconomics because macroeconomics focuses on the business cycle.

T   F   2. In the Classical view of the economy, the product market is brought into equilibrium by flexible wages, the factor market by flexible prices.

T   F   3. The Classical approach to the business cycle was laissez-faire.

T   F   4. Unemployment and inflation tend to rise and fall together.

T   F   5. Business cycles are measured using percentage changes of the real GDP.

T   F   6. *Constant* prices eliminate distortions in the GDP from inflation.

T   F   7. Most countries experienced the Great Depression with approximately the same percentage change in real GDP as the United States.

T   F   8. A growth recession occurs when the growth rate of the GDP is positive but below its long-term average.

T   F   9. During the business cycle, unemployment and production typically move in the same direction.

T   F   10. During a recession, real output must actually fall.

T   F   11. Unlike a growth recession, a recession is defined as occurring when the unemployment rate increases for two consecutive quarters.

T   F   12. Policy levers include wars, natural disasters, and trade disruptions.

T   F   13. Internal market forces include population growth, spending behavior, invention, and innovation.

T   F   14. The quantity of real output demanded rises as the price level rises, *ceteris paribus*.

T   F   15. In a diagram of aggregate demand and aggregate supply the *x*-axis is referred to as real output, real income, or real value of purchases.

T F 16. The cost effect results in a linear aggregate supply curve.

T F 17. The profit effect reflects the changes in quantity supplied that result when lower average prices fail to lower costs.

T F 18. The response of quantity supplied to higher average prices consists of (a) the cost effect resulting from costs remaining unchanged, and (b) the profit effect resulting from costs adjusting to higher average prices.

T F 19. For macroeconomic equilibrium to occur, the aggregate demand curve must intersect the aggregate supply curve.

T F 20. If, at the prevailing price level, aggregate supply exceeds aggregate demand, the price level will tend to rise.

T F 21. The full-employment GDP is the same as the equilibrium GDP.

T F 22. Both Keynesian and monetarist theories of the business cycle are supply-side theories.

T F 23. Fiscal policy is the use of tax and spending powers to shift the aggregate supply curve.

Multiple Choice: *Select the correct answer.*

_____ 1. Which of the following is inherent in the Classical view of a self-adjusting economy?
   (a) Inflexible wages.
   (b) Inflexible prices.
   (c) Say's Law.
   (d) All of the above.

_____ 2. Keynesian theory became important when Classical economic theory did not adequately explain:
   (a) A prolonged period of both inflation and unemployment.
   (b) A prolonged growth recession.
   (c) A depression.
   (d) A prolonged inflation.

_____ 3. The downswing in the business cycle is characterized by:
   (a) Higher real output.
   (b) A higher unemployment rate.
   (c) Higher prices.
   (d) All of the above.

_____ 4. *Constant prices* are used in the compution of:
   (a) The volume of production.
   (b) Real GDP.
   (c) Business cycles.
   (d) All of the above.

_____ 5. The Great Depression:
  (a) Affected the Soviet Union more than most other economies because of its failure to use the market mechanism.
  (b) Was a global depression.
  (c) Affected most countries except the Soviet Union, the United States, and Germany with the same percentage change in output.
  (d) All of the above.

_____ 6. The percentage decline in economic growth during the typical business slump in the United States has been:
  (a) Highly variable.
  (b) In the range of 6 to 8 percent.
  (c) Associated with low levels in the unemployment rate.
  (d) All of the above.

_____ 7. Which of the following is a ranking of growth rates from fastest to slowest?
  (a) Depression, recession, growth recession.
  (b) Growth recession, recession, depression.
  (c) Recession, depression, growth recession.
  (d) Recession, growth recession, depression.

_____ 8. In the aggregate demand-aggregate supply diagram:
  (a) The vertical axis measures real output.
  (b) The horizontal axis measures the average price level.
  (c) The intersection of the two marks the macro equilibrium.
  (d) All of the above.

_____ 9. Which of the following effects explains a differently shaped aggregate demand or supply curve than the other three determinants?
  (a) Profit effect.
  (b) Interest-rate effect.
  (c) Real-balances effect.
  (d) Foreign-trade effect.

_____ 10. The real-balances effect relies on the idea that as the price level falls:
  (a) Each dollar you own will purchase more goods and services.
  (b) Each bond you own will increase in value, thus increasing your wealth.
  (c) You will begin to save less because your wealth has increased.
  (d) All of the above are the case.

_____ 11. When the average price level falls in our economy, consumers tend to:
  (a) Buy more imported goods and fewer domestically produced goods, _ceteris paribus_.
  (b) Buy more imported goods and more domestic goods, _ceteris paribus_.
  (c) Buy fewer imported goods and more domestic goods, _ceteris paribus_.
  (d) Buy fewer imported goods and fewer domestic goods, _ceteris paribus_.

_____ 12. The difference between market demand and aggregate demand is:
  (a) Market demand applies to all individuals, and aggregate demand does not.
  (b) Aggregate demand applies to a specific good, and market demand does not.
  (c) Policy levers work only through market demand.
  (d) Market demand applies to a given market while aggregate demand applies to the entire economy.

_____ 13. The cost effect implies:
- (a) That greater output results in increasingly higher costs.
- (b) A curved, upward-sloping aggregate supply curve.
- (c) That higher average prices are reflected in higher costs.
- (d) All of the above.

_____ 14. As output rises, the cost effect results from:
- (a) The difficulty of producing more with limited capacity.
- (b) Tight supplies of factors of production.
- (c) Higher overtime wages.
- (d) All of the above.

_____ 15. In macro equilibrium:
- (a) Aggregate quantity demanded equals aggregate quantity supplied.
- (b) The equilibrium price level and rate of output are both stable.
- (c) Both buyers' and sellers' intentions are satisfied.
- (d) All of the above.

_____ 16. When aggregate supply exceeds aggregate demand, what will happen to the price level?
- (a) Prices will rise to a new equilibrium.
- (b) Prices will remain the same at equilibrium.
- (c) Prices will drop to a new equilibrium.
- (d) Not enough information is given to answer the question.

_____ 17. Starting from an equilibrium at less than full employment:
- (a) If aggregate supply increases, _ceteris paribus_, the economy will generally experience inflation.
- (b) If aggregate demand decreases, _ceteris paribus_, the economy will generally experience inflation.
- (c) If both aggregate demand and aggregate supply increase, output and employment should decrease, but direction of the price-level movement would be uncertain.
- (d) None of the above.

_____ 18. Which of the following groupings contains a term which does not belong?
- (a) Internal market forces, external shocks, policy levers.
- (b) Output, prices, jobs.
- (c) Aggregate demand curve shift, aggregate supply curve shift, laissez faire.
- (d) Real-balances effect, foreign-trade effect, cost effect.

_____ 19. Which of the following may be a problem of a macro equilibrium?
- (a) Undesirable inflation.
- (b) Instability of the equilibrium.
- (c) Unacceptable levels of unemployment.
- (d) Any of the above.

_____ 20. According to Keynes, policymakers should respond to a downturn by:
- (a) Cutting taxes, increasing government spending, and reducing transfers.
- (b) Cutting taxes, reducing government spending, and increasing transfers.
- (c) Cutting taxes, increasing government spending, and increasing transfers.
- (d) Raising taxes, increasing government spending, and increasing transfers.

_____ 21. Equilibrium falling short of full employment is another way of saying:
      (a)   Capacity is fully utilized.
      (b)   Unemployment levels are unacceptably high.
      (c)   The economy is on the production-possibilities curve.
      (d)   All of the above.

_____ 22. If full employment equals the macro equilibrium, which of the following best describes the macroeconomic effect of an upward shift of the aggregate supply curve, *ceteris paribus*?
      (a)   Inflation and movement toward full employment with a faster economic growth rate.
      (b)   Inflation and a lower economic growth rate.
      (c)   Recession or depression.
      (d)   A lower price level and a greater economic growth rate.

_____ 23. Keynes argued that deficient aggregate demand might originate with:
      (a)   Inadequate business investment.
      (b)   Lower consumer savings.
      (c)   Excessive government spending.
      (d)   All of the above.

_____ 24. Which of the following causes the aggregate supply curve to shift?
      (a)   Changes in consumer income.
      (b)   Changes in consumer savings.
      (c)   Changes in costs experienced by American businesses.
      (d)   None of the above.

_____ 25. Which of the following combination of shifts of aggregate demand and supply curves would definitely result in higher unemployment?
      (a)   Demand shifts left and supply shifts right.
      (b)   Demand shifts left and supply shifts left.
      (c)   Demand shifts right and supply shifts right.
      (d)   Demand shifts right and supply shifts left.

_____ 26. The reasons the economy fails to reach full employment are described correctly for which of the following groups of economists?
      (a)   Supply-side economists believe greed, rising costs, resource shortages, taxes, and regulation interfere.
      (b)   Keynesians believe inadequate aggregate demand interferes.
      (c)   Monetarists believe that inappropriate monetary policy interferes.
      (d)   All of the above.

_____ 27. An example of an economic theory that answered the failure of an earlier economic theory is the:
      (a)   Explanation by Keynes about the way "priming the pump" could eliminate a depression.
      (b)   Explanation by New Classical economists about the inability of government to adjust short-run macroeconomic outcomes.
      (c)   Use of eclecticism by politicians who do not see that a single, clear economic theory that solves all of the macroeconomic problems that face them.
      (d)   All of the above.

_____ 28. In the long run:
   (a) Rises in costs catch up with rising prices.
   (b) Sellers have no incentive to increase output.
   (c) The aggregate supply curve is vertical.
   (d) All of the above.

_____ 29. Which of the following is used in the eclectic approach to solving the business cycle?
   (a) The money supply.
   (b) Taxes and government spending.
   (c) Incentives for producers.
   (d) All of the above.

_____ 30. Which of the following macro policy strategies is the focus of the World View headline "Free Enterprise Blooms in Wenzhou, China, Out of the Party's Sight"?
   (a) Laissez faire.
   (b) Monetary policy.
   (c) Fiscal policy.
   (d) Supply-side policy.

Problems and Applications

Exercise 1

This exercise examines the effects of tax policy using aggregate supply and demand curves.

Assume the aggregate demand and supply curves are those shown in Figure 4.1. Then suppose the government reduces taxes, which causes the quantity of output demanded in the economy to rise by $1 trillion per year at every price level. Decide whether the tax change shifts aggregate demand or aggregate supply from its initial position.

Figure 4.1

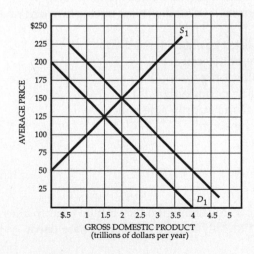

1. In Figure 4.1 draw the new aggregate demand curve (label it D_2) or aggregate supply curve (label it S_2) that results from the tax change.

2. Compute the percentage change in equilibrium GDP caused by the shift. _____

3. Suppose that the unemployment rate drops by 1 percentage point for every 5 percent increase in GDP. If the unemployment rate was 15 percent before the shift occurred, what would it be after the shift? _____

4. What is the percentage change in the equilibrium price level as a result of the tax change? _____

5. The shift that occurred in Question 1 (above) is consistent with:
   (a) Stagflation.
   (b) Inflation and a lower unemployment rate.
   (c) Deflation and a higher unemployment rate.
   (d) Lower inflation and a lower unemployment rate.

Now suppose the lower taxes also induce productivity changes and generate incentives that cause firms (sellers) to lower prices by $50 per unit of output per year after the tax change. (In Questions 6-11, compare the new equilibrium with the one you established above in Question 1.)

6. Draw the new aggregate demand curve (label it D_3) or aggregate supply curve (label it S_3) in Figure 4.1.

7. Compare the percentage change (on curve S_2 or D_2) in equilibrium GDP caused by the shift. _____

8. Suppose that the unemployment rate drops by 1 percentage point for every 5 percent increase in GDP. If the unemployment rate was 8.4 percent before the shift occurred, what would it be after the shift? _____

9. What would be the percentage change in the equilibrium price level associated with the new level of output? _____

10. This shift is consistent with:
    (a) Stagflation.
    (b) Inflation and a lower unemployment rate.
    (c) Deflation and a higher unemployment rate.
    (d) A lower price level and a lower unemployment rate.

11. The tax cut can best be characterized as:
    (a) Monetary policy only.
    (b) Fiscal policy only.
    (c) Supply-side policy only.
    (d) Both fiscal and supply-side policy.
    (e) None of the above.

Exercise 2

This exercise shows how government policy can be used to alleviate problems brought on by natural disasters. Aggregate supply and demand curves are used.

Assume the aggregate demand and supply curves are those shown in Figure 4.2. Suppose drought causes massive destruction of crops, which results in a decrease of $1 trillion of goods and services (GDP) that sellers are willing and able to provide. Decide whether the change shifts aggregate demand or aggregate supply from the initial equilibrium.

Figure 4.2

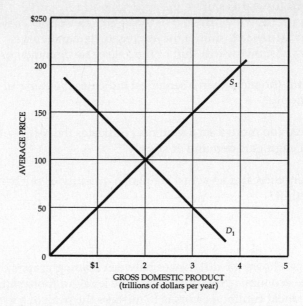

1. In Figure 4.2 draw the new aggregate demand (label it D_2) or aggregate supply curve (label it S_2) that results from the drought.

2. With which of the following is the move to the new equilibrium in Question 1 consistent?
   (a) Stagflation.
   (b) Inflation and a lower unemployment rate.
   (c) Deflation and a higher unemployment rate.
   (d) Deflation and a lower unemployment rate.

3. If the average price was held down to $100 by government price controls, there would be a (shortage, surplus) after the drought?

4. Suppose the government released some of its inventories to push the equilibrium to a GDP of $2 trillion at an average price of $100? In Figure 4.2 draw the new aggregate demand (label it D_3) or supply curve (label it S_3) that would result from the government's inventory release program.

Exercise 3

The media frequently provide information on macroeconomic events that affect aggregate demand and aggregate supply. To describe such shifts the media should provide certain kinds of information. This exercise will use one of the articles in the text to show the kind of information to look for. If your professor makes a newspaper assignment from the *Instructor's Manual*, this exercise will provide an example of how to do it.

Reread the selection on page 66 in Chapter 3 entitled "The Gulf War and Oil Prices." Ignore the graph that is used to analyze the article, which refers to the market demand and supply of oil, rather than aggregate demand and supply of goods and services.

1. Which of the following shifts in the world's aggregate demand or supply was caused by the invasion of Iraq in addition to the original invasion of Kuwait?
    (a) Leftward (upward) shift of the aggregate supply curve.
    (b) Rightward (downward) shift of the aggregate supply curve.
    (c) Leftward (upward) shift of the aggregate demand curve.
    (d) Rightward (downward) shift of the aggregate demand curve.

2. What statement (no more than a sentence) indicates the cause of a shift in aggregate demand or supply?

3. What statement (no more than a sentence) indicates the recipients of the initial impact of the change in aggregate demand or supply?

4. What statement indicates an actual change in quantity or price (no more than a sentence) owing to the shift?

Exercise 4

The following exercise shows the differences between reading graphs of percentage changes of variables (for example, the economic growth rate) and the levels of those same variables (for example, the real GDP). One of the most common errors is to mistake the peak of a graph of percentage changes for the maximum value of a variable. In this graphing exercise you will become aware of the differences between the two ways of graphing one piece of information.

1. Graph the real GDP (see the data on the inside cover of the text) in Figure 4.3a and the percentage change in real GDP in Figure 4.3b

Figure 4.3a
The real GDP

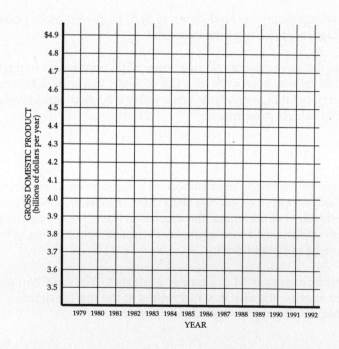

Figure 4.3b
Percentage change of the real GDP

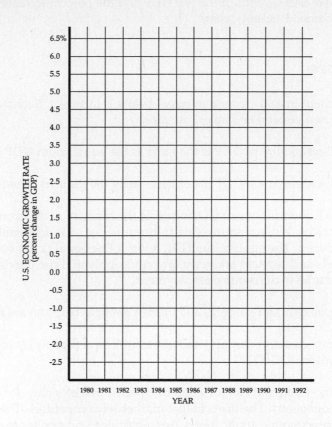

2. In Figure 4.3a of real GDP, recessions occur:
   (a) Immediately after peaks in the curve.
   (b) Immediately after troughs in the curve.
   (c) When the curve is above the *x*-axis at zero.
   (d) When the curve is below the *x*-axis at zero.

3. In Figure 4.3b of the percentage change in real GDP, recessions occur:
   (a) Immediately after peaks in the curve.
   (b) Immediately after troughs in the curve.
   (c) When the curve is above the x-axis at zero.
   (d) When the curve is below the x-axis at zero.

4. In both diagrams identify the years in which recessions occur. _____
   _____

5. In which figure (Figure 4.3a or Figure 4.3b) is it visually easier to determine when recessions occur? _____

6. Fill in the blanks in following the statements with one of the following responses: "real GDP" or "percentage change in real GDP."

   When the _____ rises, the _____ is positive.

When the _____ equals zero, then _____ reaches the bottom of a trough or the top of a peak.

7. The peaks and troughs of the real GDP and the percentage change in the real GDP occur in the (same, different) years.

Common Errors

The first statement in each "common error" below is incorrect. Each incorrect statement is followed by a corrected version and an explanation.

1. The full-employment GDP is the same as the equilibrium GDP. WRONG!

   The full-employment GDP is not necessarily the same as the equilibrium GDP. RIGHT!

   The full-employment GDP refers to the capacity of the economy to produce goods and services. When resources are fully employed, no additional goods and services can be produced. The equilibrium GDP refers to the equality between the aggregate demand for goods and services and the aggregate supply of those goods and services, not to any particular level of resource employment.

2. Aggregate demand (supply) and market demand (supply) are the same. WRONG!

   Aggregate demand (supply) and market demand (supply) involve very different levels of aggregation. RIGHT!

   Market demand can be found for specific markets only. Products in that market must be homogeneous. The firms in that market are competitors. The market demand is used for microeconomic applications. Aggregate demand applies to all markets within the economy and involves their average prices. It is not even possible to sum the market demand curves to find the aggregate demand curve because the prices of different commodities cannot be measured in the same units; an average price must be computed. Aggregate demand is used for macroeconomic applications, not microeconomic ones. The distinction between aggregate supply and market supply is similar to that between aggregate demand and market demand.

3. A downward-sloping trend of the economic growth rate indicates a recession. WRONG!

   A downward-sloping trend of the real GDP indicates a recession. RIGHT!

   The economic growth rate is measured by the *percentage change* in the real GDP. A recession occurs whenever that percentage change is negative for two quarters. By contrast, in a graph of the real GDP, without any computation of year-to-year changes, it is necessary to look for a downward dip in the real GDP to spot a recession. Three rules for the relationship between the levels and percentage changes of the real GDP should always be remembered when either graph is being examined:
   1. Whenever there is a downward slope to a graph of the real GDP, there will be a negative percentage change in real GDP.
   2. Whenever the graph of the real GDP flattens, the percentage change in the real GDP will approach zero.
   3. Whenever there is an upward slope to a graph of the real GDP, there will be a positive percentage change in real GDP.

•ANSWERS•

Key-Term Review

1.	Say's Law	8.	supply-side policy
2.	law of demand	9.	business cycle
3.	growth recession	10.	macroeconomics
4.	recession	11.	real GDP
5.	aggregate demand	12.	equilibrium (macro)
	aggregate supply	13.	inflation
6.	monetary policy	14.	*laissez-faire*
7.	fiscal policy		

True or False

1.	T	5.	T	9.	F	13.	T	17.	T	21.	F
2.	F	6.	T	10.	T	14.	F	18.	F	22.	F
3.	T	7.	F	11.	F	15.	T	19.	T	23.	F
4.	F	8.	T	12.	F	16.	F	20.	F		

Multiple Choice

1.	c	4.	d	7.	b	10.	d	13.	d	16.	c
2.	c	5.	b	8.	c	11.	c	14.	d	17.	d
3.	b	6.	a	9.	a	12.	d	15.	d		

18.   d   This grouping mixes the reasons for a downward-sloping aggregate demand curve with the reasons for an upward sloping aggregate supply curve. Other groupings are (a) determinants of the macro economy, (b) macroeconomic outcomes, and (c) the three distinct macro policy strategies (p. 100).

19.	d	21.	b	23.	a	25.	b	27.	d	29.	d
20.	c	22.	b	24.	c	26.	d	28.	d	30.	a

Problems and Applications

Exercise 1

1. See Figure 4.1 Answer, D_2.

Figure 4.1 Answer

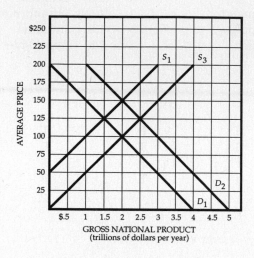

2. Equilibrium GDP before the shift is $1.5 trillion each year.
   Equilibrium GDP after the shift is $2.00 trillion each year.
   Percentage change = (2.0 - 1.5)/1.5 = 33%.

3. 33% change in output/5% = 6.6% drop in the unemployment rate.
   The new unemployment rate is 8.4% (= 15% - 6.6%).

4. Equilibrium price before the shift is 125.
   Equilibrium price after the shift is 150.
   Percentage change = (150 - 125)/125 = 20%.

5. b

6. See Figure 4.1 Answer, S_3.

7. Equilibrium GDP before the shift is $2.0 trillion
   Equilibrium GDP after the shift is $2.5 trillion.
   Percentage change = (2.5 - 2.0)/2.0 = 25%.

8. 25% change in output/5% = 5% drop in the unemployment rate.
   The new unemployment rate is 3.4% (= 8.4% - 5%).

9. Equilibrium price before the shift is 150.
   Equilibrium price after the shift is 125.
   Percentage change = (125 - 150)/150 = -17%.

10. d

11. d

Exercise 2

1. See Figure 4.2 Answer, S_2.

Figure 4.2 Answer

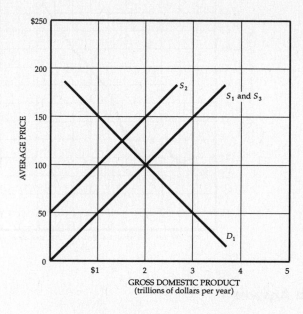

2. Since the drought causes prices to rise and the GDP to fall, its effects on the economy are consistent with stagflation.

3. shortage. The price ($100) is below the new equilibrium price of $125.

4. See Figure 4.2 Answer, S_3.

Exercise 3

1. (a) Leftward shift of the aggregate supply curve. The refusal to purchase Iraqi oil is a separate leftward shift of the aggregate demand and must be analyzed separately.

2. "After repeated pleas to Kuwait to curtail its oil production, Iraq decided to invade Kuwait and shut down its oil production." (The determinant that is changing is a reduction in the number of sellers of oil in the oil market.)

3. "and shut down its [Kuwait's] oil production" or "Effectively cutting off its [Iraq's] oil production and exports as well"

4. "reduced the world's oil supply by 4 million barrels a day and sent oil prices soaring" or "the price of oil jumped from $15 a barrel . . . to over $40 a barrel"

Exercise 4

1. See Figure 4.3a Answer and Figure 4.3b Answer

Figure 4.3a Answer

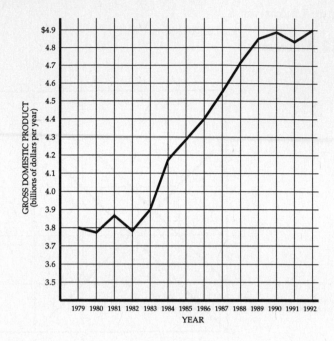

Figure 4.3b Answer

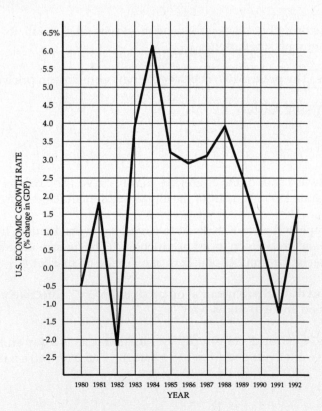

2. a

3. d

4. 1980, 1982, 1991. However, the data is annual data and recessions occur when there are two consecutive *quarters* of negative real GDP data. We cannot technically be sure that we have caught all of the periods of recession by looking at annual data.

5. Figure 4.3b

6. When the *real GDP* rises, the *percentage change in real GDP* is positive. When the *percentage change in real GDP* equals zero, then *real GDP* reaches the bottom of a trough or the top of a peak.

7. different

CHAPTER 5

Unemployment

Quick Review

Unemployment concerns policymakers because it causes people to lose their income and creates social unrest. Society also loses its potential output. In the Employment Act of 1946 a low unemployment rate became one of the country's important national goals. But unemployment is difficult to measure, its causes are numerous, and its impact is hard to gauge. Thus we need to answer several questions:

- When is a person "unemployed"?
- What are the costs of unemployment?
- What is an appropriate goal for "full employment"?

Unemployment is measured in terms of only those people in the labor force who have no job but are actively seeking employment. If you're a civilian under 16 or you're not looking for work, then you're not in the labor force and you are not considered unemployed. This criterion eliminates children, parents at home, and people in the armed forces. The number of unemployed is determined through surveys of households across the country. To find the unemployment rate, divide the number of unemployed by the number in the labor force.

Making the distinction between the labor force and the total population allows us to distinguish also between physical production possibilities, the maximum amount that could be produced with all resources and technology, and institutional production possibilities, which defines the annual output we could produce if we efficiently employed our resources within the limits imposed by available resources, technology, and social constraints on their use. The labor force is smaller than the entire population because of institutional constraints such as compulsory education or child labor laws. The institutional production-possibilities curve lies inside the physical production-possibilities curve.

Thus the country's labor-force participation rate is calculated by dividing the number of people working or seeking work by the population. Those who are unemployed do not stay unemployed, however, and how long it takes to get a new job (the duration of unemployment) is important. The duration grows longer in recessions and can be very short when the economy approaches capacity. Finally, the unemployment rate varies by a number of socioeconomic variables – race, age, sex, education, and so on. Besides causing a loss of output, unemployment imposes other costs on society as well - alcoholism, suicide, divorce, crime, and the like, are all positively related to the unemployment rate. Underemployment and discouraged workers are submerged in the unemployment rate as well. As unemployment goes up, GDP goes down. According to Okun's Law the relationship is systematic – each one percentage point increase in the unemployment rate leads to a two percentage point reduction in GDP.

Economists typically distinguish four kinds of unemployment: frictional (short-term unemployment between jobs), seasonal (unemployment that varies with the seasons), structural (caused by a mismatch of available labor with skill requirements or job locations), and cyclical (caused by deficient aggregate demand). For these reasons, several million people are unemployed in the United States during any period of time.

During the 1960s the Council of Economic Advisers thought that an unemployment rate of 4 percent provided the optimal balance between employment and price-level goals. In the 1970s and 1980s this figure was revised upward to 6 to 7 percent to reflect the increased importance of structural unemployment. Changes in the age-sex composition of the labor force, and more liberal transfer payments, were among the reasons for this revision. As structural barriers declined, President Bush (and now, President Clinton) began to accept 5.5 percent as the nation's unemployment goal.

In the foreseeable future the United States appears headed for a "skills gap" and, again, a higher structural unemployment component. Technological advance, declining industries, and corporate downsizing are all conspiring to require a more educated labor force with increased emphasis on skills not currently in evidence.

Learning Objectives

After reading Chapter 5 and doing the following exercises, you should:	True or false	Multiple choice	Problems and applications	Common errors	Pages in the text
1. Know who is included in the labor force.	1-3, 8, 12	2	4		104-106
2. Know the reasons physical production possibilities and institutional production possibilities differ.	4	5, 7			106-107
3. Understand why unemployment is a major social concern.		9-11, 13, 14, 21	3		107-112
4. Be able to calculate the unemployment rate.	5-8, 11, 13	3, 4, 11	1, 2		108
5. Be able to explain why and how the unemployment rate varies with age, sex, education, and race.	9, 14, 22				109
6. Be able to distinguish between unemployment and underemployment.	10				110
7. Be aware of programs designed to alleviate unemployment.	16	12			116
8. Be aware of the ways in which the unemployment rate may understate or overstate the true dimensions of the unemployment problem.	12			2	110-112
9. Know the meaning of "full employment."	15	8, 19, 20	4	1, 2	112, 114-118
10. Be able to distinguish the nature and causes of cyclical, frictional, structural, and seasonal unemployment.	17-23	15-18	4		112-115
11. Be able to calculate the nation's loss of output owing to rising unemployment using Okun's Law.		6-9	1		107-108
12. Know the dimensions, causes and cures of the emerging "skills gap."		1			117-119

Key-Term Review

Review the following terms; if you are not sure of the meaning of any term, write out the definition and check it against the Glossary in the text. •

cyclical unemployment
discouraged worker
frictional unemployment
full employment
institutional production possibilities
labor force
labor-force participation rate
Okun's Law

physical production possibilities
seasonal unemployment
skills gap
structural unemployment
underemployment
unemployment
unemployment rate

Fill in the blank following each of the statements below with the appropriate term from the list above.

1. When people are employed below their capabilities, they are said to be victims of _____ .

   1. _____

2. The loss of jobs when the economy fails to reach its potential is called _____ .

   2. _____

3. Official statistics sometimes understate the magnitude of the unemployment problem because they do not take into account the _____ .

   3. _____

4. Dividing the number of unemployed people by the entire labor force yields the _____ .

   4. _____

5. The labor force can get larger even though the population does not increase simply because of an increase in the _____ .

   5. _____

6. The Council of Economic Advisers has revised upward its estimate of what constitutes _____ , to be between 5 and 6 percent unemployment.

   6. _____

7. The economy's physical production possibilities exceed its _____ .

   7. _____

8. When society imposes limitations on the efficient use of workers, the result is that it cannot produce at the limit of its _____ .

   8. _____

9. Every person 16 years of age or older who is either employed for pay or actively seeking employment is considered a part of the _____ .

   9. _____

10. When the unemployment rate increases after schools close for the summer, the increase is referred to as _____ .

10. _____

11. Those who cannot find jobs because they do not possess the skills that jobs currently require suffer from _____ .

11. _____

12. Adding together structural, frictional, seasonal, and cyclical unemployment gives a gross estimate of the amount of total _____ .

12. _____

13. Joblessness that occurs as people move from one job to another is _____ .

13. _____

14. The systematic response of output (GDP) to changes in the unemployment rate is known as _____ .

14. _____

15. The looming _____ will likely cause structural unemployment to worsen in the 1990s.

15. _____

True or False: *Circle your choice.*

T F 1. Those who get discouraged and no longer seek work are counted as unemployed.

T F 2. To be counted as part of the labor force, one must be at least 16 years old.

T F 3. A homemaker with part-time paid employment is part of the labor force; one without paid employment (and who is not looking for employment) is not part of the labor force.

T F 4. The institutional production-possibilities curve lies outside the physical production-possibilities curve.

T F 5. The number of unemployed can rise simultaneously with declines in the unemployment rate.

T F 6. When the growth rate of the labor force is greater than the growth rate of employment, then the unemployment rate rises.

T F 7. To obtain the unemployment rate, divide the number counted as unemployed by the labor force.

T F 8. Everyone who is willing to work and seeking work but cannot find a job is considered unemployed.

T F 9. There is a direct (positive) relationship between educational level attained and the unemployment rate.

T F 10. A person who is employed part-time but seeks, and is qualified for, a full-time job is underemployed.

T F 11. Those who get discouraged and no longer seek work are referred to as "discouraged workers."

T F 12. Teenage unemployment is high because of teenagers' lack of job experience and marketable skills, and a minimum wage of $4.25.

T F 13. One of the main reasons for revising the full-employment rate was a change in the age and sex structure of the labor force.

T F 14. The federal government determines if you qualify for unemployment benefits.

T F 15. Frictional unemployment stems from insufficient aggregate demand.

T F 16. Those who make their living by driving snowplows are likely to suffer from seasonal unemployment.

T F 17. Someone who quits one job to take another after a short vacation is among those who are classified as "frictionally unemployed."

T F 18. When long-distance telephone operators were replaced by direct dialing, one could predict the development of structural unemployment.

T F 19. Cyclical unemployment stems from insufficient aggregate demand.

T F 20. In recent years the rapid increase in the number of teenagers and women in the labor force has led to increased structural and frictional unemployment.

T F 21. The transition from manufacturing to service industries leads to greater growth, but it also leads to greater structural unemployment.

Multiple Choice: *Select the correct answer.*

_____ 1. Which of the following is the correct rank ordering (fastest to slowest) of industry unemployment growth to the year 2000?
(a) Health services, computer services, legal services.
(b) Nursing, accounting, management and public relations.
(c) Computer services, health services, business services.
(d) Health services, accounting, nursing.

_____ 2. People enter the labor force when they:
(a) Take a full-time job.
(b) Go back to school.
(c) Return solely to household activities.
(d) Retire.

_____ 3. When the growth rate of the labor force is faster than the growth rate of unemployer then it is certain that:
(a) The unemployment rate is rising.
(b) The labor-force participation rate is rising.
(c) The percentage of the labor force that is employed is rising.
(d) The labor-force participation rate is falling.

_____ 4. When the growth rate of the population is slower than the growth rate of the labor force but is faster than the growth rate of employment, which of the following is happening?
(a) The labor-force participation rate is falling.
(b) The unemployment rate is rising.
(c) The percentage of the population that is employed is rising.
(d) None of the above.

_____ 5. Which of the following would cause the institutional production-possibilities curve to shift outward immediately?
(a) The NRC begins licensing more nuclear power plants.
(b) The federal government eliminates its student loan program.
(c) The FDA approves a chemical that enhances the production of potatoes.
(d) All of the above.

_____ 6. Okun's Law implies that every:
(a) 1 percent drop in the unemployment rate means a 3 percent rise in real GDP.
(b) 1 percent drop in the unemployment rate means a 3 percent higher economic growth rate.
(c) 1 percent increase in real GDP means a 2 percent lower unemployment rate.
(d) 1 percent increase in the economic growth rate means a 2 percent lower unemployment rate.

_____ 7. Which of the following groupings contains a term which does not belong?
(a) Population, labor force, employed workers.
(b) Physical production possibilities, institutional production possibilities, full-employment GDP.
(c) Unemployment, underemployment, discouraged workers.
(d) Seasonal, cyclical, structural.

_____ 8. Which of the following statements provides a rationale for treating a 6 percent unemployment rate rather than a 4 percent unemployment rate as the "full-employment target"?
(a) The number of teenagers seeking jobs has increased.
(b) The proportion of women in the labor force is higher than it used to be.
(c) The number of persons reentering the labor force has increased dramatically.
(d) All of the above provide such a rationale.

_____ 9. When an economy enters a recession, then:
(a) The duration of unemployment rises.
(b) The number of discouraged workers rises.
(c) The unemployment rate rises.
(d) All of the above.

_____ 10. A substantial increase in mental illness in the population:
(a) Lowers the labor-force participation rate.
(b) Raises the unemployment rate.
(c) Increases phantom unemployment.
(d) Raises underemployment.

_____ 11. Which of the following would be classified economically as a discouraged worker?
(a)   Someone who has recently been disciplined by his or her employer.
(b)   Someone who finds it difficult to be productive on the job because of bureaucratic interference.
(c)   Someone who is not actively seeking employment but who would work if offered a job.
(d)   Someone who is tired of working and decides to be unemployed and live on unemployment benefits.

_____ 12. Which of the following groups would be the most likely to qualify for unemployment benefits?
(a)   People who quit their last jobs.
(b)   People who leave the military after failing to reach a higher rank and are looking for work.
(c)   Unwed mothers who have not worked.
(d)   People who are fired from one of the three part-time jobs that they have been working.

_____ 13. Which of the following have been claimed to be side effects of increased unemployment?
(a)   Suicides, homicides, and other crimes.
(b)   Heart attacks and strokes.
(c)   Admissions to mental hospitals.
(d)   All of the above.

_____ 14. Which of the following combination of shifts in the market for low-cost beer would you most expect when unemployment increases?
(a)   Beer supply shifts leftward and beer demand shifts leftward.
(b)   Beer supply shifts leftward and beer demand shifts rightward.
(c)   Beer supply shifts rightward and beer demand shifts leftward.
(d)   Beer supply shifts rightward and beer demand shifts rightward.

_____ 15. Which of the following unemployment categories is most clearly related to the rate of growth in real GDP?
(a)   Cyclical.
(b)   Frictional.
(c)   Seasonal.
(d)   Structural.

_____ 16. Which of the following government programs would be most appropriate to counteract cyclical unemployment?
(a)   Those which stimulate economic growth.
(b)   Providing additional health services.
(c)   More job placement services.
(d)   More job training.

_____ 17. When migrant workers seek employment after the crops have been picked, the unemployment rate goes up. This situation is an example of:
(a)   Frictional unemployment.
(b)   Seasonal unemployment.
(c)   Structural unemployment.
(d)   Cyclical unemployment.

_____ 18. Which of the following contributed to an increase in the perceived level of structural unemployment?
- (a) More youth and women in the labor force.
- (b) Increased transfer payments.
- (c) Structural changes in demand.
- (d) All of the above.

_____ 19. The Council of Economic Advisors in the 1960s decided the full employment goal could best be:
- (a) Achieved with a zero unemployment rate.
- (b) Reached with a zero inflation rate.
- (c) Minimized by lowering cyclical and structural unemployment.
- (d) Monitored by watching for rising prices.

_____ 20. One In the News article is entitled "Unemployment Benefits Not for Everyone." Which of the following pieces of information might appear in such an article?
- (a) Benefits are financed by those employees who are still employed.
- (b) To qualify, you need a good reason for leaving your last job.
- (c) Local government determines who should receive the benefits.
- (d) All of the above.

_____ 21. One In the News article is entitled "Recession's Cost: Lives." Which of the following policy conclusions might be made on the basis of the article?
- (a) Economic policymakers must take health implications of their policies into account.
- (b) Reaching zero unemployment is a life-or-death justification for government economic intervention.
- (c) The cost of financing welfare benefits during recession places burdens that we will pay for the rest of our lives.
- (d) All of the above.

Problems and Applications

Exercise 1

The following exercise provides practice in categorizing the population according to their availability to the labor force and their employment.

Suppose the population of a country is 1.4 million and the labor force is 1 million, of whom 900,000 are employed. Assume that the full-employment level occurs at a 5 percent unemployment rate at a real GDP of $100 billion. Answer the indicated questions on the basis of this information:

1. What is the unemployment rate? _____

2. How many more members of the labor force must find jobs for the economy to achieve full employment? _____

3. On the basis of the information above and the revised version of Okun's Law, how much potential GDP of the economy has been lost because the economy is not at full employment? _____

4. On the basis of the information above and the revised version of Okun's Law, what is the GDP of the economy? _____

Exercise 2

This exercise shows the relationship between unemployment and the level of GDP. It is similar to the problem at the end of Chapter 5 in the text.

Suppose the data in Table 5.1 describe a nation's population.

Table 5.1
Employment and unemployment

	Year 1	Year 2
Population	400 million	460 million
Labor force	250 million	250 million
Unemployment rate	8 percent	8 percent
Number of unemployed	_____	_____
Number of employed	_____	_____
Employment rate	_____	_____

1. Fill in the blanks in the table to show the number of unemployed people and employed people as well as the employment rate (i.e., number of employed as a percentage of the total population).

2. When the population grows but the labor force remains the same size, the employment rate (rises, remains the same, falls).

3. As the percentage of people past retirement age rises in the economy, the employment rate should (rise, remain the same, fall), *ceteris paribus.*

4. The people who immigrate to the United States are generally a young, working-age population compared with the existing population of the United States. As greater immigration rates are permitted and if the unemployment rate holds constant, the employment rate would (rise, remain the same, fall), *ceteris paribus.*

Exercise 3

Articles on unemployment provide information that is often politically sensitive. This excercise will use one of the articles in the text to show the kind of information to look for. If your professor makes a newspaper assignment from the *Instructor's Manual*, this exercise will provide an example of how to do it.

Reread the In the News article on page 325 in Chapter 15 entitled "The Misery Index." Then answer the following questions:

1. What statement provides the latest unemployment data? To what group or community do the data apply?

2. What statement indicates the trend in the unemployment rate prior to the most recent data?

3. What statement indicates an interpretation of the numbers?

Exercise 4

This exercise shows how to calculate the unemployment rate and indicates the relationship between the unemployment rate and GDP.

1. Graph the unemployment rate (see the data on the inside cover of the text) on the same axis as the percentage change in the real GDP.

Figure 5.1
Unemployment and real GDP

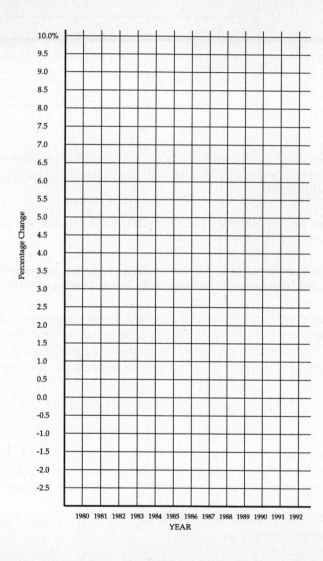

2. The relationship between the unemployment rate and the percentage change in the real GDP is best characterized as direct, inverse.

3. Which of the two indicators seems to change direction first through time – percentage change in real GDP or unemployment rate?

4. Which of the following kinds of unemployment is suggested in Figure 5.1?
   (a) Structural unemployment.
   (b) Seasonal unemployment.
   (c) Cyclical unemployment.
   (d) Frictional unemployment.

5. Which government programs would be *most* appropriate to counteract this kind of unemployment?
   (a) Increase job-placement services.
   (b) Stimulate economic growth.
   (c) Make school last all year long.
   (d) Provide more job training.

6. In what years was full employment, as defined by the Reagan administration, achieved between 1980 and 1992? _____

Common Errors

The first statement in each "common error" below is incorrect. Each incorrect statement is followed by a corrected version and an explanation.

1. The government should eliminate unemployment. WRONG!

   The government must lower unemployment at the same time that it accomplishes other goals. RIGHT!

   Under the Full Employment and Balanced Growth Act of 1978, the government sets an unemployment goal for itself, but this goal is well short of a zero unemployment rate. As we shall see in subsequent chapters, the government may have to sacrifice such goals as price stability if it lowers unemployment too much. In this chapter we have seen that it would be very difficult and even undesirable to eliminate frictional or seasonal unemployment.

2. A rise in the unemployment rate of 0.1 or 0.2 percent for a month is bad. WRONG!

   Monthly changes in the unemployment rate may not have any significant economic implications. RIGHT!

   Small changes in the unemployment rate tell us nothing about what is happening to disguised unemployment, discouraged workers, or changes in the labor force; large changes in seasonal or frictional unemployment are not necessarily bad and could not be easily remedied even if they were. Be careful in interpreting short-run changes in the unemployment rate.

•ANSWERS•

Key-Term Review

1. underemployment
2. cyclical unemployment
3. discouraged worker
4. unemployment rate
5. labor-force participation rate
6. full employment
7. institutional production possibilities
8. physical production possibilities
9. labor force
10. seasonal unemployment
11. structural unemployment
12. unemployment
13. frictional unemployment
14. Okun's Law
15. skills gap

True or False

1. F
2. T
3. T
4. F
5. T
6. T
7. T
8. F
9. F
10. T
11. F
12. T
13. T
14. F
15. F
16. T
17. T
18. T
19. T
20. T
21. T

Multiple Choice

1. c
2. a
3. c
4. b
5. d
6. a
7. b
8. d
9. d
10. a
11. c
12. b
13. d
14. d
15. a
16. a
17. b
18. d
19. d
20. b
21. a

Problems and Applications

Exercise 1

1. The unemployment rate is found as follows:
   Unemployment rate =

   $$\frac{\text{Unemployed}}{\text{Labor force}} = \frac{(\text{Labor force minus employed})}{\text{Labor force}}$$

   $$= \frac{(1{,}000{,}000 - 900{,}000)}{1{,}000{,}000} = 10\%$$

2. 50,000. The unemployment rate is 10 percent which is 5 percent above full employment. Multiplying 5 percent by the labor force of 1 million gives 50,000.

3. With 5 percent unemployment above the full employment level, Okun's Law translates into a 10 percent (5% x 3 = 15%) loss of real output.

4. $85 billion = ($100 billion in real output - $15 billion in lost real output)

Exercise 2

1. **Table 5.1 Answer**

	Year 1	Year 2
Population	400 million	460 million
Labor force	250 million	250 million
Unemployment rate	8 percent	8 percent
Number of unemployed	20 million (= 250 x 0.08)	20 million
Number of employed	230 million (= 250 - 20)	230 million
Employment rate	57.5% (= 230/400)	50% (= 230/460)

2. falls

3. fall

4. rise

Exercise 3

1. The statement "as well as high unemployment (7.1 percent)" applies to data for the United States as indicated by the source: *The Economic Report of the President*.

2. The word "high" indicates the unemployment had been higher than the historical average. The graph of the misery index shows a peak in 1980, although it includes inflation as well.

3. "Arthur Okun proposed measuring the extent of misery by adding together the inflation and unemployment rates" indicates that unemployment is undesirable. Again, the interpretation is that 7.1 percent is "high."

Exercise 4

1. **Figure 5.1 Answer**

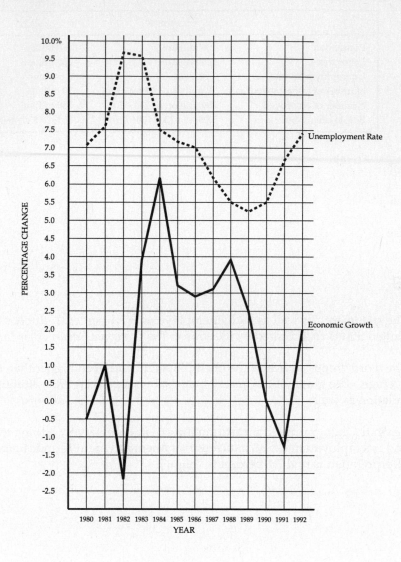

2. inverse

3. Theoretically, percentage change in real GDP should move first. At first glance the unemployment rate seems to be first. However, we are looking at the *percentage change* in real GDP, not the level of GDP. When level of GDP peaks or reaches the bottom of a trough, the percentage change in real GDP goes through the *x*-axis.

4. c

5. b

6. 1970-74, 1978, 1987, 1988, and 1989

CHAPTER 6

Inflation

Quick Review

It is generally agreed that inflation was the nation's number one problem in the 1980s. Fear of its ravaging effects led presidents and other statesmen to advocate and to take dramatic and desperate steps to tame the process. And, while inflation has retreated it is still a matter of great concern. To understand inflation we pose the following questions:

- What kind of price increases are referred to as inflation?
- What is hurt (or helped) by inflation?
- What is an appropriate goal for "price stability"?

Inflation is defined as an increase in the average level of prices; deflation, a decrease in the same measure. The average is a weighted one, so some prices may be falling while the *average* increases.

Inflation is not an equal opportunity phenomenon. It makes some worse off while at the same time conferring benefits on others. We can see this by analyzing the price, income, and wealth effects spawned by the increase in average prices.

Briefly, during an inflationary period the prices of some goods which are important to you will rise faster than the average. Your income may not rise as fast as the rate of inflation, and those who hold wealth in some forms may lose because the prices of the things they own rise more slowly than the average. Of course, if the opposite occurs, some will benefit from the inflationary process.

On a macro (economywide) level, inflation's effects are damaging too, as it is hard to make business and household decisions when you haven't a good idea of what the price level will be in the future. This leads decision makers to shorten their time horizons, diverts resources to speculative activities, and wreaks havoc on taxpayers whose tax bill is calculated in nominal terms, while their well-being is measured in real terms.

The rate of inflation is measured most frequently by using the Consumer Price Index (CPI), a weighted average of the price of a given basket of goods. Increases in the average price of the basket represent the inflationary process. Other indexes – the Producers Price Index (PPI) and the GDP deflator – can be used to answer questions about inflation too.

The oft-quoted goal of stable prices does not necessarily mean we wish to have a zero rate of change in the price level. Other macro goals, such as full employment and economic growth, must be considered too, and tradeoffs seem inevitable. Moreover, the CPI itself has some flaws which make zero inflation less desirable.

The inflationary problems experienced in the 1980s led to the development of some practical measures such as cost-of-living adjustment (COLA) clauses in various contractual arrangements and adjustable-rate mortgages (ARMs) for lenders. Still, some feel that given the capricious nature of the inflationary process, the best protection against inflation is to aim for zero inflation worldwide. Given the historical record, in which industrial countries had long periods with relatively stable prices, the idea is not as far-fetched as it may seem.

Learning Objectives

After reading Chapter 6 and doing the following exercises, you should:	True or false	Multiple choice	Problems and applications	Common errors	Pages in the text
1. Understand that inflation is measured as an increase in the *average* level of prices.	1, 3	1, 15-17, 29		1, 2	121-123
2. Understand the difference between average prices and relative prices.	2, 3, 7, 18	2, 5, 28			123
3. Be able to describe how price, income, and wealth effects accomplish redistributions in the economy.	6, 8, 18	3, 7-10, 13, 22	1, 4		124-129
4. Understand that some in society are subject to money illusion.	5, 9	6, 8, 9			129-133
5. Be able to explain why the inflationary process causes uncertainty and shortened time horizons, and diverts resources to speculative activity.	17	11, 12, 30	4		133-136
6. Be able to calculate and interpret a price index like the Consumer Price Index (CPI), and understand why other measures are also useful.	10-13, 16	16, 18-21, 29	1, 3		135-136
7. Understand why price stability does not necessarily mean a zero rate of increase in the price level.		14, 23			135-136
8. Know that when quality improvements occur, the CPI will overstate the rate of inflation.	19	14			136
9. Be able to discuss mechanisms developed to protect various groups from the redistributive effects of inflation.	5, 14	11, 24-27	2	3	137-139
10. Understand why many knowledgeable people advocate policies designed to yield zero inflation worldwide.	10	3			139-141

Key-Term Review

Review the following terms; if you are not sure of the meaning of any term, write out the definition and check it against the Glossary in the text.

adjustable-rate mortgage (ARM)
base period
bracket creep
Consumer Price Index (CPI)
cost-of-living adjustment (COLA)
deflation
inflation

inflation rate
money illusion
nominal income
price stability
real income
real interest rate
relative price

Fill in the blank following each of the statements below with the appropriate term from the list above.

1. One measure of the _____ can be found by computing the _____ , which measures the average percentage price increases that consumers face from a benchmark called the _____ .

1. _____
   _____
   _____

2. When the inflation rate is negative, the process is called _____ .

2. _____

3. When the inflation rate is low and does not vary much, we say there is _____ .

3. _____

4. A positive rate of increase in the average price level is called _____ .

4. _____

5. The _____ was invented by lenders who had experienced a negative _____ when prices rose very rapidly and they had lent at low, fixed rates of interest.

5. _____
   _____

6. Unions may try to protect members' incomes from inflation by having a _____ clause inserted in their contracts.

6. _____

7. When inflation occurs, _____ grows at a faster rate than _____ .

7. _____
   _____

8. The measures of inflation do not provide information on how the _____ of a single good changes with respect to the prices of other goods.

8. _____

9. When people fail to recognize changes in their real income because they look only at their nominal income, they are victims of _____ .

9. _____

10. When inflation pushes the nominal income of taxpayers into higher marginal tax brackets, the process is called _____ .

10. _____

True or False: *Circle your choice.*

T F 1. It is possible for individual prices to rise or fall continuously without changing the average price.

T F 2. When doctors' fees rise faster than aspirin prices, real income falls for people who visit a doctor relative to those who prescribe aspirin for themselves.

T F 3. Some price increases do not contribute to inflation because they are below the inflation rate.

T F 4. Some buyers respond to inflation by cutting back on purchases of goods and services, whereas others respond by making greater purchases of goods and services.

T F 5. If all individuals were able to anticipate inflation correctly and make appropriate adjustments in their market behavior, there would be no redistribution of real income or real wealth owing to inflation.

T F 6. Redistribution of income is a microeconomic effect of inflation.

T F 7. When a person's nominal income rises but real income falls, then average prices have risen.

T F 8. If your real income rises faster than your nominal income then you benefit from inflation.

T F 9. Money illusion results from expectations based on currentt nominal income rather than purchasing power.

T F 10. The Consumer Price Index usually increases before the Producer Price Index.

T F 11. The three major indexes used to measure inflation are the CPI, COLA, and PPI.

T F 12. From data on a price index through time, it is possible to compute the percentage changes in price, but not the actual price itself.

T F 13. The GDP deflator registers a lower inflation rate than the CPI.

T F 14. A COLA counteracts the effects of inflation on the economy by lowering the inflation rate.

T F 15. The real interest rate equals the inflation rate in the long run.

T F 16. The base period for a price index is the year against which other years are compared.

T F 17. Sudden speculative withholding of commodities owing to inflation ties up resources, causing real income to fall.

T F 18. If the prices of things you buy do not increase, but the inflation rate is 10 percent, then your real income falls, *ceteris paribus.*

T F 19. The CPI overstates the rate of inflation when the quality of the items in the market basket improves.

Multiple Choice: *Select the correct answer.*

_____ 1. If Argentina has an annual inflation rate of 606.8 percent, then 1 austral (Argentina's unit of currency) today would be equivalent to how many australs 1 year from today?
   (a) 7.60608 australs.
   (b) 0.1415 australs.
   (c) 6.068 australs.
   (d) None of the above.

_____ 2. If all relative prices remain unchanged, then:
   (a) Changes in average prices must be zero.
   (b) The prices of all goods and services must change by the same percentage.
   (c) There can be no inflation or deflation.
   (d) None of the above.

_____ 3. If there is a zero inflation rate, changes in relative prices would signal:
   (a) Changes in the economy's desirable mix of output.
   (b) Changes in how much sellers produce of different goods.
   (c) Changes in how much buyers purchase of different goods.
   (d) All of the above.

_____ 4. Income redistribution occurs during inflation because:
   (a) Not all prices rise by the same amount as average prices.
   (b) Some taxes cause inflation to hit certain income groups harder than others.
   (c) Not all groups can protect their incomes against inflation.
   (d) All of the above are the case.

_____ 5. When the inflation rate is zero, a decrease in the absolute price of a specific product is most similar to:
   (a) No increase in the price of the product when there is deflation.
   (b) The price of the product increasing faster than the inflation rate.
   (c) The price of the product remaining unchanged during inflation.
   (d) The price of the product rising at the same rate as the inflation rate.

_____ 6. We can always compute real income if we know:
   (a) The inflation rate and the growth rate of nominal income.
   (b) The inflation rate and nominal income.
   (c) The price index and nominal income.
   (d) The price index and the growth rate of nominal income.

_____ 7. Which of the following is a micro consequence of inflation that causes redistribution of income?
   (a) A price effect.
   (b) An income effect.
   (c) A wealth effect.
   (d) All of the above.

_____ 8. Suppose you get a 10 percent raise during a year in which the price level rises by 10 percent. Then over the year:
   (a) Your real income falls, but your nominal income remains unchanged.
   (b) Your real and nominal income both fall.
   (c) Your real income remains unchanged, but your nominal income rises.
   (d) Your real income remains unchanged, but your nominal income falls.

9. Nominal income always falls when real income:
   (a) Falls and there is inflation.
   (b) Falls and there is deflation.
   (c) Rises and there is inflation.
   (d) Rises and there is deflation.

10. A rise in a person's real income is consistent with that person's nominal income:
    (a) Falling and nationwide inflation.
    (b) Falling with nationwide deflation falling more slowly.
    (c) Rising faster than real income with nationwide deflation.
    (d) Rising faster than the inflation rate.

11. Which of the following groups is vulnerable to sudden deflation?
    (a) Borrowers who have loans at fixed interest rates.
    (b) Fixed-income groups.
    (c) Workers who receive fixed wages under multiyear contracts.
    (d) Mortgage lenders who make adjustable-rate mortgages.

12. Which of the following happenings can characterize the reactions of consumers or businesses to the uncertainties caused by inflation?
    (a) Consumers cut back on consumption because they fear that future cost increases will make it difficult to make payments on what they consume.
    (b) Consumption increases as consumers try to buy products before their prices rise.
    (c) Businesses decrease investment spending in an attempt to avoid being caught with unprofitable plant and equipment.
    (d) All of the above can characterize their reactions.

13. Which of the following is a micro consequence of inflation?
    (a) Increased uncertainty.
    (b) Shortened time horizons.
    (c) The wealth effect.
    (d) All of the above.

14. The reason that policymakers are reluctant to force the economy to a zero percent inflation rate is that:
    (a) There would be unacceptable levels of unemployment if the economy were controlled by fiscal policy.
    (b) Wasteful quality changes and new products would be designed to escape price controls if controls were used.
    (c) Shortages of some products would be likely if there were wage-price controls.
    (d) All of the above.

15. At the beginning of 1950 the CPI was 24.1. At the end of 1990 it was 130.7. Which of the following most closely approximates the forty-year rate of inflation?
    (a) 110 percent
    (b) 130 percent
    (c) 450 percent
    (d) 550 percent

16. The inflation rate is:
    (a) The percentage change in an index of average prices between two points in time.
    (b) An index of average prices.
    (c) The rate of increase in the price of a single good.
    (d) All of the above.

17. From data on a price index through time, it is possible to compute:
    (a) A product's actual price and percentage price changes.
    (b) A product's actual price but not the percentage price changes through time.
    (c) The percentage changes in price, but not the actual price itself.
    (d) Neither the actual price, nor the percentage price changes through time.

18. Which of the following groupings contains terms that do not reflect a common theme?
    (a) PPI, CPI, GDP deflator.
    (b) COLA, GDP deflator, interest rate.
    (c) Growth recession, depression, per capita GDP.
    (d) Money illusion, inflation, bracket creep.

19. The CPI and PPI do not rise simultaneously because:
    (a) Prices and interest rates are inversely related.
    (b) One measures prices immediately after production while the other measures consumer prices.
    (c) The deflator is computed by an agency different from the one for other indexes.
    (d) One is a measure of mortgage interest rates and the other measures inflation.

20. If you were interested in charting prices charged by producers of energy, which of the following would you use?
    (a) The CPI.
    (b) The PPI.
    (c) The GDP deflator.
    (d) The COLA.

21. Assume that real income weighted by output is going to be computed by the following formula:

$$\text{Real income} = \frac{\text{nominal income}}{\text{price index}}$$

Which index would you use in the formula?

    (a) GDP deflator.
    (b) Consumer Price Index.
    (c) Producer Price Index.
    (d) Interest rate.

22. A dozen Topps football trading cards cost $0.18 in 1975 and $0.45 in 1990. Suppose during the same period a price index for the economy rose from 15.00 to 30.00. Buyers of Topps trading cards, relative to nonbuyers, would experience:
    (a) A lower real income as a result of the price effect.
    (b) A higher real income as a result of the price effect.
    (c) A lower nominal income as a result of the wealth effect.
    (d) A lower nominal income as a result of the income effect.

23. In the Full Employment and Balanced Growth Act of 1978 Congress set an inflation goal of 3 percent rather than 0 percent because:
    (a) It was concerned that a zero percent inflation would cause severe unemployment.
    (b) It is not possible to achieve a zero percent inflation goal.
    (c) It is the responsibility of the president of the United States, not Congress, to set the inflation target.
    (d) None of the above.

_____ 24. COLAs are desired because:
   (a) The real value of wages can be maintained, since COLAs correct for the effects of inflation.
   (b) COLAs help dampen inflation.
   (c) COLAs help stimulate employment.
   (d) All of the above.

_____ 25. A cost-of-living adjustment (COLA) clause is intended:
   (a) To protect workers from unexpected changes in relative prices.
   (b) To provide income automatically to cover workers when the unemployment rate goes up.
   (c) To prevent a redistribution of income when the average level of prices is falling.
   (d) None of the above.

_____ 26. Suppose you have a COLA of 5 percent per year and your income this year is $30,000. If the inflation rate is 5 percent annually, what is the approximate value of your nominal salary five years from now?
   (a) $30,000.
   (b) $38,288.
   (c) $24,197.
   (d) None of the above.

_____ 27. Universal indexing fails to protect people from inflation because:
   (a) Indexing typically lags inflation.
   (b) Not all prices rise by the same amount.
   (c) There would be redistributions under any system.
   (d) All of the above.

_____ 28. One In the News article in the text states: "The College Board survey also found tuition and fee increases again outpaced inflation." Relative to other parents, parents of college-bound students experience:
   (a) A relative decline of real income.
   (b) A relative rise in real income.
   (c) A relative decline in nominal income.
   (d) A relative rise in nominal income.

_____ 29. How is the impact of a given price change on the Consumer Price Index computed?
   (a) Multiply the base period times the weight assigned to the item.
   (b) Divide the weight assigned to the item by the change in the price of the item.
   (c) Multiply the weight assigned to the item by the percentage change in the price of the item.
   (d) None of the above is correct.

_____ 30. Inflation may cause the economy to operate inside the production-possibilities curve because:
   (a) People waste resources when they hoard in anticipation of inflation.
   (b) Firms withhold resources in anticipation that the relative price of resources will be higher than the inflation rate.
   (c) The government takes strong inflationary countermeasures that result in less than full-employment real income.
   (d) All of the above can cause the economy to operate inside the production-possibilities frontier.

_____ 31. Which of the following occurrences is *not* an effect of a sudden burst of inflation?
  (a)   The economy is pushed inside the production-possibilities curve.
  (b)   Morale in the economy is lowered.
  (c)   Government receives lower taxes because of lower real incomes.
  (d)   Production and consumption incentives are distorted.

Problems and Applications

Exercise 1

This exercise shows how to compute changes in real income. It is similar to problem 2 for Chapter 6 in the text.

1. Suppose that between 1980 and 2000, the average consumer's nominal income increases from $18,000 to $36,000. Table 6.1 lists the prices of a small market basket purchased in both of those years. Assuming that this basket of goods is representative of all goods and services purchased, compute the percentage change in real income between 1980 and 2000. _____

Table 6.1
Price of a small market basket in 1980 and 2000

Item	Quantity (units per year)	Price in 1980 (dollars per unit)	Price in 2000 (dollars per unit)
Coffee	20 pounds	$ 3	$ 8
Tuition	1 payment	4,000	20,000
Pizza	100 pizzas	8	6
VCR rental	75 days	15	4
Vacation	2 weeks	300	1,000

2. If the market basket is representative of what actually happens to consumers over the period, the consumers have experienced the effects of (inflation, deflation).

3. The consumers have seen their nominal income (rise, fall).

4. The consumers have seen their real income (rise, fall).

5. T F There has been inflation in three of the products but deflation in the other two.

Exercise 2

This exercise shows how important a cost-of-living adjustment clause (COLA) can be and demonstrates the income, price, and wealth effects of inflation.

1. Suppose you expect to have an annual nominal income of $20,000 from 1990 through 2000. Compute the purchasing power of $20,000 in each year shown in Table 6.2. Use an inflation rate of 7 percent per year, which was the average inflation rate in the United States in the 1970s. For example, to find the real value of your $20,000 income in 1991, you would discount $20,000 as follows:

$$\text{Real value of \$20,000 in 1991} = \frac{\$20,000}{(1+7\%)} = \$18,692$$

To find the real value for 1992, it is necessary to square the discount factor.

$$\text{Real value of \$20,000 in 1992} = \frac{\$20,000}{(1.07)^2} = \$17,469$$

For 1993 it would be

$$\text{Real value of \$20,000 in 1993} = \frac{\$20,000}{(1.07)^3} = \$16,326$$

Compute column 1 in Table 6.2.

Table 6.2
Real value of $20,000 annual income

Year	(1) Real value of a $20,000 nominal income	(2) Nominal income with a 7 percent COLA	(3) Real income with a 7 percent COLA
1995	$_____	$_____	$_____
2000	_____	_____	_____

2. Suppose there is a COLA which raises income automatically by 7 percent per year. In column 2 of Table 6.2 compute the nominal income that would be received if a person had a COLA of 7 percent per year.

   With a COLA it becomes necessary to multiply income by a factor $(1 + .07)$. For example, the nominal income in 1992 would be

   $$\text{Nominal income in 1991} = \$20,000\,(1.07) = \$21,400$$

   and for 1992 it would be

   $$\text{Nominal income in 1992} = \$20,000\,(1.07)^2 = \$22,898$$

3. Compute the real value of the income with a COLA of 7 percent, assuming an inflation rate of 7 percent per year. Place the answers in column 3 of Table 6.2. (*Hint:* It is necessary to discount to find the real income as was done in column 1 and to multiply as was done in column 2.)

4. T   F   The real income stays the same when there is an inflation rate of 7 percent and a COLA of 7 percent.

5. T   F   If you did not have COLA and the inflation rate was 7 percent per year for 10 years, you would be able to buy the equivalent of about half as many goods with your $20,000 annual income.

For the following three problems, suppose there is inflation.

6. With no assets (such as a home) and without a COLA, you experience (negative, positive) (wealth effects, income effects, price effects).

7. Suppose you negotiate a COLA that protects your income completely against the 5 percent inflation rate, but after you purchase a house, you find that its value does not increase through time. You will experience (negative, positive) (wealth effects, income effects, price effects).

8. After selling your house, suppose you rent an apartment. Suddenly you discover that rents are going up 10 percent a year. Even though your COLA protects your income, you find that it takes a larger and larger fraction of your budget to pay the rent. Under these circumstances you experience (negative, positive) (wealth effects, income effects, price effects).

Exercise 3

This exercise provides practice in computing price indexes, using base years, and percentage changes.

1. Compute the percentage change in price for each of the commodities in Table 6.3 from the year indicated in parentheses to 1990. Then use the early year, price in parentheses in the table as the base-year price and enter the price index in 1990 for each commodity in the last column of the table.

Table 6.3
Prices

	Early price	(Base year)	1990 price	Percent change	Index
Polaroid camera	$150.00	(1963)	$42.75	_____	_____
Ballpoint pen	89¢	(1965)	29¢	_____	_____
Microwave oven	$400.00	(1972)	$89.00	_____	_____
Compact Disc player	$1000.00	(1977)	$250.00	_____	_____

2. Place a star by the commodity in Table 6.3 that had the largest percentage decline in price.

3. Place brackets around the commodity in Table 6.3 with the smallest percentage decline in price.

4. Place two stars next the commodity in Table 6.3 that had the largest price index relative to its base year.

5. What is the range in which the price index falls relative to the base years for all of the products in Table 6.3?

Lowest _____   Highest _____

Exercise 4

Articles on inflation are as politically sensitive as those reporting unemployment numbers. The former often provide selected information on average price increases throughout the economy. This exercise will use one of the articles in the text to show the kind of information to look for. If your professor makes a newspaper assignment from the *Instructor's Manual*, this exercise will provide an example of how to do it.

Reread the article from *The Wall Street Journal* on page 132 in Chapter 6 entitled "Inflation and the Weimar Republic." then answer the following questions:

1. What sentence provides the inflation data for the worst period of inflation? To what group or community do these data apply?

2. What sentences indicate the trend in the inflation rate prior to the hyperinflation?

3. What statement indicates the government's interpretation of the numbers?

Exercise 5

This exercise compares the dynamics of two different measures of the inflation rate.

1. On the back inside cover of the text you will find data on the percentage changes in the GDP deflator and the percentage changes in the Consumer Price Index. In Figure 6.1, graph these indexes, showing time from 1970 to the present on the horizontal axis (*x*-axis) and percentage changes on the vertical axis (*y*-axis).

Figure 6.1
Measures of inflation: CPI and GDP deflator

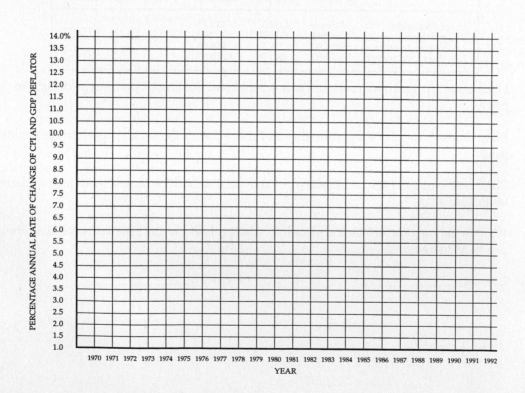

Label each curve.

2. The two indexes are (directly, inversely) related to each other.

3. Which index tends to have the widest swings? _____

4. Which index usually reaches its peak or trough first? _____

5. The CPI frequently (lags, leads) the movements of the GDP deflator.

Common Errors

The first statement in each "common error" below is incorrect. Each incorrect statement is followed by a corrected version and an explanation.

1. When the price of a product rises, there is inflation. WRONG!

   When an average of prices rise, there is inflation. RIGHT!

   The price of a single product may rise while an average of prices of all products falls. Such adjustment in relative prices is essential to the most *efficient* distribution of goods and services through the market. When the average of all prices is rising, however, distribution may not be efficient and capricious redistributions of income may occur.

2. As long as price increases do not exceed the inflation rate, they do not contribute to inflation. WRONG!

   Every price increase contributes to a rise in the inflation rate. RIGHT!

   Since the inflation rate is an average of all price increases, the increase in any price by any amount raises the average. Firms that buy commodities from other firms that raise prices will in turn pass the increase on to their own customers; an increased price may have indirect effects in raising the inflation rate.

3. Indexation such as a COLA clause in a contract protects the *economy* against the effects of inflation. WRONG!

   Indexation institutionalizes inflation. RIGHT!

   Indexation can protect the real incomes of specific groups for which indexation is applied. In other words, it can address some of the micro consequences of inflation. However, if everyone's income is not indexed, then even the micro consequences may not be adequately addressed. In fact, indexation can lead under such circumstances to dramatic changes in relative prices. Furthermore, indexation may lead to anticipation of higher rates of inflation; high current inflation rates may guarantee higher future rates owing to indexation.

Crossword Puzzle

Select the economic term in the following list that corresponds with each of the defintions and descriptions below. Then fit the term or one of the words within it into the crossword puzzle at the number indicated.

absolute price level
adjustable-rate mortgage
Consumer Price Index
cost-of-living adjustment
deflation
demand
GDP
GDP deflator
speculation

inflation rate
money illusion
nominal income
price stability
Producer Price Index
profit
real income
relative price

Across

5. The measure you would use if you wanted to find the average price increases charged directly by businesses for commodities.

6. A form of borrowing in which the interest rate varies with the market.

7. If you wanted a measure of GDP that was not distorted by inflation, you would compute this.

110

11. A clause you might want in a contract to protect you from the effects of inflation.

13. The difference between revenue and cost.

15. If you want to find how much your household costs are rising, this measure of price movements will be just what you're looking for.

16. The average price increases of goods and services.

17. What people are willing and able to buy at different prices during a given time period, *ceteris paribus*.

Down

1. What you might engage in if you expect prices of certain commodities to increase greatly in the future—enough to make it worthwhile to hold the commodities off the market.

2. A measure of output for a nation's economy.

3. Even when price indexes are going down, this price may go up.

4. The price index used to calculate real income from nominal income.

8. One of three goals established in the Employment Act of 1946 and the Full Employment and Balanced Growth Act of 1978.

9. What you look at when you want to know how much money to shell out to buy a product.

10. The measure of national welfare that impresses many people because they do not realize that it grows because of inflation, not just because of increased production.

12. A decrease in average prices.

14. When nominal income, not real income, is used as a basis for market choice.

•ANSWERS•

Key-Term Review

1. inflation rate
   Consumer Price Index
   base period
2. deflation
3. price stability
4. inflation
5. adjustable-rate mortgage (ARM)
   real interest rate

6. cost-of-living adjustment (COLA)
7. nominal income
   real income
8. relative price
9. money illusion
10. bracket creep

True or False

1. T	5. T	8. F	11. F	14. F	17. T
2. T	6. T	9. T	12. T	15. F	18. F
3. F	7. T	10. F	13. T	16. T	19. T
4. T					

Multiple Choice

1. a   [1 austral x (1 + 6.0608) = 7.60608 australs next year, which has the same buying power as 1 austral this year.]

2. b	7. d	12. d	17. c	22. a	27. d
3. d	8. c	13. c	18. b	23. a	28. a
4. d	9. b	14. d	19. b	24. a	29. d
5. c	10. d	15. c	20. b	25. d	30. d
6. c	11. a	16. a	21. a	26. b	31. c

Problems and Applications

Exercise 1

1. The first step is to find the total expenditure on the items for each year.

$$
\begin{array}{rcl}
& 1980 & \\
20 \text{ pounds x } \$3 \text{ per pound} & = & \$60 \\
1 \text{ year x } \$4{,}000 \text{ per year} & = & 4{,}000 \\
100 \text{ pizzas x } \$8 \text{ per pizza} & = & 800 \\
75 \text{ days x } \$15 \text{ per day} & = & 1{,}125 \\
2 \text{ weeks x } \$300 \text{ per week} & = & \underline{600} \\
& = & \$6{,}585
\end{array}
$$

$$
\begin{array}{rcl}
& 2000 & \\
20 \text{ pounds x } \$8 \text{ per pound} & = & 160 \\
1 \text{ year x } \$20{,}000 \text{ per year} & = & 20{,}000 \\
100 \text{ pizzas x } \$6 \text{ per pizza} & = & 600 \\
75 \text{ days x } \$4 \text{ per day} & = & 300 \\
2 \text{ weeks x } \$1000 \text{ per week} & = & \underline{2{,}000} \\
& = & \$23{,}060
\end{array}
$$

2. inflation (average prices have risen)
3. rise

4. fall The percentage change in real income is $\dfrac{\$10{,}285 - \$18{,}000}{\$18{,}000} = -42.9\%$

5. F   Inflation and deflation apply to an average of prices, not the specific products themselves.

Exercise 2

1. See Table 6.2 Answer.

Table 6.2 Answer

Year	(1)	(2)	(3)
1995	$14,259	$28,052	$20,000
2000	10,167	39,344	20,000

Note: Your answers should be close but need not be exactly the same as those in the table. Discrepancies depend on how precisely you carried out the calculations.
For the year 2000, $20,000 must be "discounted" by the factor $(1 + 0.07)^{10}$, which is 1.967. Therefore, $20,000/1.967 = $10,167.

2. See Table 6.2 answer (column 2). In column 2 the $20,000 should be *multiplied* by 1.07^5 for 1995; by 1.07^{10} for 2000.

3. See Table 6.2 answer (column 3). In column 3, the amount is both multiplied and divided by the same factor.

4. T

5. T

6. negative income effects

7. negative wealth effects

8. negative price effects

Exerise 3

1.- 4. **Table 6.3 Answer**

	Early price	(Base year)	1990 price	Percent change	Index
Polaroid camera	$150.00	(1963)	$42.75	-71.5%	28.5
Ballpoint pen	89¢	(1965)	29¢	-67.4%	32.6
Microwave oven	$400.00	(1972)	$89.00	-77.7%	22.3
Compact Disc player	$1,000.00	(1977)	$250.00	-75.0%	25.0

5. Lowest = .223   Highest = .326

Exercise 4

1. The last sentence of the second paragraph describes the worst period of the hyperinflation. The data apply to Germany.

2. The first two paragraphs describe the trend of inflation before and after World War I.

3. The government is mentioned only at the end of the article in an understatement: "57 years later government policy is still colored by this experience with hyperinflation."

Exercise 5

1. **Figure 6.1 Answer**

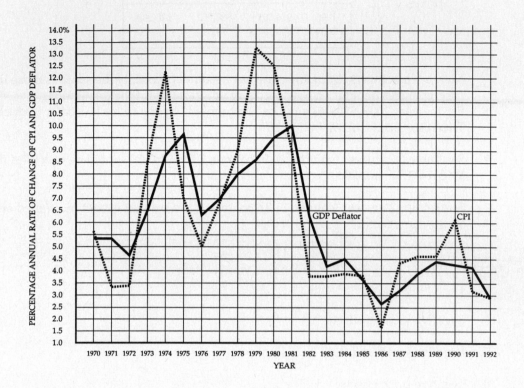

2. directly
3. Consumer Price Index
4. Consumer Price Index
5. leads

Crossword Puzzle Answer

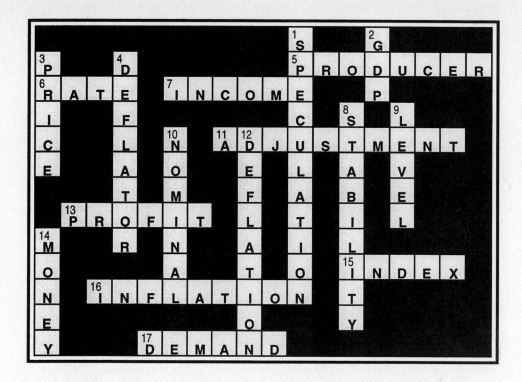

Across

5. *Producer* Price Index
6. adjustable-*rate* mortgage
7. real *income*
11. cost-of-living *adjustment*
13. *profit*
15. Consumer Price *Index*
16. *inflation* rate
17. *demand*

Down

1. *speculation*
2. *GDP*
3. relative *price*
4. GDP *deflator*
8. price *stability*
9. absolute price *level*
10. *nominal* income
12. *deflation*
14. *money* illusion

CHAPTER 7

National-Income Accounting

Quick Review

In this chapter, we begin the task of measurement in the economy. We want to know some basic information, including:

- How much output do we produce in a year?
- How much income is generated from production of these goods and services?
- Where does all of the output and income go?

National-income accounting is a process by which we measure the nation's economic activity. Several national-income aggregates allow the national-income accountant to add together the production of goods and services using dollar value as a single common denominator.

The most often used economic aggregate is gross domestic product (GDP) – the total market value of all final goods and services produced within a nation's borders over a year. When our total output is calculated in dollar terms and compared with *what could have been* produced by the economy over the same period, appropriate economic policies can be developed.

The GDP does not include all types of transactions. It includes only those involving production of new products and services; for example, sales of new cars are included, but sales of used cars are not. The transactions must be at arm's length; paying Junior for mowing the lawn is not included in the GDP. Illegal transactions, the services of homemakers, and bartering are not included in the GDP. There is also a large underground economy that the GDP never captures. Finally, only transactions involving goods and services that are sold for final consumption are included—whether they are purchased by households, business, government, or foreign buyers. Intermediate goods are not included in the GDP in order to avoid distortions resulting from double counting.

The GDP serves as an excellent standard for comparing different economies and the changes in the output of a single economy over time. There are, however, several alternative measures of output, each calculated with a different purpose in mind. The net domestic product (NDP) corrects for the using up of capital and therefore serves as a better measure of the changes in the production possibilities of the economy. When indirect business taxes are subtracted from net domestic product, we get national income, which shows what the factors of production earned in the process of producing the nation's output. Finally, to find out how much of the income earned is received, we calculate personal income and disposable income, the latter being how much is available to spend.

GDP is a price-times-quantity measure. It can increase because prices go up, because quantities go up, or both. Because our standard of living is based on real goods and services, we distinguish between real GDP and nominal GDP. When prices are rising, we deflate the GDP by dividing by an appropriate index. When prices fall, we inflate it. When comparing the output of different countries, it is good practice to divide GDP by population to find the income per capita.

Learning Objectives

After reading Chapter 7 and doing the following exercises, you should:	True or false	Multiple choice	Problems and applications	Common errors	Pages in the text
1. Know the purposes of national-income accounting.	1	1			143-144
2. Be able to describe the different measures of output and income.	1, 12-14, 16, 17, 19, 20	3, 12, 16, 17		1, 2	144
3. Know why the GDP per capita is computed.	3, 4	6, 11	1	2	145-146
4. Be able to explain the conceptual problems encountered in estimating GDP.	5, 7, 10, 11, 15, 17, 18	2, 4, 5, 9, 10, 14, 16		1, 3	144-149
5. Be familiar with the underground economy.		5, 8			147
6. Know the difference between real GDP and nominal GDP and be able to caluclate each.	6, 8, 9	13, 15, 25-27	1, 3		149-151
7. Know the definitions and uses of the important national-income aggregates.		17-24, 28			151, 147-159
8. Be able to calculate GDP and other aggregates from a given set of data on the national accounts.			2, 3		156
9. Be able to distinguish GDP and NDP.	10, 11				152

Key-Term Review

Review the following terms; if you are not sure of the meaning of any term, write out the definition and check it against the Glossary in the text.

depreciation	national income (*NI*)
disposable income (*DI*)	national-income accounting
exports	net domestic product (NDP)
GDP per capita	net investment
gross domestic product (GDP)	nominal GDP
gross investment	personal income (*PI*)
imports	production possibilities
inflation	real GDP
intermediate goods	saving
investment	value added

Fill in the blank following each of the statements below with the appropriate term from the list above.

1. Those goods that are to be processed further before final sale are _____ .

   1. _____

2. Final purchases of goods and services by the business sector are referred to as _____ .

   2. _____

3. The major national-income aggregate used to measure an economy's total economic activity is _____ .

   3. _____

4. The major aggregate used to compare economic well-being across international boundaries is _____ .

   4. _____

5. Gross domestic product unadjusted for changes in the price level is called _____ .

   5. _____

6. At each stage of production there is an increase in _____ .

   6. _____

7. An increase in the general level of prices is referred to as _____ .

   7. _____

8. The value of the capital stock used up in producing this year's GDP is an estimate of _____ .

   8. _____

9. Gross domestic product adjusted for changes in the general level of prices is referred to as _____ .

   9. _____

10. That part of GDP that is "earned" by factors of production is called _____ .

    10. _____

11. The national-income aggregate that measures what the household sector has left to spend or save after taxes is _____ .

    11. _____

12. If you add net investment to depreciation, you get _____ .

    12. _____

13. The aggregate that measures the *addition* to the nation's capital stock is called _____ .

    13. _____

14. Disposable income plus personal taxes is called _____ .

    14. _____

15. Technology and resources are the most important constraints on the economy's _____ .

    15. _____

16. Goods and services produced in the United States but purchased by foreigners are _____ .

16. _____

17. Goods and services produced by foreigners but purchased by buyers in the United States are _____ .

17. _____

18. _____ is the process by which the nation's aggregate economic activity is measured.

18. _____

19. The amount of current output that society can consume without reducing next year's production possibilities is best measured by _____ .

19. _____

20. Whatever households do not spend out of their disposable income is referred to as _____ .

20. _____

True or False: *Circle your choice.*

T F 1. Without prices, it would be impossible to add up the outputs produced in different sectors of the economy in a meaningful way.

T F 2. Both the GNP and the GDP include production in the United States by subsidiaries of foreign firms in the same way.

T F 3. Comparisons of per capita GDP across international boundaries provide information on the distribution of GDP within each country.

T F 4. While the United States has the highest standard of living based on the real GDP per capita, it does not have the world's highest real GDP.

T F 5. Eliminating intermediate goods from the calculation of GDP results in double counting.

T F 6. In periods of rising prices, real GDP will rise more slowly than nominal GDP.

T F 7. The exclusion of homemaker services from the GDP means that the gap in the standard of living between developing countries and developed countries is probably smaller than the numbers would indicate.

T F 8. Real GDP and nominal GDP are equal during the base year for which an index is constructed.

T F 9. In periods of falling prices, nominal GDP must be inflated to obtain real GDP.

T F 10. Depreciation figures used in the calculation of GDP are based on actual measures of the deterioration of equipment, plant, capital, and the like.

T F 11. For the nation's capital stock to grow, net investment must be positive.

T F 12. Government spending currently claims about one-fifth of the U.S. GDP.

T F 13. Consumption expenditures by households account for roughly two-thirds of GDP.

T F 14. When imports exceed exports, net exports are positive.

T F 15. The reason state and local government expenditures are not included in GDP is that they are expenditures for intermediate goods and services.

T F 16. National income is a measure of the incomes "earned" by the factors of production in the process of producing the GDP.

T F 17. The total value of market incomes must equal the total value of final output, or GDP.

T F 18. The GDP accounts have two sides: one focuses on expenditure (the demand side), and the other focuses on income (the supply side), and the two sides are equal only when the market is at equilibrium.

T F 19. Consumption expenditure plus personal saving equals disposable income.

T F 20. Retained corporate earnings are an example of income that is earned but not received by the owners of the factors of production.

Multiple Choice: *Select the correct answer.*

_____ 1. A basic function of the national-income-accounting system is to:
    (a) Identify economic problems.
    (b) Provide an objective basis for evaluating policy.
    (c) Provide a framework for policy.
    (d) All of the above.

_____ 2. Prices are used in national accounting to:
    (a) Add the values of output from different sectors of the economy.
    (b) Compare the value of output of one period with that of another.
    (c) Provide an index to measure the rate of inflation.
    (d) All of the above.

_____ 3. GDP can be found by:
    (a) Adding up the spending by business, government, households, and foreigners, and subtracting imports.
    (b) Adding up the "value added" at every stage of production in the economy.
    (c) Adding up all of the receipts of households, government, and business.
    (d) All of the above.

_____ 4. Which of the following are treated differently in computing GNP as compared with GDP?
    (a) Goods produced by American firms located in the United States which have been acquired by foreign firms.
    (b) Goods produced by U.S. firms in foreign countries.
    (c) Goods produced by foreign firms in the United States.
    (d) All of the above.

5. Suppose apples cost consumers $1 per pound and oranges cost consumers $2 per pound. What combined contribution does the production of 1,000 pounds of apples and 1,000 pounds of oranges make to the GDP?
   (a) $3,000.
   (b) $2,000.
   (c) $1,000.
   (d) None of the above.

6. If the real U.S. GDP was $4,142.6 billion in 1989 and the U.S. population was 248.8 million, the per capita real GDP would have been closest to:
   (a) $16,650 per person.
   (b) $1,665 per person.
   (c) $6,006 per person.
   (d) $60,059 per person.

7. The underground economy includes:
   (a) All intermediate goods.
   (b) All unreported income.
   (c) All net exports.
   (d) All imports.

8. The underground economy exists because:
   (a) People wish to avoid taxes.
   (b) Illegal activities are profitable and such activities are disguised to avoid detection.
   (c) It is difficult to trace many transactions.
   (d) All of the above.

9. A housewife takes over the job of a deceased family member in running the family business and hires help to clean house and babysit. As a result, the GDP of the economy, *ceteris paribus*:
   (a) Remains unchanged, since the amount of productive activity remains unchanged.
   (b) Rises by the amount paid to house cleaners and babysitters.
   (c) Falls by the household work left undone by the house cleaners and babysitters.
   (d) Falls by the amount of income generated previously by the deceased family member.

10. Suppose sugar cane costs a penny a pound. But the ounce of sugar produced from that pound is worth $1. If 1,000,000 ounces of sugar is produced annually in the United States what is the contribution of sugar cane and sugar to the GDP?
    (a) $1000.
    (b) $101,000.
    (c) $1,000,000.
    (d) $1,010,000.

11. If both the prices and the quantities of all final goods and services produced doubled from one year to the next and population remained constant, then:
    (a) Nominal GDP would be four times as large in the second year as in the first.
    (b) Real GDP would be twice as large in the second year as in the first.
    (c) On the average, the population could be twice as well off in the second year as in the first.
    (d) All of the above would be the case.

_____ 12. Which of the following groupings contains a word which does not belong?
(a) GDP, NDP, net investment.
(b) Illegal drug trade, cash income of workers, sales revenue of small businesses.
(c) Sum of value added, GDP, $C + I + G + (X - M)$.
(d) Consumers, business, government.

_____ 13. Assume that nominal GDP is $1,000 in period 1 and $2,000 in period 2. If prices in period 2 are half as high as in period 1, real GDP in period 2:
(a) Is $2,000 measured in first-period prices.
(b) Is $1,000 measured in first-period prices.
(c) Is $4,000 measured in first-period prices.
(d) Cannot be determined from the data.

_____ 14. The value of goods that have been produced but not sold during the period:
(a) Increases business inventories and GDP for the period.
(b) Reduces GDP because the goods have not been sold.
(c) Neither increases nor decreases GDP.
(d) Is included in the next period's GDP when the goods are sold.

_____ 15. The nominal GDP in 1992 was $5950.7 billion. The implicit GDP deflator was 121.6 in 1992 (1987=100). What was 1992 GDP stated in 1987 prices?
(a) Less than $4,500 billion.
(b) Approximately $4,894 billion.
(b) Approximately $5,951 billion.
(c) Approximately $7,236 billion.

_____ 16. The total value of output produced by the economy and the total value of income generated by the economy:
(a) Differ by the amount of profits earned by corporations.
(b) Are equal.
(c) Differ by the amount of taxes collected by all levels of government.
(d) Differ by the amount of depreciation that occurs in the economy.

_____ 17. Transfer payments are part of personal income but not of national income because:
(a) Personal income is a "receipts concept."
(b) Personal income is an "earnings concept."
(c) National income is a "receipts concept."
(d) None of the above is an adequate explanation.

_____ 18. National income is a measure of:
(a) How well the economy is doing on a gross basis.
(b) The incomes earned by the factors of production in producing GDP.
(c) The incomes received by the factors of production in producing GDP.
(d) None of the above.

_____ 19. Which of the following must be subtracted from national income to obtain personal income?
(a) Undistributed corporate profits.
(b) Social security taxes.
(c) Corporate profit taxes.
(d) All of the above.

20. Personal income is the best measure of:
    (a) How well the economy is doing on a sustained basis.
    (b) The incomes earned by the factors of production in producing GDP.
    (c) The incomes received by households.
    (d) The relative standard of living of the populations of different countries.

21. Saving equals:
    (a) Gross investment.
    (b) Net investment.
    (c) Depreciation minus the capital consumption allowance.
    (d) None of the above.

22. DI is the most practical way to:
    (a) Measure how much income households can spend and save.
    (b) Measure how much output can be consumed on a sustainable basis.
    (c) Make international comparisons of the standard of living.
    (d) Analyze the growth rate of the economy over time.

23. Social security payments are:
    (a) Transfer payments.
    (b) Added, along with other things, to national income to get personal income.
    (c) Payments received for which no current good or service is rendered in return.
    (d) All of the above.

24. Businesses return purchasing power to the circular flow in the form of:
    (a) Retained earnings.
    (b) Depreciation charges.
    (c) Business investment.
    (d) Profit.

One World View article in the text (Chapter 3) reported about Poland:

"The price of electricity, natural gas and central heating went up by as much as 70 percent on New Year's Day as part of Poland's program to eliminate communist-era subsidies that kept the price of goods artificially low. . . The new increases have stung a population already severely pinched by unemployment and the new, real-world prices for food, rents and other services."

25. The most likely implication from this passage is that Poland is experiencing:
    (a) Both a higher real GDP and a higher nominal GDP.
    (b) A higher real GDP, but a lower nominal GDP.
    (c) A lower real GDP, but a higher nominal GDP.
    (d) Both a lower real GDP and a lower nominal GDP.

26. On the basis of this passage, the most likely implication about per capita real GDP and government share of GDP is that Poland is experiencing:
    (a) Higher per capita GDP but lower government share.
    (b) Higher per capita GDP and higher government share.
    (c) Lower per capita GDP and lower government share.
    (d) Lower per capita GDP and higher government share.

_____ 27. If the Polish government is encouraging free enterprise and lowers taxes, which of the following would be the long-run implication for the size of the underground economy and the share of investment in the GDP?
   (a) The underground economy should become smaller, and investment share should rise.
   (b) The underground economy should become smaller, and investment share should fall.
   (c) The underground economy should become larger, and investment share should rise.
   (d) The underground economy should become larger, and investment share should fall.

_____ 28. If the Polish government is encouraging free enterprise in Poland and lowers taxes on both firms and households, then which of the following would be the longirun implication for the national accounts?
   (a) The difference between NDP and *NI* should narrow, but the difference between *PI* and *DI* should widen.
   (b) The difference between NDP and *NI* should narrow, and the difference between *PI* and *DI* should narrow.
   (c) The difference between NDP and *NI* should widen, and the difference between *PI* and *DI* should widen.
   (d) The difference between NDP and *NI* should widen, but the difference between *PI* and *DI* should narrow.

Problems and Applications

Exercise 1

This exercise shows the relationship between nominal GDP and real GDP, and provides practice in computing percentage changes over time. Completing this exercise will help you with the problems for Chapter 7 in the text.

Each January the president's Council of Economic Advisers prepares *The Economic Report of the President*. It summarizes the essential features of the economy's performance and the policy initiatives that are likely to be undertaken. This exercise shows the kind of information that is developed for this publication.

Table 7.1 presents the Commerce Department estimates of GDP.

1. Table 7.1 shows the real GDP and the GDP deflator for each of the years indicated. Calculate nominal GDP and place it in the appropriate column.

Table 7.1
Real GDP, GDP deflator, and per capita GDP, 1982-91

(1) Year	(2) GDP deflator	(3) Real GDP (in billions of dollars per year)	(4) Nominal GDP (in billions of dollars per year)	(5) Percentage growth in nominal GDP	(6) Percentage growth in real GDP	(7) U.S. population (in millions)	(8) Real GDP per capita
1982	83.8	3,760.3	$_____	---- %	---- %	232.2	$_____
1983	87.2	3,906.6	_____	_____	_____	234.3	_____
1984	91.0	4,148.5	_____	_____	_____	236.3	_____
1985	94.4	4,279.8	_____	_____	_____	238.5	_____
1986	96.9	4,404.5	_____	_____	_____	240.7	_____
1987	100.0	4,539.9	_____	_____	_____	242.8	_____
1988	103.9	4,718.6	_____	_____	_____	245.0	_____
1989	108.5	4,838.0	_____	_____	_____	247.3	_____
1990	113.2	4,877.5	_____	_____	_____	249.9	_____
1991	117.8	4,821.0	_____	_____	_____	252.7	_____

Source: *The Economic Report of the President*, 1993, Table B-2, Table B-3, Table B-29

2. From the information in Table 7.1, calculate the percentage growth in nominal and real GDP for each of the years 1983-92 and insert your answers in the appropriate columns. Use the following formula:

$$\text{Percentage growth in real GDP} = \frac{\text{GDP}_{n+1} - \text{GDP}_n}{\text{GDP}_n} \times 100\%$$

where n = beginning year
  $n + 1$ = next year

For example, from 1983 to 1984 the real GDP increased by the following percentage:

$$\frac{\text{GDP}_{n+1} - \text{GDP}_n}{\text{GDP}_n} \times 100\% = \frac{4148.5 - 3906.6}{3906.6} \times 100\% = 6.2\%$$

3. T F   When nominal GDP grows, real GDP grows.

4. By what nominal dollar amount did nominal GDP grow from 1982 to 1991? _____

5. By what amount did real GDP grow from 1982 to 1991? _____

6. The U.S. population for the years 1983-92 is presented in column 7 of Table 7.1. Calculate the real GDP per capita in column 8.

7. T F   When real GDP rises, real GDP per capita also rises.

Exercise 2

This problem is designed to help you learn the way the national-income aggregates are determined and to reinforce your understanding of their relationship to one another. It will also help you with the problem 3 for Chapter 7 in the text.

Table 7.2
U.S. national-income aggregates, 1984 (billions of dollars per year)

Personal consumption expenditures	$2,460.3
Gross private domestic investment	718.9
Exports	302.4
Imports	405.1
Federal government purchases	310.9
State and local government purchases	389.9
Depreciation	433.2
Indirect business taxes	309.5
Social security taxes	325.0
Retained earnings	63.8
Corporate profits tax liability	94.0
Net interest	307.9
Transfer payments	437.8
Personal taxes	395.1

Source: *The Economic Report of the President*, 1993.

1. On the basis of the information provided in Table 7.2, calculate the national-income aggregates for 1984 and insert the amounts in Table 7.3. Complete Table 7.3 by calculating the percent increases in nominal value.

Table 7.3
U.S. national-income aggregates
(billions of dollars per year)

Economic aggregate	1984	1989	Percent increase in nominal value
GDP	$_____	$5,250.8	_____%
NDP	_____	4,686.4	_____
NI	_____	4,249.5	_____
PI	_____	4,380.3	_____
DI	_____	3,787.0	_____

2. Which national-income aggregate increased by the greatest percentage? _____ .

3. What percentage of the GDP was accounted for by government purchases in 1984? _____

   In 1989? _____ (*Note*: Federal government purchases in 1989 were $409 billion.)

Exercise 3

The data in this exercise was selected to show the importance of the inflation adjustment. The percentage change in nominal GDP is compared with the percentage change in real GDP.

1. Graph the percentage change in nominal GDP and real GDP (see the data on the inside cover of this Study Guide) on the same axis in Figure 7.1.

Figure 7.1
Percentage change of Nominal and Real GDP

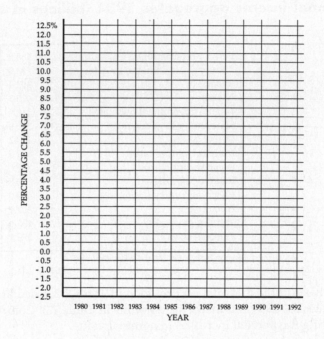

2. The relationship between the percentage change in real GDP and the percentage change in the nominal GDP is best characterized as (direct, inverse). _____

3. What accounts for the difference between the two measures of the GDP?

   _____

4. Is the percentage change in nominal GDP negative in each year in which there is a recession?_____

5. In which years do recessions appear to occur?

   _____

Common Errors

The first statement in each "common error" below is incorrect. Each incorrect statement is followed by a corrected version and an explanation.

1. Income and output are two entirely different things. WRONG!

    Income and output are two sides of the same coin. RIGHT!

    This is fundamental. Every time a dollar's worth of final spending takes place, the seller must receive a dollar's worth of income. It could not be otherwise. Remember, profits are used as a balancing item. Don't confuse the term "income" with the term "profit." Profits can be negative, whereas output for the economy cannot.

2. Comparisons of per capita GDP between countries tell you which population is better off. WRONG!

    Comparisons of per capita GDP between countries are only indicators of which population is better off. RIGHT!

    Simple comparisons of per capita GDP ignore how the GDP is distributed. A country with a very high per capita GDP that is unequally distributed may well provide a standard of living that is below that of another country with a lower per capita GDP which is more equally distributed. There are other problems with comparisons of per capita GDP as a result of exchange-rate distortions, and differences in mix of output in two countries, and how the economy is organized. GDP per capita is an indicator only of the amount of goods and services each person could have, not what each person does have.

3. Value added is a measure of a firm's profit. WRONG!

    Value added includes all factor payments to land, labor, and capital in addition to the residual (profit) that goes to the entrepreneur for taking risks. RIGHT!

    In computing value added, a firm subtracts *from* total revenue the cost of items sold to the firm in "arm's-length" transactions. There are additional cost items that normally would be subtracted to calculate "profit" but which are not subtracted in the computation of value added. Those items include the cost of capital, land, and labor. When value added for all economic units is combined, the total of payments to capital (interest), land (rent), labor (wages), and risk taking (profits) will equal the total gross national product.

•ANSWERS•

Key-Term Review

1. intermediate goods
2. investment
3. gross domestic product (GDP)
4. GDP per capita
5. nominal GDP
6. value added
7. inflation
8. depreciation
9. real GDP
10. national income (*NI*)
11. disposable income (*DI*)
12. gross investment
13. net investment
14. personal income (*PI*)
15. production possibilities
16. exports
17. imports
18. national-income accounting
19. net domestic product (NDP)
20. saving

True or False

1. T	5. F	9. T	12. T	15. F	18. F
2. F	6. T	10. F	13. T	16. T	19. T
3. F	7. T	11. T	14. F	17. T	20. T
4. F	8. T				

Multiple Choice

1. d	3. d	5. a	7. b	9. b	11. d
2. d	4. d	6. a	8. d	10. c	

12. a   Net investment is not a measure of total national product. Other topics include (b) transactions in the underground economy that are not picked up by GNP accounting, (c) alternative measures of the GNP, and (d) groups to whom the GNP is distributed.

13. c	16. b	19. d	22. a	25. c	27. a
14. a	17. a	20. c	23. d	26. c	28. b
15. b	18. b	21. d	24. c		

Problems and Applications

Table 7.1 Answer

Year	Nominal GDP (in billions of dollars per year)	Percentage growth in nominal GDP	Percentage growth in real GDP	Real GDP per capita per year
1982	$3,151.1	__%	__%	$16,194
1983	3,406.6	8.1	3.9	16,673
1984	3,775.1	10.8	6.2	17,556
1985	4,040.1	7.0	3.2	17,945
1986	4,268.0	5.6	2.9	18,299
1987	4,539.9	6.4	3.1	18,698
1988	4,902.6	8.0	3.9	19,260
1989	5,249.2	7.1	2.5	19,563
1990	5,521.3	5.2	0.8	19,521
1991	5,679.1	2.9	-1.2	19,078

1. See Table 7.1 Answer, column 4.

2. See Table 7.1 Answer, columns 5 and 6.

3. F

4. $2,527.9 billion

5. $1060.7 billion

6. See Table 7.1 Answer, column 8.

7. F

Exercise 2

1.GDP = C + I + G + (X - M)
GDP = 2460.3 + 718.9 + (310.9 + 389.9) + (302.4 - 405.1)
GDP = 3777.3

Gross domestic product (GDP)	3777.3
Less depreciation	(433.2)
Net domestic product	3344.1
Less indirect business taxes	(309.5)
National income (NI)	3034.6
Less corporate taxes	(94.0)
Less retained earnings	(63.8)
Less social security taxes	(325.0)
Plus transfer payments	437.8
Plus net interest	307.9
Personal income (PI)	3295.7
Less personal taxes	(395.1)
Disposable incomes (DI)	2902.4

Table 7.3 Answer

Economic aggregate	1984 (billions of dollars per year)	Percent increase in nominal value
GDP	$3,777.3	39.0%
NDP	3,344.1	40.1
NI	3,034.6	40.0
PI	3,297.5	32.8
DI	2,902.4	30.5

2. NDP

3. 1984 : 8.2%
   1989 : 7.8%

Exercise 3

1. **Figure 7.1 Answer**

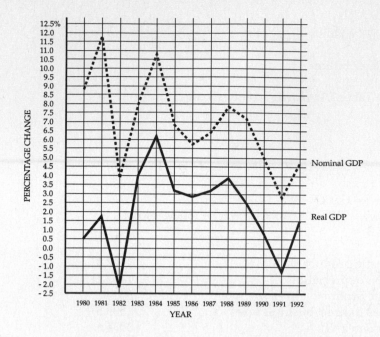

2. direct

3. Inflation (as measured by the GDP deflator)

4. Nominal GDP gives no indication of a recession; it's positive each year.

5. 1980, 1982, and 1991. However, a recession occurs when real GDP growth is negative for two quarters in a row, and, because this is annual data, we can't be absolutely sure that we have all of the recessions. Theoretically it could be possible, though unlikely, that a negative number could occur without two quarters in a row being negative.

CHAPTER 8

Aggregate Spending

Quick Review

The Great Depression caused economists to change the way they thought about the macroeconomy. John Maynard Keynes concluded that a *market-driven economy* could fall into a recessionary trap *and* that the problem was on the demand side of the economy. He posed the following questions:

- What are the components of aggregate demand?
- What determines the level of spending for each component?
- Will there ever be enough demand to maintain full employment?

Macroequilibrium only requires that aggregate supply equal aggregate demand, but the goal of full employment requires that the equilibrium occur at a unique level of output and price level. Keynes was concerned about the four components of aggregate demand?

- Consumption (*C*).
- Investment (*I*).
- Government spending (*G*).
- Net exports *(X - IM)*.

He questioned whether they would be sufficient to generate full employment and, if they were not, wondered if they would shift so as to solve the problem. He focused first on consumption and concluded that it is determined mostly by disposable income.

Disposable income must be divided into two parts – that which is spent and that which is saved. The amount spent out of any level of disposable income can be anticipated using the consumption function (a Keynesian invention) of the form $C = a + bY_D$, where the coefficients a and b describe consumer behavior. Here a depends on wealth, credit, age, and the like. and is referred to as "autonomous spending"; b is the percentage of current disposable income which will be spent.

Income which is not spent is, by definition, saved. Household saving is a leakage from the circular flow of income as are business saving, imports, and taxes. If the economy is to prosper, some way must be found to inject the income which "leaks out" back into the income stream. There are several injections. Investment spending is done by firms as they purchase final output, and this category depends on interest rates, expectations, the development of new technologies, and innovation *but not* on current income. Government purchases (federal, state, and local) are a significant force in the economy, and decisions on how much to spend are made independently of real income. Foreign buyers purchase exports from the U.S. economy; Americans gladly purchase imports from foreign countries. The difference is called net exports. We can summarize as follows:

$$\text{Aggregate expenditure} = C + I + G + (X - IM)$$

Using spending categories, we can predict how much spending will take place at any level of income, and whether it will be sufficient to create full employment. Obviously, twin problems loom – aggregate spending may be too little and a recessionary gap may develop, or it may be too much and an inflationary gap may ensue. The former causes cyclical unemployment; the latter, demand-pull inflation.

Learning Objectives

After reading Chapter 8 and doing the following exercises, you should:	True or false	Multiple choice	Problems and applications	Common errors	Pages in the text
1. Know the Keynesian theory of aggregate spending.	1, 3, 4		1	1	167-170, 180-184
2. Understand the difference between aggregate demand and aggregate spending.	2, 5, 6	2, 3, 17	1		166
3. Know how to find the average and marginal propensities to consume.	9-14	4, 5, 7, 13	1	4	168
4. Be able to interpret the consumption function.	16	8-14, 19, 26, 27, 31	1, 2, 5		170-172
5. Know how to use the aggregate spending function and the 45-degree line to calculate saving or dissaving.	8, 9, 16, 17	6, 12, 15, 16		5	172-173
6. Be able to graph a recessionary or an inflationary gap, explain what occurs, and describe appropriate government intervention.	16, 18, 19	1, 28	2, 4		185-186
7. Explain the role of saving, its relation to investment, and the effect it has on equilibrium income.	8	1, 6, 15, 16, 20, 21, 29, 30	1, 3, 4	2	175-180
8. Be able to describe the determinants of C, I, G, and (X - IM).	7	14, 20, 22-26	1-3, 6	2, 6	180-184
9. Understand the nature and role of both leakages and injections.	15-17	6, 18, 22	1-4	6	175-180
10. Be able to graph the aggregate expenditure function and determine the resulting level of income.	2, 5, 16	3, 27	3	3	183-185

Key-Term Review

Review the following terms; if you are not sure of the meaning of any term, write out the definition and check it against the Glossary in the text.

aggregate demand
aggregate spending
aggregate supply
average propensity to consume (*APC*)
business saving
consumption
consumption function
cyclical unemployment
demand-pull inflation
disposable income (*DI*)
dissaving

equilibrium (macro)
full-employment GDP
inflationary gap
injection
investment
leakage
marginal propensity to consume (*MPC*)
marginal propensity to save (*MPS*)
recessionary gap
saving

Fill in the blank following each of the statements below with the appropriate term from the list above.

1. The formula $C = a + bY_D$ is referred to as the
    _____ .   1. _____

2. In this formula, b is the same thing as the
    _____ .   2. _____

3. The formula $C + I + G + (X - IM)$ represents
    _____ .   3. _____

4. I in this formula represents _____ .   4. _____

5. C in the formulas represents _____ .   5. _____

6. Dividing C by _____ gives the _____ ,
    which is the percentage of the consumer's   6. _____
    income that is spent on consumption.   _____

7. The excess of disposable income over
    consumption is _____ .   7. _____

8. Saving is considered a _____ because it is
    income not spent directly on domestic output.   8. _____

9. When consumption exceeds disposable income,
    there is _____ .   9. _____

10. When desired aggregate spending is less than
    _____ , there is a _____ , which means
    that inventories will accumulate and there will   10. _____
    be fewer jobs. This type of unemployment is   _____
    often referred to as _____ .   _____

11. _____ is established at the price-output combination at which _____ equals _____ .

11. _____
_____
_____

12. If the economy is at full employment and aggregate demand rises above full-employment GDP, then there is an _____ .

12. _____

13. A rise in average prices due to excessive demand for goods and services is called _____ .

13. _____

14. Investment is an _____ into the income stream.

14. _____

15. The ratio of the change in saving to a change in disposable income is known as the _____ .

15. _____

16. The sum of depreciation allowances and retained earnings is referred to as gross _____ .

16. _____

True or False: *Circle your choice.*

T F 1. Keynes believed that if market participants were unwilling to buy all the output produced, the government would have to intervene if the economy were to pull itself out of a recessionary gap.

T F 2. The four components of aggregate spending are the same as those for aggregate demand.

T F 3. Most economists recognize that a short-run macro failure is possible.

T F 4. Most economists believe that equilibrium output can fall short of full-employment output in the short run.

T F 5. Aggregate demand curves and aggregate expenditure curves are drawn on the same set of axes, with real output on the *x*-axis and average price on the *y*-axis.

T F 6. The aggregate supply curve represents the total quantity of output supplied at alternative average price levels in a given time period, *ceteris paribus*.

T F 7. The largest component of aggregate spending is government spending.

T F 8. An individual, like an economy, cannot spend more than current income.

T F 9. When all disposable income is spent on consumption, the marginal propensity to consume is zero.

T F 10. The question "What fraction of added disposable income is spent on consumption?" can be answered by calculating the marginal propensity to consume.

T F 11. $APC = 1 - APS$.

T F 12. If consumers are optimistic, the marginal propensity to save rises.

T F 13. The *APS* is negative whenever there is dissaving.

T F 14. The marginal propensity to consume in the United States has been fairly constant since 1970.

T F 15. Because saving is a leakage, a sudden increase in saving necessarily results in lower equilibrium income for society, *ceteris paribus*.

T F 16. Full-employment GDP is any rate of production that allows prices to remain stable.

T F 17. The household sector is the only sector of the economy that saves.

T F 18. An inflationary gap implies that desired injections at full employment exceed desired leakages.

T F 19. If full-employment output is greater than desired spending at full employment there is a recessionary gap.

Multiple Choice: *Select the correct answer.*

_____ 1. Equilibrium (macro) always occurs at the output at which:
  (a) The aggregate expenditure curve intersects the 45-degree line.
  (b) The aggregate demand curve intersects the aggregate supply curve.
  (c) The price-quantity combination at which aggregate demand equals aggregate supply.
  (d) All of the above.

_____ 2. Which of the following groups contains a term which does not belong?
  (a) Aggregate demand, aggregate supply, aggregate spending.
  (b) Investment, government expenditure, exports.
  (c) Saving, taxes, imports.
  (d) Changes in expectations, changes in government spending or taxes, changes in interest rates.

_____ 3. Total spending:
  (a) Rather than real output was used in models developed by Keynes.
  (b) Is given by the formula $P \times Q$ where P stands for price and Q for real output.
  (c) Is the same as the real value of output if price is constant over time.
  (d) All of the above.

_____ 4. The average propensity to consume is:
  (a) Total consumption in a given period divided by total disposable income.
  (b) C/Y_D.
  (c) That part of the average consumer dollar that goes to the purchase of final goods.
  (d) All of the above.

_____ 5. If, in the aggregate, consumers spend 90 cents out of every extra dollar received:
  (a) The *APC* is 1.11.
  (b) The *APC* is 0.90.
  (c) The *MPS* is 0.10.
  (d) The *MPC* is 0.10.

_____ 6. Personal saving is:
   (a)   Negative above the income at which consumption and income are equal.
   (b)   Disposable income less consumption.
   (c)   The part of disposable income spent on goods and services during the current period of time.
   (d)   All of the above.

_____ 7. The difference between the marginal propensity and the average propensity to consume reflects:
   (a)   Why people fail to devote the same percentage of extra income to saving that they devote from their total income to total saving.
   (b)   A large, autonomous consumption component in the consumption function that is not affected by income.
   (c)   The difference between *APS* and *MPS*.
   (d)   All of the above.

_____ 8. Suppose a consumption function is given as $C = 100 + 0.5Y$. The marginal propensity to consume is:
   (a)   0.2.
   (b)   0.5.
   (c)   50.
   (d)   100.

Figure 8.1
Alternate consumption functions

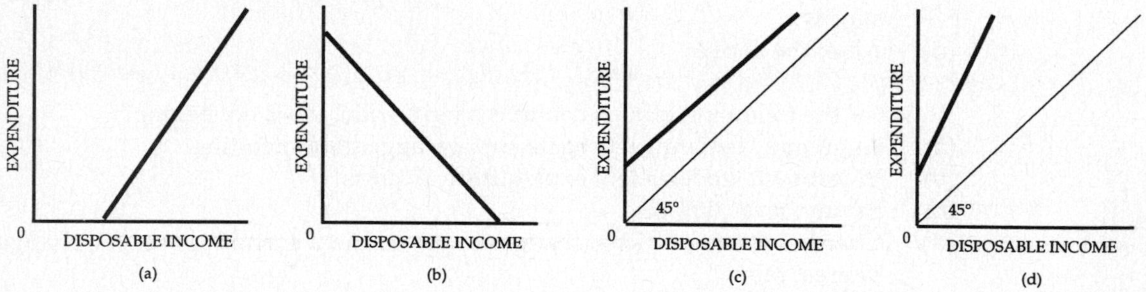

(a)   (b)   (c)   (d)

Use Figure 8.1 to answer questions 9 - 13.

_____ 9. Which diagram in Figure 8.1 best represents a plausible graph of the consumption function?
   (a)   (b)   (c)   (d)

_____ 10. Which diagram in Figure 8.1 suggests that there is no consumption expenditure at an income level of zero?
   (a)   (b)   (c)   (d)

_____ 11. Which diagram in Figure 8.1 shows that consumption does not rise with income?
   (a)   (b)   (c)   (d)

_____ 12. Which diagram in Figure 8.1 shows that the economy always consumes more than its income?
   (a)   (b)   (c)   (d)

_____ 13. Which diagram in Figure 8.1 shows the marginal propensity to consume as being negative?
(a)   (b)   (c)   (d)

_____ 14. Autonomous consumption is found where the consumption function intersects the:
(a)   Vertical axis.
(b)   Horizontal axis.
(c)   45-degree line.
(d)   Aggregate spending curve.

_____ 15. When there is dissaving, then it must be true that:
(a)   Consumption minus disposable income is negative.
(b) MPS is negative.
(c) APS is negative.
(d)   All of the above.

_____ 16. In graphs with disposable income on the horizontal axis and expenditures on the vertical axis, a 45-degree line represents:
(a)   The potential growth path for consumption.
(b)   A line marking where aggregate demand and supply intersect for equilibrium (macro).
(c)   The points on which aggregate expenditure equals disposable income.
(d)   All of the above.

_____ 17. An increase in taxes could best be represented by a graph of the aggregate demand curve:
(a)   Shifting leftward while an aggregate expenditure curve would shift downward.
(b)   Shifting leftward while an aggregate expenditure curve would shift upward.
(c)   Shifting rightward while an aggregate expenditure curve would shift downward.
(d)   Shifting rightward while an aggregate expenditure curve would shift upward.

_____ 18. Which of the following is a leakage?
(a)   Savings.
(b)   Imports.
(c)   Taxes.
(d)   All of the above.

_____ 19. A change in autonomous consumption would correspond to:
(a)   A shift of both a graph of the consumption function and the aggregate demand curve.
(b)   A shift of a graph of the consumption function and a movement along the aggregate demand curve.
(c)   A movement along a graph of the consumption function and a shift of the aggregate demand curve.
(d)   A movement along both a graph of the consumption function and the aggregate demand curve.

_____ 20. When an economy is at full employment but consumers, government, businesses, and the foreign sector do not buy the full amount of output, then:
(a)   Inventories accumulate.
(b)   There is an inflationary gap.
(c)   The economy will sustain itself at its potential GDP.
(d)   All of the above.

_____ 21. Which of the following terms does not belong?
  (a) Retained earnings.
  (b) Depreciation allowances.
  (c) Dividends.
  (d) Business saving.

_____ 22. If desired leakages exceed desired injections, then:
  (a) Keynesians believe government has a responsibility to increase injections by spending more.
  (b) Classical economists believe the economy will self-adjust.
  (c) The economy cannot sustain itself at full employment.
  (d) All of the above.

_____ 23. Which of the following would _not_ be included in investment spending?
  (a) The purchase of a new share of stock issued by IBM.
  (b) The purchase of a house built five years ago but which had never been occupied.
  (c) The purchase of a used Sears delivery van by a small business.
  (d) All of the above.

_____ 24. Which of the following causes a movement along the investment demand curve?
  (a) A change in expectations.
  (b) A change in technology.
  (c) A change in the rate of interest.
  (d) The current level of income.

_____ 25. The x-axis for a graph of an investment demand curve is labeled with:
  (a) The average price of investment goods.
  (b) The interest rate.
  (c) Planned investment.
  (d) Depreciation.

_____ 26. In a graph with income along the x-axis and expenditure along the y-axis, which of the following expenditure curves is most likely to be positively sloped?
  (a) Government spending.
  (b) The consumption function.
  (c) The investment function.
  (d) The export function.

_____ 27. The aggregate expenditure curve has the same slope as the consumption function if it is assumed that:
  (a) Investment is autonomous with respect to income.
  (b) Government expenditures are autonomous with respect to income.
  (c) Net exports are autonomous with respect to income.
  (d) All of the above.

_____ 28. The amount by which the desired rate of total expenditure at full employment exceeds full-employment output refers to the:
  (a) GDP gap.
  (b) Recessionary gap.
  (c) Inflationary gap.
  (d) Budget deficit.

Use Figure 8.2 to answer questions 29 and 30.

Figure 8.2
Investment demand curves

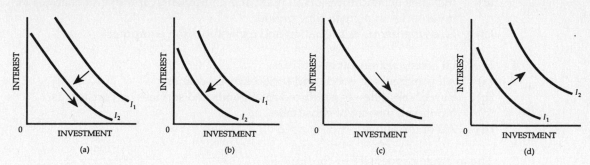

(a)   (b)   (c)   (d)

_____ 29. Which diagram shows how investment responds to expectations that the economy is about to enter a recession, causing firms to expect a decline in sales?
(a)   (b)   (c)   (d)

_____ 30. Which diagram shows what happens to investment as the interest rate falls?
(a)   (b)   (c)   (d)

_____ 31. A World View article in the text has the headline "Japan's Consumers Go on a Spending Spree, and Economy Booms." Which of the following statements best represents the change indicated in this headline?
(a)   The consumption function has shifted downward because consumers are saving less.
(b)   The aggregate demand curve has shifted leftward because leakages have increased.
(c)   The investment demand curve has shifted leftward because of the change in saving.
(d)   None of the above.

Problems and Applications

Exercise 1

This exercise emphasizes the use of definitions in computing the marginal propensity to consume, the average propensity to consume, and saving.

1. The consumption function is:
(a) $C = a + bY_D$.
(b)   A mathematical relationship indicating the rate of consumer spending that will take place at various income levels.
(c)   An algebraic relationship that shows consumption is influenced by disposable income.
(d)   All of the above.

2. Personal saving is:
(a)   That part of current disposable income not spent on goods and services in a given time period.
(b)   Disposable income less consumption.
(c)   Positive above the break-even level of income.
(d)   All of the above.

3. Net investment:
    (a) Occurs when money is used to purchase shares of stock.
    (b) Includes expenditures on only new plant and equipment (capital) and changes in inventories in a given time period.
    (c) Includes expenditures on all plant and equipment (capital) and changes in inventories in a given time period.
    (d) Is saving minus depreciation and expenditure on equipment.

4. Personal consumption expenditure is:
    (a) All purchases of goods and services by consumers.
    (b) Purchases of newly produced final goods and services by consumers.
    (c) Nontaxed income of consumers.
    (d) All of the above.

5. The average propensity to consume is:
    (a) Total consumption in a given period divided by total disposable income.
    (b) The percentage of total disposable income spent on consumption.
    (c) That part of the average consumer dollar that goes to the purchase of final goods.
    (d) All of the above.

6. The marginal propensity to consume is:
    (a) That part of the average consumer dollar that goes to the purchase of final goods.
    (b) The change in consumption divided by the change in disposable income.
    (c) The fraction of each additional (marginal) dollar of consumption spent on disposable income.
    (d) All of the above.

7. Using the consumption schedule in Table 8.1, complete columns 4, 5, and 7, and then compute the average propensity to consume and the marginal propensity to consume in columns 3 and 6.

Table 8.1
Marginal and average propensity to consume
(billions of dollars per year)

(1) Disposable income	(2) Total Consumption	(3) Average propensity to consume	(4) Change in consumption	(5) Change in income	(6) Marginal propensity to consume	(7) Saving
$ 0	$ 200	___				$_____
400	500	_____	$300	$400	_____	_____
1,200	1,100	_____	_____	_____	_____	_____

8. What is the equilibrium level of disposable income if investment is $100 billion and government spending and net exports are zero? _____

Exercise 2

This exercise provides practice in using the consumption function and in identifying shifts and movements along the consumption expenditure curve.

1. Assume the following consumption function:

$$C = \$200 \text{ billion} + 0.75\, Y_D$$

In Table 8.2, compute a consumption schedule from the formula.

Table 8.2
Computation of a consumption schedule
(billions of dollars per year)

Disposable income (Y_D)	Consumption not changing with income (a)	+	Additional spending at higher income (bY_D) (0.75 x col. 1)	=	Total consumption (C)
$ 0	_____		_____		$_____
400	_____		_____		_____
1,200	200		0.75 x 1,200		1,100

2. Using the consumption schedule in Table 8.2, draw the consumption function in Figure 8.3 and label it 1. The curve should pass through point B if it is correctly drawn.

3. In Table 8.3 fill in the schedule for the consumption function $C = \$300 \text{ billion} + 0.75\, Y_D$.

4. What is the marginal propensity to consume in Table 8.3? _____

Table 8.3
Consumption function shift
(billions of dollars per year)

Disposable income (Y_D)	Consumption not changing with income (a)	+	Additional spending at higher income (bY_D) (0.75 x col. 1)	=	Total consumption (C)
$ 0	$300		_____		$_____
400	300		_____		_____
800	300		_____		_____
1,200	300		_____		_____

5. Using the schedule in Table 8.3, graph the consumption function in Figure 8.3 (label it 2) and draw a 45-degree line from the origin.

6. For simplicity, suppose the aggregate expenditure curve for the economy is the same as its consumption function (there are no government, business, or foreign sectors). If full employment is $1,200 billion, then the shift moves the economy from:
    (a)   A recessionary gap to an inflationary gap.
    (b)   An inflationary gap to a recessionary gap.
    (c)   Equilibrium (macro) to an inflationary gap.
    (d)   A recessionary gap to equilibrium (macro).

7. T F   In Figure 8.3 the shift in the consumption function shows that at any given level of disposable income, consumption will be greater and savings will be less.

Figure 8.3
Consumption functions

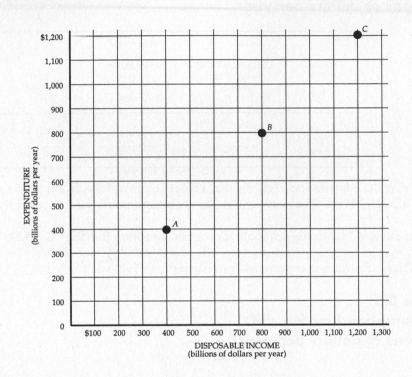

Choose the diagram in Figure 8.4 that best represents the shift or movement along a consumption curve that accompanies each of the events described in problems 8-11. (*Hint*: Try to figure out how each event affects the amount of consumption goods demanded.)

Figure 8.4

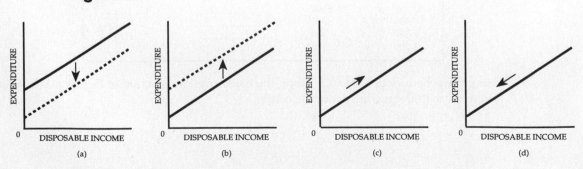

8. A recession occurs. _____

9. U.S. imports increase, so there is less consumption of U.S. goods at every level of income. _____

10. People expect that inflation will get out of hand, so they decide to buy more goods today before prices rise. _____

11. People have more disposable income so they consume more. _____

Exercise 3

This exercise offers practice in graphing aggregate spending curves using information about consumption and investment. It also relates the level of aggregate spending to interest rates.

1. Use the information in Table 8.4 to graph the demand curve for investment goods in Figure 8.5.

Table 8.4
Demand schedule for investment goods

Interest rate (percent)	Investment goods (billions of dollars per year)
20%	$ 0
15	50
10	100
5	200
0	300

Figure 8.5

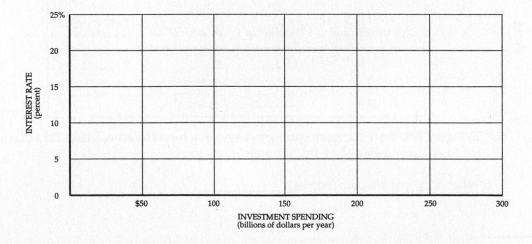

2. As interest rates rise, the investment demand curve shows, *ceteris paribus*:
   (a) That people find it worthwhile to invest in capital goods that will appreciate in value.
   (b) That since capital goods must now yield a higher rate of return to be profitable, fewer new capital goods and inventories are worth buying.
   (c) That as it becomes more expensive to borrow, more savings are used for investment and therefore the total amount of investment increases.
   (d) All of the above.

3. Use Figure 8.5 to determine investment at each of the income levels in Table 8.5 when the interest rate is 10 percent. (*Hint:* Remember that investment is insensitive to current income.)

Table 8.5
Investment schedule
(billions of dollars per year)

Disposable income	Investment goods
$ 0	$_____
400	_____
800	_____
1,200	_____

4. Assume that the consumption function is $C = \$200$ billion $+ 0.75\ Y_D$ and that the interest rate is 20 percent. Fill in Table 8.6 to determine the aggregate spending schedule. (Assume that government expenditures and net exports are zero.)

Table 8.6
Aggregate spending schedule
(billions of dollars per year)

(1) Disposable income	(2) Consumption	(3) Investment	(4) Aggregate spending (2) + (3) = (4)
$ 0	$_____	$_____	$_____
400	_____	_____	_____
800	_____	_____	_____
1,200	_____	_____	_____

5. In Figure 8.6, draw the aggregate spending curve from the schedule in Table 8.6 and label it 1; then draw a 45-degree line through the origin.

6. What is the equilibrium income? _____

Figure 8.6

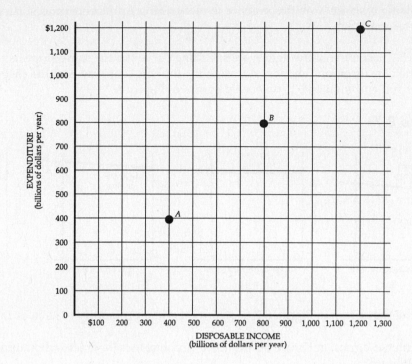

7. Suppose that in Table 8.4 the interest rate fell to 10 percent and the consumption function remained $C = \$200$ billion $+ 0.75 \, Y_D$. Fill in Table 8.7 to find the new aggregate spending schedule.

Table 8.7
Aggregate spending schedule
(billions of dollars per year)

(1) Disposable income	(2) Consumption	(3) Investment	(4) Aggregate spending (2) + (3) = (4)
$ 0	$_____	$_____	$_____
400	_____	_____	_____
800	_____	_____	_____
1,200	_____	_____	_____

8. In Figure 8.6, draw the aggregate spending curve based on Table 8.7 and label it 2.

9. What is the new equilibrium income? _____

10. When the interest rate fell by 10 percentage points, then:
    (a) Investment rose by $100 billion and equilibrium income rose by $100 billion per year.
    (b) Investment rose by $100 billion and equilibrium income rose by $400 billion per year.
    (c) Investment fell by $100 billion and equilibrium income fell by $100 billion per year.
    (d) Investment fell by $100 billion and equilibrium income fell by $400 billion per year.

Exercise 4

The following exercise provides practice in recognizing equilibrium and sorting out inflationary gaps from recessionary gaps.

In Figure 8.7 assume that the aggregate spending curve has the same slope as the curve representing the consumption function. Also assume that the economy is at the disposable income which achieves full employment, Y_f, in each diagram of Figure 8.7.

Figure 8.7

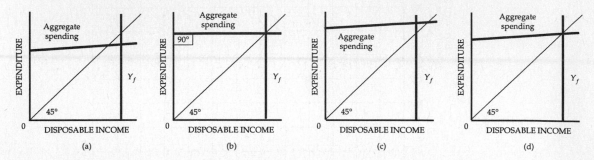

(a)   (b)   (c)   (d)

1. Which diagram in Figure 8.7 depicts a marginal propensity to save of 1.00? _____

2. Which diagram in Figure 8.7 depicts a circumstance in which substantial inventories are piling up? _____

3. Which diagram in Figure 8.7 is most likely to correspond to a situation of widespread bidding wars in different markets? _____

4. Which diagram in Figure 8.7 depicts equilibrium income equal to full-employment income and a marginal propensity to consume that is greater than zero? _____

5. Which diagram in Figure 8.7 depicts a circumstance in which workers are being laid off? _____

6. Which diagram in Figure 8.7 is most likely to correspond to a negative economic growth rate for the economy? _____

Exercise 5

The media continually present information about events that shift aggregate expenditures for our economy. This exercise will use one of the articles in the text to show the kind of information to look for. If your professor makes a newspaper assignment from the *Instructor's Manual*, this exercise will provide an example of how to do it.

Reread the the World View article on page 178 in the text, "Japan's Consumers Go on a Spending Spree, and Economy Booms," written for the *Wall Street Journal*. Then answer the following questions. Use Figure 8.8 to answer question 1.

Figure 8.8

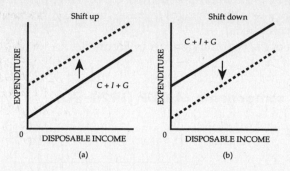

(a)   (b)

1. Which diagram in Figure 8.8 best represents the shift in aggregate expenditure that the article is describing? _____

2. Which of the following changes best represents the change to the circular flow?
    (a)   More of a leakage.
    (b)   Less of a leakage.
    (c)   More of an injection.
    (d)   Change in consumption.

3. What phrase or sentence in the article provides evidence of a shift in a leakage, injection, or consumption?

4. What passage (no more than a sentence) indicates the change in income that results from the shift?

Exercise 6

This exercise will show just how much more important government has become in the economy over time.

1. For the years shown in Table 8.8, collect the data from the inside cover of the text for two components of the GDP indicated. Place the results in the appropriate blanks. Find the share of each expenditure in the GDP by dividing it by the GDP for that year.

Table 8.8
Aggregate Spending

Year	Personal consumption expenditures (billions of dollars per year)	Percent of GDP	Government purchases (billions of dollars per year)	Percent of GDP	Total nominal GDP (billions of dollars per year)
1929	_____	_____	_____	_____	_____
1940	_____	_____	_____	_____	_____
1950	_____	_____	_____	_____	_____
1960	_____	_____	_____	_____	_____
1970	_____	_____	_____	_____	_____
1980	_____	_____	_____	_____	_____
1990	_____	_____	_____	_____	_____

2. Which component of GDP has grown the most since 1929? _____

3. In a graph of a production-possibilities curve with public goods on the *x*-axis and private goods on the *y*-axis, the changes through time suggest a movement along the curve toward (*x*-axis, *y*-axis).

4. Graph each of the two components in Figure 8.9.

Figure 8.9
Expenditure components of GDP (1929-90)

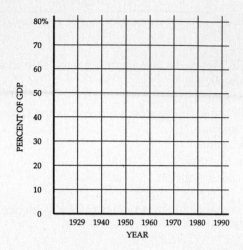

5. Why do the graphs of these two components differ from those shown in Figure 8.9 in the text?_____

Crossword Puzzle

Select the economic term in the following list that corresponds with each of the definitions and descriptions below. Then fit the term or one of the words within it into the crossword puzzle at the number indicated. Some of the words in the list are used twice (as indicated in parentheses).

aggregate demand
aggregate spending
aggregate supply
average propensity
   to consume (2)
consumption
consumption function
cyclical unemployment

demand-pull inflation
disposable income
dissaving
45-degree line
full-employment GDP
inflationary gap
investment
leakage

marginal propensity to consume
marginal propensity to save (2)
nominal income
potential GDP
recessionary gap
saving
stabilization problem

Across

1. The amount of goods and services that people can buy after personal taxes have been deducted from personal income.

6. The proportion of the next dollar of income that people tend not to consume.

7. The excess of aggregate spending over a 45-degree line at full-employment income.

10. Consumption + government + investment + net exports.

11. An algebraic representation which shows that what people consume depends on their disposable income.

13. Diversion of income from the circular flow.

14. The percentage of the next dollar of income that is spent for final goods and services by households.

16. The one type of inflation for which excessive buying is the cause.

20. Expenditures for capital (including residential construction and increases in inventories).

22. The percentage of disposable income spent on final goods and services by households.

23. The total quantity of output buyers are willing and able to buy at alternative price levels in a given time period, *ceteris paribus*.

24. The total quantity of output sellers are willing and able to sell at alternative price levels in a given time period, *ceteris paribus*.

Down

2. The part of disposable income that is not consumed.

3. The percentage of total income devoted to consumption.

4. The shortfall of aggregate spending from a 45-degree line at full-employment income.

5. When aggregate demand fails to reach the full-employment level, the labor force suffers from _____ .

8. A synonym for full-employment GDP.

9. The tradeoff between growth and price stability.

12. The extinction of final goods and services.

15. When income is low, people have to engage in _____ .

17. The change in saving divided by the change in income.

18. A measure of income that can be distorted by sudden changes in inflation.

19. The curve that shows where expenditures equal income.

21. The total market value of final goods and services at maximum employment with stable prices.

Common Errors

The first statement in each "common error" below is incorrect. Each incorrect statement is followed by a corrected version and an explanation.

1. The economy can spend no more than its income. WRONG!

   The economy *can* spend more than its income. RIGHT!

   The economy can spend more than its income by drawing down inventories of both public and private goods or by consuming capital (allowing it to depreciate) without replacing it. If the economy consumes more than its income, it will actually dissave and experience negative investment.

2. When a person invests in stocks, investment expenditure is increased. WRONG!

   The purchase of stocks has only an indirect relationship to investment expenditure in the economy. RIGHT!

   Investment expenditure refers to purchases of new capital goods (plant, machinery, and the like), inventories, or residential structures. A purchase of stock, represents a transfer of ownership from one person to another. Sometimes such purchases are called "financial investments," but they do not represent economic investment.

3. The aggregate expenditure curve is the same as the aggregate demand curve. WRONG!

   The aggregate expenditure curve and aggregate demand curve are related to each other only indirectly. RIGHT!

   The aggregate expenditure curve and aggregate demand curve are two quite different concepts. They have different units on the axes: aggregate spending represents the intended expenditures at each *income* level; aggregate demand represents quantity demanded at each average price level for all goods and services.

4. The marginal propensity to consume is consumption divided by income. WRONG!

   The average propensity to consume is consumption divided by income. RIGHT!

   There is a big difference between total consumption and a change in consumption. While the average propensity to consume involves total consumption and total income, the marginal propensity to consume involves changes in consumption and changes in income.

5. Dissaving is the difference between the 45-degree line and aggregate expenditure curves. WRONG!

Dissaving is the difference between a curve representing the consumption function and the 45-degree line. RIGHT!

Both saving and dissaving are defined as the difference between disposable income and consumption. The 45-degree line shows the points at which expenditure equals income. So, when consumption expenditure equals income (the consumption function intersects the 45-degree line), there is zero saving. When the consumption expenditure exceeds income (the consumption function is above the 45-degree line), there is dissaving. But at higher incomes, we expect consumption expenditure to be below income (the consumption function falls below the 45-degree line), and there will be saving.

6. Aggregate spending rises when people buy more imports. WRONG!

Aggregate spending falls when people buy more imports, *ceteris paribus*. RIGHT!

Students often think of imports as expenditures and therefore believe that increased spending on imports will have the same effect on the economy as an increase in consumption. Expenditures on imports, however, do not generate domestic income. If imports increase, they do so at the expense of purchases of U.S. goods, meaning fewer jobs in the United States. Because employment declines, there is less income with which to purchase goods; consumption falls and so does aggregate spending.

•ANSWERS•

Key-Term Review

1.	consumption function	10.	full-employment GDP
2.	marginal propensity to		recessionary gap
	consume (*MPC*)		cyclical unemployment
3.	aggregate spending	11.	equilibrium (macro)
4.	investment		aggregate demand
5.	consumption		aggregate supply
6.	disposable income (*DI*)	12.	inflationary gap
	average propensity to	13.	demand-pull inflation
	consume (*APC*)	14.	injection
7.	saving	15.	marginal propensity to save (*MPS*)
8.	leakage	16.	business saving
9.	dissaving		

True or False

1.	T	5.	F	8.	F	11.	T	14.	T	17.	F
2.	T	6.	T	9.	F	12.	F	15.	T	18.	T
3.	T	7.	F	10.	T	13.	F	16.	F	19.	T
4.	T										

Multiple Choice

1. a   Aggregate spending is shown on different axes than aggregate demand or aggregate supply. Other topics include (b) injections, (c) leakages, and (d) determinants of aggregate demand.

2.	d	7.	d	12.	d	17.	a	22.	d	27. d
3.	d	8.	b	13.	b	18.	d	23.	d	28. c
4.	d	9.	c	14.	a	19.	a	24.	c	29. b
5.	c	10.	a	15.	c	20.	a	25.	c	30. c
6.	b	11.	b	16.	c	21.	c	26.	b	31. d

Problems and Applications

Exercise 1

1. d   2. d   3. b   4. b   5. d   6. b

7. **Table 8.1 Answer**

(3) Average propensity to consume	(4) Change in consumption	(5) Change in income	(6) Marginal propensity to consume	(7) Saving
undefined				- $200
1.25	$300	$400	0.75	- 100
0.92	600	800	0.75	100

8. $1,200

Exercise 2

1. **Table 8.2 Answer**

(Y_D)	(a)	+	(bY_D)	=	(C)
$ 0	$200		0.00		$ 200
400	200		0.75 x 400		500
1,200	200		0.75 x 1,200		1,100

2. **Figure 8.3 Answer**

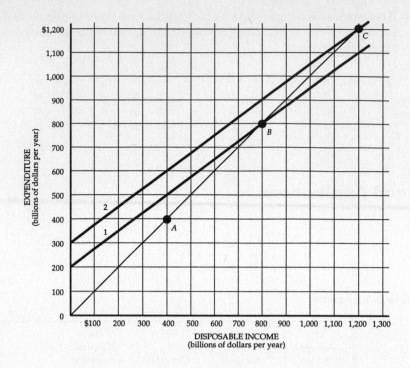

3. **Table 8.3 Answer**

(Y_D)	(a)	$+$	(bY_D)	$=$	(C)
$ 0	$300		0.75 x 0		$ 300
400	300		0.75 x 400		600
800	300		0.75 x 800		900
1,200	300		0.75 x 1,200		1,200

4. 0.75. The marginal propensity to consume is the change in consumption (e.g., $600 - $300 billion per year) divided by the corresponding change in income ($400 - $0 billion per year).

5. See Figure 8.3 Answer, line 2.

6. d Notice that the consumption function intersects the 45-degree line at full employment ($1,200 billion) after the shift, which means equilibrium has been achieved.

7. T

8. d   9. a   10. b   11. c

156

Exercise 3

1. **Figure 8.5 Answer**

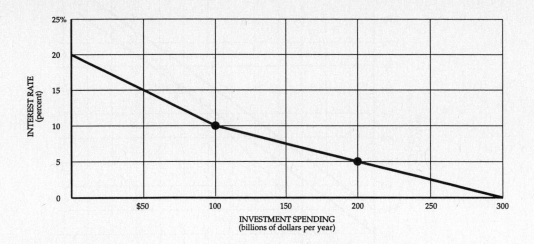

2. b

3. **Table 8.5 Answer**

Disposable income	Investment goods
$ 0	$100
400	100
800	100
1,200	100

4. **Table 8.6 Answer**

Disposable income	Consumption	Investment	Aggregate spending
$ 0	$ 200	$0	$ 200
400	500	0	500
800	800	0	800
1,200	1,100	0	1,100

5. **Figure 8.6 Answer**

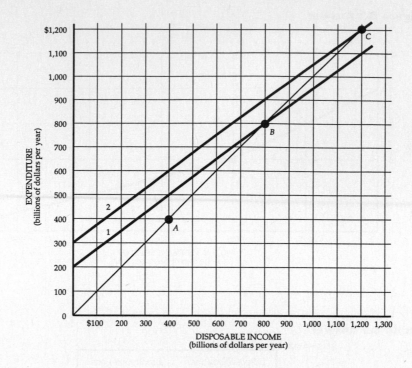

6. $800 billion per year (where the 45-degree line and the aggregate spending curve cross)

7. **Table 8.7 Answer**

Disposable income	Consumption	Investment	Aggregate spending
$ 0	$ 200	$100	$ 300
400	500	100	600
800	800	100	900
1,200	1,100	100	1,200

8. See Figure 8.6 Answer, line 2.

9. $1,200 billion per year (where the 45-degree line and the aggregate spending curve intersect)

10. b

Exercise 4

1. b   2. a   3. c   4. d   5. a   6. a

Exercise 5

1. a
2. b   If less saving or d if more consumption.
3. "Many Japanese, young and old, are giving up the self-sacrificing ways of the past" indicates an increase in consumption.

4. Higher income is indicated by the statement: "The result: a booming economy."

Exercise 6

1. **Table 8.8 Answer**

Year	Personal consumption expenditures (billions of dollars per year)	Percent of GDP	Government purchases (billions of dollars per year)	Percent of GDP	Total nominal GDP (billions of dollars per year)
1929	77.5	75.2%	8.6	8.3%	103.1
1940	71.2	71.2	15.8	15.8	100.0
1950	182.7	63.7	39.5	13.8	287.0
1960	322.4	62.8	99.8	19.4	513.4
1970	648.5	64.2	212.7	21.0	1,017.7
1980	1,748.1	64.6	496.1	18.3	2,708.0
1990	3,748.4	57.5	1,043.2	16.0	6,522.2

2. Government expenditures
3. *x*-axis toward greater public goods

4. **Figure 8.9 Answer**

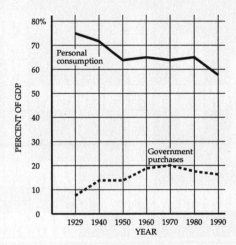

5. In Figure 8.9 in the text, the *x*-axis is disposable income (output), but in the diagram here, time is on the *x*-axis. The *y*-axis shows percent of GDP.

Crossword Puzzle Answer

Across

1. *disposable* income
6. marginal propensity to *save*
7. inflationary *gap*
10. *aggregate* spending
11. consumption *function*
13. *leakage*
14. *marginal* propensity to consume
16. demand-*pull* inflation
20. *investment*
22. average propensity to *consume*
23. aggregate *demand*
24. aggregate *supply*

Down

2. *saving*
3. *average* propensity to consume
4. *recessionary* gap
5. *cyclical* unemployment
8. *potential* GDP
9. stabilization *problem*
12. *consumption*
15. *dissaving*
17. marginal propensity to *save*
18. nominal *income*
19. 45-degree *line*
21. *full*-employment GDP

CHAPTER 9

Potential Instability

Quick Review

This chapter describes how the economy responds to imbalances between desired spending and desired production. The following questions are addressed:

- How do producers respond to an imbalance between output and sales?
- How do consumers respond to changes in output and income?
- What macro outcomes will these responses create?

Imbalances between saving and investment are likely sources of aggregate expenditure imbalance. A two-sector model (households and business) is the easiest way to examine the imbalance. Actual investment consists of two components:

$$\text{Actual investment} = \text{desired investment} + \text{undesired investment}$$

If desired saving exceeds desired investment at full employment, the economy experiences a recessionary gap. This "excess saving" causes inventory accumulation for business, which is *undesired investment*. As inventories pile up, prices fall, more workers are let go, wages fall, capacity is allowed to deteriorate, and interest rates fall.

The recessionary gap is measured at full employment as either the amount by which desired saving exceeds desired investment or as the amount by which full-employment output exceeds desired spending.

Any recessionary gap is compounded by the multiplying effect into a much larger cutback in production and employment. If the economy is at full employment when a recessionary gap suddenly emerges, we can predict how far the economy will fall below full employment by the following:

$$\text{Total change in spending} = \text{multiplier} \times \text{initial change in aggregate spending}$$

where the last term is equal to the recessionary gap.

The inflationary gap is also measured at full employment as the amount by which desired spending exceeds full-employment output or the amount by which desired investment exceeds desired saving. In this case inventories are drawn down, prices rise, more people are hired, wages rise, there is an attempt to expand capacity, and interest rates rise. The problem here also is the accompanying multiplier effects. Keynes felt that a market-driven economy would fail to achieve equilibrium at full employment when there was a recessionary or an inflationary gap.

A weakness of the Keynesian model is that it does not separate out real output effects from price effects. To do this, we need to use the aggregate-demand – aggregate-supply framework introduced in Chapter 4. That model allows us to focus on both the real output gap (measured horizontally) and the required change in the price level (measured vertically) necessary to achieve the desired macro equilibrium. The multiplier determines how far the aggregate demand curve shifts, while the slope of the aggregate supply curve determines how much of the shift is dissipated into price changes.

It is clear that saving and investment play a critical role in achieving short-run macro stability. Moreover, saving is required to release resources in a fully employed economy so that net investment (a requirement for economic growth) can take place in the long run.

Learning Objectives

After reading Chapter 9 and doing the following exercises, you should:	True or false	Multiple choice	Problems and applications	Common errors	Pages in the text
1. Be able to define and calculate both a recessionary gap and an inflationary gap.	1, 6, 10, 14, 17	4, 5, 8, 10, 16, 17	6		192, 199
2. Understand the critical distinction between desired investment and actual investment.	3-5	1, 7, 11, 15	1	1, 2	191-194
3. Be able to describe how the economy responds to a recessionary gap.	9, 10	2, 4		2	194-200
4. Be able to describe the multiplier process and calculate the multiplier.	7-9	6, 12-15, 22	1-3		194-198
5. Understand the possible divergence between equilibrium GDP and full-employment GDP.	10-13, 15, 17	3, 14, 18, 24, 25	1	3	198-200
6. Be able to describe and demonstrate price and output effects and the inflation-unemployment tradeoff in an AS-AD framework.		19-21, 23	4		202-204
7. Understand the dual role of saving, that is, as a leakage in the short run and as a source of resources for net investment and growth in the long run.	2, 18	8-10, 26-31	5, 7	1	204-205

Key-Term Review

Review the following terms; if you are not sure of the meaning of any term, write out the definition and check it against the Glossary in the text.

aggregate demand (AD)
aggregate supply (AS)
consumption function
cyclical unemployment
demand-pull inflation
equilibrium (macro)
equilibrium GDP

full employment
GDP gap (real)
inflationary gap
marginal propensity to consume (*MPC*)
multiplier
real GDP
recessionary gap

Fill in the blank following each of the statements below with the appropriate term from the list above.

1. When the economy is experiencing cyclical unemployment, the difference between aggregate spending and income at full employment is equal to the _____ .

    1. _____

2. $C = a + b\, Y_D$ is the formula for the _____ .

    2. _____

3. _____ requires that _____ and _____ be equal at a particular price level and level of output.

    3. _____
       _____
       _____

4. The level of GDP at which aggregate spending equals income is known as _____ .

    4. _____

5. 1 - *MPS* indicates the _____ .

    5. _____

6. The type of inflation that can be caused by too much government spending is known as _____ .

    6. _____

7. $\dfrac{1}{1 - MPC}$ gives the value of the _____ .

    7. _____

8. When total desired spending at full employment exceeds full-employment output, there is an _____ .

    8. _____

9. The type of unemployment that is reduced by expanding aggregate spending is _____ .

    9. _____

10. Macro equilibrium can occur when the economy is producing less than the _____ level of _____ .

    10. _____
        _____

11. The _____ is the difference between the full employment level of real output and the equilibrium level of real output.

    11. _____

True or False: *Circle your choice.*

T F 1. A Classical economist would say that the Great Depression would have come to an end without government interference if the free market had simply been allowed a chance to adjust.

T F 2. Because saving is a leakage, reductions in saving result in higher equilibrium income for society, *ceteris paribus*.

T F 3. Investment is more volatile than consumption spending.

T F 4. In a purely private economy, the difference between desired saving and desired investment is a measure of the undesired change in inventory.

T F 5. A change in expectations is represented by a movement along the aggregate spending curve.

T F 6. If an inflationary gap exists, cyclical unemployment will rise as firms try to raise inventory levels.

T F 7. The impact of the multiplier depends on the time period over which the multiplier works.

T F 8. In a purely private economy without exports or imports, the *MPS* may be calculated if the multiplier is known.

T F 9. The cumulative decrease in total spending resulting from the appearance of a recessionary gap at full employment is equal to the GDP gap multiplied by $1/(1 - MPC)$.

T F 10. By definition, equilibrium GDP occurs when there is full employment in an economy.

T F 11. Equilibrium GDP is the most desired level of GDP for an economy.

T F 12. There is only one output at which equilibrium (macro) can occur.

T F 13. At the full employment rate of output there is no cause for further changes in output or prices, because all output produced is being sold.

T F 14. When there is an inflationary gap, there are excess purchases of goods and services, and consumers bid up prices by competing for those goods and services.

T F 15. The real GDP gap is the same in both the aggregate-supply – aggregate-demand and "Keynesian cross" models as long as the aggregate supply curve is upward-sloping.

T F 16. The aggregate supply curve rises more steeply as it approaches full employment, and larger shifts in aggregate demand are needed to increase real output by any given amount.

T F 17. The GDP gap is larger than a recessionary gap.

T F 18. The paradox of thrift shows that saving is undesirable for an economy.

Multiple Choice: *Select the correct answer.*

_____ 1. Injections include:
   (a) Investment.
   (b) Business saving.
   (c) Consumer saving.
   (d) None of the above.

_____ 2. A recessionary gap emerges when:
   (a) Desired spending at full employment exceeds full-employment output.
   (b) Desired saving falls short of desired investment at full employment.
   (c) $C + I + G$ falls short of Y_F.
   (d) Desired injections exceed desired leakages.

Use the diagrams in Figure 9.1 to answer the questions 3-6. Assume the consumption function has the same slope as the aggregate spending curve. Also assume the economy is at the disposable income which achieves full employment, Y_F, in each diagram of Figure 9.1.

Figure 9.1

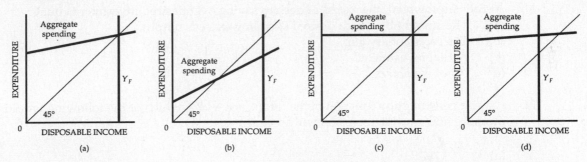

_____ 3. In which diagram is full-employment income equal to the equilibrium income and the marginal propensity to save is 100 percent?
   (a)   (b)   (c)   (d)

_____ 4. In which diagram is a recessionary gap in evidence?
   (a)   (b)   (c)   (d)

_____ 5. In which diagram would autonomous aggregate spending be lowest if there were no income?
   (a)   (b)   (c)   (d)

_____ 6. In which diagram would the multiplier be lowest?
   (a)   (b)   (c)   (d)

_____ 7. Which of the following would be excluded from analysis of a purely private economy?
   (a) Taxes.
   (b) Consumption.
   (c) Saving.
   (d) Investment.

8. The output at which a graph of the consumption function intersects the 45-degree line is the output at which:
    (a) Saving is zero.
    (b) Macro equilibrium is achieved.
    (c) Full employment is achieved.
    (d) Desired investment equals desired saving.

9. Suppose an economy can be described by the consumption function $C = 20 + 0.85 \times Y$. Saving (S) would be:
    (a) $S = -20 + 0.85 \times Y$.
    (b) $S = 20 + 0.85 \times Y$.
    (c) $S = -20 + 0.15 \times Y$.
    (d) None of the above.

10. Suppose an economy can be described by the consumption function $C = 20 + 0.85 \times Y$. At an income of 100 saving (S) would be:
    (a) -5.
    (b) 45.
    (c) 105.
    (d) None of the above.

11. At full employment, the excess of desired saving over desired investment equals:
    (a) The amount by which desired spending exceeds output.
    (b) The recessionary gap.
    (c) Actual investment.
    (d) All of the above.

12. Using a consumption function of the form $C = a + bY_D$, which of the following would best measure how much a recession will spread?

    (a) $\dfrac{1}{1 - MPS}$

    (b) $\dfrac{1}{1 - b}$

    (c) $\dfrac{1}{1 - MPC}$

    (d) All of the above.

13. When output exceeds desired spending, which of the following is included in the Keynesian adjustment process?
    (a) Producers cut output and employment.
    (b) Lost income causes a decline in consumer spending.
    (c) Lower consumer spending results in losses of income.
    (d) All of the above.

14. Which of the following does not belong?
    (a) Undesired inventory depletion.
    (b) Declining real GDP.
    (c) Demand-pull inflation.
    (d) Falling unemployment.

_____ 15. In which of the following cases would cyclical unemployment be the highest?
   (a)   Undesired inventory depletion.
   (b)   Total value of goods supplied exceeds the total value of goods demanded.
   (c)   Demand-pull inflation.
   (d)   Desired investment exceeds desired saving.

_____ 16. Which of the following groupings contains a term which does not belong?
   (a)   Multiplier, $1/(1-MPC)$, $1/MPS$.
   (b)   Recessionary gap, inflationary gap, equilibrium GDP.
   (c)   Cyclical unemployment, recessionary gap, deflation.
   (d)   Full employment, inflationary gap, low inventories.

_____ 17. Where there is an inflationary gap, there are not enough:
   (a)   Goods available and consumers bid up prices.
   (b)   Resources available and businesses bid wages.
   (c)   Savings and investors bid up interest rates.
   (d)   All of the above.

_____ 18. In an economy that is below full employment, a rise in income becasue of increased government spending definitely leads to, *ceteris paribus*:
   (a)   Higher desired saving and higher desired investment.
   (b)   Higher desired saving but no change in desired investment.
   (c)   No change in desired saving but higher desired investment.
   (d)   No change in desired saving and no change in investment.

_____ 19. Which of the following is a limitation of the "Keynesian cross"?
   (a)   It fails to differentiate between price and output effects.
   (b)   It is incapable of illustrating multiplying effects.
   (c)   It implies full employment is achieved through self-adjustment of the economy.
   (d)   All of the above.

_____ 20. As the aggregate supply curve rises more steeply as it approaches full employment:
   (a)   Price changes become smaller.
   (b)   Larger and larger shifts in aggregate demand are needed to increase real output.
   (c)   Changes in real output become more important relative to price changes.
   (d)   All of the above.

_____ 21. In graphs of the aggregate demand curve and the aggregate spending curve:
   (a)   x-axis is measured in real output and disposable income, respectively.
   (b)   y-axis is measured in average prices and expenditures, respectively.
   (c)   Full employment is represented by a full employment demand curve and vertical line, respectively.
   (d)   All of the above.

_____ 22. At an *MPC* of 0.50, an increase of $2 billion in autonomous consumption would cause:
   (a)   An initial increase of $1 billion in income.
   (b) $2 billion in multiplier effects.
   (c)   Income to change by a total of $4 billion.
   (d)   None of the above.

_____ 23. A rightward shift in the aggregate demand curve will cause:
   (a) Both higher prices and higher output if the aggregate supply curve is upward-sloping.
   (b) Higher prices, but not higher output, if the aggregate supply curve is vertical.
   (c) No change in prices, but higher output, if the aggregate supply curve is horizontal.
   (d) All of the above.

_____ 24. Increased saving:
   (a) Lowers income, *ceteris paribus*.
   (b) Makes larger actual investment possible.
   (c) Increases the economic growth rate in the long run.
   (d) All of the above.

_____ 25. Which of the following In the News reports from the text comes closest to describing the effect of the multiplier?
   (a) "The layoffs touch almost every corner of the country" – from an article about the auto industry.
   (b) "Inventory Buildup Could Pose Threat for Some Big Companies."
   (c) "I don't like six-per-cent unemployment, either. But I can live with it."
   (d) "The way I look at it, there's a price tag on everything. You want a high standard of living, you settle for a low quality of life."

For questions 26-31, select the letter of the diagram in Figure 9.2 that best describes each situation, *ceteris paribus*.

Figure 9.2
Shifts of aggregate supplu and demand

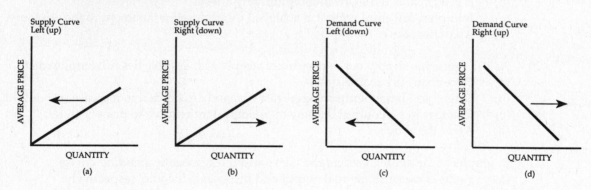

_____ 26. Savings increases.

_____ 27. A new technology increases productivity.

_____ 28. Autonomous consumption rises.

_____ 29. Taxes are reduced.

_____ 30. Imports rise.

_____ 31. Environmental legislation makes it more costly for businesses to manufacture goods.

Problems and Applications

Exercise 1

This exercise shows how market forces lead the economy to equilibrium income. It is similar to an exercise at the end of Chapter 9 in the text.

Use Figure 9.3 to answer the following problems.

Figure 9.3
Full employment and equilibrium

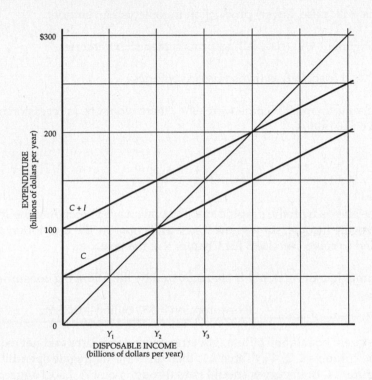

Problems 1-8 concern an economy starting at an annual income level of Y_3 in Figure 9.3.

1. People save _____ billion worth of income per year.

2. Businesses desire to invest _____ billion worth of income per year.

3. There is _____ billion of undesired investment per year.

4. Because of undesired investment, inventories will (accumulate, fall).

5. Firms will (raise, lower) production to eliminate inventories.

6. Employment will (rise, fall) as inventories are eliminated.

7. Income (GDP) will tend to (rise, fall) as inventories are eliminated.

8. If full-employment income were at Y_3, there would be (a recessionary , an inflationary) gap of $50 billion.

Problems 9-16 concern an economy at income level Y_1 over a single year.

9. People save _____ billion of income per year.

10. Firms desire to invest _____ billion of income per year.

11. There is:
    (a) $50 billion of unused output (undesired investment).
    (b) $50 billion shortage of output to meet desired investment.

12. Undesired inventories will (accumulate, fall).

13. Firms will (raise, lower) production to replenish inventories.

14. Employment will (rise, fall) as firms replenish inventories.

15. GDP will (rise, fall) as firms raise inventories.

16. If full-employment income were at Y_1, there would be (a recessionary, an inflationary) gap of $50 billion.

Exercise 2

This exercise shows both the graphic and algebraic ways to compute the influence of aggregate spending on aggregate income, shows how to use and compute the multiplier, and provides practice in the skills needed to solve exercise 3 for Chapter 9 in the text.

1. Assume that an economy is characterized by the following consumption function:

$$\text{Consumption} = \$30 \text{ billion} + 0.75\, Y_D$$

While investment equals $30 billion, government expenditures and net exports are assumed to be zero. Complete columns 2, 3, 4 in Table 9.1; then draw the aggregate spending curve and 45-degree line in Figure 9.4. Both curves should pass through point A. Label aggregate spending TE_1.

Table 9.1
Aggregate spending schedule
(billions of dollars per year)

(1) Disposable income (Y_D)	(2) Consumption (C)	(3) Investment (I)	(4) Aggregate spending (C + I)	(5) MPC
$ 0	_____	_____	_____	----
120	_____	_____	_____	_____
240	_____	_____	_____	_____

Figure 9.4

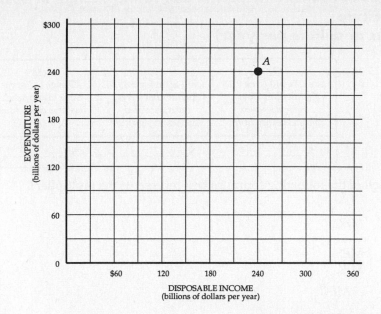

2. Fill in the marginal propensity to consume for each shift of disposable income level in Table 9.1.

3. T   F   The marginal propensity to consume changes with income in this example.

4. Businesses suddenly decide to invest $30 billion less. Complete Table 9.2, which shows this change. Assume the consumption function does not cange and graph the new aggregate spending curve in Figure 9.4 and label it TE_2.

Table 9.2
Aggregate spending schedule with a fall of $30 billion in investment (billions of dollars per year)

(1) Disposable income	(2) Consumption	(3) Investment	(4) Aggregate spending (2) + (3) = (4)
$ 0	$_____	$_____	$_____
120	_____	_____	_____
240	_____	_____	_____

5. Fill in Table 9.3, which shows the changes in equilibrium income when the businesses suddenly invest less.

171

Table 9.3
Changes in equilibrium income due to the change in business expenditure
(billions of dollars per year)

(1) *(see TE₁ in Figure 9.4)* *Equilibrium income* *before decreased* *business expenditure*	(2) *(see TE₂ in Figure 9.4)* *Equilibrium income* *after decreased* *business expenditure*	(3) *Change in income* *due to decreased* *business expenditure* *(2) - (1) = (3)*
$_____	$_____	$_____

6. Which of the following formulas best represents the multiplier?

   (a) $\dfrac{1}{MPC}$

   (b) $\dfrac{MPS}{MPC}$

   (c) $1 - MPC$

   (d) $\dfrac{1}{1 - MPC}$

7. If the $MPC = 0.75$ and investment expenditures fall by $30 billion, equilibrium income will change by:
   (a) $40 billion.
   (b) $22.5 billion.
   (c) $120 billion.
   (d) $30 billion.

8. Does your answer to problem 7 correspond to the third column in Table 9.3? _____

9. T F The diagram showing a shift in aggregate spending predicts the same change in income as would be predicted using the multiplier.

10. T F As long as full employment is not reached, the multiplier magnifies changes in aggregate spending into much larger changes in real income.

Exercise 3

The following exercise shows how the multiplier works and two ways of calculating it—an easy way and a hard way. It will help you with problem 2 for chapter 9 in the text.

1. Suppose the economy were at full employment but suddenly experienced a $216 billion recessionary gap. Investment plans are cancelled. Follow the impact of this sudden change through the economy in Table 9.4, as in Table 9.1, p. 196 in the text. Assume the marginal propensity to consume is 5/6.

Table 9.4

Spending cycles		Amount (billions of dollars per year)	Cumulative decrease in aggregate spending (billions of dollars per year)
First cycle:	recessionary gap emerges	$216	$216
Second cycle:	consumption drops by MPC x gap		
Third cycle:	consumption drops by $MPC2$ x gap		
Fourth cycle:	consumption drops by $MPC3$ x gap		
Fifth cycle:	consumption drops by $MPC4$ x gap		
Sixth cycle:	consumption drops by $MPC5$ x gap		
Seventh cycle:	consumption drops by $MPC6$ x gap		

2. What will be the final cumulative impact on aggregate spending? (*Hint:* The eighth cycle is $[5/6]^7$ x $216 billion = $60 billion, which brings the cumulative change in aggregate spending to $994 billion. Continue the cycles.)

3. Compute the multiplier.

4. Multiply the $216 billion by the multiplier.

Exercise 4

This exercise will help show the tradeoff between inflation and unemployment in public policy. It also provides practice in using the aggregate demand and supply tools.

The aggregate demand curve and aggregate supply curve for all of the goods in an economy are presented in Figure 9.5. The economy is assumed to be on aggregate demand curve *B* in the current fiscal year.

Figure 9.5

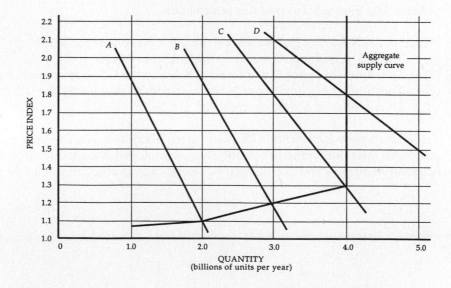

1. Four aggregate demand curves are shown in Figure 9.5, corresponding to four alternative government policies for the coming fiscal year. Indicate the equilibrium price index for each policy in Table 9.5.

Table 9.5
Equilibrium prices for four government policies

Aggregate demand curve	A	B	C	D
Equilibrium price index	_____	_____	_____	_____

2. Suppose the price index is currently 1.2, as shown by demand curve *B* in Figure 9.5. Compute the inflation rate under each of the four policies assuming the supply curve remains unchanged. The formula is

$$100 \times \frac{\text{equilibrium price index - 1.2}}{1.2}$$

Enter your answers for each policy in the appropriate blank of column 1 in Table 9.6.

Table 9.6
Inflation rates, equilibrium output, and unemployment rates under four government policies

Aggregate demand curve	(1) Equilibrium price change (percent)	(2) Equilibrium output (billions of units per year)	(3) Unemployment rate (percent)
A	_____%	_____	_____%
B	_____	_____	_____
C	_____	_____	_____
D	_____	_____	_____

3. In Table 9.6 (column 2) indicate the equilibrium output associated with each of the policies. Use Figure 9.5 to find this information.

4. Which of the following *best* represents the U.S. unemployment rate?
   (a)   The U.S. population divided by the U.S. labor force.
   (b)   The number of people employed divided by the U.S. population.
   (c)   The number of people counted as unemployed divided by the U.S. labor force.
   (d)   The number of people unemployed divided by the U.S. population.

5. Table 9.7 shows a *hypothetical* U.S. population, labor force, number of people who are employed, and number of people who are unemployed at each output level for the economy. Compute the unemployment rate at each production rate in the table.

Table 9.7
Computation of the unemployment rate

	Production rate (billions of units per year)		
	2	3	4
U.S. population (millions)	200	200	200
Labor force (millions)	100	100	100
Number of people unemployed (millions)	15	8	5
Number of people employed (millions)	85	92	95
Unemployment rate (percent)	___	___	___

6. Using the information in Table 9.7, complete column 3 in Table 9.6, which shows the unemployment rate corresponding to each government policy.

7. Which of the four aggregate demand curves places the economy closest to full-employment output and moderate inflation?
    (a)   Aggregate demand curve A.
    (b)   Aggregate demand curve B.
    (c)   Aggregate demand curve C.
    (d)   Aggregate demand curve D.

8. The government's dilemma is:
    (a)   That it cannot reach an unemployment level of 5 percent without experiencing inflation of at least 8 percent.
    (b)   That it cannot achieve stable prices (0 percent increase) without experiencing an unemployment rate of 8 percent or more.
    (c)   That when it holds inflation below 8 percent, unemployment increases.
    (d)   Expressed by all of the above statements.

Exercise 5

After completing the previous exercise, you can see how the "Keynesian cross" model compares to the aggregate-supply – aggregate-demand model.

We'll use the data on aggregate supply and demand from the previous exercise and see what the Keynesian model adds and what it loses by focusing on spending rather than on price and output separately.

1. Table 9.8 is based on data borrowed from the previous exercise.

Fill in the equilibrium price indexes and output data (see Tables 9.5 and 9.6 in Exercise 4). To find spending (column 3) in terms of price and quantity, remember that spending equals quantity x price.

   You will need to fill in column 5 of Table 9.8 for real output and column 6 for spending with a similar calculation, using policy B for the base comparison. For example, for real output, you would use the following formula:

$$100 \text{ x } \frac{\text{equilibrium price index } - \text{ } 3.0}{3.0}$$

Table 9.8
Equilibrium Prices, Output, and Spending

	Policy equilibrium			Percent change in		
	Price (1)	Output (2)	Spending (3)	Price (4)	Output (5)	Spending (6)
A	——	——	——	——	——	——
B	——	——	——	——	——	——
C	——	——	——	——	——	——
D	——	——	——	——	——	——

2. What is full-employment output? _____ What is the expenditure at full employment income that achieves relatively stable prices? _____

3. Suppose the consumption of the economy is given by $C = 1$ billion $+ 0.5\ Y_D$ and investment (I) is $0.8 billion. Calculate equilibrium spending at full-employment: _____

4. With which government policy in Table 9.8 does this spending correspond? (circle one)
    A   B   C   D

5. Draw the aggregate spending curve in Figure 9.6.

Figure 9.6

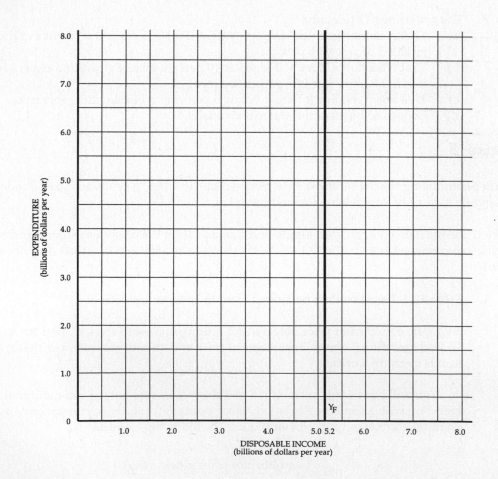

EXPENDITURE (billions of dollars per year)

DISPOSABLE INCOME (billions of dollars per year)

6. This policy results in (choose just one):
   (a)   a recessionary gap of _____.
   (b)   an inflationary gap of _____.
   (c)   equilibrium income equal to full employment.

7. Suppose government policy raises interest rates, which causes investment to fall from $0.8 billion to $0.1 billion and leaves the consumption function unchanged. Repeat 3-5 above using the new data, and place your answers in Table 9.9.

8. Realizing the damage that is occuring in the economy, suppose the government lowers interest rates which causes investment to rise from $0.1 billion to $1.6 billion and leaves the consumption function unchanged. Repeat steps 3-5 above, and place your answers in Table 9.9.

9. The government is so successful that consumer sentiment improves and lifts autonomous consumption to $2.0 billion, which is double its original value. The new consumption function is, therefore, $C = \$2.0$ billion $+ 0.5 Y_D$. Investment remains at $1.6 billion. Repeat steps 3-5 above, and place your answers in Table 9.9.

Table 9.9
Policy, Equilibrium, and Gaps

Problems	Policy	Equilibrium	Inflation/ recessionary gap
3-6	B	_____	_____
7	A	_____	_____
8	C	_____	_____
9	D	_____	_____

10. Use Table 9.10 to compare the "Keynesian cross" model (used in this exercise) with the AS–AD (used in the previous exercise). Place an X in the appropriate column to indicate which model you think does the best job in analyzing each item lested in the table.

Table 9.10
Aggregate-Supply – Aggregate- Demand versus Keynesian cross

Best model for analysis		
AS AD	Keynesian cross	Item analyzed
_____	_____	Size of the multiplier and multiplying effect
_____	_____	Impacts of components of demand and spending on inflation
_____	_____	Effect of income on expenditures
_____	_____	Impacts of technological change and other supply determinants on productivity and efficiency of the economy
_____	_____	Relationship of spending to the consumption function and autonomous injections
_____	_____	Analysis of shortages and surpluses due to goverment policy
_____	_____	Impacts of output on unemployment

Exercise 6

The media continually provide information that can help us determine if the economy is experiencing an inflationary or recessionary gap. This exercise will use one of the articles in the text to show the kind of information to look for. If your professor makes a newspaper assignment from the *Instructor's Manual*, this exercise will provide an example of how to do it.

Figure 9.7
Inflationary and recessionary gaps

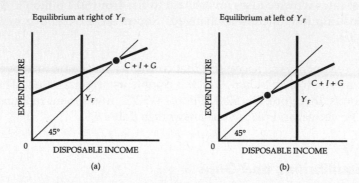

(a)   (b)

Reread the World View article on page 194 in the text entitled "Layoffs at Big Three Spreading" from *USA Today* (January 5, 1990, p. 1B) Then answer the following questions. Use Figure 9.6 to answer question 1.

1. On the basis of the information in the article which diagram in the figure best represents the condition of the economy? _____

2. The article provides evidence of (a recessionary gap, an inflationary gap).

3. What is the word, phrase, or sentence (no more than a sentence) in the article that provides evidence for your choice?

Exercise 7

This exercise shows what actually happens to investment and saving in the United States over time.

1. For the years shown in Table 9.11, collect the nominal data from the inside cover of the text for investment and consumption. Find personal saving from the data provided. Divide saving by disposable income for each year and place the result in the appropriate column.

Table 9.11
Aggregate pending (billions of dollars)

Year	Gross private domestic investment	Personal consumption	Other personal outlays	Total disposable income	Personal saving	Saving as a percentage of income
1960	_____	_____	7.5	360.5	_____	_____
1970	_____	_____	18.5	723.0	_____	_____
1980	_____	_____	51.0	1,952.9	_____	_____
1990	_____	_____	118.9	4,042.9	_____	_____

2. Since the sixties, the share of saving from disposable income has (risen, fallen, stayed constant).

3. How can saving and investment be different? _____
_____

4. Graph both saving and investment in Figure 9.8

Figure 9.8
Investment and saving (1960-90)

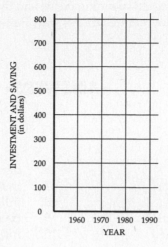

5. Why do the graphs of these two components differ from that in Figure 9.6, p.192 in the text?_____

Common Errors

The first statement in each "common error" below is incorrect. Each incorrect statement is followed by a corrected version and an explanation.

1. Since saving and investment must be the same by definition, a closed economy must be at equilibrium because investment equals saving. WRONG!

   Intended investment equals intended saving at equilibrium in a closed economy. RIGHT!

   If there are excess inventories or if people are forced to save because they cannot spend on desired goods and services, then the income level may be different from equilibrium income. Do not confuse actual investment and actual saving with intended investment and intended saving.

2. If consumers save more, interest rates will fall and investment will rise. WRONG!

   When consumption falls as a result of increased saving, investment may be discouraged. RIGHT!

   Interest rates *may* fall because of increased saving. However, Keynes showed that businesses may invest less when they expect to sell less. The lower consumption which results from increased saving may actually cause businesses to reduce investment.

3. Equilibrium GDP and full-employment GDP are always the same. WRONG!

   Equilibrium GDP and full-employment GDP are determined in different ways. RIGHT!

   Equilibrium GDP occurs where the aggregate spending curve and the 45-degree line intersect. The full-employment GDP occurs at the GDP level where the market supply and market demand curves for labor are in equilibrium. For most purposes, we can consider the two levels to be independent of each other.
   Be careful! While it is possible to determine the equilibrium GDP or income level by glancing at the aggregate spending curve and the 45-degree line, it is not possible to determine full-employment GDP this way. Full-employment GDP is shown simply as a vertical line.

•ANSWERS•

Key-Term Review

1.	recessionary gap	6.	demand-pull inflation
2.	consumption function	7.	multiplier
3.	equilibrium (macro)	8.	inflationary gap
	aggregate demand (*AD*)	9.	cyclical unemployment
	aggregate supply (*AS*)	10.	full-employment
4.	equilibrium GDP		real GDP
5.	marginal propensity to	11.	GDP gap (real)
	consume (*MPC*)		

True or False

1.	T	4.	T	7.	T	10.	F	13.	F	16.	T
2.	T	5.	F	8.	T	11.	F	14.	T	17.	T
3.	T	6.	F	9.	F	12.	T	15.	F	18.	F

Multiple Choice

1.	a	4.	b	7.	a	10.	a	12.	d	14.	b
2.	c	5.	b	8.	a	11.	b	13.	d	15.	b
3.	c	6.	c	9.	c						

16. b Full-employment GDP, not equilibrium GDP, is responsible for determing the existence of an inflationary or recessionary gap. Other topics include (a) ways to calculate the multiplier, (c) effects of equilibrium GDP being below full employment GDP, and (d) effects of equilibrium GDP exceeding full employment GDP.

17.	d	20.	b	23.	d	26.	c	28.	d	30.	c
18.	b	21.	d	24.	d	27.	b	29.	d or b	31.	a
19.	a	22.	c	25.	a						

Problems and Applications

Exercise 1

1. $100 [= $300 (45-degree line) - $200 (*C* line)]

2. $50 [= $250 (*C* + *I* line) - $200 (*C* line)]

3. $50 [= $100 (problem 1) - $50 (problem 2)]

4. accumulate

5. lower

6. fall

7. fall

8. a recessionary

9. $0 [= $100 (45-degree line) - $100 (*C* line)]

10. $50 [= $150 (*C* + *I* line) - $100 (*C* line)]

11. b

12. fall

13. raise

14. rise

15. rise

16. an inflationary

Exercise 2

1. See Table 9.1 Answer and Figure 9.4 Answer.

Table 9.1 Answer

Disposable income (Y_D)	Consumption (C)	Investment (I)	Aggregate spending (C + I)	MPC
$ 0	30 + 0.75 x 0 = $30	$30	$ 60	---
120	30 + 0.75 x 120 = $120	30	150	$\frac{120 - 30}{120 - 0} = 0.75$
240	30 + 0.75 x 240 = $210	30	240	$\frac{210 - 120}{240 - 120} = 0.75$

Figure 9.4 Answer

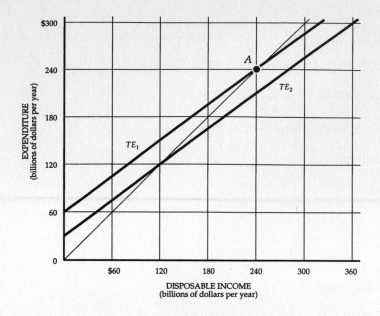

2. See Table 9.1 Answer, column 5.
3. F
4. See Table 9.2 Answser and Figure 9.4 Answer, TE_2.

Table 9.2 Answer

Disposable income	Aggregate spending
$ 0	$ 30
120	120
240	210

5. **Table 9.3 Answer**

(1)	(2)	(3)
$240	$120	- $120

6. d   7. c   8. yes   9. T   10. T

Exercise 3

1. **Table 9.4 Answer**

Spending cycles	Amount (billions of dollars per year)	Cumulative decrease in aggregate spending
First cycle:	$216	$216
Second cycle:	180	396
Third cycle:	150	546
Fourth cycle:	125	671
Fifth cycle:	104	775
Sixth cycle:	87	862
Seventh cycle:	72	934

2. $1,296 billion per year

3. $\text{Multiplier} = \dfrac{1}{1 - 5/6} = 6$

4. 6 x $216 billion per year = $1,296 billion per year

Exercise 4

1. **Table 9.5 Answer**

Aggregate demand curve	A	B	C	D
Equilibrium price index	_____	_____	_____	_____

2. See Table 9.6 Answer, column 1.

Table 9.6 Answer

Aggregate demand curve	(1) Equilibrium price change (percent)	(2) Equilibrium output (billions of units per year)	(3) Unemployment rate
A	- 8.3%	2.0	15%
B	0.0	3.0	8
C	8.3	4.0	5
D	50.0	4.0	5

3. See Table 9.6 Answer, column 2.

4. c

5. **Table 9.7 Answer**

Production rate (billions of units per year)	2	3	4
Unemployment rate (percent)	15	8	5

6. See Table 9.6 Answer, column 3.

7. c

8. d

Exercise 5

1. **Table 9.8 Answer**

	Policy equilibrium			Percent change in		
	Price (1)	Output (2)	Spending (3)	Price (4)	Output (5)	Spending (6)
A	1.1	2.0	2.2	-8.3%	-33%	-39%
B	1.2	3.0	3.6	0	0	0
C	1.3	4.0	5.2	8.3%	33%	44%
D	1.8	4.0	7.2	50.0%	0	100%

2. Output is 4.0 billion units. Expenditure is $5.2 billion.

3. $3.6 billion. Since $Y = C + I$ then:
   $Y = (\$1 \text{ billion} + 0.5 \times Y) + \$0.8 \text{ billion}$ which is solved by placing the Y term on the left:
   $Y - 0.5 \times Y = \$1.8 \text{ billion}$ which is $Y(1 - 0.5) = \$1.8 \text{ billion}$
   Simplifying on the left leads to the solution: $Y = \$3.6 \text{ billion}$.

4. *B*

5. **Figure 9.6 Answer**

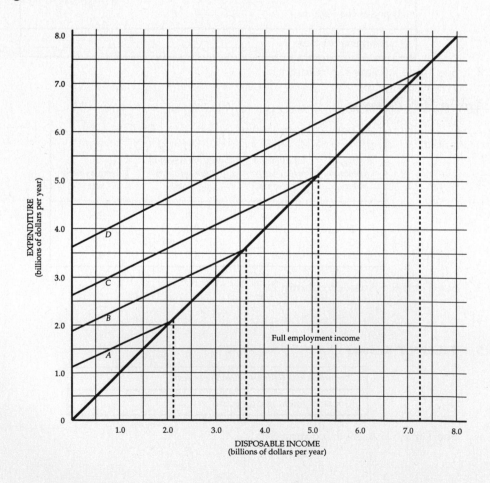

6. (a) a recessionary gap of $0.8 billion(= 5.2 - 3.6/multiplier).

7.-9. **Table 9.9 Answer**

Problems	Policy	Equilibrium	Inflationary/recessionary gap
3-6	B	$3.6 billion	Recessionary: $0.8 billion
7	A	$2.2 billion	Recessionary: $1.5 billion
8	C	$5.2 billion	Equilibrium = Full employment
9	D	$7.2 billion	Inflationary: $1.0 billion = $3.6 - $2.6 billion

10. **Table 9.10 Answer**

Best model for analysis		Item analyzed
AS AD	Keynesian cross	
___	X	Size of the multiplier and multiplying effect
X	___	Impacts of components of demand and spending on inflation
___	X	Effect of income on expenditures
X	___	Impacts of technological change and other supply determinants on productivity and efficiency of the economy
___	X	Relationship of spending to the consumption function and autonomous injections
X	___	Analysis of shortages and surpluses due to goverment policy
X	___	Impacts of output of umemployment

Exercise 6

1. b

2. a recessionary gap

3. Possible answers: "quarter of the nation's autoworkers - 133,500—who have been getting layoff notices since December," or "automakers struggling to cut production to meet falling demand," or "The layoffs touch almost every corner of the country."

Exercise 7

1. **Table 9.11 Answer**

Year	Gross private domestic investment	Personal consumption	Other personal outlays	Total disposable income	Personal saving	Saving as a percentage of income
1960	78.7	332.4	7.5	360.5	20.6	5.7
1970	150.3	646.5	18.0	722.0	57.5	8.0
1980	467.6	1748.1	51.0	1,952.9	153.8	7.9
1990	799.5	3748.4	118.9	4,042.9	175.6	4.3

2. fallen

3. The key equation is $I + G + X = S + T + IM$. The government deficit $(G - T)$ takes away from saving, but business does substantially more saving than is indicated in personal saving which is measured here. However, the foreign sector also lowers investment since net exports $(X - IM)$ are negative.

4. **Figure 9.8 Answer**

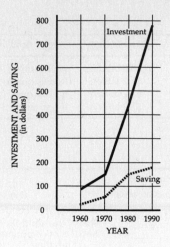

5. The graph that you have drawn in Figure 9.8 has time on the *x*-axis. The graph in the text shows income on the *x*-axis, indicating how investment and saving change as income changes.

CHAPTER 10

Fiscal Policy

Quick Review

Keynesian theory strongly suggests that there is often too little aggregate demand to achieve full-employment output or too much aggregate demand, which causes inflation. This dim view of an unregulated economy's ability to achieve society's employment, output, and price-level goals leads directly to the idea of government intervention. We discuss the following questions:

- Can government spending and tax policies help ensure full employment?
- What policy actions will help fight inflation?
- What are the risks of government intervention?

Federal tax revenues are gigantic, and have grown from $650 *million* to over $1.5 *trillion* in this century. Today the most important sources of federal revenue are, in descending order, the personal income tax, the social security tax, and the corporate income tax.

Government spending has grown even faster than tax revenues, spurred by New Deal programs during the Great Depression, then the massive military effort during World War II and other subsequent military commitments. The desirability of such a large government share must be weighed in terms of the opportunity cost of what must be forgone in the private sector. Roughly half of the federal government's spending now goes for the purchase of goods and services used in government programs and services ranging from national defense to the EPA.

The rest of the budget is used either to provide income transfers or to pay interest on the public debt. The initial effects of income transfers and paying interest on the debt are different from the effects of purchases. The government doesn't buy anything with transfers; purchasing is left for the transfer recipients who then decide what they will purchase.

Fiscal policy can influence the level of aggregate demand by:

- Purchasing more or fewer goods and services.
- Raising or lowering taxes.
- Changing the level of income transfers.

Suppose that aggregate demand is insufficient to create full employment output. In terms of the aggregate-demand – aggregate-supply framework, the intersection is to the left of the full-employment level of income. Since the AS curve is upward-sloping, we must distinguish between:
  - The GDP gap, the difference between equilibrium GDP and the GDP required for full employment, and

- The aggregate-demand shortfall, the difference between the quantity demanded and the quantity supplied at the equilibrium price level— the amount of additional AD needed to achieve full employment.

The required increase in AD does not all come from government purchases. Successive rounds of spending, kicked off by the initial government purchases, ripple through the economy through the multiplier process. The value of the multiplier is calculated by:

$$1/(1 - MPC)$$

The multiplier can be used to estimate the fiscal stimulus required to get the economy to full employment by the following:

$$\text{Desired fiscal stimulus} = (AD \text{ shortfall}/\text{the multiplier})$$

The same thing could be accomplished with a tax cut which can again be estimated in two steps. First determine the desired fiscal stimulus and then determine the desired tax cut with:

$$\text{Desired taxcut} = (\text{desired iscal stimulus}/MPC)$$

A tax cut of a given size will be less expnsionary than a spending increase of the same size because part of the tax cut leaks out before the first private-sector spending takes place. That is reflected in the changed denominator.

But what if aggregate demand is excessive and the economy is suffering from inflation? Then the process must be reversed and the economy slowed down by the appropriate amount of fiscal restraint:

- Cuts in government spending.
- Increased taxes.
- Reduced income transfers.

The desired fiscal restraint mirrors the discussion above in all respects except the desired direction of change. First, calculate the desired fiscal restraint; then determine the appropriate reduction in government spending or increase in taxes.

In addition to the level of income and unemployment, we must worry about the content of GDP. While Keynes tried to analyze the first, economists and policy makers are continually trying to address the second.

Learning Objectives

After reading Chapter 10 and doing the following exercises, you should:	True or false	Multiple choice	Problems and applications	Common errors	Pages in the text
1. Know the major sources of federal government revenue.	1, 3	1			208-209
2. Know the history of federal government expenditures.	2, 3	1			209-210
3. Be able to distinguish the effects of government purchases from those of government transfers.	4, 10	2			210
4. Understand how the components of fiscal policy (T,G) can be used to stabilize the economy.	5	3, 4, 8			211

Learning Objectives cont.	True or false	Multiple choice	Problems and applications	Common errors	Pages in the text
5. Be able to describe the AD shortfall.		5	1, 3		212
6. Be able to calculate the AD shortfall, the multiplier, and the desired fiscal stimulus.	6, 7, 15	7, 9, 10-14, 17, 20, 21, 26, 27	1, 3	1	212-214
7. Be able to explain why tax cuts are less expansionary than increases in government purchases of an equal size.	8, 9, 11, 12	7, 9, 13, 15, 16, 18, 19	1, 2	1	214-219
8. Understand that fiscal restraint of a predictable size is required when aggregate demand is excessive.	14	6, 22, 24			219-222
9. Be able to explain why changes in transfer payments are seldom used to provide fiscal stimulus (or restraint).	13				222
10. Be able to explain how fiscal stimulus can be offset by the "crowding out" of private expenditure.	3, 16	23		1	222-223
11. Be able to describe Joan Robinson's concern for the content of GDP.	16-18	23, 25	4		223-225

Key-Term Review

Review the following terms; if you are not sure of the meaning of any term, write out the definition and check it against the Glossary in the text.

AD excess
AD shortfall
aggregate demand
aggregate supply
crowding out
disposable income

fiscal policy
income transfers
macro equilibrium
marginal propensity to consume (*MPC*)
multiplier
real GDP gap

Fill in the blank following each of the statements below with the appropriate term from the list above.

1. Congress may initiate new spending programs to counteract the effects of recession; this is referred to as the use of _____ .

   1. _____

2. _____ is the idea that government borrowing reduces the private sector's ability to borrow and spend.

   2. _____

3. When the government cuts back its spending, the _____ causes household after-tax disposable income to fall by more than the cutback in government expenditures.

3. _____

4. The _____ determines the size of the multiplier.

4. _____

5. The intersection of the _____ curve and the _____ curve determine _____ .

5. _____
_____
_____

6. _____ is what households have to spend or to save.

6. _____

7. The _____ is a measure of the additional aggregate demand needed to create full employment.

7. _____

8. The _____ is the amount by which aggregate demand must be reduced to eliminate inflationary pressures in the economy.

8. _____

9. Social security payments are an example of _____ .

9. _____

10. If the economy is not at full employment a _____ will exist.

10. _____

True or False: *Circle your choice.*

T F 1. The ranking of the size of tax revenues received by the federal government (from highest to lowest) would be corporate taxes, social security payroll taxes, income taxes, and customs taxes.

T F 2. The ranking of the size of federal government expenditures (from highest to lowest) would be defense, social security payments, health.

T F 3. The government's share of the economy today is greater than it has ever been.

T F 4. Government purchases become part of aggregate demand only when those who sold goods and services to the government decide to spend their added income.

T F 5. The inflationary gap in the Keynesian cross is larger than the shortfall in aggregate demand.

T F 6. Increasing government expenditures by the amount of the AD shortfall will achieve full employment only if the aggregate supply curve is flat.

T F 7. When government spending increases, saving also increases as a result of the multiplier process.

T F 8. A dollar of government purchases is less stimulative than a dollar of tax cuts.

T F 9. An increase of government purchases by $50 billion and a tax hike of $50 billion may stimulate the economy by $50 billion.

T F 10. If the federal government balanced its budget, its tax revenues would be equal to government purchases.

T F 11. The balanced-budget multiplier has a numerical value of 1.

T F 12. The budget must be balanced for the balanced-budget multiplier to equal 1.

T F 13. The cumulative fiscal stimulus of increased transfer payments is given by
$$\text{fiscal stimulus} = MPC \times \text{increase in transfer payments}$$

T F 14. When there is excess aggregate demand, then the GDP gap is negative.

T F 15. When there is excessive aggregate demand, desired fiscal restraint equals the AD excess divided by the multiplier.

T F 16. The ratio of $(C + I)$ to the GDP has risen dramatically in the twentieth century in the United States.

T F 17. The opportunity cost of public expenditure in terms of private expenditure is a key to understanding the "first crisis of economic theory."

T F 18. The opportunity cost of public expenditure in terms of private expenditure is a key to understanding the "second crisis of economic theory."

Multiple Choice: *Select the correct answer.*

_____ 1. Over the period 1902 through the 1990s, the federal government was able to expand:
(a) From a 2 percent share of the economy to a 20 percent share.
(b) From 14,000 employees to 5 million.
(c) Because the Sixteenth Amendment gave it the power to tax incomes.
(d) All of the above.

_____ 2. Which of these government expenditures does not belong?
(a) Defense spending.
(b) Social security payments.
(c) Health purchases.
(d) Highway expenditures.

_____ 3. Which of the following is an application of fiscal policy?
(a) Increasing purchases of goods and services.
(b) Increasing taxes.
(c) Increasing income transfers.
(d) All of the above.

_____ 4. Which of the following does not belong?
(a) Output.
(b) Jobs.
(c) A policy lever.
(d) International balances.

_____ 5. In a diagram of aggregate demand and supply curves, the GDP gap is measured:
   (a) As the vertical distance between the equilibrium price and the price at which the aggregate demand would intersect aggregate supply at full employment.
   (b) As the horizontal distance between the equilibrium output and the full employment output.
   (c) As the horizontal distance between the aggregate demand and the aggregate supply curves at the equilibrium price.
   (d) None of the above.

_____ 6. When the macro equilibrium is above full employment, fiscal policy should be targeted to shift aggregate demand by the amount of the:
   (a) AD shortfall.
   (b) GDP gap.
   (c) Excess AD.
   (d) Vertical difference between aggregate expenditure and the 45-degree line.

_____ 7. In the Keynesian model, the assumption that the price level remains unchanged means that, until full employment is achieved:
   (a) The AD shortfall and GDP gap are the same.
   (b) Price changes cannot be distinguished from real output changes.
   (c) The aggregate supply curve appears as horizontal.
   (d) All of the above.

_____ 8. Fiscal policy works principally through shifts of:
   (a) The aggregate supply curve.
   (b) The aggregate demand curve.
   (c) The full-employment output line.
   (d) The 45-degree line.

_____ 9. Assuming an *MPC* of 0.50, the change in total spending for the economy as a result of a $100 billion new government spending injection would be:
   (a) $200 billion.
   (b) $100 billion.
   (c) $50 billion.
   (d) None of the above.

_____ 10. To eliminate the AD shortfall of $100 billion when the economy has an *MPC* of 0.80, the government should increase its purchases by:
   (a) $20 billion.
   (b) $100 billion.
   (c) $500 billion.
   (d) $800 billion.

_____ 11. When the government tries to correct for an aggregate demand shortfall in the economy, it must take into account that:
   (a) The total change in spending equals the government's spending and the multiplying effects of that spending.
   (b) The desired stimulus should be set at the AD shortfall multiplied by the marginal propensity to save.
   (c) Prices will rise unless the GDP gap equals the AD shortfall.
   (d) All of the above.

_____ 12. $1/(1 - MPC)$ multiplied by a new spending injection gives the:
   (a) MPC.
   (b) Multiplier.
   (c) Total change in income generated from the new spending.
   (d) First-round income that is gained from the new spending.

_____ 13. The AD shortfall divided by the multiplier is equal to the:
   (a) MPC.
   (b) Desired fiscal stimulus.
   (c) Total gain in income generated from lower spending.
   (d) First-round consumption that is lost from higher taxes.

_____ 14. An MPC of 0.8 means a $100 tax hike:
   (a) Reduces consumption in the first round by $20.
   (b) Reduces consumption in the first round by $80.
   (c) Increases consumption in the first round by $20.
   (d) Increases consumption in the first round by $80.

_____ 15. An MPS of 0.25 means a $100 tax increase ultimately causes:
   (a) Spending to fall by $25.
   (b) Spending to fall by $300.
   (c) Spending to rise by $75.
   (d) Spending to rise by $400.

_____ 16. The desired tax cut necessary to close an AD gap is given by:
   (a) AD shortfall/multiplier.
   (b) AD shortfall/MPC.
   (c) (AD shortfall/multiplier)/MPC.
   (d) None of the above.

_____ 17. The desired fiscal stimulus that will eliminate an AD gap should equal the:
   (a) Change in government purchases.
   (b) Desired tax cut x MPC.
   (c) Desired income transfer x MPC.
   (d) All of the above.

_____ 18. If the government institutes a $100 million tax rebate and simultaneously cuts government expenditure by $100 million, then:
   (a) Income in the economy will remain unchanged.
   (b) Income will rise because government cutbacks in expenditures occur so slowly.
   (c) People will spend only a part of their tax rebate, so income will eventually fall by $100 million.
   (d) Not enough information is given to answer the question.

_____ 19. For the balanced-budget multiplier to equal 1:
   (a) The budget need not be balanced, but the changes in taxes and spending must be equal.
   (b) The budget must be balanced before the changes in taxes and spending take place.
   (c) The budget must be balanced and the change in spending must equal the change in taxes.
   (d) The budget must be balanced, but the changes in taxes and spending may be unequal amounts.

_____ 20. Suppose the consumption function is $C = 100 + 0.8Y$. If the government stimulates the economy with $100 billion in increased government purchases, aggregate expenditure would rise by:
    (a) $500 billion.
    (b) $400 billion.
    (c) $80 billion.
    (d) $20 billion.

_____ 21. Suppose the consumption function is $C=100+.75Y$. If the government stimulates the economy with $100 billion in increased income transfers, aggregate expenditure would rise by:
    (a) $20 billion.
    (b) $80 billion.
    (c) $400 billion.
    (d) $500 billion.

_____ 22. In a diagram of aggregate demand and supply curves, excess AD is measured:
    (a)   As the vertical distance between the equilibrium price and the price at which the aggregate demand would intersect aggregate supply at full employment.
    (b)   As the horizontal distance between the equilibrium output and the full-employment output.
    (c)   As the horizontal distance between the aggregate demand at full employment and the aggregate supply curve at the equilibrium price.
    (d)   None of the above.

_____ 23. Crowding out occurs when the government:
    (a)   Increases taxes, thus causing a decrease in consumption.
    (b)   Issues debt, thus making it more difficult for the private sector to issue debt.
    (c)   Prints money, which displaces currency.
    (d)   Does all of the above.

_____ 24. With the economy experiencing low unemployment and rapidly rising inflation, the government should respond with a tax:
    (a)   Cut in the amount of the desired fiscal restraint/MPC.
    (b)   Cut in the amount of the desired fiscal stimulus.
    (c)   Increase in the amount of the desired fiscal stimulus.
    (d)   Increase in the amount of the desired fiscal restraint/MPC.

_____ 25. Which of the following is associated with the "second crisis of economic theory"?
    (a)   How should the peace dividend be used?
    (b)   Men can be hired to dig holes and then to fill them back up again.
    (c)   Should the economy be allowed to self-adjust?
    (d)   Full Employment and Balanced Growth Act of 1978.

_____ 26. One World View article in the text had the headline "Japan Readies $70 Billion Plan to Stimulate Economy." Assume that the MPC for Japan is 0.80. How much of an AD shortfall is the government likely to eliminate?
    (a) $14 billion.
    (b) $56 billion.
    (c) $87.5 billion.
    (d) $350 billion.

_____ 27. One World View article in the text had the headline "Japan Readies $70 Billion Plan to Stimulate Economy." What is the most likely effect of this policy?
(a) U.S. aggregate supply curve shifts leftward.
(b) U.S. aggregate supply curve shifts rightward.
(c) U.S. aggregate demand curve shifts leftward.
(d) U.S. aggregate demand curve shifts rightward.

Problems and Applications

Exercise 1

This exercise shows how to use the aggregate demand and supply curves to analyze macro equilibrium, the AD shortfall, excess AD, and the GDP gap. It will help with problem 4 for Chapter 10 of the text.

Table 10.1
Aggregate demand and supply*

Price Index (1)	Aggregate Supply (Qs) (2)	Aggregate Demand (Qd) Full Employment (3)	Aggregate Demand (Qd) AD1 (4)	Aggregate Demand (Qd) AD2 (5)
2.6	24	-	-	-
2.2	23	0	-	14
1.8	22	6	0	22
1.0	18	18	8	-
0.8	16	21	10	-
0.6	12	24	12	-
0.4	4	27	14	-

* Quantity is measured in billions of units in columns 2 through 5.

1. Use the first two columns in Table 10.1 to draw the aggregate supply curve for an economy in Figure 10.1. Then use columns 1 and 3 to draw the aggregate demand curve at full employment. Label the aggregate supply curve *AS* and the aggregate demand curve at full employment AD_F.

Figure 10.1
Aggregate demand and supply

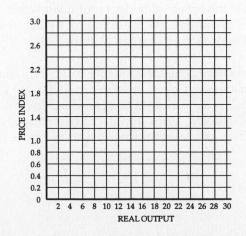

2. When macro equilibrium is achieved at full employment, the full-employment real output is _____. The corresponding full-employment price index is _____.

3. Now draw the aggregate demand curve corresponding to columns 1 and 4 labeling it AD_1. For this aggregate demand curve, the equilibrium is _____. The corresponding equilibrium price index is _____.

4. The shift from the full-employment equilibrium income to AD_1 would most likely have been caused by which of the following government policies?
   (a) The government lowers interest rates.
   (b) The government cuts taxes.
   (c) The government cuts its expenditures.
   (d) The government raises tariffs, which increases the cost of imports.
   (e) The government subsidizes exports to help domestic firms sell abroad.
   (f) The government eliminates IRAs and other instruments that encourage saving which results in greater autonomous consumption.

5. In Figure 10.1 indicate the GDP gap, which is _____ billion units of output, and the AD (excess, shortfall), which is _____ billion units of output.

6. Now draw the aggregate demand curve corresponding to columns 1 and 5 labeling it AD_2. For this aggregate demand curve, the equilibrium real output is _____. The corresponding equilibrium average price index is _____.

7. The shift from the full employment equilibrium income to AD_2 would most likely have been caused by which of the following government policies?
   (a) The government increases taxes.
   (b) The government provides tax incentives to encourage more saving.
   (c) The government eliminates investment tax credits, which results effectively in higher taxes on investment goods.
   (d) A trade agreement is approved, which suddenly results in U.S. exports rising faster than imports.
   (e) Foreign governments place limits on U.S. exports.
   (f) Government cuts back on its expenditures.

8. In Figure 10.1 indicate the GDP gap, which is _____ units of output, and the AD (excess, shortfall), which is _____ units of output.

Exercise 2

This exercise shows how the balanced-budget multiplier works in terms of the Keynesian cross. It will also give you a chance to compare the usefulness of the Keynesian cross model with aggregate-supply – aggregate-demand approach of Chapter 10 in the text.

1. Figure 10.2 shows the aggregate spending curve, TE_1, facing an economy in the first year of a new administration. Government expenditures are $100 billion while taxes are only $50 billion. To balance the budget, Congress decides to cut government spending from $100 billion to $50 billion. Draw the new aggregate spending curve and label it TE_2. (*Hint:* It should pass through one of the three points in Figure 10.2.)

Figure 10.2

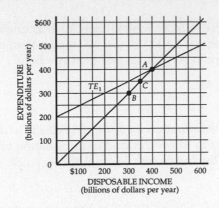

DISPOSABLE INCOME
(billions of dollars per year)

2. Suppose the new president discovers Congress has acted too severely and decides to stimulate the economy by proposing tax rebates. Since government expenditures were cut $50 billion, the president proposes to give $50 billion back to consumers in tax rebates during the next year. What is the marginal propensity to consume on the basis of Figure 10.2? _____
    (*Hint:* Look at the slope of the aggregate spending curve.)

3. How much of the rebate will be spent on consumption? _____
    (*Hint:* The MPC tells how much consumption changes for an extra dollar of disposable income.)

4. Assume that only $25 billion out of the $50 billion rebate appears as increased consumption; draw the new aggregate spending curve in Figure 10.2 and label it TE_3.
    (*Hint:* It should pass through one of the three points in Figure 10.2.)

5. T   F   When cuts in government expenditures are balanced by tax rebates of an equal amount, equilibrium income remains unchanged. (*Hint:* Compare TE_1 and TE_3 in Figure 10.2.)

6. Let's see if these fiscal policy actions (the cut in government expenditures and taxes) are an improvement over doing nothing. Complete Table 10.2. Assume full-employment income is $500 billion per year.

Table 10.2
Effects of cutback and rebate on the economy
(billions of dollars per year)

	(1) Before cutback and rebate	(2) After cutback and rebate	(3) Change (2) - (1)
Equilibrium income	$400	$_____	$_____
Recessionary gap	50	_____	
Government spending	100	50	- 50
Taxes	50	$50 - $50 rebate = $0	_____
Deficit	50	_____	_____

7. T   F   In this example, by taking actions that would seem to move toward a balanced budget, the government does not change the deficit at all, lowers income, and increases unemployment.

8. T   F   In this example, taxes are lowered, but more people are out of work or are receiving lower incomes.

9. T   F   If there were automatic stabilizers such as unemployment insurance and welfare, the government deficit would be smaller than it was before the cut in government expenditures and the tax rebate.

Exercise 3

The media often provide information on multiplier effects in the economy. This exercise will use one of the articles in the text to show the kind of information to look for. If your professor makes a newspaper assignment from the *Instructor's Manual*, this exercise will provide an example of how to do it.

Reread the In the News article "Layoffs at Big Three Spreading" (p. 194 of the text).

1. What sentence indicates the cause of the change of income in the economy?

2. Can the cause of the change in income be classified as an injection, a leakage, or consumption?

3. Does the change mean there is more or less of the injection, leakage, or consumption?

4. What group initially experiences the change in income?

5. What is the change in spending resulting from the change in income?

6. What evidence of secondary changes in income are reported?

Exercise 4

This exercise will show you how the elements of fiscal policy, receipts and expenditures, compare with each other and the GDP of the economy over time.

1. Calculate the surplus or deficit using the data on government receipts and expenditures in the first two columns of Table 10.3. (Surpluses are positive numbers; deficits are negative numbers.)

2. Divide the deficit by gross domestic product for each year and place the result in the last column. You have just found the deficit as a percentage of the GDP.

Table 10.3
Deficit/GDP ratio

Year	(1) Government receipts	(2) Government expenditures	(3) Deficit	(4) GDP	(5) Deficit/ GDP
1960	138.2	135.2	____	513.4	____
1970	299.8	311.2	____	1010.7	____
1980	825.7	861.0	____	2208.0	____
1990	1,704.4	1,840.5	____	6522.8	____

3. Graph the deficit as a percentage of GDP in Figure 10.3.

Figure 10.3
Deficit as a percentage of GDP
(1960-90)

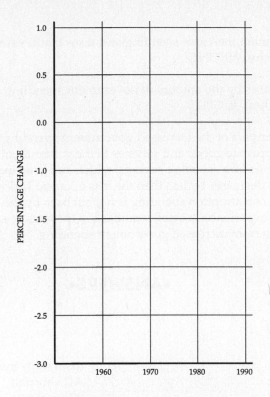

4. Fill in the following blanks on the basis of your observations.

    Since 1960 the U.S. governments (federal, state, and local) have moved from running a
    _____ (surplus,deficit) to a persistent _____ (surplus,deficit).
    Government _____ (receipts, outlays) have been rising faster than
    _____(receipts, outlays). The trend in the deficit fas been
    _____ (downward, upward). Since 1960 the deficit has been a
    _____ (constant, rising, falling) percentage of GDP.

Common Errors

The first statement in each "common error" below is incorrect. Each incorrect statement is followed by a corrected version and an explanation.

1. Government deficits always lead to inflation. WRONG!

    Government deficits may result from government spending to reach full employment with price stability. RIGHT!

    You should focus on what is happening to aggregate supply and demand, not just deficits, when looking for the sources of inflation. By looking at the deficit, you cannot tell if there is adequate aggregate demand in the economy. If there is a shortfall in aggregate demand, government spending and resulting deficits may restore full employment with price stability! If there is an excess aggregate demand, demand-pull inflation can result from increased consumption, investment, or export expenditures, just as much as from increased government spending. It is all too easy to point the finger at the government and forget the contribution to inflation of all the other sectors of the economy.

2. If the government increases spending and taxes by the same amount, there will be no effect on income. WRONG!

Income increases by the amount of government spending, even if taxes are increased by the same amount. RIGHT!

The full impact of the increased government spending turns into income for the people who provide goods and services to the government. Part of the increased taxes, however, comes from people's savings, which had been leakages from the economy. So consumption decreases by less than the loss of taxes. This in turn means that income generated by consumption spending is not cut back by the amount of taxes. Therefore, the economy experiences a smaller cutback in incomes as a result of increased taxes than from stimulus from increased government spending.

•ANSWERS•

Key-Term Review

1.	fiscal policy	6.	disposable income
2.	crowding out	7.	AD shortfall
3.	multiplier	8.	AD excess
4.	marginal propensity to consume (MPC)	9.	income transfers
		10.	real GDP gap
5.	aggregate demand aggregate supply macro equilibrium		

True or False

1. F   2. F   3. F   4. F   5. F

6. F   It's necessary to consider the multiplier.

7. T   8. F

9. T   This reflects the government budget multiplier. See page 217 of the text.
10. F   There is a difference between purchases and expenditures.

11. T   13. F   15. T   16. F   17. F   18. T
12. F   14. T

Multiple Choice

1.	d	4.	c	7.	d	9.	a	11.	d	13.	b
2.	b	5.	b	8.	b	10.	a	12.	c	14.	b
3.	d	6.	c								

15. b $(-b/1 - b) \times 100 = -0.75/1 - 0.75 \times 100 = -300$

16. c   The desired fiscal stimulus is the AD shortfall divided by the multiplier. However, a tax cut has to be larger than the desired fiscal stimulus by the amount, desired fiscal stimulus/MPC.

17. d   18. c   19. a

20. a   The MPC is 0.8 from the equation. The formula is, then, change in spending x multiplier.

21. c   Be careful of the difference between income transfers and government purchases. The formula for transfers is (MPC x change) x multiplier = 0.8 x 100 x 5).

22. c   23. b   24. d   25. a   26. d   27. d

Problems and Applications

Exercise 1

1. See Figure 10.1 Answer, AS and AD_F.

Figure 10.1 Answer

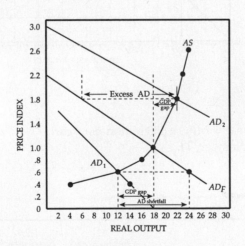

2. At full employment, the price index is 1.0 at an output of 18 units.

3. See Figure 10.1 Answer, AD_1. At AD_1, the price index is 0.6 at an output of 12 units.

4. c   We are looking for more of a leakage or less of an injection, and we find lower government expenditures, which is less of an injection.

5. See Figure 10.1 Answer. GDP gap = 6.0 units; AD shortfall = 12 units.

6. See Figure 10.1 Answer, AD_2. At AD_2, the price index is 1.8 at an output of 22 units.

7. d   We are looking for more of a leakage or less of an injection, and we find lower government expenditures, which is less of an injection.

8. See Figure 10.1 Answer. GDP gap = 4.0 units; excess AD = 16 units.

Exercise 2

1. See Figure 10.2 Answer, TE_2.

Figure 10.2 Answer

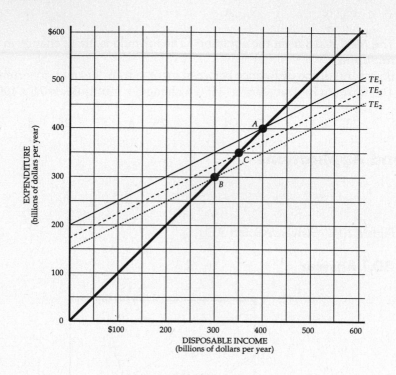

2. $MPC = 0.5$
3. $25 billion per year = MPC \times $50 billion per year
4. See Figure 10.2 Answer, TE_3.
5. F

6. **Table 10.2 Answer**

	(1) Before cutback and rebate	(2) After cutback and rebate	(3) Change (2) - (1)
Equilibrium income	$400	$350	- $50
Recessionary gap	50	75	25
Government spending	100	50	- 50
Taxes	50	0	- 50
Deficit	50	50	0

7. T   8. T   9. F

Exercise 3

1. The passage that indicates the original change that is hurting the automakers is the statement, "'The Big Three will emerge from their latest slump,' he said summarily, 'when the customers come back to the showrooms.'" Also, "automakers struggling to cut production to meet falling demand" indicates the source of the change in automaker income.

2. The change in income should be caused by a change in a leakage (savings, taxes, or imports) or an injection (investment, exports, or government expenditure), or consumption (see Chapters 8 and 9). In this case, consumption of auto buyers has changed.

3. There is less consumption.

4. The automakers experience the change.

5. The automakers are purchasing the services of fewer workers.

6. The income of the automakers will be lower, as indicated by the references to layoffs in each of the last three paragraphs of the article.

Exercise 4

1-3. **Table 10.3 Answer**

Year	(3) Deficit	(4) GDP	(5) Deficit/ GDP
1960	3.0	513.4	+ 0.7
1970	- 11.4	1,010.7	- 1.1
1980	- 35.3	2,708.0	- 1.3
1990	- 136.1	5,522.2	- 2.5

4. **Figure 10.3 Answer**

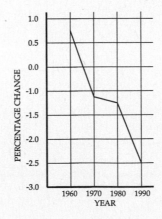

5. surplus, deficit, outlays, receipts, upward, rising

CHAPTER 11

Deficits and Debt

Quick Review

This chapter concerns federal budget deficits and the national debt. The focus is on the following questions:

- How do deficits arise?
- What harm, if any, do deficits cause?
- Who will pay off the national debt?

When the federal government's revenues fall short of its expenditures in any fiscal year, the U.S. Treasury issues IOUs (e.g., Treasury bonds) and sells them to cover the difference. The difference is called the "deficit." It is a "flow" concept because it has a time dimension. If you add up all of the Treasury's IOUs that are outstanding, the sum is the national debt. It is a stock concept, because it can be measured at a point in time.

Budget deficits are closely related to fiscal policy. At present, nearly 80 percent of the budget is for "uncontrollables": spending programs that are locked in from previous legislative commitments *and* whose value changes with the state of the economy. These automatic stabilizers (like unemployment compensation) increase as the economy slows and decrease during economic expansions. Only 20 percent of the federal budget is "controllable." This is why economists and policymakers distinguish between "cyclical deficits," due to economic conditions, and the "structural deficit," which is the deficit which would result if the economy were at full employment. It is the latter which is used to determine whether fiscal policy is expansionary or restrictive.

Most citizens are overwhelmed by the size of the debt (currently more than $4 trillion) and concerned about its effects in the present and in the future. Some of this apprehension is unfounded. After all, while the national debt is a liability of the government (and its citizen-taxpayers), it represents an asset to those who own it. Nearly 90 percent is owned "internally" by banks and other financial institutions, the Federal Reserve, and the like. The interest earned from holding government debt is an important source of income for many private individuals.

Most of the debt that accrued in the first 200 years of our history was incurred to fight wars or recessions. In the 1980s, however, the debt exploded because of the recessions in 1981 and 1984 and massive tax cuts. The ratio of the national debt to the GDP rose dramatically. This rise signals a reduced ability to pay the interest on the debt.

Only about 2 percent of the debt is owned by foreigners, but foreign ownership is an important concern. Payments on foreign holdings of U.S. debt mean that dollars must flow out of the country, which in turn has an impact on exchange rates. Debt that is purchased and held by foreigners allows us to avoid opportunity costs by providing the wherewithal to import goods and services. But, if foreigners in the future turn in their bonds for dollars and use them to increase their imports from us, future generations will have less output to consume. This situation *would* be a real burden.

The national debt will never be paid off; when some of it comes due, the Treasury just issues more IOUs to obtain funds. This "refinancing" is done routinely. The debt also has to be "serviced"—interest must be paid to those who own it. The interest payments restrict the government's ability to spend and redistribute income from taxpayers to bondholders without imposing opportunity costs.

Only when the debt takes resources that would be employed other places *or* causes resources to be misallocated does society incur an opportunity cost. When government purchases goods and services, the resources used to produce them are denied to the rest of society. But society owns what the government buys, so the cost is borne in the present, and future generations will reap some of the benefits from the sacrifice today. Even when transfer payments are financed by selling bonds, few resources are used and the real cost is very small.

When government uses resources that would otherwise be used by the private sector, however, the mix of output is definitely changed. This is referred to as "crowding out." Rates of investment and economic growth may both be slowed when government borrowing pushes interest rates up. This situation has a serious impact. Because of crowding out, future generations will have less capital to work with and thus less productive capacity. Of course, some of the things that government purchases benefit future generations too. The debate about the debt is, then, less about passing a burden on to future generations than about the relative role of public versus private spending.

Some believe that "deficit ceilings" are a way to slow down or eliminate growth in the debt. The Gramm-Rudman Act of 1985 called for lower deficits each year until a balanced budget is achieved, and automatic spending cutbacks if Congress fails to keep the deficit below the ceiling. President Bush and the Congress developed a new set of rules for reducing the deficit with the Budget Enforcement Act of 1990, but those rules expired in 1993.

Learning Objectives

After reading Chapter 11 and doing the following exercises, you should:	True or false	Multiple choice	Problems and applications	Common errors	Pages in the text
1. Understand how budget deficits come into existence and the relationship between deficits and the national debt.	1, 4, 13, 14	2, 4, 7, 8, 10, 19, 23, 29	1	2, 3	227-229
2. Be able to discuss the recent history of the national debt.	20	10	2		227-229, 235-238
3. Be able to distinguish between discretionary spending and that called "uncontrollable."	2, 3, 10, 23	1, 11, 13, 26	3		230
4. Be able to describe the operation and importance of automatic stabilizers.	2, 3, 6-8, 10	14, 28	3		230-231
5. Be able to distinguish cyclical deficits from structural deficits.	3, 5, 7, 9-12	14-18, 26	3		231-233
6. Understand the economic effects of deficits and be able to explain "crowding out."	21, 22			1	233-235
7. Understand the history of the national debt and how it reached its present size.	17, 18	8		2, 3	235-238
8. Know who owns the debt, and understand the implications of internal and external ownership.	17, 18, 24	20, 21, 24, 25			238-240

Learning Objectives cont.	True or false	Multiple choice	Problems and applications	Common errors	Pages in the text
9. Be able to explain the difference between real and imagined burdens of the debt.	17	5, 6, 9, 20, 21, 25	2	1, 2, 3	240-244, 246-248
10. Understand that the only way to stop the debt from growing is to eliminate budget deficits.	5, 15, 19, 25, 26	3	2, 4		245-246

Key-Term Review

Review the following terms; if you are not sure of the meaning of any term, write out the definition and check it against the Glossary in the text.

asset
automatic stabilizers
budget deficit
budget surplus
crowding out
cyclical deficit
debt ceiling
debt servicing
deficit ceiling
deficit spending

discretionary fiscal spending
external debt
fiscal year
internal debt
liability
national debt
opportunity cost
refinancing
structural deficit
Treasury bonds

Fill in the blank following each of the statements below with the appropriate term from the list above.

1. When the federal government spends more than it receives in tax revenue, the difference is called a _____ .

1. _____

2. Budget deficits lead to an accumulation of IOUs called the _____ .

2. _____

3. The bonds that are owned by foreign households and institutions are known as _____ .

3. _____

4. The bonds that are owned by U.S. households and institutions are known as _____ .

4. _____

5. Most discussions concerning the national debt focus on the debt as a _____ .

5. _____

6. People often neglect the fact that the debt is an _____ to those who own it.

6. _____

7. To provide funds for _____ and to retire bonds as they mature, the Treasury engages in _____ , that is, selling new bonds to retire old bonds.

7. _____
_____

8. _____ on the balance sheet of the Federal Reserve System are used to conduct open-market operations.

8. _____

9. Any real burden of the debt must result in an _____ for society.

9. _____

10. The president and the Congress prepare the budget for each _____ .

10. _____

11. The Gramm-Rudman Act sought to address this problem by imposing a _____ on Congress.

11. _____

12. The imposition of a _____ has been unsuccessful in halting growth in the national debt.

12. _____

13. The _____ hypothesis suggests that the debt influences where the economy is with reference to the production-possibilities curve.

13. _____

14. If tax revenues fall short of federal expenditures, government has engaged in _____ ; a _____ occurs when tax revenues exceed government spending.

14. _____
_____

15. A _____ comes about because of the operation of _____ .

15. _____
_____

16. The _____ is measured as though the economy were at full employment.

16. _____

17. Roughly 20 percent of the federal budget allows for _____ .

17. _____

True or False: *Circle your choice.*

T   F   1. Deficit spending results whenever the government uses fiscal policy to stimulate the economy.

T   F   2. When income falls, the budget deficit rises because of automatic increases in government spending for transfer payments and because tax revenues decline when unemployment increases.

T   F   3. By attempting to reduce the deficit during a recession, the government will worsen the recession, *ceteris paribus.*

T F 4. The government finances the deficit by borrowing directly from the private sector and the banking system.

T F 5. In Keynes's view, a balanced budget would be appropriate only if all other injections and leakages were in balance and the economy was in full employment.

T F 6. Automatic stabilizers reduce government expenditures when the budget is in deficit.

T F 7. A 1 percentage point increase in the unemployment rate narrows the deficit.

T F 8. A 1 percentage point increase in the inflation rate narrows the deficit.

T F 9. Part of the deficit arises from cyclical changes in the economy; the rest is the result of discretionary fiscal policy.

T F 10. The cyclical deficit narrows when unemployment increases or inflation subsides.

T F 11. The structural deficit is calculated as if the economy were at full employment.

T F 12. Discretionary fiscal policy is stimulative if the structrual deficit is shrinking (or the surplus is growing).

T F 13. The national debt is a stock concept, as opposed to annual deficits, which are a flow concept.

T F 14. The national debt equals the sum total of annual deficit flows.

T F 15. The only way to prevent the national debt from growing is to balance the federal budget annually or to run a surplus.

T F 16. The Budget Enforcement Act requires any new spending initiatives to be financed by higher taxes or cutbacks in other programs.

T F 17. National wealth is reduced when the federal government borrows money by selling bonds.

T F 18. Bonds owned by financial institutions represent indirect ownership of the national debt by the private sector.

T F 19. The debt would cease to grow if debt refinancing was unnecessary.

T F 20. When the government refinances a portion of the debt, the debt must grow larger, *ceteris paribus*.

T F 21. In general, deficit financing tends to change the mix of output in the direction of more public-sector goods and fewer private-sector goods.

T F 22. The national debt is an asset to those who own it and a liability of the federal government.

T F 23. Interest rates are an "uncontrollable" expenditure in the federal budget.

T F 24. When foreigners add to their debt holdings, U.S. residents can consume more than they produce.

T F 25. A debt ceiling is invoked whenever tax revenues fall short of government expenditures.

T F 26. The Budget Enforcement Act required any new spending initiatives to be financed by higher taxes or cutbacks in other programs.

Multiple Choice: *Select the correct answer.*

_____ 1. The government can best eliminate an AD shortfall by:
   (a)   Increasing government spending and raising taxes.
   (b)   Increasing government spending and lowering taxes.
   (c)   Decreasing government spending and raising taxes.
   (d)   Decreasing government spending and lowering taxes.

_____ 2. Treasury bonds are:
   (a)   An asset on the balance sheet of the Federal Reserve System.
   (b)   A liability on the balance sheet of the U.S. Treasury.
   (c)   An asset on the balance sheet of a commercial bank.
   (d)   All of the above.

_____ 3. If the federal government balanced its budget every year, it would have to:
   (a)   Raise taxes and spending in a recession.
   (b)   Lower taxes and spending in a recession.
   (c)   Lower spending and raise taxes in a recession.
   (d)   Do none of the above.

_____ 4. Deficit spending results whenever the government:
   (a)   Faces interest expense from government debt amassed from previous deficits.
   (b)   Must finance expenditures greater than its tax revenue.
   (c)   Refinances the debt.
   (d)   All of the above.

_____ 5. To pay off the debt would require that:
   (a)   Current government expenditures be less than current government receipts.
   (b)   The federal government run a budget surplus.
   (c)   There be a transfer of revenue from taxpayers to bondholders.
   (d)   All of the above.

_____ 6. *Ceteris paribus,* if taxpayers and bondholders are different people and taxpayers have a higher *MPC* than bondholders, if taxes are increased to pay off the national debt:
   (a)   Spending will fall.
   (b)   Unemployment will be lower.
   (c)   Inflation will increase.
   (d)   All of the above.

_____ 7. Deficit spending is financed in the same year by:
   (a)   Taxes.
   (b)   Borrowing from the banking system and the private sector.
   (c)   U.S. treasury bonds.
   (d)   All of the above.

_____ 8. Deficit spending is most likely to result from a government policy of:
   (a) Tax hikes, spending cutbacks, benefit reductions, and a booming economy.
   (b) Tax hikes, spending cutbacks, benefit reductions, and an economy in recession.
   (c) Tax cuts, spending hikes, benefit hikes, and an economy in recession.
   (d) Budget balancing and a booming economy.

_____ 9. If, in equilibrium, planned saving equals planned investment and exports are equal to imports, the government would:
   (a) Run a trade deficit.
   (b) Run a federal surplus.
   (c) Engage in deficit financing.
   (d) Have a balanced budget.

_____ 10. Which of the following is the best measure of the size of government?
   (a) Government expenditure - government revenue/GDP.
   (b) Government expenditure + government revenue/GDP.
   (c) Government expenditure/GDP.
   (d) GDP per capita.

_____ 11. The term "discretionary fiscal spending" refers to:
   (a) Current spending to which Congress has not already committed itself and which Congress can control.
   (b) That part of the current revenues and expenditures which is determined by prior decisions.
   (c) Automatic stabilizers which operate whenever the economy moves away from full employment.
   (d) The idea that Congress will gain control over the federal budget only if it starts over each fiscal year.

_____ 12. Examples of discretionary fiscal spending include:
   (a) Income taxes.
   (b) Unemployment benefits.
   (c) Social security payments.
   (d) Expenditures for highways.

_____ 13. Uncontrollables:
   (a) Include the major automatic stabilizers.
   (b) Limit the use of discretionary fiscal policy.
   (c) Make it difficult to achieve short-run stimulus or restraint.
   (d) All of the above.

_____ 14. Which of the following items in the federal budget definitely moves the budget toward greater deficit in response to higher inflation?
   (a) Social security payroll taxes.
   (b) Indexed retirement and social security benefits.
   (c) Medicaid.
   (d) Food stamps.

_____ 15. Which of the following is the best indication that the government fiscal policy is stimulative?
   (a) The total deficit increases.
   (b) The structural deficit increases.
   (c) The cyclical deficit increases.
   (d) None of the above.

16. Suppose that full employment requires a GDP of $2 trillion and that the tax revenue received by the federal government is always one-fifth of GDP. Then if planned government expenditure is $400 billion:
    (a) The structural deficit is zero.
    (b) The structural deficit is $200 billion.
    (c) The structural surplus is $200 billion.
    (d) None of the above.

17. The cyclical deficit increased $53 billion while the structural deficit increased by only $15 billion from 1989 to 1990. President Bush was criticized for not doing more to end the recession. The data show that relative to the total deficit, President Bush:
    (a) Pursued a small, restrictive discretionary policy.
    (b) Pursued a large, restrictive discretionary policy.
    (c) Pursued a small, stimulative discretionary policy.
    (d) Pursued a large, stimulative discretionary policy.

18. The cyclical deficit increased $53 billion while the structural deficit increased by only $15 billion from 1989 to 1990. The total deficit:
    (a) Fell by $38 billion.
    (b) Grew by $38 billion.
    (c) Grew by $68 billion.
    (d) Not enough data is supplied to determine the total deficit.

19. The national debt increased in the 1990s as a result of:
    (a) Military expenditures for the cold war.
    (b) The bailout of the failed S&Ls.
    (c) Massive tax cuts.
    (d) All of the above.

20. If the interest rate is 10 percent, the federal government expenditures are $1 trillion, and the federal government's tax revenues are $700 billion, then the interest payment for the next year on the *additional* federal debt would be:
    (a) $25 billion.
    (b) $30 billion.
    (c) $70 billion.
    (d) $100 billion.

21. If the interest payment on the total federal debt is $100 billion and the average annual interest rate on the debt is 10%, then the debt would be:
    (a) $10 billion.
    (b) $100 billion.
    (c) $1 trillion.
    (d) None of the above.

22. Which of the following owns the largest amount of the federal debt?
    (a) Foreigners.
    (b) Federal agencies in the executive branch of government.
    (c) State and local governments.
    (d) The Federal Reserve System.

23. *Ceteris paribus*, when the Treasury refinances the debt:
    (a) The debt gets larger.
    (b) The debt gets smaller.
    (c) The size of the debt does not change.
    (d) It is not possible to determine what happens to the debt.

_____ 24. Externally held U.S. debt results in:
  (a)   A burden to the United States when newly issued bonds are sold to foreigners.
  (b)   A burden to the United States when bonds are cashed in and proceeds are used to buy goods and services produced in the United States.
  (c)   A burden incurred by outsiders when bonds are sold in the United States.
  (d)   No burden to the United States.

_____ 25. The real burden of externally held debt is:
  (a)   Incurred when the newly issued bonds are sold to foreigners.
  (b)   Incurred in the future when foreigners sell the bonds and use the proceeds to buy goods and services from the United States.
  (c)   Incurred by third countries if those who own the bonds sell them and use the proceeds to purchase goods and services from those countries.
  (d)   None of the above.

_____ 26. Which of the following limited discretionary spending and raised taxes on the basis of the structural deficit?
  (a)   Balanced Budget and Emergency Deficit Control Act of 1985.
  (b)   Gramm-Rudman Act.
  (c)   The Budget Enforcement Act.
  (d)   None of the above.

_____ 27. Which of the following groupings contains a term that does not belong?
  (a)   Less spending, tax hikes, reduced transfers.
  (b)   Automatic stabilizers, uncontrollables, deficit spending.
  (c)   Total budget deficit, cyclical deficit, structural deficit.
  (d)   More spending, tax cuts, increased transfers.

_____ 28. Which of the following groupings contains a term which does not belong?
  (a)   Taxes, government expenditures, transfer payments.
  (b)   Deficit spending, structural deficit, budget surplus.
  (c)   Welfare payments, income taxes, unemployment benefits.
  (d)   Interest payments, social security benefits, Medicare.

_____ 29. An In the News article in the text carried the headline "Treasury Plans to Borrow $27 Billion." It explained: "The $27 billion to be raised includes $14.9 billion in new cash and $12.1 billion to pay off maturing securities." The $12.1 billion represents:
  (a)   A federal budget surplus.
  (b)   A lowering of the federal deficit.
  (c)   Retirement of bonds, which reduces the federal debt.
  (d)   Refinancing of the federal debt.

Problems and Applications

Exercise 1

After doing this exercise you should understand the relationships among deficits, bonds, debt, and interest payments. You should see how continual deficits lead to larger and larger interest payments and larger and larger debt. Keep in mind that it is difficult to eliminate deficits when interest payments are an important factor contributing to the deficits. This problem is similar to the problem at the end of Chapter 11 in the text.

1. Suppose the federal government expenditures in the year 2000 are $1 trillion and taxes are $800 billion. Compute the deficit and place the answer in column 1 of Table 11.1 for the year 2000.

Table 11.1
Deficits, bonds, debts, and interest payments
(billions of dollars per year)

Year	(1) Deficit	(2) Newly issued bonds	(3) Total debt	(4) Interest payment
1999	$0	$0	$0	$0
2000	_____	_____	_____	_____
2001	_____	_____	_____	_____
2002	_____	_____	_____	_____
2003	_____	_____	_____	_____
2004	_____	_____	_____	_____
2005	_____	_____	_____	_____
2006	_____	_____	_____	_____
2007	_____	_____	_____	_____

2. To finance the deficit, the government must sell bonds of an equivalent amount to cover the revenue shortfall. What is the dollar amount necessary to finance the debt? Place the answer in column 2 of Table 11.1 for the year 2000.

3. Assume that up to 1999 the government had zero debt (as shown in the 1999 row of Table 11.1). What is the total debt after the government has borrowed to cover the deficit in the year 2000? Place the answer in column 3 of Table 11.1 for the year 2000.

4. What will be the interest payment on the total debt in the year 2000 if the interest rate is 10 percent per year? Place the answer in column 4 of Table 11.1 for the year 2000. Assume all bonds are sold January 1 with interest due December 31.

5. For the years 2001 through 2007, the government spends $1 trillion each year plus any interest payment on the previous years' debt and receives tax revenues of only $800 billion each year. The interest rate is still 10 percent per year. Fill in the rest of Table 11.1.

6. Graph and label the deficit (column 1 of Table 11.1) and interest payment (column 4) in Figure 11.1.

Figure 11.1

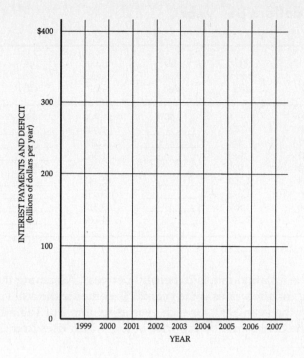

7. T F With continual deficits, interest payments on past deficits will become a bigger part of current deficits, *ceteris paribus*.

8. T F In this example, if both taxes and government expenditures increased at 5 percent per year as a result of bigger government, both the deficit and the debt would become smaller.

9. T F If taxes and government expenditures increased at 5 percent per year and the inflation rate was 5 percent per year, the nominal debt would become larger.

Exercise 2

This exercise focuses on the ratio of the debt to GDP, which is an important measure of the burden of the public debt. It shows, too, how important inflation rates are to this burden. Finally, it demonstrates how inflation is an alternative to taxation as a mechanism to finance government deficits. This exercise builds on the data from the previous exercise.

1. Column 1 of Table 11.2 shows the growth of the nominal debt resulting from continual deficits (numbers are from the previous exercise). Graph and label the nominal debt in Figure 11.2. Assume that the government is disciplining itself to a deficit ceiling of $200 billion per year on noninterest payments each year (see previous exercise).

Table 11.2
Debt, income, and inflation
(billions of dollars per year)

Year	(1) Nominal debt	(2) Real debt	(3) Nominal GDP	(4) Real GDP	(5) Debt/ GDP
1999	$ 0	$0	$ 800	$960	$_____
2000	200	_____	1,000	_____	_____
2001	420	_____	1,250	_____	_____
2002	662	_____	1,563	_____	_____
2003	928	_____	1,953	_____	_____
2004	1,221	_____	2,441	_____	_____
2005	1,543	_____	3,052	_____	_____
2006	1,897	_____	3,815	_____	_____
2007	2,287	_____	4,768	_____	_____

2. Suppose the inflation rate is 20 percent per year. Assuming that the base year for computing inflation rates is the year 2000, compute the real value of the debt in constant dollars (for the year 2000) for each year in column 2 of Table 11.2. This is done by dividing the debt figure by the price index, which rises from 1.2 in 2001 to 1.2^2 in 2002, and so on.

3. Graph and label the real value of the debt in Figure 11.2.

Figure 11.2

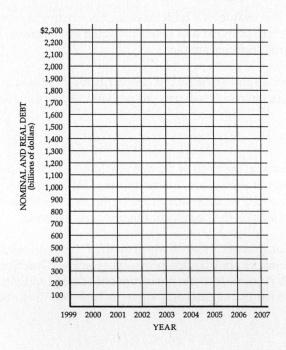

4. T   F   As the price level rises in this example, the real value of the debt also rises.

5. T   F   Inflation and holding down the size of the deficit both lower the real value of the debt immediately.

6. In column 3 of Table 11.2 the nominal GDP for each year is presented. It grows at the rate of 25 percent per year. Compute the real GDP in column 4 the same way you computed the real value of the debt in column 2.

7. T   F   The economy is in a recession over the period 2000 to 2007.

8. The ratio of the nominal debt (column 1) to the nominal GDP (column 3) is a measure of the burden that the debt places on the economy. Compute this ratio in column 5 of Table 11.2.

9. T   F   While the real value of the debt continues to rise, the burden of the debt on the economy eventually begins to fall.

Exercise 3

Many of the reports on fiscal policy implicitly involve major changes in the deficit and debt. This exercise will uses one of the articles in the text to show the kind of information to look for. If your professor makes a media assignment from the *Instructor's Manual*, this exercise will provide an example of how to do it.

Reread the World View article on page 214 in Chapter 10 entitled "Japan Readies $70 Billion Plan to Stimulate Economy" from the *Washington Post* (August 27, 1992).

1. The major change in fiscal policy involves:
   (a)   Government purchases.
   (b)   Income transfers.
   (c)   Government revenues.

2. Which sentence refers to the change in fiscal policy?

3. The change in fiscal policy involves (an increase, a decrease) of (a leakage, an injection).

4. The impact of the change in fiscal policy, *ceteris paribus* on the deficit is an (increase, decrease) of a (surplus, deficit)

5. What words refer to a decision-maker who is responsible for the change in the fiscal policy?

Exercise 4

The following exericse shows you how the debt and servicing of the debt has changed relative to the GDP through time.

1. For the years shown in Table 11.3 collect the data (nominal GDP, prime rate, interest payments) from the endcovers of the text , and place the data in the appropriate column. Calculate the debt as a percentage of GDP for each year, and place the results in column 3.

2. Suppose the government had the same opportunity cost of its funds as the most solid corporate clients. Those clients must pay the "prime rate" when they borrow from banks. Calculate the annual interest payments (column 5) that the government would make to cover the opportunity cost of borrowing at the prime rate.

3. To see what burden these interest payments impose on the economy, divide the interest payments by GDP in column 6.

Table 11.3
Federal debt and interest payments.

	(1)	(2)	(3)	(4)	(5)	(6)
Year	Debt	GDP	Debt/GDP ratio (%)	Prime rate	Interest payments	Interest/GDP ratio (%)
1960	290.5	___	___	___	___	___
1970	380.9	___	___	___	___	___
1980	908.5	___	___	___	___	___
1990	3206.3	___	___	___	___	___

SOURCE: *The Economic Report of the President,1993,* Table B-74 on page 435.

Figure 11.3
Debt and GDP

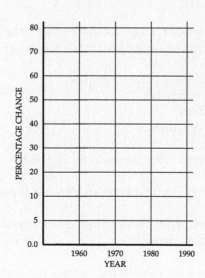

4. In Figure 11.3 graph and label both the debt/GDP ratio and the interest/GDP ratio.

5. Why was the debt/GDP ratio so large in 1960? _____

6. Why was the debt/GDP ratio growing so fast during the eighties? _____

Crossword Puzzle

Select the economic term in the following list that corresponds with each of the defintions and descriptions below. Then fit the term or one of the words within it into the crossword puzzle at the number indicated. Some of the words in the list do not fit the puzzle.

built-in surplus
crowding out
cyclical unemployment
deficit spending
demand-pull inflation
discretionary fiscal spending
disposable income
equilibrium GDP
fiscal policy
fiscal year

inflationary gap
injections
leakage
marginal propensity to consume
marginal propensity to save
multiplier
real GDP
recessionary gap
structural deficit
aggregate expenditure

Across

3. The collection of points which represent at different income the real output multiplied by an index of average prices for the whole economy.

7. The state of government finances if the economy is producing at the potential GNP level under prevailing fiscal policy.

9. The government's _____ begins on October 1.

10. The change in consumption divided by the change in income.

12. Expenditures that the president and Congress can increase or cut back relatively easily.

15. What you have left to spend after taxes.

18. A measure of output corrected for inflation.

19. If the government decides to increase expenditures when aggregate demand equals income at full employment, the increased expenditures will produce an _____ .

21. The government's use of taxes and expenditures to stabilize the economy.

Down

1. The difference between government taxes and expenditures that would exist if the economy were at full employment.

2. Flows of current income that are not used for expenditures on goods and services that are currently produced.

4. Increases in aggregate expenditures at each level of income.

5. The factor that is used to find the total impact of an increase in government expenditures.

6. The use of borrowed funds to finance government expenditures above tax revenues.

8. Increases in average prices due to excessive expenditures.

11. The income level at which aggregate demand equals the 45-degree line.

13. What occurs in private bond markets when government has to finance a large debt.

14. Loss of jobs due to inadequate aggregate demand.

16. The state of government finances if actual expenditures are less than actual taxes.

17. The change in the amount of saving divided by the change in income.

20. The excess of income over aggregate expenditure at full-employment income.

Common Errors

The first statement in each "common error" below is incorrect. Each incorrect statement is followed by a corrected version and an explanation.

1. Our grandchildren will feel the burden of the deficit. WRONG!

    Our grandchildren may feel the burden of the debt. RIGHT!

    Deficit and debt are concepts that are often confused. While deficits occur becasue of the excess of expenditures over taxes during a given year, the debt can be calculated at any given point in time and represents the cumulative effect of running deficits over our entire history. It is the debt on which transfers such as interest payments are made, not the deficit. Such transfers may result in opportunity costs. However, a deficit may reflect expenditures on capital that future generations will need and thus may not be the source of the burden.

2. The national debt must be paid off eventually. WRONG!

    The national debt is paid off continually through refinancing. RIGHT!

    No Treasury bond has a maturity date more than thirty years in the future. Some bonds have maturity dates that come much sooner—in ten or twenty years. Treasury bills are sold at auction and have maturity dates of 360 days or less with 30-day intervals (i.e., 30, 60, 90, and so on). Suppose the federal government has balanced budgets for the next thirty years. The entire debt will come due at some point. What will happen? It would be refinanced as it comes due and replaced with new debt with other maturities.

3. There is nothing "behind" the national debt. WRONG!

    The federal government owns many physical assets and has the ability to tax. RIGHT!

    The proceeds of bond sales by the federal government are used to do many things, including the purchase of many assets. Every item owned by the federal government—from the White House to Old Faithful—is an asset that could be sold to help pay off the national debt. Stealth bombers, office buildings, computers, and the like, are all assets that were needed over the years and are as much an asset as the debt is a liability. By raising taxes, the government can at least theoretically run a surplus and pay off the debt.

•ANSWERS•

Key-Term Review

1.	budget deficit	10.	fiscal year
2.	national debt	11.	deficit ceiling
3.	external debt	12.	debt ceiling
4.	internal debt	13.	crowding out
5.	liability	14.	deficit spending
6.	asset		budget surplus
7.	debt servicing	15.	cyclical deficit
	refinancing		automatic stabilizers
8.	Treasury bonds	16.	structural deficit
9.	opportunity cost	17.	discretionary fiscal spending

True or False

1.	F	6.	F	11.	T	15.	T	19.	T	23.	T
2.	T	7.	F	12.	F	16.	T	20.	F	24.	T
3.	T	8.	T	13.	T	17.	F	21.	T	25.	F
4.	T	9.	T	14.	T	18.	T	22.	T		
5.	T	10.	F								

Multiple Choice

1.	b	6.	a	11.	a	16.	a	20.	b	24.	b
2.	d	7.	d	12.	d	17.	c	21.	c	25.	b
3.	c	8.	c	13.	d	18.	c	22.	b	26.	c
4.	b	9.	d	14.	b	19.	b	23.	c		
5.	d	10.	c	15.	b						

27. b   see answer to 27 on page 9

28. c   Two items are transfers while the other is a type of tax. Other topics include (a) government expenditure items, (b) budget deficit components, and (d) uncontrollables.

29. d

Problems and Applications

Exercise 1

1.-5. **Table 11.1 Answer.**

Table 11.1 Answer

Year	(1) Deficit	(2) Newly issued bonds	(3) Total debt	(4) Interest payment
2000	$200	$200	$ 200	$ 20 = (0.10 x 200)
2001	220	220	420 = (200 + 220)	42 = (0.10 x 420)
2002	242	242	662 = (420 + 242)	66 = (0.10 x 662)
2003	266	266	928 = (662 + 266)	93 = (0.10 x 928)
2004	293	293	1,221 = (928 + 293)	122 = (0.10 x 1,221)
2005	322	322	1,543 = (1,221 + 322)	154 = (0.10 x 1,543)
2006	354	354	1,897 = (1,543 + 354)	190 = (0.10 x 1,897)
2007	390	390	2,287 = (1,897 + 390)	229 = (0.10 x 2,287)

6. **Figure 11.1 Answer**

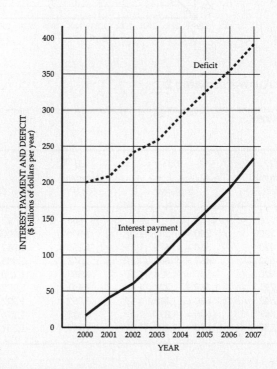

7. T   Compare relative sizes of columns 1 and 4 in Table 11.1 Answer.

8. F   9. T

Exercise 2

1. See Figure 11.2 Answer, Nominal debt.

Figure 11.2 Answer

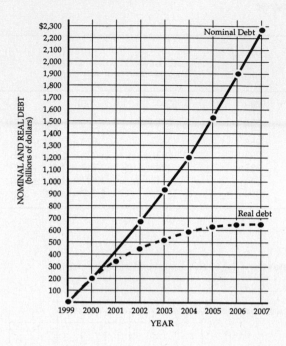

2. See Table 11.2 Answer, column 2.

Table 11.2 Answer

Year	(1) Nominal debt	(2) Real debt		(3) Nominal GDP	(4) Real GDP		(5) Debt/ GDP
1999	$ 0	$ 0		$ 800	$ 960		
2000	200	200 =	$200/(1.0)^0$	1,000	1,000 = 1,000/1.000		0.20
2001	420	350 =	$420/(1.1)^1$	1,250	1,042 = 1,250/1.200		0.34
2002	662	460 =	$662/(1.2)^2$	1,563	1,085 = 1,563/1.440		0.42
2003	928	537 =	$928/(1.3)^3$	1,953	1,130 = 1,953/1.728		0.48
2004	1,221	589 =	$1,221/(1.4)^4$	2,441	1,177 = 2,441/2.074		0.50
2005	1,543	620 =	$1,543/(1.5)^5$	3,052	1,227 = 3,052/2.488		0.51
2006	1,897	635 =	$1,897/(1.6)^6$	3,815	1,278 = 3,815/2.986		0.50
2007	2,287	638 =	$2,287/(1.7)^7$	4,768	1,331 = 4,768/3.583		0.48

(*Hint:* To calculate the real value of the debt, divide the nominal debt for each year by the appropriate price index, which grows as follows: 1 x 1.2 = 1.2; 1.2 x 1.2 = 1.44; 1.2 x 1.44 = 1.7, and so on. For the year 2000, the real value of the debt is 200 divided by 1.2^0; for 2001, it is420 divided by 1.2^1; for 2002, it is 662 divided by 1.2^2 = 1.44l; and so on.)

3. See Figure 11.2 Answer, real debt.

4. T Notice that a positive inflation rate dampens the increase in the real value of the debt in Figure 11.2 Answer.

5. F While the real debt grows at a lower rate because of both instruments, the change is very gradual.

6. See Table 11.2 Answer, column 4.

7. F Notice that column 4 is rising at about 5 percent per year, which is relatively fast growth for the United States.

8. See Table 11.2 Answer, column 5.

9. T Notice how column 5 starts to fall in the year 2006, while the real debt is still rising by 2007.

Exercise 3

1. a

2. "The biggest item in it is a major new public works spending plan for infrastructure improvements."

3. increase; injection

4. increase; surplus. Remember that Japan was the only surplus country listed in the World View article on p. 229 of the text "U.S. Deficits Not Unusually Large."

5. "Japan's government"

Exercise 4

1.-3. **Table 11.3 Answer**

Year	(1) Debt	(2) GDP	(3) Debt/GDP ratio (%)	(4) Prime rate	(5) Interest payments	(6) Interest/GDP ratio (%)
1960	290.5	513.4	57	4.82	14	2.7
1970	380.9	1010.7	38	7.91	30	3.0
1980	908.5	2708.0	34	5.27	139	5.1
1990	3206.3	5522.2	58	10.01	321	5.8

SOURCE: *Economic Report of the President*, Table B-74 on page 435 (January, 1993)

4. **Figure 11.3 Answer**

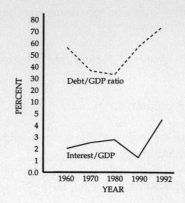

5. The United States was still recovering from the Korean War and was in the midst of the cold war.

6. The Reagan administration built up the military and cut taxes.

Crossword Puzzle Answer

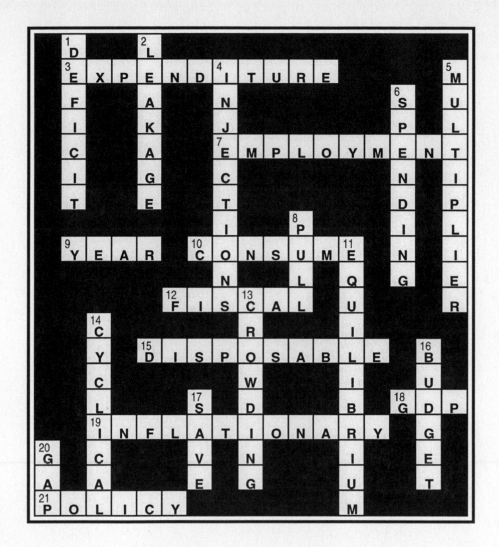

Across

3. aggregate *expenditure*
7. full-*employment* budget
9. fiscal *year*
10. marginal propensity to *consume*
12. descretionary *fiscal* spending
15. *disposable* income
18. real *GDP*
19. *inflationary* gap
21. fiscal *policy*

Down

1. structural *deficit*
2. *leakage*
4. *injections*
5. *multiplier*
6. deficit *spending*
8. demand-*pull* inflation
11. *equlibrium* GNP
13. *crowding* unemployment
14. *cyclical* unemployment
16. *budget* surplus
17. marginal propensity to *save*
20. recessionary *gap*

CHAPTER 12
Money and Banks

Quick Review

Money is clearly very important to the operation of the U.S. economy. The study of money begins with some very basic questions:

- What is money?
- How is money created?
- What role do banks play in the circular flow of income and spending?

Let's begin by examining what money does for us. Money has three functions; it serves as a

- Medium of exchange: is accepted as payment for goods and services (and debts).
- Store of value: can be held for future purchases.
- Standard of value: serves as yardstick for measuring the prices of goods and services.

Money consists of all of those things that are generally acceptable as a medium of exchange. The narrowest definition of the "money supply" is $M1$, the sum of currency held by the public and balances held in transactions accounts and traveler's checks. The most watched monetary aggregate is $M2$. It includes $M1$ as well as savings accounts, certain time deposits, money-market mutual funds, and the like. Most of the basic money supply, $M1$, is in the form of transactions-account balances, commonly referred to as checking accounts. Most of the checking accounts come into existence when banks perform their lending function. When you borrow from a bank, you receive an increase in your checking account. You have more money, and no other member of the public has less. Thus the money supply expands.

Our banking system is based on the fractional-reserve principle. The Federal Reserve System (the "Fed") requires banks to maintain reserves equal to some fraction of their transactions-account liabilities. As a result of this reserve requirement and the fact that banks may lose reserves to other banks via the check-clearing process, a single bank can safely make loans only to the extent of its excess reserves. The banking system, however, can make loans equal to a multiple (1/reserve requirement) of any existing reserves. Banks and other depository institutions control the money supply by making loans and creating transactions-account balances. Banks also hold savings accounts and thus assist in the transfer of purchasing power from savers (those who choose not to spend all of their incomes) to borrowers (those who wish to spend more than their incomes).

The Monetary Control Act of 1980 ended a set of regulations that discriminated among financial institutions. The changes set in motion by the act (which continue today) have blurred the distinction between commercial banks and other depository institutions. There have been significant and well-publicized problems in the financial sector in recent years. Fraud, inflation, high interest rates, and falling oil prices all conspired to wreak havoc among the S&Ls and banks. While some of the losses suffered by depositors were covered by deposit insurance, others were not. So many S&Ls failed that Congress had to appropriate ever larger sums for the "bailout." The Resolution Trust Corporation (RTC) was created to manage the loans of failed financial institutions. The financial debacle witnessed the failure of the FSLIC, the agency which was supposed to insure S&L deposits. The problem is still with us today.

Learning Objectives

After reading Chapter 12 and doing the following exercises, you should:	True or false	Multiple choice	Problems and applications	Common errors	Pages in the text
1. Know the basic characteristics, history, and functions of money.	1, 3-5	7, 9, 24	3, 4	3	253-256
2. Know some of the differences between various accounts permitting transfer by check.	2, 6				256
3. Understand that the Monetary Control Act of 1980 caused changes in the way financial institutions conduct their business.		21			271-273
4. Be familiar with the composition and various definitions of the money supply.	7, 10	5, 10, 23	4		254-259
5. Be able to summarize the important differences between banks and other financial institutions.	11	11, 12, 20	1-3	4	260
6. Know how banks create money with new loans.	8, 9, 12, 13	14-19	1-3	2	259-269
7. Know the reason for the reserve requirement.	14-16, 21	1, 6, 8, 26			268
8. Know the difference between required and excess resserves.	17-19, 21	3, 4, 8, 13-19, 22, 29, 30	1, 2		263-266
9. Be able to work through the steps of deposit creation using balance sheets (T-accounts).	12, 13, 22	13-19, 26, 30	1, 2	1, 4	264
10. Be able to calculate the money multiplier.	20, 21	2, 13, 19	1, 2		267
11. Know the history of recent financial crises.	23	21, 27, 28			271-273

Key-Term Review

Review the following terms; if you are not sure of the meaning of any term, write out the definition and check it against the Glossary in the text.

aggregate demand
bank reserves
barter
deposit creation
excess reserves
money

money multiplier
money supply (M1, M2)
required reserves
reserve ratio
transactions account

Fill in the blank following each of the statements below with the appropriate term from the list above.

1. To exchange goods and services, an economy without a monetary system must use _____ .

   1. _____

2. When banks make loans, they expand the money supply by balancing loan creation with _____ .

   2. _____

3. A bank account that permits direct payment to a third party is called a _____ .

   3. _____

4. The reserves that a bank must have on its books are its _____ .

   4. _____

5. Something that is generally accepted in exchange for goods and services and that can be used as a standard and store of value is _____ .

   5. _____

6. The ratio of reserves to deposits is the _____ .

   6. _____

7. Bank reserves beyond those required by government regulation are known as _____ .

   7. _____

8. Cash is a very small part of the _____ .

   8. _____

9. The inverse of the reserve ratio is sometimes called the _____ .

   9. _____

10. By making loans, banks can influence the level of _____ in the economy.

    10. _____

11. _____ are assets held by a bank to fulfill its deposit obligations.

    11. _____

True or False: *Circle your choice.*

T F 1. Before the Civil War, state-chartered banks issued their own currencies.

T F 2. Credit cards are a form of money.

T F 3. Money eliminates the need to exchange goods directly through barter.

T F 4. When you purchase $5 worth of gasoline, money is serving as a medium of exchange.

T F 5. In times of rising prices, money serves as a good store of value.

T F 6. The terms "transactions- account balances" and "checking accounts" mean the same thing.

T F 7. M1 is made up of the dollar value of all coin, currency, and transaction account balances in existence, whether held by the public or by banks.

T F 8. When you get a loan at a bank, the bank creates money.

T F 9. Banks transfer money from savers to spenders by lending funds held on deposit.

T F 10. Time deposits at commercial banks are part of M1.

T F 11. A commercial bank is one that accepts deposits only from commercial establishments.

T F 12. When you withdraw money from your checking account, the money supply gets smaller.

T F 13. When you deposit cash or coins in a bank, you are increasing the money supply by the amount of your deposit divided by the required reserve ratio.

T F 14. The minimum-reserve ratio is established by the Federal Reserve System.

T F 15. "Fractional reserves" refers to the fact that reserves are a small fraction of total transactions-account balances.

T F 16. The higher the legal minimum-reserve ratio, the greater the lending power of the banks.

T F 17. To calculate required reserves, multiply the minimum-reserve ratio by the amount of transactions-account balances on the bank's balance sheet.

T F 18. If the minimum-reserve ratio is 20 percent, then $1 of reserves can support $5 in transactions-account balances.

T F 19. Total reserves minus required reserves equals excess reserves.

T F 20. Each bank in a multibank system is free to expand its loans by an amount equal to the money multiplier times its excess reserves.

T F 21. The amount any bank in a multibank system can lend is equal to its excess reserves.

T F 22. If people preferred to hold cash and stopped using checks, banks would not be able to acquire or maintain reserves and would be forced to halt lending.

T F 23. Federal deposit insurance provides an incentive for banks to take more safe, secure loans rather than risky ones.

Multiple Choice: *Select the correct answer.*

_____ 1. Which of the following sets the legal minimum-reserve ratio?
   (a)   The commercial banks.
   (b)   The U.S. Treasury.
   (c)   The Federal Reserve System.
   (d)   None of the above.

_____ 2. If the minimum-reserve ratio is 25 percent, the money multiplier is:
   (a)   25.
   (b)   5.
   (c)   4.
   (d)   Not enough information is given to answer the question.

_____ 3. A bank's required-reserve ratio is:
   (a)   A bank's transactions-account balances divided by its reserves.
   (b)   The minimum ratio a bank must maintain between its reserves and its loans.
   (c)   The amount of a bank's reserves above required reserves.
   (d)   (1/money multiplier).

_____ 4. Which of the following is the correct way to calculate excess reserves?
   (a)   Total reserves minus required reserves.
   (b)   The minimum-reserve requirement times transactions account balances.
   (c)   Total reserves minus the legal minimum-reserve ratio.
   (d)   None of the above.

_____ 5. M1 refers to:
   (a)   The money-supply concept.
   (b)   Currency held by the public plus transactions-accounts balances.
   (c)   The smallest of the money-supply aggregates watched by the Fed.
   (d)   All of the above.

_____ 6. The purpose of the legal minimum-reserve requirement is:
   (a)   To provide safety to depositors.
   (b)   To provide control of the money supply by the Fed.
   (c)   To prevent bankers from calling in loans.
   (d)   None of the above.

_____ 7. A paper currency has been issued by the U.S. government continuously since:
   (a)   The War of Independence in 1776.
   (b)   The Constitution was written.
   (c)   The Civil War.
   (d)   The creation of the FDIC and FSLIC in 1933.

_____ 8. When you pay off a loan at the bank:
   (a)   The money supply becomes smaller.
   (b)   The money supply becomes larger.
   (c)   There is no change in the money supply.
   (d)   More information is needed to determine the money-supply effect.

_____ 9. Money:
   (a)   Promotes efficient division of labor.
   (b)   Is a mechanism for transforming current income into future purchases.
   (c)   Facilitates the continuous series of exchanges that characterize a market economy.
   (d)   All of the above.

_____ 10. Which of the following appears in $M1$ but not in $M2$?
      (a)   Credit-union share drafts.
      (b)   Treasury bills.
      (c)   Money-market mutual funds.
      (d)   U.S. savings bonds.

_____ 11. Which of the following institutions was established as a vehicle for channeling savings of small savers into investments?
      (a)   Commercial banks.
      (b)   Savings and loan associations.
      (c)   Mutual savings banks.
      (d)   Credit unions.

_____ 12. Which of the following is _not_ an essential function of a "bank"?
      (a)   It must accept deposits.
      (b)   It must offer certificates of deposit to be included in $M2$.
      (c)   It must offer check-writing services.
      (d)   It must make loans.

_____ 13. If none of the banks in the banking system have any excess reserves before the Fed lowers the minimum legal reserve ratio from 16 percent to 12 percent:
      (a)   The banks will then be able to make loans.
      (b)   Excess reserves will then exist.
      (c)   The Fed is engaging in an expansionary policy.
      (d)   All of the above are the case.

_____ 14. Suppose the total amount of transactions accounts on the books of all of the banks in the system is $1 million and the minimum-reserve ratio is 0.10. The amount of required reserves for the banking system is, then:
      (a) $10,000,000.
      (b) $1,000,000.
      (c) $900,000.
      (d) $100,000.

_____ 15. Suppose that conditions remain as in question 14 and the minimum-reserve requirement is raised to 20 percent. In order to meet the new requirement, the banks in the system will need an _additional_:
      (a) $10,000,000 of reserves.
      (b) $1,000,000 of reserves.
      (c) $900,000 of reserves.
      (d) $100,000 of reserves.

_____ 16. If the banking system described in question 14 (the reserve requirement is 0.10) has no excess reserves and you deposit $100 in cash:
      (a)   Your bank can lend $90.
      (b)   Your bank can lend $10.
      (c)   Your bank can lend $900.
      (d)   Your bank can lend none of the above.

_____ 17. Given the situation in question 16, all of the banks in the banking system could expand loans by:
      (a) $1,000.
      (b) $900.
      (c) $100.
      (d) $10.

_____ 18. If the banks lend the maximum legal amount in questions 16 and 14, the total maximum expansion in the money supply is:
(a) $1,000.
(b) $100.
(c) $900.
(d) None of the above.

_____ 19. The money supply becomes smaller when:
(a) The reserve requirement is lowered.
(b) People begin to use checking accounts instead of cash.
(c) More loans are paid off than are created.
(d) All of the above.

_____ 20. Which of the following is a source of profits for banks?
(a) Securities.
(b) Reserves.
(c) Cash in the vault.
(d) All of the above.

_____ 21. The Monetary Control Act of 1980:
(a) Created sharper distinctions among various financial institutions.
(b) Eliminated many forms of competition among financial institutions.
(c) Required banks to pay interest on checking accounts.
(d) Did none of the above.

_____ 22. Suppose a monopoly banking system has $100,000 in deposits, a required reserve ratio of 10 percent, and total bank reserves for the whole system of $25,000. Then the whole system can make new loans in the amount of:
(a) $10,000.
(b) $15,000.
(c) $150,000.
(d) None of the above.

_____ 23. The alternative measures of the money supply are all intended to reflect:
(a) Variations in liquidity and accessibility of assets.
(b) Whether deposits are domestic or international.
(c) How often depositors use their accounts.
(d) All of the above.

_____ 24. In Russia many consumers prefer to use cigarettes rather than money as:
(a) A medium of exchange.
(b) A standard of value.
(c) A store of value.
(d) All of the above.

_____ 25. For the Russian people, using cigarettes rather than rubles allows them to:
(a) Avoid long lines in stores.
(b) Buy the items they wish from others who prefer to have cigarettes rather than goods.
(c) Maintain wealth in a form not subject to change by the government.
(d) All of the above.

26. Which of the following are constraints on the deposit-creation process of the banking system?
    (a) The willingness of consumers and businesses to continue using and accepting checks rather than cash.
    (b) The willingness of consumers, businesses, and government to borrow money.
    (c) The Federal Reserve System.
    (d) All of the above.

27. Which of the following would acquire the assets and deposits of a failed S&L, and then seek to sell the assets and/or the entire institution?
    (a) The Federal Reserve.
    (b) The RTC.
    (c) The FDIC.
    (d) The FSLIC.

28. Deposit insurance:
    (a) Lowers the bankruptcy rate for banks.
    (b) Lowers the number and magnitude of bank runs.
    (c) Must be subsidized and run by the government in order to have credibility.
    (d) All of the above.

29. Suppose a bank has $2 million in deposits, a required reserve ratio of 20 percent, and reserves of $500,000. Then it has excess reserves of:
    (a) $200,000.
    (b) $300,000.
    (c) $400,000.
    (d) None of the above.

30. Suppose a bank has $100,000 in deposits, a required reserve ratio of 5 percent, and bank reserves of $45,000. Then it can make new loans in the amount of:
    (a) $40,000.
    (b) $5,000.
    (c) $2,500.
    (d) None of the above.

31. Which of the following groupings contains a term that does not belong?
    (a) Coin, currency, transactions- account balances.
    (b) $M1$, $M2$, L.
    (c) Money multiplier, reserve ratio, aggregate demand.
    (d) Savings and loans, credit unions, mutual savings banks.

Problems and Applications

Exercise 1

Use the information from the T-account in Table 12.1 to answer problems 1-10.

Table 12.1
Bank of Arlington

Assets		Liabilities	
Loans	$1,000,000	Transactions deposits	$1,000,000
Securities	200,000		
Member bank reserves	200,000		
Other assets	100,000		
		Ownership claims	500,000
Total	$1,500,000	Total	$1,500,000

1. Suppose that the Bank of Arlington is just meeting its reserve requirement. The reserve requirement must be _____.

2. To be in a position to make loans, the Bank of Arlington must acquire some (required reserves/excess reserves).

3. If we assume that the reserve ratio is changed to 10 percent, the Bank of Arlington would have required reserves of _____ and excess reserves of _____.

4. With a 10 percent reserve ratio, the Bank of Arlington is in a position to make new loans totaling _____.

5. Suppose the Bank of Arlington makes a loan of $100,000. The $100,000 is then spent so that it does not return to the Bank of Arlington but goes instead to the Bank of Cambridge. After this transaction, transactions accounts of the Bank of Arlington will be _____; its total reserves will be _____; its excess reserves will be _____; its required reserves will be _____.

6. The Bank of Cambridge had zero excess reserves before receiving the $100,000 deposits. Because of the 10 percent reserve requirement, the required reserves for the bank rise by _____.

7. Excess reserves for the Bank of Cambridge after the $100,000 deposit are _____.

8. If it makes the full amount of loans possible under the reserve requirement, the Bank of Cambridge will cause $M1$ to increase by _____.

9. Altogether, the Bank of Arlington and the Bank of Cambridge made loans and created transactions-account balances of _____.

10. If this process were to continue to the maximum, the amount of loans made on the basis of the $100,000 initial excess reserves of the Bank of Arlington would be _____, and the amount of transactions-account balances created would be _____.

Exercise 2

This exercise is very much like Table 12.3 in the text (p. 264), but the reserve requirement has been changed. Assume Bank A, below, is a monopoly bank.

1. Complete Table 12.2 on the basis of the following:

    $100 in cash is deposited in Bank A. (Assume cash is counted as reserves.)

    The reserve requirement is 0.10.

    The bank begins with zero excess reserves.

Table 12.2
Transactions-account-balance creation

	Change in transactions deposits	Change in total reserves	Change in required reserves	Change in excess reserves	Change in lending capacity
If $100 in cash is deposited in Bank A, then Bank A acquires	$_____	$_____	$_____	$_____	$_____
If loan made and deposited in Bank B, then Bank B acquires	_____	_____	_____	_____	_____
If loan made and deposited in Bank C, then Bank C acquires	_____	_____	_____	_____	_____
If loan made and deposited elsewhere, then Bank D acquires	_____	_____	_____	_____	_____
If loan made and deposited elsewhere, then Bank E acquires	_____	_____	_____	_____	_____
If loan made and deposited elsewhere, then Bank F acquires	_____	_____	_____	_____	_____
If loan made and deposited elsewhere, then Bank G acquires	_____	_____	_____	_____	_____
And if process continues indefinitely, changes will total	_____		_____		_____

2. The money multiplier in Table 12.3 in the text is 5 and the money multiplier in this exercise is _____.

3. Suppose that the initial transaction had been a withdrawal of $100 in cash (reserves) and the banking system had been all loaned up (had no excess reserves). As a result of the initial withdrawal, _____ of reserves would have been lost. Required reserves would have been reduced by _____ and the banking system would be deficient by _____. Assuming no other way to get reserves, the banking system would have to call in loans of _____.

Exercise 3

The topic of often money appears throughout the newspaper. A little practice from this exercise will help you see evidence of money as a store of value, a standard of value, and a medium of exchange.

If your professor makes a newspaper assignment from the *Instructor's Manual*, this exercise will provide an example of how to do it.

Reread the article "Goodbye Rubles, Hello Baubles: Russians Rush to Get Rid of Cash" on page 255 of the text.

1. Which form of money ($M1$, $M2$,... etc.), would be the smallest measure including the type of money described in the article.

2. What is the first passage that specifically refers to money and provides evidence of the type of money that you indicated in problem 1 above?

3. Which passage shows money performing (or failing to perform) as a medium of exchange?

4. The ruble is (succeeding, failing) to perform the function of medium of exchange.

5. Which passage shows money performing (or failing to perform) as a standard of value?

6. The ruble is (succeeding, failing) to perform the function of a standard of value.

7. Which passage shows money performing (or failing to perform) as a store of value?

8. The ruble is (succeeding, failing) to perform the function of a store of value.

Exercise 4

This exercise illustrates graphically the relationship between money and nominal GDP. This relationship will mean much more when we examine the equation of exchange in Chapters 13 and 14.

1. Graph the percentage change in nominal GDP (see the data on the inside cover of the text) on the same axis as the percentage change in $M2$ shown in Figure 12.1.

Figure 12.1
M2 and economic growth rates

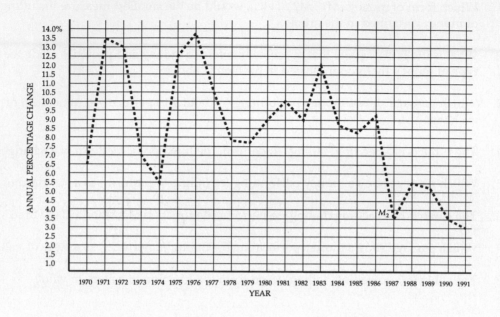

2. The relationship between the nominal GDP and the percentage change in $M2$ is best characterized as (direct, inverse).

3. We will see that GDP and money are related to each other by definition (equation of exchange). But here you can see that money seems to lead GDP growth rates by two years. Look at the peaks of money in 1971, 1976, 1983, and 1986, that have corresponding peaks in the growth rate for the years 1973, 1978, 1984, and 1988. Also note simultaneous years 1974, 1981, and 1988.

Common Errors

The first statement in each "common error" below is incorrect. Each incorrect statement is followed by a corrected version and an explanation.

1. Banks can't create money. WRONG!

   Banks can and do create money. RIGHT!

   It should be obvious by now that banks and other depository institutions are very important participants in the money-supply process. They create money by granting loans to borrowers and accomplish their role by adding to their customers' transactions accounts. The accounts are money just as much as the printed money in your wallet is money. The banks create (supply) money, but only in response to borrowers' demands for it. Without customers "demanding" loans, banks wouldn't be able to create money at all.

2. Banks hold your deposits in their vaults. WRONG!

    Banks don't hold your deposits in their vaults. (And neither do other depository institutions.) RIGHT!

    You can look at this two ways. First, when you deposit your paycheck, there's nothing for the bank to "hold" in its vault, except the check, and that is returned to the person who wrote it. Second, if you deposited coin or cash, it's all put together and you can't distinguish any one person's deposit from any other person's deposit. Even then, when "cash in vault" becomes too large, much of it is shipped away by armored truck to the Federal Reserve Bank. (This is described in Chapter 13.) Thus, banks don't hold your deposits in their vaults.

3. Gold and silver are intrinsically valuable and are necessary to secure the value of a currency. WRONG!

    Money can serve as a store of value, a standard of value, and a medium of exchange without being backed by gold and silver. RIGHT!

    While precious metals such as gold and silver have frequently been used to back currencies, they do not back the dollar today. Like other commodities, their value in terms of dollars continually fluctuates in response to supply and demand conditions. International monetary authorities have attempted to "demonetize" the precious metals and have been successful in holding the price of these metals down in terms of the major currencies. Nevertheless, during periods of calamity and fear, these precious metals are hoarded because people believe these items have intrinsic value; they then do take the role of a store of value.

4. Banks are irresponsible if they fail to store all of the money that is deposited with them so that it is available on demand. WRONG!

    Banks must lend most of the money that is deposited with them so that they can earn and pay interest on the those deposits. RIGHT!

    If banks allowed money just to sit in the vault, no productive use could be made of the money. Banks are useful as the intermediary between savers, who have the money, and investors, who wish to make the capital goods that will provide future income for the economy. That means they must put the money of savers to use, which means the money is not there for the savers at all times.

•ANSWERS•

Key-Term Review

1.	barter	7.	excess reserves
2.	deposit creation	8.	money supply ($M1$, $M2$)
3.	transactions account	9.	money multiplier
4.	required reserves	10.	aggregate demand
5.	money	11.	bank reserves
6.	reserve ratio		

True or False

1.	T	3.	T	5.	F	7.	F	9.	T	11.	F
2.	F	4.	T	6.	T	8.	T	10.	F	12.	F

13. F Review page 261 of the text. Remember that cash in the bank vault is not counted as part of the money supply, but your new transactions-account balance in the amount of the money in the bank vault now would be.

14.	T	16.	F	18.	T	20.	F	22.	T	23.	F
15.	T	17.	T	19.	T	21.	T				

Multiple Choice

1.	c	6.	b	11.	c	16.	a	21.	d	26.	d
2.	c	7.	c	12.	b	17.	b	22.	c	27.	b
3.	d	8.	a	13.	d	18.	c	23.	a	28.	b
4.	a	9.	d	14.	d	19.	c	24.	d		
5.	d	10.	c	15.	d	20.	a	25.	d		

29. d $100,000 = $500,000 - (0.2 x $2 million)
30. a $40,000 = $45,000 - (0.5 x $100,000)
31. c Aggregate demand is not directly linked to the reserve ratio or the money multiplier. Other groupings are (a) kinds of money, (b) money-supply measures, and (d) financial institutions.

Problems and Applications

Exercise 1

1. 0.20

2. excess reserves

3. $100,000; $100,000

4. $100,000

5. $1,000,000; $100,000; 0; $100,000

6. $10,000

7. $90,000

8. $90,000

9. $190,000

10. $1,000,000; $1,000,000

Exercise 2

1. **Table 12.2 Answer**

	Change in transactions deposits	Change in total reserves	Change in required reserves	Change in excess reserves	Change in lending capacity
If $100 in cash is deposited in Bank A, then Bank A acquires	$ 100.00	$100.00	$ 10.00	$ 90.00	$ 90.00
If loan made and deposited in Bank B, then Bank B acquires	90.00	90.00	9.00	81.00	81.00
If loan made and deposited in Bank C, then Bank C acquires	81.00	81.00	8.10	72.90	72.90
If loan made and deposited else-where, then Bank D acquires	72.90	72.90	7.29	65.61	65.61
If loan made and deposited else-where, then Bank E acquires	65.61	65.61	6.56	59.05	59.05
If loan made and deposited else-where, then Bank F acquires	59.05	59.05	5.91	53.15	53.15
If loan made and deposited else-where, then Bank G acquires	53.15	53.15	5.32	47.84	47.84
And if process continues indefi-nitely, changes will total	1,000.00		100.00		900.00

2. 10

3. $100; $10; $90; $900

Exercise 3

1. The article is talking mainly about cash. The smallest monetary aggregate that includes cash is $M1$ in the United States. Although all other forms of money include cash, $M1$ is the smallest measure of money that includes cash. Since Russia has such poorly developed financial institutions, transactions accounts and other forms of money are much less important.

2. "That the exchange rate for the *ruble* would be slashed to know the waning value of their *currency*." Another passage that refers specifically to cash is "anything that would turn the crumpled bank notes in their hands into something with lasting value."

3. "The only way for this to be worth gold is to buy gold with it. And that's exactly why I'm waiting here."

4. Succeeding (marginally). This passage indicates that rubles are being used as a medium of exchange, but the fact that the individual has to stand in line indicates that rubles are not fully responsible for rationing.

5. "The people standing there . . . did not need the official announcement . . . that the exchange rate for the *ruble* would be slashed to know the waning value of their *currency*."

6. failing. The standard of value represented by the ruble is "waning," which means that the standard is changing.

7. "anything that would turn the crumpled bank notes in their hands into something with lasting value"

8. failing. The passage quoted in problem 7 shows implicitly that the ruble does not hold its value.

Exercise 4

1. **Figure 12.1 Answer**

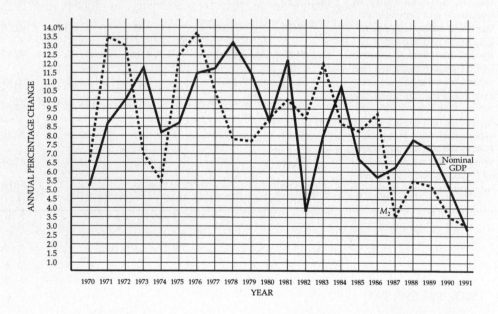

2. There is a direct relationship between money and nominal GDP.

CHAPTER 13

The Federal Reserve System

Quick Review

In the preceding chapter we saw how money was created and received strong signals that money must be controlled. In this chapter we examine these questions:

- How does government control the amount of money in the economy?
- Which government agency is responsible for exercising this control?
- How are banks and bond markets affected by the government's policies?

The answer to all of these questions rests with the Federal Reserve System, the central bank of the United States. All banks are subject to the reserve requirements imposed by the Fed. The Fed is independent of congressional whims and has a structure which is unique among the world's central banks because it is made up of twelve regional Federal Reserve banks. Alan Greenspan chairs the Board of Governors and is the chief spokesman for the Fed.

The Federal Reserve System has three basic tools with which to control the money supply: open-market operations, changes in the reserve requirement, and changes in the discount rate. Open-market operations are implemented by the Open Market Committee, and are the most important. To increase the size of the money supply, the Open Market Committee orders the purchase of government securities (bonds) in the open market. These purchases increase bank reserves and lending potential and may have the additional effect of raising bond prices (lowering yields).

The Fed could accomplish the same objective, although with less certainty, by lowering the discount rate. A lower discount rate encourages member banks to borrow reserves and acquire lending potential. The Fed can also modify reserve requirements, but these are not changed often or by large amounts. When the reserve requirement is raised, excess reserves are transformed into required reserves; when the reserve requirement is lowered, required reserves are transformed into excess reserves. In addition, there is an inverse relationship between the size of the reserve requirement and the size of the money multiplier.

There are occasions when the Fed will restrain the economy with a "tight money" policy—by selling bonds in the open market, raising reserve requirements and raising the discount rate. In practice, restraint is basically applied through open-market operations.

The idea of what constitutes a "bank" has changed dramatically in the last fifteen years. Before 1980, the Fed's power over the money supply was weakening because so many financial institutions remained outside its control. As a result, Congress passed the Monetary Control Act of 1980 to allow the Fed to reassert control over the money supply and foster competition among financial institutions. Over the intervening period banks have declined in importance while "nonbanks" have grown more important. The nonbanks hold accounts and make loans too. Banks now must compete more vigorously against money-market mutual funds, brokerage houses, foreign and domestic corporations, and so on. Banks are certainly less important than they used to be.

Learning Objectives

After reading Chapter 13 and doing the following exercises, you should:	True or false	Multiple choice	Problems and applications	Common errors	Pages in the text
1. Be familiar with the organization, structure, and purposes of the Federal Reserve System.	1-4, 16-18	9, 10, 12, 20		1, 2	275-277
2. Know how the reserve requirement can be changed to achieve a money-supply objective.	6-8	3-5, 26	1, 5	1, 2	277-279
3. Know what the money multiplier is and how it is used.		6, 27	1-3		278
4. Know the meaning of "federal funds" and the "federal funds rate."	10	8, 11, 13, 18	8		221
5. Know how the discount rate can be changed to achieve a given policy objective.	2, 5, 8, 9	14, 16	3	2	281
6. Understand the distinction between the interest rate on a bond and the yield from a bond.	15	1, 15, 23-25	4, 6	3	284
7. Be able to demonstrate the inverse relationship between interest rates and bond prices.	14	1, 15, 22, 24	4	3	284
8. Understand how the Fed's activities in the bond market alter portfolio decisions of bond sellers and bond buyers.	11, 14				283-286
9. Know how the Open Market Committee can achieve a given policy objective by buying or selling securities.	12, 13	7	2	2, 4	282-287
10. Know the background and provisions of the Monetary Control Act of 1980 and recent changes in the structure of the financial system.	19, 20	12, 17, 19, 21			288-290

Key-Term Review

Review the following terms; if you are not sure of the meaning of any term, write out the definition and check it against the Glossary in the text.

bond
discount rate
discounting
excess reserves
monetary policy
money multiplier

money supply ($M1$, $M2$)
open-market operations
portfolio decision
required reserves
yield

Fill in the blank following each of the statements below with the appropriate term from the list above.

1. When a member bank borrows from the Federal Reserve Bank in its district, it is engaging in _____ .

    1. _____

2. When the Federal Reserve System engages in open-market operations, it must do so by inducing banks and individuals to make the appropriate _____ .

    2. _____

3. Those reserves a bank holds over and above what are required are called _____ .

    3. _____

4. The rate of interest that the Fed charges on loans to member banks is called the _____ .

    4. _____

5. When the Fed buys or sells government securities, it is engaging in _____ .

    5. _____

6. A certificate acknowledging the existence of a debt and the amount of interest to be paid each year until the agreed date of repayment is called a _____ .

    6. _____

7. The Open Market Committee attempts to elicit the appropriate portfolio responses from banks and members of the public by altering the bond _____ .

    7. _____

8. Those reserves that a bank must hold against its demand liabilities are referred to as _____ .

    8. _____

9. The inverse of the required reserve ratio is the _____ .

    9. _____

10. The discount rate, reserve requirements, and open-market operations are all instruments of _____ .

    10. _____

11. The main function of the Federal Reserve
System is to control the _____ .   11. _____

True or False: *Circle your choice.*

T F   1. The Federal Reserve System consists of one central bank and eleven branches.

T F   2. When commercial banks borrow from each other, the process is called "discounting."

T F   3. The Federal Reserve banks hold deposits of banks and other business firms.

T F   4. All depository institutions are subject to reserve requirements established by the Federal
           Reserve System.

T F   5. The most powerful monetary-policy tool available to the Fed is the power to change the
           discount rate.

T F   6. If the Fed wishes to create the conditions under which the money supply can be
           increased, it can reduce the reserve requirement.

T F   7. When the reserve requirement is increased, excess reserves are reduced.

T F   8. The Fed changes the reserve requirement by changing the discount rate.

T F   9. The discount rate is the rate of interest charged by banks that lend in the federal funds
           market.

T F 10. The federal funds rate is the rate of interest the Fed pays on member bank reserves.

T F 11. Banks that are short of reserves can acquire reserves by selling securities.

T F 12. The buying and selling of federal government securities by the Fed is known as "open-
           market operations."

T F 13. To increase the lending capacity of banks, the Fed buys securities.

T F 14. The Fed's activities in the bond market influence bankers' portfolio decisions.

T F 15. The value of a bond is found by dividing the face amount of the bond by the current
           market rate of interest.

T F 16. All U.S. banks are subject to reserve requirements established by the Fed.

T F 17. The size of the reserve requirement is positively related to the dollar volume of the
           transactions accounts on a bank's balance sheet.

T F 18. Federal Reserve System requirements are structured to give a competitive advantage to
           smaller banks.

T F 19. The United States returned to the gold standard with the passage of the Monetary
           Control Act of 1980.

T F 20. The Fed's control of the banks has decreased since 1980, and the importance of banks
           relative to other institutions has increased.

Multiple Choice: *Select the correct answer.*

_____ 1. Suppose a 1-year note issued today bearing interest at 5 percent has a par value of $1,000 and the current market rate of interest is 5 percent. The price at which it would sell *today* is:
    (a)   ($1,000) (0.05).
    (b)   ($1,000) (1.05).
    (c) $1,000/0.05.
    (d)   None of the above.

_____ 2. Which of the following is *not* one of the tools of monetary policy used by the Fed?
    (a)   Expulsion from Fed membership.
    (b)   Changing the reserve requirement.
    (c)   Changing the discount rate.
    (d)   Performing open-market operations.

_____ 3. Suppose the banking system has $1 million of reserves when the reserve requirement is 0.20. What is the volume of demand deposits in the system if there are no excess reserves to begin with?
    (a) $200,000.
    (b) $500,000.
    (c) $5,000,000.
    (d) $2,000,000.

_____ 4. Suppose the Fed raised the reserve requirement to 0.25 in question 3. Then the banks in the system would be *deficient* in reserves by:
    (a) $2,500,000.
    (b) $1,250,000.
    (c) $250,000.
    (d) $1,000,000.

_____ 5. Suppose the banking system is in the condition described in question 3, and the Fed lowers the reserve requirement to 0.15. Then the banking system has:
    (a)   Excess reserves of $250,000.
    (b)   Required reserves of $750,000.
    (c)   The potential to create $250,000 x 1/0.15 of new loans.
    (d)   All of the above.

_____ 6. In Question 5, the money multiplier is:
    (a)   1/0.15.
    (b)   0.15/1.
    (c)   (1)(0.15).
    (d)   None of the above.

_____ 7. When the Fed wishes to increase the excess reserves of the member banks, it:
    (a)   Buys securities.
    (b)   Raises the discount rate.
    (c)   Raises the reserve requirement.
    (d)   None of the above.

_____ 8. Federal funds are:
    (a)   Tax revenues collected by the Fed.
    (b)   Bank deposits held in Federal Reserve banks.
    (c)   The source of funds for revenue sharing.
    (d)   Reserves loaned by one bank to another.

_____ 9. Which of the following is a service performed by the Federal Reserve banks?
   (a) Clearing checks between commercial banks.
   (b) Holding reserves of commercial banks.
   (c) Providing currency to commercial banks.
   (d) All of the above.

_____ 10. In which of the following ways can bank reserves be held?
   (a) Deposits at the district Federal Reserve bank.
   (b) Cash in the bank's own vault.
   (c) Deposits held at other commercial banks.
   (d) Both (a) and (b).

_____ 11. The Federal Reserve System can provide reserves to the banking system by all of the following _except_:
   (a) Buying securities in the open market.
   (b) Lending to member banks.
   (c) Lending federal funds to member banks.
   (d) Reducing the reserve requirements.

_____ 12. The reserve requirements imposed by the Fed:
   (a) Are the same for all member banks.
   (b) Vary with the size of the bank's capital account.
   (c) Vary with the value of the bank's transactions-account liabilities.
   (d) Vary from as low as 2 percent to as high as 25 percent.

_____ 13. If a bank in New York borrows federal funds from a bank in San Francisco:
   (a) Lending potential goes up in New York.
   (b) Lending potential goes down in San Francisco.
   (c) Lending potential for the banking system does not change.
   (d) All of the above.

_____ 14. When the Fed raises the discount rate, this action:
   (a) Raises the cost of borrowing reserves to member banks.
   (b) Is a signal that the Fed is moving toward a slower growth rate for the money supply.
   (c) Is a signal that interest rates may rise generally.
   (d) Does all of the above.

_____ 15. Suppose you buy a bond issued by General Motors. Which of the following _best_ describes your financial situation?
   (a) General Motors will have to redeem the bond at maturity for an amount stated on the face of the bond.
   (b) General Motors owes you an amount equal to the market value of the bond.
   (c) General Motors owes you an amount equal to the interest on the bond.
   (d) You own part of General Motors.

_____ 16. Suppose the Federal Reserve system requires a minimum reserve ratio of 0.10 _and there are no excess reserves in the system._ Also suppose banks respond to each percentage point change in the discount rate by changing the amount of borrowing of reserves from the Fed by $40 million. If the Fed raises the discount rate by 3 percentage points, then the potential for additional loans changes by:
   (a) Positive $4 million.
   (b) Negative $1.2 billion.
   (c) Positive $12 million.
   (d) Positive $1.2 billion.

17. Eurodollars are:
    (a)   Typically, dollars spent by U.S. residents traveling in Europe.
    (b)   Dollar deposits on the books of European financial institutions.
    (c)   Dollars owed by European borrowers to U.S. lending institutions.
    (d)   Dollars borrowed by U.S. firms to make investments in European financial institutions.

18. The federal funds market is a market in which:
    (a)   The reserve requirement does not apply.
    (b)   Government securities are bought and sold.
    (c)   Reserves are discounted outside the Fed's control.
    (d)   All of the above.

19. The basic reason Congress passed the Monetary Control Act of 1980 was that:
    (a)   Banks demanded authority to pay interest on checking accounts.
    (b)   Credit unions demanded to be subject to Federal Reserve regulation.
    (c)   Savings and loan associations paid rates of interest that gave them a competitive advantage over mutual funds.
    (d)   The Fed's ability to control the money supply had diminished.

20. Which of the following is subject to regulation by the Fed?
    (a)   All commercial banks.
    (b)   Savings and loan associations.
    (c)   Savings banks.
    (d)   All of the above.

21. Which of the following has come into competition with banks since the Monetary Control Act of 1980?
    (a)   AT&T, GM, Sears, and other credit card issuers.
    (b)   Eurodollars lent by foreign banks.
    (c)   S&Ls.
    (d)   All of the above.

22. When interest rates fall:
    (a)   Bond prices rise.
    (b)   Bond yields rise.
    (c)   The face value of bonds rises.
    (d)   None of the above.

23. An example of an interest rate is:
    (a)   The prime rate.
    (b)   The discount rate.
    (c)   The federal funds rate.
    (d)   All of the above.

24. Suppose a bond issued by IBM that matures in the year 2020 in the amount of $1,000 has a current yield of 10 percent and pays $200 of interest annually. What should be the current selling price of the bond, *ceteris paribus?*
    (a)   Less than $1,000.
    (b) $1,000.
    (c) $1,200.
    (d) $2,000.

_____ 25. If the annual interest rate printed on the face of a bond with a par value of $1,000 is 10 percent and you purchase the bond for $800, what is the implied annual yield on the bond?
   (a) 10 percent or less.
   (b) 12.5 percent.
   (c) 20 percent.
   (d) 25 percent.

_____ 26. Suppose the Federal Reserve System has total transactions accounts of $10 billion, a minimum reserve ratio of 0.10, and there are no excess reserves in the system. If the Fed wishes to *stimulate* the economy by changing the money supply by $10 billion, it can best do so by:
   (a) Lowering the discount rate enough to increase reserves by $20 billion.
   (b) Buying enough securities from banks to raise reserves by $20 billion.
   (c) Lowering the minimum reserve ratio from 0.10 to 0.05.
   (d) None of the above.

_____ 27. Which of the following groupings contains a term which does not belong?
   (a) Check clearing, holding bank reserves, providing loans.
   (b) Reserve requirements, discount rates, open-market operations.
   (c) 1/reserve ratio, money multiplier, 1/*MPS*.
   (d) Board of Governors, Federal Reserve Banks, Open Market Committee.

Problems and Applications

The first three exercises demonstrate how monetary policy might work in a hypothetical situation.

Exercise 1

This exercise is similar to the problem 5 for Chapter 13 in the text, which shows how to understand the accounts for the entire banking system. The focus of this exercise is the reserve requirement.

Suppose the Fed wishes to expand $M1$. Carefully read the assumptions below and then work through the exercise step-by-step to achieve the policy objective. Assume that:

- The banks in the system initially have $240 million of transactions-deposit liabilities.
- The banking system initially has no excess reserves.
- The initial reserve requirement is 0.25.
- The banks make loans in the full amount of any excess reserves that they acquire.
- No cash is drained out of the system.
- The combined balance sheet of the banks in the system is as shown in Table 13.1.

Table 13.1
Balance sheet of banking system when reserve requirement is 0.25 (millions of dollars)

Total reserves	$ 60	Transactions accounts	$240
Required, $60			
Excess, $0			
Securities	80		
Loans	100		
Total	$240	Total	$240

1. Suppose the Fed lowers the reserve requirement to 0.20. How many dollars of excess reserves does this create? _____

2. How large are required reserves now? _____

3. How large are total reserves? _____

4. What is the additional lending capacity of the banking system as a result of the change in the reserve requirement from 0.25 to 0.20? _____

5. Assume the banks fully utilize their new lending capacity. Reconstruct the balance sheet in Table 13.2 to show the new totals for the accounts affected in the total banking system.

Table 13.2
Balance sheet of banking system when reserve requirement is 0.20 (millions of dollars)

Total reserves	$_____	Transactions accounts	$_____
Required, _____			
Excess, _____			
Securities	_____		
Loans	_____		
Total	$_____	Total	$_____

6. So far the money supply ($M1$) has expanded by _____ .

7. Total reserves have gone up by _____ .

8. Loans have gone up by _____ .

Exercise 2

Like problem 5 for Chapter 13 in the text, this exercise shows how the money supply can be changed. The focus of this exercise is open-market policy.

Suppose the Fed wants to expand the money supply using open-market operations and it is faced with the balance sheet of the banking system as shown in Table 13.3. Suppose further that:

- The banking system initially has no excess reserves.
- The reserve requirement is 0.20.
- The banks make loans in the full amount of any excess reserves that they acquire.
- No cash is drained out of the system.

Table 13.3
Balance sheet of banking system
(millions of dollars)

Total reserves	$ 60	Transactions accounts	$300
Required, $60			
Excess, $0			
Securities	80		
Loans	160		
Total	$300	Total	$300

1. Suppose the Open Market Committee buys $10 million of securities from the commercial banking system. In Table 13.4 show the changes and new totals for the various accounts on the balance sheet of the commercial banks after this transaction but before any new loans are made or called in.

Table 13.4
Balance sheet of commercial banking system after OMC buys $10 million of securities
(millions of dollars)

Total reserves	$_____	Transactions accounts	$_____
Required, _____			
Excess, _____			
Securities	_____		
Loans	_____		
Total	$_____	Total	$_____

2. Suppose the banking system now expands its loans and transactions accounts by the maximum amount it can on the basis of its _____ in excess reserves.

3. In Table 13.5 complete the balance sheet for the banking system showing the new totals for all of the accounts after loans have been made. (*Remember*: The reserve ratio is 0.20.)

Table 13.5
Balance sheet of banking system after expansion of loans and deposits
(millions of dollars)

Total reserves	$_____	Transactions accounts	$_____
Required, _____			
Excess, _____			
Securities	_____		
Loans	_____		
Total	$_____	Total	$_____

4. As a result of the open-market operations, the money supply has expanded by a total of _____ .

5. Total reserves have gone up by _____ .

6. Loans have increased by _____ .

Exercise 3

This exercise demonstrates what might happen when the Fed lowers the discount rate.

Suppose the Fed wants to expand the money supply by changing the discount rate. It is faced with the balance sheet of the banking system as shown in Table 13.6. Carefully read the assumptions below and then work through the exercise step-by-step to achieve the policy objective. Assume that:

- The banking system initially has no excess reserves.
- The initial reserve requirement is 0.20.
- The banks in the system respond to each percentage point drop in the discount rate by borrowing $2 million from the Fed.
- The banks make loans in the full amount of any excess reserves that they acquire.
- No cash is drained out of the system.

Table 13.6
Balance sheet of banking system
(millions of dollars)

Total reserves	$ 70	Transactions accounts	$350
Required, $70			
Excess, $0			
Securities	70		
Loans	210		
Total	$350	Total	$350

1. Suppose that the Fed now lowers the discount rate by 1 percentage point and that the banking system responds as indicated in the third assumption above. As a result of this policy initiative, the banks in the system will now borrow _____ from the Fed, all of which is (excess/required) reserves. On the basis of this lending potential, the banks together can expand their loans by _____ .

2. In Table 13.7 assume the banks have made the additional loans. Complete the balance sheet to show the final effect of the change in the discount rate.

Table 13.7
Final balance sheet of banking system
(millions of dollars)

Total reserves	$_____	Transactions accounts	$_____
Required, _____			
Excess, _____			
Securities	_____		
Loans	_____	Discounts payable to Fed	_____
Total	$_____	Total	$_____

3. The effect of lowering the discount rate is an increase in the money supply of _____ .

Exercise 4

It is very important that the inverse relationship between bond prices and bond yields be understood. The following problems will help you nail down this important concept.

1. Suppose that today you purchased from AT&T a bond with a par value of $1,000 that would mature in 1 year, bearing interest at 8 percent. In 1 year AT&T would pay you _____ for return of principal and _____ of interest for letting them use your purchasing power. The yield on the bond is _____ percent.

2. Suppose that a company called Similar Firm was offering bonds paying 10 percent interest. If you paid $1,000 for a bond from Similar Firm, at the end of 1 year you would receive _____ for return of principal and _____ in interest, and the yield would be _____ percent.

3. All other things being equal, which bond would be the best buy?

4. To earn a yield of 10 percent, how much would the price of the AT&T bond have to fall? (*Hint:* The formula for finding the new bond price is:

$$\frac{\text{Principal} + \text{interest}}{\text{New price of bond}} = (1 + \text{bond yield})$$

The bond was issued with a par value of $1,000 and paid $80 of interest annually. To compete with the obligations of Similar Firm, the price must fall enough to provide a yield of 10 percent. Find the new price of the bond.

5. T F Although the interest rate on the AT&T bond is 8 percent, its price will fall enough to raise the yield to 10 percent.

6. As the price of the AT&T bond goes down, the yield goes (down/up), even though the face value and the original interest rate do not change.

(The message here is clear. Bond prices and bond yields move in opposite directions. When interest rates on new bonds have risen, you won't be able to sell old bonds for what you paid for them. But there is a lower price that will make them competitive with

256

any newly issued bonds. Similarly, if interest rates have fallen, the price of old bonds will have risen.)

Exercise 5

The media often provide information about changes in policy by the Federal Reserve System. This exercise will use one of the articles in the text to show the kind of information to look for. If your professor makes a newspaper assignment from the *Instructor's Manual*, this exercise will provide an example of how to do it.

Reread the In the News article on page 280 in Chapter 13 entitled "Fed Cuts Deposit-Reserve Requirements" from the *Wall Street Journal*. Then answer the following questions.

1. What central monetary authority is mentioned in the article?

2. What phrase in the article indicates the monetary instrument that is being used by the central monetary authority?

3. Which instrument is being used?
   (a) Reserve requirement.
   (b) Open-market operations.
   (c) Discount rate.
   (d) Other (Specify: _____)

4. What passage (not more than a sentence) indicates in what direction the monetary instrument(s) is being used by the central monetary authority to change the money supply?

5. The change in monetary policy (lowers, raises) the quantity of money relative to what it would have been without the change in policy.

Exercise 6

This exercise shows how closely related the discount rate is to the prime rate, one of the key interest rates used in the private sector.

1. Graph the prime rate and the discount rate from 1970-1992 in Figure 13.1 (see the data on the inside cover of the text).

Figure 13.1
Interest rates

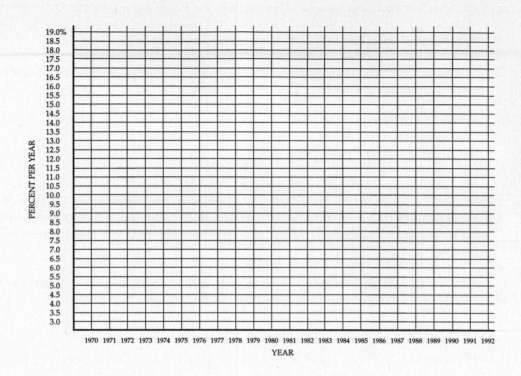

2. The relationship between the prime rate and the discount rate is best characterized as (direct,inverse).

3. If the prime rate (leads, follows) the discount rate, the Federal Reserve would apparently follow the direction of the private financial markets.

4. Which of the two indicators (prime rate, discount rate) has the largest swings? _____

5. Which of the two indicators (prime rate, discount rate) is lowest? _____ Why is it lowest? _____

Common Errors

The first statement in each "common error" below is incorrect. Each incorrect statement is followed by a corrected version and an explanation.

1. Bank reserves are required for the safety of depositors' money. WRONG!

    Bank reserves are for control of the money supply. RIGHT!

    Many people have the idea that bank reserves provide for the safety of depositors' money. They don't. The statistics in Chapter 11 indicate that the amount of demand deposits is several times larger than that of reserves. Reserves are for control of the money supply. The FDIC provides for safety of deposits by insuring them. Reserves are not principally for depositors' safety.

2. Deposits of cash are necessary to start the process of lending and deposit creation. WRONG!

    To start the lending process, the banks must acquire reserves from outside the banking system. RIGHT!

    Many find it difficult to understand that for deposit creation to occur, the banking system needs only to acquire reserves from outside the system or be able to stretch existing reserves further. It may acquire reserves by selling a security to the Fed or by borrowing from the Fed. An individual bank, however, may acquire reserves from another bank. So to the extent that it has increased its reserves, another bank's reserves have shrunk. Thus, the system has no more reserves after the transaction than it had before, and so the system's lending capacity is unchanged.

3. Rising interest rates make existing bonds more valuable. WRONG!

    Bond prices and interest rates are inversely related. RIGHT!

    The relationship between the price of a bond maturing in 1 year and the "yield" (which is usually close to current market interest rates) is given by

    $$\frac{\text{Current market price of bonds}}{} = \frac{\text{face value of the bond} \times (1 + \text{bond interest rate})}{(1 + \text{current interest rate})}$$

    There are two interest rates involved here: the interest rate stated on the bond when it is issued and the current market interest rate which can change before the bond matures. The price of bonds moves in the opposite direction (i.e., inversely) to movements in market rates of interest.

4. When the Fed sells government bonds in open-market operations, it is increasing the money supply. WRONG!

    When the Fed sells government bonds, the buyers pay with reserves, which means there are fewer reserves and less money. RIGHT!

    The key here is to realize that payment of reserves to the Fed means that there are fewer reserves available to the entire banking system. By selling bonds the Fed is tightening monetary policy.

•ANSWERS•

Key-Term Review

1.	discounting	5.	open-market operations	9.	money multiplier
2.	portfolio decision	6.	bond	10.	monetary policy
3.	excess reserves	7.	yield	11.	money supply ($M1$, $M2$)
4.	discount rate	8.	required reserves		

True or False

1.	F	5.	F	9.	F	12.	T	15.	F	18.	T
2.	F	6.	T	10.	F	13.	T	16.	T	19.	F
3.	F	7.	T	11.	T	14.	T	17.	T	20.	F
4.	T	8.	F								

Multiple Choice

1. d The price *today* would be $1000.

2.	a	7.	a	11.	c	15.	a	19.	d	23. d
3.	c	8.	d	12.	c	16.	b	20.	d	24. d
4.	c	9.	d	13.	d	17.	b	21.	d	25. b
5.	d	10.	d	14.	d	18.	a	22.	a	26. c
6.	a									

27. c. The marginal propensity to save (*MPS*) does not apply to the money multiplier. Topics of other groupings are (a) services performed by Fed banks, (b) the Fed's levers, and (d) different organizations within the Fed.

Problems and Applications

Exercise 1

1. $12 million
2. $48 million
3. $60 million
4. $60 million
5. **Table 13.2 Answer**

Total reserves	$ 60	Transactions accounts	$300
Required, $60			
Excess, $0			
Securities	80		
Loans	160		
Total	$300	Total	$300

6. $60 million
7. Zero
8. $60 million

Exercise 2

1. **Table 13.4 Answer**

Total reserves	$ 70	Transactions accounts	$300
Required, $60			
Excess, $10			
Securities	70		
Loans.	160		
Total	$300	Total	$300

2. $10 million

3. **Table 13.5 Answer**

Total reserves	$ 70	Transactions accounts	$350
Required, $70			
Excess, $0			
Securities	70		
Loans	210		
Total	$350	Total	$350

4. $50 million

5. $10 million

6. $50 million

Exercise 3

1. $2 million; excess; $10 million

2. **Table 13.7 Answer**

Total reserves	$ 72	Transactions accounts	$360
Required, $72			
Excess, $0			
Securities	70		
Loans	220		2
Total	$362	Total	$362

3. $10 million

Exercise 4

1. $1,000; $80; 8

2. $1,000; $100; 10

3. Similar Firm

4. $982 [= ($1,000 + $80)/1.10]

5. T

6. up

Exercise 5

1. The Federal Reserve Board

2. The title, "Deposit-Reserve Requirments"

3. a

4. "The Fed cut to 10% from 12% the percentage of checking-account deposits that banks are required to hold as reserves."

5. raises

Exercise 6

1. **Figure 13.1 Answer**

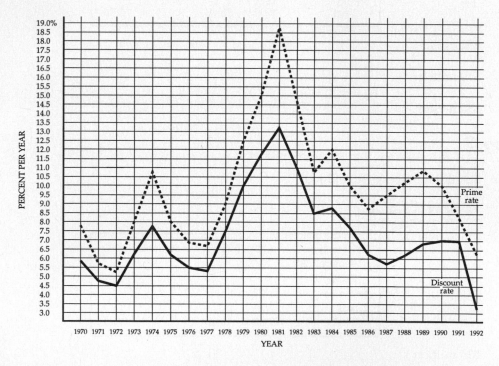

2. direct

3. leads

4. prime rate

5. discount rate. Banks borrow at the discount rate and lend at the prime rate. They would make no profit if there were no differential between the discount rate and the prime rate.

CHAPTER 14

Monetary Policy

Quick Review

In this chapter, the focus is on monetary policy and the Fed's role in attempting to move the economy toward its macroeconomic goals. Specifically, we look for answers to the following questions:

- What is the relationship between the money supply and aggregate demand?
- How can the Fed use its control of the money supply to alter macro outcomes?
- How effective is monetary policy, compared with fiscal policy?

By controlling the banks' ability to make loans ("create money"), the Federal Reserve System controls the money supply. The amount of money in the economy, however, reflects money demand as well as money supply.

The demand for money has three components:
1. The transactions demand, which reflects normal needs for coin, currency, and checking accounts in order to buy and sell goods and services.
2. The precautionary demand, which is what people feel they need for potential emergencies and other unforeseen needs that may arise.
3. The speculative demand, in which money is held temporarily as a secure liquid asset in anticipation of profiting from changes in interest rates.

Both the level of GDP and interest rates influence transactions and precautionary demand. Speculative demand, however, is most influenced by interest rates. It is the interest rate (price of money) that connects the demand for money with the supply of money. The equilibrium rate of interest is the rate that equates the quantity of money demanded with the quantity of money supplied.

If the Fed wishes to stimulate aggregate spending, it will drive down interest rates by expanding the money supply. This lower interest rate stimulates components of aggregate demand (e.g., investment), which are influenced by interest rates. The success of monetary policy depends on the elasticity of the demand for money and the sensitivity of the spending decisions to changes in interest rates.

One way to visualize the transmission mechanism from the money market to aggregate demand is as follows: An increase in the money supply will, *ceteris paribus*, drive the interest rate down and stimulate greater investment spending, thus shifting the aggregate demand curve to the right. There are constraints to be considered though and things might not work so smoothly. Will the banks be willing to lend? Will the increase in the money supply force the interest rate down, or will it fall into the Keynesian liquidity trap? Will low expectations leave the business sector without incentives to increase investment? Or if monetary restraint is being applied and the money supply is reduced, might expectations be so buoyant that firms and households borrow more in spite of higher interest rates? Finally, since the money market is a global one, if domestic interest rates get too high, will borrowers look abroad? There is substantial controversy over the transmission mechanism implied by the use of monetary policy. Monetarists believe that the link is direct. They use the equation of exchange ($MV = PQ$) to demonstrate this. Assuming V is constant, any increase in M must be translated into greater spending regardless of what happens to interest rates. The Monetarists further assert that Q is constant as well, creating a vertical aggregate supply curve at the natural rate of unemployment. Thus, greater M translates into greater P. Monetarists, as a result, advocate steady, predictable changes in the money supply in contrast to the Keynesian manipulations.

Monetarists and Keynesians alike argue that monetary policy can affect nominal, if not real, interest rates. When interest rates rise, some market participants. (e.g., corporations) fare better than others. This influences the content of GDP and can influence the distribution of income as well. The monetarist-Keynesian debate hinges on which policy lever (M or V) is likely to be effective. Monetarists and Keynesians are led to radically different views as to the efficacy of monetary *and* fiscal policy.

Learning Objectives

After reading Chapter 14 and doing the following exercises, you should:	True or false	Multiple choice	Problems and applications	Common errors	Pages in the text
1. Understand the opportunity cost of holding idle funds.	1		7	1	293
2. Know the determinants of the transactions, precautionary, and speculative demands for money.	2, 3, 6, 7	3, 5, 6, 9			293-294
3. Be able to graph money-market equilibrium.	9	2, 5, 9, 13	1		294-295
4. Understand how changes in the money supply lead to changes in the interest rate.	10, 11, 21	7, 10	1, 5		296
5. Understand how changes in the money supply are transmitted to aggregate demand.	9-11	7, 10, 14-19	1, 3, 5	1	296-298
6. Be able to contrast expansionary and restrictive monetary-policy initiatives.	10, 11, 13	13, 14, 16-19	4, 5		296-299
7. Be able to describe the constraints on *both* expansionary and restrictive monetary policy.	7, 12, 13	10, 15, 22, 28, 30	5	3	299-301
8. Understand the equation of exchange and the assumptions on which it is based.	18, 16	4, 8, 24, 25			302
9. Understand the relationship between the natural rate of unemployment and the aggregate supply curve.	4	22, 27	1		304-305
10. Know the mechanism by which changes in M affect GDP in the monetarist model.	8	4, 24, 25, 27			304-305

Learning Objectives, cont.	True or false	Multiple choice	Problems and applications	Common errors	Pages in the text
11. Understand and be able to calculate the real rate of interest.	1, 14, 15, 24	11, 20	7	2	305
12. Be able to contrast Keynesian and monetarist views of how monetary policy works.	5, 16-18, 20, 21, 23	1, 4, 7, 16-19, 22, 25, 26, 29	1-4, 6	3	305-308
13. Be able to articulate the effects of monetary policy on the mix of output and the distribution of income.	5	4, 23, 28			308-309
14. Be able to contrast Keynesian and monetarist views of monetary and fiscal policy.	8, 19, 20	4, 25, 26	2-4		309-315

Key-Term Review

Review the following terms; if you are not sure of the meaning of any term, write out the definition and check it against the Glossary in the text.

aggregate demand	monetary policy
crowding out	natural rate of unemployment
demand for money	portfolio decision
equation of exchange	precautionary demand for money
equilibrium rate of interest	real rate of interest
income velocity of money (V)	speculative demand for money
interest rate	transactions demand for money
liquidity trap	

Fill in the blank following each of the statements below with the appropriate term from the list above.

1. The implicit cost of holding money in idle balances is measured by the _____ .

   1. _____

2. The total quantity of money the public is willing and able to hold at various rates of interest, *ceteris paribus*, is called the _____ .

   2. _____

3. When the average level of prices is rising, the nominal rate of interest exceeds the _____ .

   3. _____

4. Dividing GDP by the number of dollars in circulation yields the _____ .

   4. _____

5. The belief that when government expands the size of its budget it merely replaces private spending that would otherwise have taken place is embodied in the concept called _____ .

   5. _____

6. Choosing among alternative ways of holding assets is essentially a _____ .

6. _____

7. That part of the money balances that the public holds in anticipation of making usual market purchases is referred to as the _____ .

7. _____

8. That part of one's money balances held in case an emergency should arise is called the _____ .

8. _____

9. That part of the money supply held with the idea of capitalizing on interest-rate (bond-price) movements is called the _____ .

9. _____

10. When the Fed wishes to close a recessionary gap by purchasing securities in the open market, it is engaging in an expansionary _____ .

10. _____

11. One reason that monetary policy may be unable to lower interest rates is the possible existence of a _____ .

11. _____

12. That rate of interest that equates the demand for money with the supply of money is called the _____ .

12. _____

13. The mathematical statement that $MV = PQ$ is called the _____ .

13. _____

14. Structural forces in the economy establish the _____ in the labor market.

14. _____

15. To be effective in achieving price and employment goals, monetary policy must influence the level of _____ .

15. _____

True or False: *Circle your choice.*

T F 1. People who hold idle money balances incur no costs.

T F 2. Money held for the purpose of making normal expenditures is called the transactions demand.

T F 3. The transactions demand for money depends primarily on the level of GDP.

T F 4. The assumption of a natural rate of unemployment implies that M is stable in the equation of exchange.

T F 5. Monetarists believe an increase in government spending will lead to the "crowding out" of an equal amount of private spending.

T F 6. The speculative demand for money depends on anticipated changes in bond prices.

T F 7.   The speculative demand curve for money flattens out when the interest rate is very low.

T F 8.   Keynes believed that fiscal policy to eliminate a recession should lower V.

T F 9.   If the interest rate in the money market is below equilibrium, bond prices will fall when the market moves toward equilibrium.

T F 10. When the Fed increases the supply of securities (by selling in the open market), interest rates rise.

T F 11. When the Fed buys securities, causing interest rates to fall, investment spending increases, thus expanding GDP.

T F 12. If the interest rate is in the liquidity-trap range, monetary policy is ineffective.

T F 13. Whether restrictive monetary policy is effective or not depends on its ability to reduce aggregate spending.

T F 14. If you lend $100 at the beginning of the year at 8 percent and prices are constant, at the end of the year you'll have $108 of real purchasing power.

T F 15. To find the real rate of return on an investment, always subtract the rate of inflation from the nominal interest rate.

T F 16. If velocity grows at 3 percent per year, inflation is 3 percent per year, and the money supply grows at 3 percent per year, real GDP does not grow at all.

T F 17. Monetarists argue that fiscal policy is ineffective in changing the level of aggregate spending.

T F 18. The monetarist proposition that "only money matters" rests on the assumption that velocity (V) is constant.

T F 19. From the monetarist point of view, reducing taxes merely "crowds out" an equivalent amount of private spending when the proceeds are spent.

T F 20. Monetarists feel the Fed should control interest rates; Keynesians feel the Fed should control the money supply.

T F 21. Consumer expectations regarding future price levels are important in determining the effectiveness of monetary policy.

T F 22. The natural rate of unemployment used to be 4 percent but has been raised to 6 percent.

T F 23. Keynesians view high interest rates as a symptom of inflation, not a cure.

T F 24. If the real interest rate is 9 percent and anticipated inflation falls from 4 percent to 2 percent, the nominal interest rate would decline from 13 percent to 9 percent.

Multiple Choice: *Select the correct answer.*

_____ 1. In the Keynesian model, the effectiveness of monetary policy depends on which of the following?
   (a)   The Fed's ability to influence bond prices.
   (b)   The sensitivity of interest rates to changes in the money supply.
   (c)   The sensitivity of investment spending to changes in interest rates.
   (d)   All of the above.

_____ 2. The measure on the y-axis is the:
   (a)   Interest rate for money supply and demand curves.
   (b)   Interest rate for investment demand and supply curves.
   (c)   Average price for aggregate demand and supply curves.
   (d)   All of the above.

_____ 3. Which of the following is thought to be *most* sensitive to changes in the rate of interest?
   (a)   The transactions demand for money.
   (b)   The speculative demand for money.
   (c)   The precautionary demand for money.
   (d)   Aggregate supply.

_____ 4. Which of the following positions can be attributed to the Monetarists?
   (a)   "Only money matters."
   (b)   "Velocity is constant."
   (c)   "Government expenditures crowd out private expenditures."
   (d)   All of the above are monetarist positions.

_____ 5. Those who hold idle balances for speculative purposes are willing to incur the opportunity costs of doing so because they expect:
   (a)   Interest rates are going to rise.
   (b)   Bond yields are going to fall.
   (c)   Bond prices are going to rise.
   (d)   All of the above.

_____ 6. Precautionary balances are held:
   (a)   To take advantage of future changes in bond prices.
   (b)   To make anticipated expenditures.
   (c)   To handle emergencies.
   (d)   To do none of the above.

_____ 7. If the supply curve of money is vertical, what should happen to the equilibrium interest rate and equilibrium quantity of money as a result of a recession, *ceteris paribus*?
   (a)   Equilibrium interest rate should go up.
   (b)   Equilibrium interest rate should go down, but equilibrium quantity would remain unchanged.
   (c)   Both equilibrium interest rate and equilibrium quantity should go up.
   (d)   Equilibrium interest rate should go down, and equilibrium quantity should go up.

_____ 8. Which of the following is a series of events used by Keynesians to describe the steps by which expansionary monetary policy works in the short run?
   (a)   Increase in M, decrease in interest rate, increase in I.
   (b)   Decrease in interest rate, increase in M, increase in I.
   (c)   Increase in M, decrease in I, decrease in interest rate.
   (d)   Increase in M, increase in interest rate, increase in I.

9. By adding together the speculative, transactions, and precautionary demands for money, one can obtain:
   (a) The market demand curve for money.
   (b) The Keynesian liquidity trap.
   (c) The monetarist demand-for-money curve.
   (d) None of the above.

10. When the money market is in equilibrium in the liquidity trap:
    (a) The demand for money is perfectly insensitive to interest rates.
    (b) An increase in the money supply does not affect interest rates.
    (c) There is no speculative demand for money.
    (d) Investment spending falls to zero.

11. Monetarists believe that increased taxes:
    (a) Lower interest rates.
    (b) Crowd out investment.
    (c) Raise the deficit.
    (d) Lower real output.

12. There is an inverse relationship between the quantity of money demanded and:
    (a) The price of money.
    (b) The interest rate.
    (c) The opportunity cost of owning money.
    (d) All of the above.

13. Equilibrium in the market for money is found where:
    (a) The quantity of money demanded equals the quantity of money supplied.
    (b) Planned saving equals planned investment.
    (c) Aggregate spending equals full-employment output.
    (d) Leakages equal injections.

14. When the Fed increases the money supply, *ceteris paribus*, in an economy with a multiplier of 10, and both the money demand curve and investment demand curve are downward-sloping:
    (a) The rate of investment spending increases.
    (b) Consumer spending increases.
    (c) Saving increases.
    (d) All of the above.

15. Monetary policy will be most effective if:
    (a) The demand curve for money is horizontal and the investment demand curve is downward-sloping.
    (b) The demand curve for money is downward-sloping but the investment demand curve is vertical.
    (c) The demand curve for money and the investment demand curve are downward-sloping, but neither is vertical nor horizontal.
    (d) The demand curve for money and the investment demand curve are vertical or both curves are horizontal.

16. What should happen to the equilibrium interest rate and the corresponding rate of investment if the Fed lowers the minimum reserve ratio?
    (a) Equilibrium interest rate and the rate of investment should both go up.
    (b) Equilibrium interest rate should go up, and the rate of investment should go down.
    (c) Equilibrium interest rate should go down, and the rate of investment should go up.
    (d) Equilibrium interest rate and the rate of investment should both go down.

_____ 17. In a graph showing aggregate demand and aggregate supply, what should happen to the equilibrium price level and rate of output if the Fed raises the minimum reserve ratio?
   (a)   Equilibrium price level and rate of output should both go down.
   (b)   Equilibrium price level should go down, and equilibrium rate of output should go up.
   (c)   Equilibrium price level should go up, and equilibrium rate of output should go down.
   (d)   Equilibrium price level and rate of output should both go up.

_____ 18. Which of the following would be most consistent with the direction of changes which should result when the Fed lowers the discount rate, _ceteris paribus?_
   (a)   Slower inflation (or more deflation) and more unemployment.
   (b)   Slower inflation (or more deflation) and a movement toward full employment.
   (c)   Greater inflation and a movement toward full employment.
   (d)   Greater stagflation (higher inflation and higher unemployment).

_____ 19. Suppose the minimum reserve ratio is 0.20 and there are no excess reserves. If the government sells $20 billion worth of government securities in the open market, then, for the total banking system, there will be:
   (a)   A $100 billion increase in lending capacity.
   (b)   A $100 billion decrease in lending capacity.
   (c)   A $200 billion increase in reserves.
   (d)   A $200 billion decrease in reserves.

_____ 20. If the nominal interest rate is 8 percent and anticipated inflation falls from 8 percent to 4 percent, the real interest rate would change from:
   (a)   16 to 12 percent.
   (b)   8 to 4 percent.
   (c)   Zero to -4 percent.
   (d)   Zero to 4 percent.

_____ 21. As a result of Fed sales of securities in its open-market operations, there should be:
   (a)   A greater AD shortfall or a greater excess AD.
   (b)   A greater AD shortfall or a smaller excess AD.
   (c)   A smaller AD shortfall or a greater excess AD.
   (d)   A smaller AD shortfall or a smaller excess AD.

_____ 22. The effectiveness of restrictive monetary policy will be lessened by the existence of:
   (a)   High real rates of interest.
   (b)   High nominal rates of interest.
   (c)   Low real rates of interest.
   (d)   Low nominal rates of interest.

_____ 23. Which of the following impacts characterizes monetary policy?
   (a)   Uneven effects across various industries and governments.
   (b)   No effect on government spending, but across-the-board effects on industries and households.
   (c)   No effect on consumption.
   (d)   No generalizations can be made about the influence of monetary policy.

_____ 24. The equation of exchange can be stated in which of the following ways?
   (a) $MV = PQ$.
   (b) $P = (MV)/Q$.
   (c) $V = (PQ)/M$.
   (d)   All of the above.

_____ 25. Monetarists argue that:
  (a) M is constant.
  (b) V is constant.
  (c) P is constant.
  (d) Q is constant.

_____ 26. Which of the following *most* accurately describes the monetarist view on the effectiveness of economic policy tools?
  (a) Fiscal policy is very powerful.
  (b) Fiscal policy and monetary policy are very effective.
  (c) Monetary policy is very powerful.
  (d) Wage and price controls are more effective than monetary policy.

_____ 27. The Keynesian counterargument to monetarism is based largely on which of the following ideas?
  (a) The Fed can alter interest rates and therefore economic activity.
  (b) "Crowding out," even if it did occur, would not be important because people would be working.
  (c) Velocity is certainly not constant and may even be quite volatile.
  (d) All of the above are Keynesian arguments.

_____ 28. Which of the following is the most defensible conclusion from examining the history of V through time?
  (a) Over short periods velocity seems constant, but over long periods it is volatile.
  (b) Over long and short periods velocity seems volatile.
  (c) Velocity seems unstable over short periods but fairly stable over long periods.
  (d) Over both long and short periods, velocity is stable.

_____ 29. The Fed adopted fixed money-supply targets as a policy goal from 1979 to 1982. The Fed abandoned the money-supply targets:
  (a) Because interest rates rose to undesired levels.
  (b) Because the economy went into a deep recession.
  (c) Because it wanted greater flexibility in policy-making.
  (d) For all of the above reasons.

_____ 30. Which of the following groupings contains a term which does not belong?
  (a) Speculative, precautionary, transactions.
  (b) Money, prices, income velocity of money.
  (c) Liquidity trap, expectations, inelastic investment demand.
  (d) Increase in money supply, reduction in interest rate, increase in aggregate spending.

Problems and Applications

Exercise 1

The Keynesian mechanism for the influence of money on aggregate demand is illustrated here, with practice in using money supply and demand, investment demand, and aggregate supply and demand curves. The exercise should help tie these tools together with the equation of exchange, the consumption function, the multiplier, full employment, and macro equilibrium. It will be particularly useful before you try the third problem in the text for Chapter 14.

1. Suppose conditions in the money market are as indicated in Table 14.1a. Plot the demand and supply of money in Figure 14.1a. The demand curve should pass through point *A*. Label the curves *D* and S_1.

Table 14.1a
Money demand and supply

Interest rate (percent)	Total demand for money (billions of dollars)	Supply of money (billions of dollars)
0	$160	$110
1	150	110
2	140	110
3	130	110
4	120	110
5	110	110
6	100	110

Figure 14.1a
Money Demand and Supply Curves

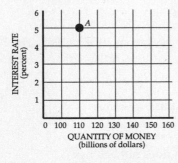

Figure 14.1b
Investment Demand Curves

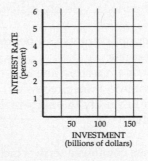

Figure 14.1c
Alternate Aggregate Demand Curves

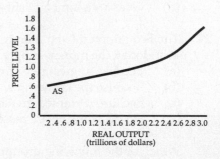

2. The equilibrium rate of interest in Figure 14.1a is _____ percent. The equilibrium quantity of money is _____ .

3. Investment demand is presented in Table 14.1b. Draw the corresponding investment demand curve in Figure 14.1b. Label the point with an (*A*) represents the quantity of investment demanded at the equilibrium interest rate.

Table 14.1b
Investment demand

Interest rate (percent)	Investment Quantity Demanded ($billions per year)
5	50
4	100
3	150

272

4. Suppose the Fed increases the money supply by $10 billion. In Figure 14.1a, draw the new money supply curve and label it *S2*. In Figure 14.1b label the new point that with a (*B*) that represents the quantity of investment goods demanded at the new money supply.

5. Suppose the economy is characterized by the consumption function $C = \$20$ billion + $0.95 \times Y$ and government expenditure is $30 billion.
    (a) The *MPC* is _____ .
    (b) The multiplier is _____.
    (c) Fill in columns 2-4 of Table 14.1c for the two levels of money supply in column 1. To do this, remember that you must solve for equilibrium expenditure (income) with the following equation: $Y = C + I + G$ (see the answer at the end of this chapter if you need a further hint).

Table 14.1c
Money impact on aggregate demand

Money Supply ($billions) (1)	Equilibrium interest rate (percent) (2)	Quantity of Investment ($billions) (3)	Equilibrium Spending ($trillions) (4)	Aggregate Demand Curve (AD#1, AD#2, AD#3, AD#4) (5)	Money Velocity (V) (6)
$110	_____	_____	_____	_____	_____
$120	_____	_____	_____	_____	_____

6. If full-employment real output is $2.5 trillion, the aggregate demand curve labeled _____ in Figure 14.1c will achieve full employment at macro-equilibrium.
    (a) The expenditure at this full-employment macro equilibrium would be _____ . (*Hint*: Expenditure equals price times real output)
    (b) Place the label of the aggregate demand curve that achieves full employment at the macro equilibrium in the appropriate row of column 5 of Table 14.1c (*Hint*: Look at the expenditure level, not real output.)
    (c) The money supply which achieves this macro equilibrium would be _____ .

7. Which of the remaining aggregate demand curves in Figure 14.1c would be achieved if the money supply set by the Fed were $110 billion? _____

8. Complete Table 14.1c (column 6) for the money velocity, *V*, using the equation of exchange and the information in the other columns of the table. The increased money supply has:
    (a) Increased velocity and raised expenditures more than proportionately to the money supply as predicted by Keynesians.
    (b) Left velocity unchanged and raised only prices, as predicted by the Monetarists.
    (c) Been ineffective because investment is insensitive to the interest rate and the interest rate is insensitive to the money supply.
    (d) None of the above.

9. The AD (shortfall, excess) at a money supply of $110 billion is _____ . Show this on Figure 14.1c. The AD gap is _____ . Also show this on the graph.

10. If aggregate supply were fixed (vertical) at the output level of $2.0 trillion, what would price have been if the money supply were raised from $110 to $120 billion? _____

11. Why is it that a $10 billion increase in the money supply can result in a $.50 trillion increase in real output?

Exercise 2

This exercise will help you check your understanding of how monetary and fiscal policy affect the economy.

1. Consider each of the statements in Table 14.2. Decide whether you think each was made by a Monetarist or a Keynesian, and place a check in the appropriate column. If you have difficulty, reread Table 14.1 and 14.2 in the text (pp. 311-312).

Table 14.2
Comparing Keynesian and monetarist views on monetary policy

	Monetarist	Keynesian
1. An increase in government spending will raise total spending.	_____	_____
2. A reduction in taxes will leave real output unaffected.	_____	_____
3. Real interest rates are determined by real growth.	_____	_____
4. Prices may be affected by increases in G or reductions in T.	_____	_____
5. Changes in the money supply definitely affect both the price level and aggregate spending.	_____	_____
6. Changes in M definitely affect changes in the normal interest rate.	_____	_____
7. Changes in M may cause changes in V and Q.	_____	_____
8. Changes in M definitely cannot lower the unemployment rate.	_____	_____
9. The liquidity trap may prevent the nominal interest rate from falling.	_____	_____
10. Monetary and fiscal policy must be used together to stabilize aggregate demand.	_____	_____

Exercise 3

The following exercise provides further practice in the relationship between monetary policy and changes in aggregate demand.

Table 14.3
Money supply and demand for money

Nominal interest rate (% per year)	Money demand ($ billions)	Supply of money ($ billions)
2	320	240
4	280	240
6	240	240
8	200	240

On the basis of Table 14.3, answer the indicated questions. Assume for every 1 percentage point decline in the interest rate, aggregate spending shifts upward by $20 billion. Also assume the marginal propensity to consume is 0.25.

1. In Table 14.3, the equilibrium interest rate is _____ percent per year.
2. If the interest rate in Table 14.3 is 8 percent, then there is a (surplus, shortage) of money, and the interest rate will (rise, fall, remain constant).
3. If the anticipated inflation rate is 4 percent, then at the equilibrium nominal interest rate in Table 14.3, the real interest rate will be _____ percent per year.
4. If the real rate of interest is negative then, *ceteris paribus*:
   (a) The nominal interest rate is negative.
   (b) Monetary policy is tight.
   (c) The inflation rate is negative.
   (d) It pays to borrow.

5. Suppose the Fed buys $8 billion worth of securities on the open market and that the reserve requirement is 0.2. If the money supply expands to its maximum potential then the new equilibrium rate of interest in Table 14.3 would be, *ceteris paribus*, _____ percent per year.
6. The change in the equilibrium interest rate in Table 14.3 as a result of the Fed's purchase of $8 billion worth of securities would be _____ percentage points.
7. If every 1 percentage point decline in the interest rate causes investment to increase by $20 billion and if the marginal propensity to consume is 0.25, then a 3 percentage point change in the interest rate would cause income to change by _____ .

Exercise 4

The following exercise shows how to use supply and demand curves to analyze money-market outcomes. You will observe the connection between the supply of money, the demand for money, and interest rates. If your professor makes a media assignment from the *Instructor's Manual*, this exercise will help you analyze articles to find changes in money supply and demand.

For each of the following nine statements decide what shift would occur in the money market. Choose the letter of the diagram in Figure 14.2 that matches the shift. Then indicate with an arrow whether the equilibrium interest rate and equilibrium quantity of money should rise (⇑) or fall (⇓) as a result of the shift you identified.

Figure 14.2
Money market

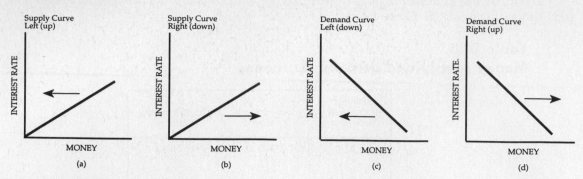

Keep in mind that the *demand* for money changes as people receive larger incomes, as the velocity of money changes, and as the inflation rate changes. The *supply* of money is determined by the actions of the Federal Reserve System, the willingness of the financial system to make loans, and individual perceptions of the future course of the economy. Also, the interest rate can be considered the price of money. It shows the additional payment required in the future when one borrows in the present.

	Shift (Figure 14.2 diagram letter)	Equilibrium interest rate	Equilibrium quantity of money
1. Economists have discussed and have tried to verify the existence of a "political business cycle" in which the Federal Reserve tries to prevent excessive unemployment in an election year. What is the effect of such actions by the Fed?			
2. In 1972, an election year, such an expansion of the money supply did occur and contributed to a very high rate of inflation. What policies should the Fed chairman have proposed to curb the inflation rate?			
3. In 1974, OPEC raised the price of oil precipitously. A recession occurred in the United States.			
4. The dollar declined in value relative to other currencies. Foreigners were worried about holding dollars because of the high U.S. inflation rate and tried to obtain West German marks, gold, and so on, to hold as substitutes for the dollar.			

	Shift (Figure 14.2 diagram letter)	Equilibrium interest rate	Equilibrium quantity of money
5. During the 1974-75 recession, the U.S. banking system was shocked as foreign debts became difficult to collect, real estate investments went bad, and the oil market collapsed. Fear of further collapses made bankers less willing to lend.	_____	_____	_____
6. The new chairman of the Federal Reserve Board of Governors applied a "credit crunch" to the economy to prevent unnecessary borrowing and to slow down the double-digit rate of inflation.	_____	_____	_____
7. The economy entered a recession in 1980 and again in 1990-91.	_____	_____	_____
8. The Reagan administration found itself running huge deficits that had to be financed with money-supply increases.	_____	_____	_____
9. Greenspan tightens monetary policy through open-market operations.	_____	_____	_____

Exercise 5

The following exercise shows how to use supply and demand curves to analyze what happens in the bond market. It also demonstrates how the bond market is related to deficits, debt, the interest rate, and monetary policy.

In each of the circumstances below, analyze the impact and decide what would happen in the market for bonds. Match the letter of the appropriate diagram in Figure 14.3 to each of the ten events. Then for each circumstance, indicate with an arrow whether the equilibrium price of bonds in the United States will rise (⇑) or fall (⇓). Do the same for interest rates and the equilibrium quantity of bonds.

Figure 14.3
Shifts of the supply and demand curves for bonds

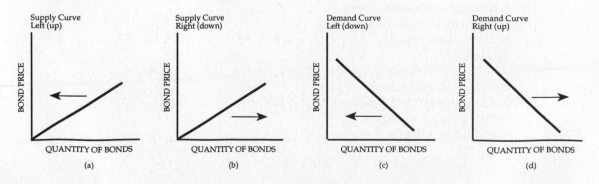

Remember that the demand for bonds will increase as people receive larger incomes, desire greater wealth, or try to increase their savings. The supply of bonds is determined by government (including the Fed in open-market operations) and private firms as they attempt to increase or decrease their debts. Keep in mind also that interest rates move in the direction opposite to that of bond prices (remember Exercise 4 of Chapter 13).

	Shift (Figure 14.3 diagram letters)	Equilibrium price of bonds	Interest rates	Equilibrium quantity of bonds
1. The Clinton administration is running large federal deficits that must be financed with new debt.	_____	_____	_____	_____
2. Foreigners view the United States as a safe haven to park their unused cash. There is a sudden shift in preferences toward holding debt of the U.S. government and U.S. corporations.	_____	_____	_____	_____
3. The auto industry must make massive purchases of new technology to compete with the Japanese. It (the auto industry) enters the capital markets to "float" their new debt.	_____	_____	_____	_____
4. A major nuclear facility is not completed and the bonds used to finance it become worthless. Bondholders suddenly flee from the bond market.	_____	_____	_____	_____
5. Foreign interest rates fall, but American rates remain the same. Foreign investors switch their preferences from foreign debt to American debt to earn a higher return.	_____	_____	_____	_____
6. A predicted recession scares firms away from financing and installing new capital equipment.	_____	_____	_____	_____
7. The stock market takes a sudden plunge. Anticipating a further plunge, investors sell stock and buy bonds.	_____	_____	_____	_____

	Shift (Figure 14.3 diagram letters)	Equilibrium price of bonds	Interest rates	Equilibrium quantity of bonds
8. There is a sudden surge in the inflation rate. Anticipating higher interest rates, investors steer clear of the bond market.	_____	_____	_____	_____
9. The United States issues bonds with smaller denominations, which makes it possible for a larger number of buyers to hold U.S. securities.	_____	_____	_____	_____
10. Greenspan tightens monetary policy through open-market operations.	_____	_____	_____	_____

Exercise 6

The media often feature articles about changes in government policies that affect the money supply or about events that change the demand for money. This exercise will use one of the articles in the text to show the kind of information to look for. If your professor makes a newspaper assignment from the *Instructor's Manual*, this exercise will provide an example of how to do it.

Reread the In the News article on page 307 in Chapter 14 entitled "Money Is Free!" from the *Wall Street Journal*. Then answer the following questions.

1. Which of the four diagrams in Figure 14.2 best represents what the author wants the Fed to do?

2. What passage (no more than a sentence) specifically indicates what the author suggests should be done to the money supply?

3. What passage indicates the determinant of the recommended change in money supply or money demand?

4. What single sentence indicates the effect on interest rates that results from the shift of supply or demand?

Exercise 7

This exercise shows you how closely interest rates and the inflation rate are related to each other.

1. On the back inside cover of the text you will find data on the prime interest rate. Graph the prime interest rate and the Consumer Price Index in Figure 14.4. Figure 14.4 shows time on the horizontal axis (x-axis) from 1970 to 1992 and percentage changes on the vertical axis (y-axis).

Figure 14.4
Inflation and interest rates, 1970-92

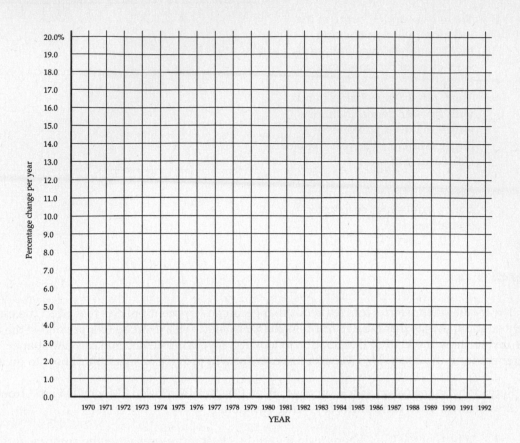

2. The two indexes are (directly, inversely) related to each other.

3. The difference between the interest rate and the inflation rate is a measure of which of the Terms to Remember at the end of Chapter 14?

4. Which series usually is highest? _____

5. In which years is the inflation rate above the prime interest rate? _____

6. Are borrowers or lenders favored when the inflation rate is above the prime interest rate? _____Why? _____
_____

Common Errors

The first statement in each "common error" below is incorrect. Each incorrect statement is followed by a corrected version and an explanation.

1. When the interest rate goes down, the demand for money increases. WRONG!

    When the interest rate goes down, the quantity of money demanded increases. RIGHT!

    Don't fail to distinguish between a change in demand and a change in quantity demanded. Remember that each demand schedule (speculative, transactions, precautionary) is drawn on the assumption of *ceteris paribus*. Unless there is a change in one of the things held constant (e.g., expectations), there will be no change in demand when the interest rate falls, only a change in quantity demanded.

2. High nominal rates of interest mean high real rates of interest. WRONG!

    High nominal interest rates and high real interest rates do not necessarily coincide. RIGHT!

    High nominal interest rates and high real interest rates will coincide only if the average level of prices is not changing rapidly enough to offset the differential. For example, if the nominal rate is 10 percent and prices are rising at 10 percent, the real rate of interest is zero.

3. Monetary policy is easy to determine and to administer. WRONG!

    Monetary policy is difficult to determine and to administer. RIGHT!

    One could easily get the idea that monetary policy is easy to administer and that the Fed always knows the rate at which the money supply should grow. This is not so. Many variables intervene to make monetary policy difficult to prescribe and implement. Such variables include timing and the duration of a given policy, unanticipated events on the fiscal side, and problems abroad. The Fed's policymakers analyze the data available and do the best they can to achieve a given objective, which often involves compromises. The process is much more difficult than turning a printing press on and off.

•ANSWERS•

Key-Term Review

1. interest rate
2. demand for money
3. real rate of interest
4. income velocity of money (V)
5. crowding out
6. portfolio decision
7. transactions demand for money
8. precautionary demand for money
9. speculative demand for money
10. monetary policy
11. liquidity trap
12. equilibrium rate of interest
13. equation of exchange
14. natural rate of unemployment
15. aggregate demand

True or False

1.	F	5.	T	9.	T	13.	T	17.	T	21.	T
2.	T	6.	T	10.	T	14.	T	18.	T	22.	F
3.	T	7.	T	11.	T	15.	T	19.	F	23.	F
4.	F	8.	F	12.	T	16.	F	20.	F	24.	F

Multiple Choice

1.	d	6.	c	11.	a	16.	c	21.	b	26.	c
2.	d	7.	b	12.	d	17.	a	22.	c	27.	c
3.	b	8.	a	13.	a	18.	c	23.	a	28.	c
4.	d	9.	a	14.	d	19.	b	24.	d	29.	d
5.	a	10.	b	15.	c	20.	d	25.	b	30.	c

Problems and Applications

Exercise 1

Figure 14.1a Answer   Figure 14.1b Answer   Figure 14.1c Answer

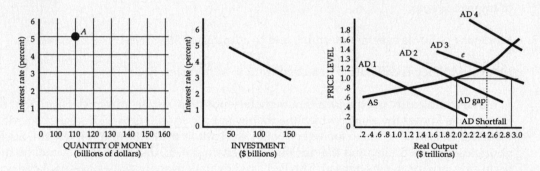

1. See Figure 14.1a Answer.

2. 5; $110 billion

3. See Figure 14.1b Answer.

4. See Figure 14.1a Answer and Figure 14.1b Answer above.

5. (a) *MPC* = 0.95 from the consumption function.
    (b) The multiplier equals $1/(1 - MPC) = 1/(1 - .95) = 20$.
    (c) See Table 14.1c Answer, columns 2-4., With substitution $Y = C + I + G$ becomes $Y = (20 + 0.95 \times Y) + I + 30$. Manipulating the Y term to one side of the equation provides the solution, $Y = (20 + 30 + I)/.05$, which goes into column 4 for different levels of I (found in column 3).

Table 14.1c Answer

Money supply (billions of dollars) (1)	Equilibrium interest rate (percent) (2)	Quantity of investment (billions of dollars) (3)	Equilibrium spending (trillions of dollars) (4)	Aggregate demand curve (5)	Money velocity (V) (6)
$110	5%	$ 50	$2.0	AD_2	18.2 [=(2)(1)/(0.11)]
$120	4	100	3.0	AD_3	25.0 [=(2.5)(1.2)/(0.12)]

6. AD_3
   - (a) $3.0 trillion (= $2.5 trillion x 1.2)
   - (b) See Table 14.1c Answer, column 5.
   - (c) $120 billion.

7. AD_2, because the expenditure is $2.0 trillion which is the same as the expenditure at macro equilibrium for AD_2 (= P x Q = 1.0 x $2.0 trillion).

8. See Table 14.1c Answer, column 6.
   - (d) Column 1 contains the amount of money and column 4 contains the amount of spending = GDP = price x real output. Solving for velocity, V, from the equation of exchange gives: $V = P$ x Q/M. The result is shown in column 6 of Figure 14.1c. The velocity increases from 18.2 to 25. The slope of the aggregate supply curve is inconsistent with the monetarist (who believe there is a vertical aggregate supply curve) and with the Keynesian (a flat AS curve up to full employment) assumptions.

9. shortfall; $0.9 trillion (= $2.9 - $2.0 trillion at a price of 1.0); $0.5 trillion (= $2.5 - $2.0 trillion)
   See Figure 14.1c Answer, AD shortfall and AD gap.

10. about 1.35 (see point e in Figure 14.1c)

11. Interest rates are highly sensitive to the money supply in Figure 14.1a. Investment is highly sensitive to interest rates, as indicated by the very flat investment demand curve in Figure 14.1b. Then the multiplier (= 20) takes that change in investment and multiplies it enormously. If any one of these assumptions were wrong, the effect would be much smaller.

Exercise 2

1. **Table 14.2 Answer**

	Monetarist	Keynesian
1.		x
2.	x	
3.	x	
4.		x
5.	x	
6.	x	
7.		x
8.	x	
9.		x
10.		x

Exercise 3

1. 6
2. surplus, fall
3. 2
4. d
5. 4
6. -2
7. $240 billion

Exercise 4

Type of shift (Figure 14.2 diagram letter)		Equilibrium interest rate	Equilibrium quantity of money
1.	b	⇓	⇑
2.	a	⇑	⇓
3.	c	⇓	⇓
4.	c	⇓	⇓
5.	a	⇑	⇓
6.	a	⇑	⇓
7.	c	⇓	⇓
8.	b	⇓	⇑
9.	a	⇑	⇓

Exercise 5

Shift (Figure 14.3 diagram letter)		Equilibrium price of bonds	Interest rates	Equilibrium quantity of bonds
1.	b	⇓	⇑	⇑
2.	d	⇑	⇓	⇑
3.	b	⇓	⇑	⇑
4.	?			
5.	d	⇑	⇓	⇑
6.	a	⇑	⇓	⇓
7.	d	⇑	⇓	⇑
8.	c	⇓	⇑	⇓
9.	d	⇑	⇓	⇑
10.	b	⇓	⇑	⇑

Exercise 6

1. a (tighten the money supply)

2. "The longer the Fed delays in starting to curb money growth . . ." suggests the author's opinion of what should be done.

3. This passage is indicative: "In particular, the observation ought to be of interest to the Federal Reserve's Open Market Committee, which meets today to set money growth

targets. . ." The *determinant* is the Federal Reserve System in its role of specifying the supply of money targets and therefore its purchases or sales of bonds.

4. "That is why interest rates will not go down, nor the dollar recover meaningfully, until inflation is reduced." By tightening the money supply, the Fed should reduce inflation, which would eventually allow the interest rate to fall. The author implicitly assumes the reader understands these relationships.

Exercise 7

1. **Figure 14.4 Answer**

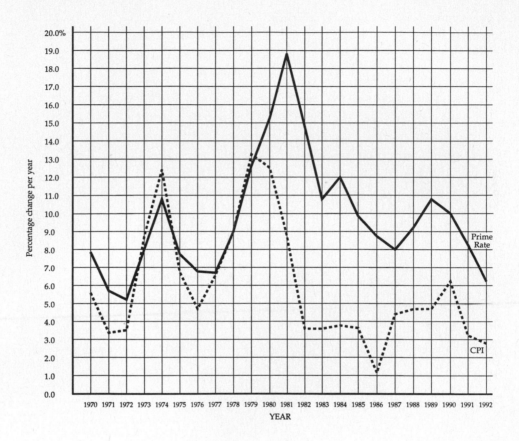

2. directly

3. real rate of interest

4. prime interest rate.

5. 1973, 1974, and 1979

6. Borrowers are favored because the value of their debt is less in real terms as a result of inflation even after their interest payments are computed. They actually make money from borrowing!

CHAPTER 15

Supply–Side Policies

Quick Review

This chapter identifies some supply-side policy options which can be used to affect macro outcomes by examining two questions:

- How does the aggregate supply curve affect macro outcomes?
- How can the aggregate supply curve be shifted?

Again we rely on the equation of exchange;
$$MV = PQ$$
where M = the quantity of money
V = velocity of circulation
P = average price of goods
Q = goods sold in a period

The demand-side levers are on the left-hand side of the equation. The responses of the economy to demand side policies depend on the slope of the aggregate supply curve. Monetarists view the aggregate supply as vertical at the natural rate of unemployment; a strict Keynesian view is that it is flat until full employment is reached. The consensus view accepts a rather smooth, upward-sloping curve which turns vertical at full employment.

It is obvious that an output–price level tradeoff exists with the consensus view in cases where either stimulus or restraint is being applied. This is made visual by the so-called Phillips curve, which plots the unemployment rate against the rate of change in price level. Evidence shows that during the 1970s, the Phillips curve shifted to the right, indicating a worsening of the tradeoff. The economy thus suffered from stagflation—simultaneous and unacceptable levels of inflation and unemployment. Fortunately, this was reversed in the mid 1980s when both measures fell.

On the other hand, it is obvious that a shift in the aggregate supply curve provides improvement in employment (and output), while leading to a reduction in the price level. The question then is how to trigger the desired shift from the supply side. Here are some options:
- Supply-side tax cuts.
- Deregulation.
- Elimination of structural bottlenecks.
- Wage–price controls.

Each type of policy change has been used at one time or another to combat stagflation.

Supply-side tax cuts are incentive-based and work on the assumption that people and firms will produce more if they get to keep a larger fraction of what they earn. Keynesian demand-side tax cuts emphasize the spending that takes place when more of every dollar earned becomes disposable income. In both cases the marginal tax rate plays a pivotal role. Some have even gone so far as to suggest that tax cuts will cause such an increase in productivity that tax revenue (generated by increased output) might actually increase. This is the idea behind the Laffer curve.

Supply-siders favor tax cuts to provide incentives to encourage saving *and* investment, thus providing for long-term growth in capital stock. Human capital incentives are important too, as they emphasize the quality of the labor force and attack structural employment barriers, thus helping shift the aggregate supply curve to the right. Worker training, spending on education and affirmative-action programs, and the like, all have positive impact on the stock of human capital. Deregulation of both product and factor markets has provided a powerful stimulus to aggregate supply since the process began in the 1980s, because it eliminates barriers to the efficient employment of resources, thus reducing costs at every level of output. Finally, emphasis on infrastructure, which was somewhat taken for granted in this country, enhances aggregate supply by reducing costs in transportation, communication, and so on. Though still impressive by international standards, public investment fell during the 1970s and early 1980s. President Clinton has embraced many supply-side policies, including his proposed "Rebuild America Fund" for investment in the nation's infrastructure.

Learning Objectives

After reading Chapter 15 and doing the following exercises, you should:	True or false	Multiple choice	Problems and applications	Common errors	Pages in the text
1. Understand why the success of demand-side policies depends on the aggregate-supply response.	1, 2	1, 2, 4, 30	2		319-321
2. Understand the nature of the inflation–unemployment tradeoff and the Phillips curve.	5, 7, 9		1, 4	2	321-323, 356-357
3. Be aware of the implications of an upward-sloping aggregate supply curve for the use of demand-side policies.	1-4, 8, 10	2, 5, 11, 12	2, 4		322-323
4. Be able to describe why the Phillips curve might shift, using the AS-AD framework.	6	3, 6-10, 12, 29	1, 4		323-326
5. Understand the basic supply-side options for improving the inflation–unemployment tradeoff.		3, 6, 13			326
6. Understand why marginal tax rates affect work incentives, investment, and saving.	11-17	14-21, 31, 32	3	3	327-332
7. Be able to describe human capital and its relationship to structural unemployment.	20	13, 23, 24, 28, 31	2	1	333-334
8. Understand why deregulation of factor and product markets influences aggregate supply.	18-21	13, 22, 25, 26, 31	2		334-338
9. Understand the importance of maintaining infrastructure to aggregate supply.	19	27, 31			338-341

Key-Term Review

Review the following terms; if you are not sure of the meaning of any term, write out the definition and check it against the Glossary in the text.

aggregate supply
equation of exchange
human capital
infrastructure
investment
labor productivity
Laffer curve
marginal tax rate

Phillips curve
saving
stagflation
structural unemployment
tax elasticity of supply
tax rebate
transfer payments

Fill in the blank following each of the statements below with the appropriate term from the list above.

1. Students pursuing a college degree are investing in _____ .

1. _____

2. The relationship between the rate of inflation and the unemployment rate is shown in graphic form by a _____ .

2. _____

3. Highways, bridges, telephone systems, and the like, are part of a nation's _____ .

3. _____

4. Output per unit of labor time is known as _____ .

4. _____

5. A worsening of both inflation and unemployment is called _____ .

5. _____

6. The total quantity of final goods sellers are willing and able to sell at alternative price levels per unit of time, *ceteris paribus*, is _____ .

6. _____

7. Joblessness caused by lack of skills or a mismatch between skills and job locations is known as _____ .

7. _____

8. Disposable income minus consumption is called personal _____ .

8. _____

9. A lump-sum refund of taxes from the government is called a _____ .

9. _____

10. The tax rate imposed on the last dollar of income is the _____ .

10. _____

11. Expenditures on new plant and equipment constitute _____ .

11. _____

12. The relationship $MV = PQ$ is called the _____ .

12. _____

13. The ratio of the percentage change in quantity supplied to the percentage change in tax rates is called the _____ .

13. _____

14. The _____ shows the relationship between tax revenues and tax rates.

14. _____

15. Unemployment compensation and social security payments are good examples of _____ .

15. _____

True or False: *Circle your choice.*

T F 1. The tools of supply-side macroeconomic policy are on the right side of the equation of exchange.

T F 2. Below full employment, the Keynesians believe that increased aggregate demand raises output only, not prices (*P*).

T F 3. Fiscal- and monetary-policy initiatives designed to restrain the economy lead to higher prices and higher output.

T F 4. If the aggregate demand curve is upward-sloping, all leftward shifts of the aggregate supply curve increase both prices and output.

T F 5. The labels for axes found on the graph of the Phillips curve are the "prices" on the *x*-axis and "unemployment rate" on the *y*-axis.

T F 6. A leftward shift of the aggregate supply curve results in stagflation.

T F 7. The Phillips curve shows an inverse relationship between unemployment and the rate of inflation.

T F 8. The "misery index" is a measure of stagflation.

T F 9. A series of rightward shifts of aggregate demand defines the movements along a Phillips curve.

T F 10. The highest value of the misery index experienced in the United States was in 1980.

T F 11. The marginal tax rate can be found by dividing taxes by income.

T F 12. A marginal tax rate which falls with higher incomes indicates a progressive system of taxation.

T F 13. A progressive tax system provides more incentives to work than a system with constant marginal tax rates.

T F 14. From the supply-side perspective, tax rebates are a one-time windfall that have no effect on marginal tax rates.

T F 15. Arthur Laffer believed that tax cuts which lowered marginal tax rates would lead to higher tax revenues.

T F 16. A reduction in tax rates will yield larger tax revenues only if the absolute value of the tax elasticity of supply is greater than 1.0.

T F 17. Because of the paradox of thrift, supply-side economists encourage investment incentives, but not savings incentives.

T F 18. Fewer opportunities to gain work experience contribute to greater structural unemployment among women and minorities than in other groups.

T F 19. The percentage of GDP devoted to investment in infrastructure in the United States has been highly variable, but has trended upward since 1960.

T F 20. Affirmative action and transfer programs shift the aggregate supply curve upward when they require specific numbers of different groups to be used so that it is not possible to hire the best person for a given job.

T F 21. If the minimum wage is increased, the cost of production also increases.

Multiple Choice: *Select the correct answer.*

_____ 1. Monetarists argue that:
(a) Greater aggregate demand results in higher P, but not lower unemployment.
(b) V is constant.
(c) The aggregate supply curve is vertical.
(d) All of the above.

_____ 2. Attempts to lower the inflation rate through demand-side policies will aggravate current unemployment, as can be illustrated by a leftward shift of the:
(a) Phillips curve.
(b) Aggregate demand curve.
(c) Aggregate supply curve.
(d) Aggregate spending curve.

_____ 3. Lower unemployment and a lower inflation rate can best be achieved with:
(a) A rightward shift of the Phillips curve.
(b) A rightward shift of the aggregate supply curve.
(c) A rightward shift of the aggregate demand curve.
(d) None of the above.

_____ 4. According to the Keynesians, the aggregate supply curve is:
(a) First horizontal, then upward-sloping, and finally vertical.
(b) Vertical.
(c) Horizontal until full employment is reached, and then it becomes vertical.
(d) Upward-sloping.

_____ 5. Monetary and fiscal stimuli should result in:
(a) A leftward shift in aggregate demand.
(b) A movement down the Phillips curve toward a higher unemployment rate.
(c) A lower unemployment rate but a higher inflation rate.
(d) All of the above.

_____ 6. Supply-side policies are designed to achieve:
  (a)   A leftward shift in the Phillips curve.
  (b)   A rightward shift of the aggregate supply curve.
  (c)   Both a lower inflation rate and a lower unemployment rate.
  (d)   All of the above.

_____ 7. In contrast to Monetarists and Keynesians, the Supply-siders focus on policies designed to:
  (a)   Move leftward along the Phillips curve.
  (b)   Raise inflation and lower unemployment.
  (c)   Increase the left side of the equation of exchange.
  (d)   Shift the Phillips curve leftward.

_____ 8. After the 1960s, the United States experienced:
  (a)   An outward shift of the Phillips curve.
  (b)   Stagflation.
  (c)   Higher inflation and higher unemployment rates.
  (d)   All of the above.

_____ 9. Which of the following would be most likely to result in a rightward shift of the Phillips curve?
  (a)   Worker training programs.
  (b)   War in a fully-employed economy.
  (c)   Lower structural unemployment.
  (d)   Government deregulates industries, allowing greater competition.

_____ 10. In which of the following are the changes consistent?
  (a)   Stagflation, leftward shift of Phillips curve, rightward shift of aggregate supply curve.
  (b)   Lower inflation and higher unemployment rates, movement along the Phillips curve, leftward shift of aggregate demand curve.
  (c)   Higher inflation rate with higher output, rightward shift of the Phillips curve, rightward shift of aggregate demand curve.
  (d)   All of the above are consistent.

_____ 11. The misery index is a measure of:
  (a)   The sum of the x and y coordinates of the Phillips curve.
  (b)   A measure of the difference between full employment and actual employment.
  (c)   The ratio of the actual inflation rate to an average of past levels of inflation.
  (d)   A graph through time of the amount of variation in the GDP of the economy.

_____ 12. Which of the following leads unequivocally to a larger value of the misery index?
  (a)   A movement along the Phillips curve.
  (b)   An outward shift of the aggregate demand curve.
  (c)   Stagflation.
  (d)   A rightward shift of the money supply curve.

_____ 13. Which of the following policies is a supply-side lever?
  (a)   Tax incentives for saving.
  (b)   Deregulation.
  (c)   Human capital investment.
  (d)   All of the above.

14. Tax cuts serve the purpose from the:
    (a) Keynesian viewpoint to inject disposable income to stimulate the economy.
    (b) Supply-side viewpoint to increase work incentives.
    (c) Monetarist viewpoint to alter the mix of output in the economy.
    (d) All of the above.

15. Which of the following groups believes that tax cuts work through investment to achieve economic expansion?
    (a) Keynesians.
    (b) Monetarists.
    (c) Supply-siders.
    (d) All of the above.

16. Moving from a progressive tax system to a system of constant marginal tax rates would:
    (a) Result in a rightward shift of the Phillips curve.
    (b) Increase work incentives.
    (c) Shift the aggregate supply curve to the left.
    (d) Move the economy down the investment demand curve.

17. Which of the following is policy which was based on a supply-side justification?
    (a) The New Deal of Franklin Roosevelt.
    (b) World War II.
    (c) The Reagan tax cut of 1981-84.
    (d) The Clinton plan to reduce the deficit.

18. Suppose the government gives you the following formula for calculating your income tax: tax = $10,000 + 0.60 x (everything over $1,000). Then the marginal tax rate is:
    (a) 0.40.
    (b) 0.60.
    (c) $1,000.
    (d) $10,000.

19. If a new tax policy raises the tax rate 2 percent but causes the quantity to supplied to fall by 10%, the absolute value of the tax elasticity of supply is:
    (a) 0.5.
    (b) 2.
    (c) 5.
    (d) 10.

20. The Laffer curve implies that tax revenue:
    (a) Increases when taxes are cut and the absolute value of the tax elasticity of supply is greater than 1.
    (b) Is maximized when the absolute value of the tax elasticity of supply is equal to zero.
    (d) Is maximized when the absolute value of the tax elasticity of supply is equal to minus 1.
    (d) Is maximized when the absolute value of the tax elasticity of supply is equal to the price elasticity of supply.

21. Which of the following is a tax incentive for saving advocated by supply-side economists?
    (a) Investment tax credit.
    (b) Elimination of the capital gains tax.
    (c) IRAs.
    (d) All of the above.

_____ 22. Which of the following programs cause unemployment?
(a) Agricultural acreage restrictions by the government.
(b) The minimum wage.
(c) More regulation by the government.
(d) All of the above.

_____ 23. The method for eliminating structural unemployment when the economy is at full employment is through:
(a) Fiscal policy.
(b) Monetary policy.
(c) Human-resource programs.
(d) None of the above.

_____ 24. Labor productivity is measured as:
(a) The dollar value of output per unit of labor.
(b) The output per unit of labor.
(c) The hourly wage rate divided by output per labor hour.
(d) The dollar value of inputs per unit of output.

_____ 25. According to supply-side theory, which of the following would cause a rightward shift in the aggregate supply curve?
(a) Lifting trade restrictions.
(b) Increasing transfer payments to the unemployed.
(c) Eliminating government-funded training programs for the structurally unemployed.
(d) Eliminating job-search assistance.

_____ 26. Which of the following regulates the environment?
(a) FDA.
(b) OSHA.
(c) ICC.
(d) EPA.

_____ 27. Declining investment in infrastructure:
(a) Will lead to greater delays and higher opportunity costs.
(b) Has characterized the United States since 1960.
(c) Shifts both aggregate demand and aggregate supply.
(d) All of the above.

_____ 28. Which of the following is an example of investment in human capital?
(a) The Fair Labor Standards Act of 1938.
(b) The Surface Transportation Act of 1991.
(c) Head Start.
(d) FDA.

_____ 29. A World View article in the text reported: "Swedish officials say they will cut the top [marginal tax] rate from 72% to 50% by 1991." Even if the total tax revenues remained unchanged, the Swedish Phillips curve would be affected in which of the following ways?
(a) A movement along the Phillips curve toward more unemployment.
(b) A movement along the Phillips curve toward greater inflation.
(c) A rightward shift of the Phillips curve.
(d) A leftward shift of the Phillips curve.

Using the diagram in Figure 15.1 answer questions 30 and 31.

Figure 15.1

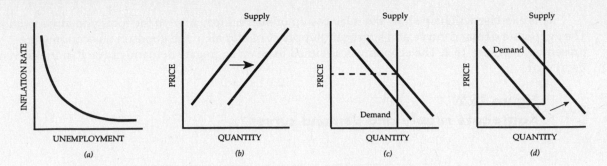

_____ 30. Choose the letter of the diagram in Figure 15.1 which Monetarists would be most willing to use to illustrate the effect of an increase in the quantity of money on the aggregate supply curve or aggregate demand curve.
   (a)   (b)   (c)   (d)

_____ 31. Choose the letter of the diagram that illustrates the effects of supply-side policies designed to increase the capacity of the economy.
   (a)   (b)   (c)   (d)

_____ 32. Which of the following groupings contains a term which does not belong?
   (a) Prohibitive range, absolute value of tax elasticity of supply greater than 1.0, lower tax rates mean more tax revenues.
   (b) Higher misery index, more stagflation, rightward shift in Phillips curve.
   (c) Supply-side tax cuts, deregulation, human capital investment.
   (d) Tax credits, elimination of capital gains tax, IRAs.

Problems and Applications

Exercise 1

This exercise will help show the relationship of the Phillips curve to the tools you already know. The aggregate demand curve and aggregate supply curve for all of the goods in an economy are presented in Figure 15.2. The economy is assumed to be on aggregate demand curve *B* in the current fiscal year.

Figure 15.2
Aggregate supply and demand curves

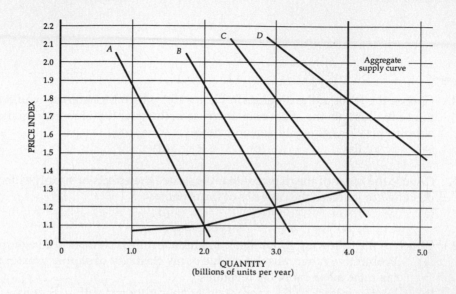

1. Four aggregate demand curves are shown in Figure 15.2, corresponding to four alternative government policies for the coming fiscal year.

   For the following four government policies, choose the aggregate demand curve in Figure 15.2 that best portrays the expected impact of each policy. Place the letter of your choice in the blank provided.

   _____ Money supply is expanded, taxes are cut, government increases its expenditures.
   _____ Government does nothing.
   _____ Government decides to balance the budget by reducing government spending and by raising taxes.
   _____ Government increases expenditures and cuts taxes.

2. Indicate the equilibrium price index and output for each policy in Table 15.1.

Table 15.1
Equilibrium prices for four government policies

Aggregate demand curve	A	B	C	D
Equilibrium price index	_____	_____	_____	_____
Equilibrium output	_____	_____	_____	_____

3. Suppose the price index is currently 1.2 at an equilibrium output of 3 billion units per year as shown by aggregate demand curve B in Figure 15.2. Compute the inflation rate under each of the four policies assuming the supply curve remains the same and place the answer for each policy in column 2 of Table 15.2. The formula is,

$$100 \times \frac{\text{equilibrium price index} - 1.2}{1.2}$$

Table 15.2
Inflation rates, equilibrium output, and unemployment rates under four government policies

Aggregate demand curve	Unemployment rate (1)	Percentage change in price (2)	Percentage change in output (3)
A	15%	_____	_____%
B	8%	_____	_____
C	5%	_____	_____
D	5%	_____	_____

4. Similarly for output, assume that the status quo is 3.0 billion units as shown by aggregate demand curve B. The percentage change in output for each policy is given by the formula

$$100 \times \frac{\text{equilibrium price index} - 3.0}{3.0}$$

Enter your answers for each policy in the appropriate blank of column 3 in Table 15.2.

5. Place a check under the appropriate column in Table 15.3 to indicate the aggregate demand curve that best achieves each of the macroeconomic outcomes listed.

Table 15.3
Macroeconomic o utcomes

(Place check mark)	Aggregate Demand Curve			
	1	2	3	4
Depression	____	____	____	____
Deflation	____	____	____	____
Highest unemployment	____	____	____	____
Recession	____	____	____	____
Zero inflation	____	____	____	____
Full employment	____	____	____	____
Price stability	____	____	____	____
Maximum output	____	____	____	____
Highest inflation	____	____	____	____

On the basis of your answer to the first question of the exercise, which matches government policy with each of the four aggregate demand curves in Figure 15.2, answer problems 6-10.

6. If the government tries to balance the budget, it will generate a (negative, zero, positive) economic growth rate with a (low, high, full-employment) unemployment rate and (deflation, constant prices, price stability, moderate inflation, hyperinflation).

7. If the government stimulates the economy only with fiscal policy, then it will generate a (negative, zero, positive) economic growth rate with a (low, high, full-employment) unemployment rate and (deflation, constant prices, price stability, moderate inflation, hyperinflation).

8. If the government stimulates the economy with both fiscal and monetary policy, then it will generate a (negative, zero, positive) economic growth rate with a (low, high, full-employment) unemployment rate and (deflation, constant prices, price stability, inflation, hyperinflation).

9. Full employment occurs between aggregate demand curve (a, b, c, d) and aggregate demand curve (a, b, c, d).

10. In Figure 15.3 graph the points that represent the data in columns 1 and 2 of Table 15.2 and then connect them with a curved line. What is this curve called? _____

Figure 15.3

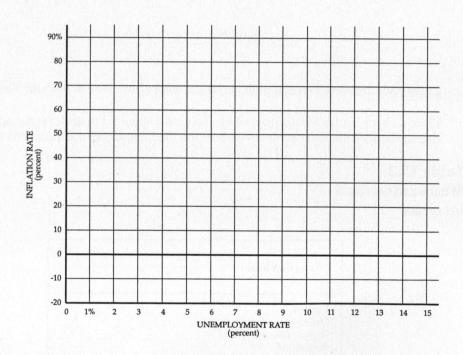

Exercise 2

The following exercise provides practice in shifts of the Phillips curve and the effects of monetary, fiscal, and supply-side policies.

1. Which of the following is the *best* indication that stagflation is occurring?
   - (a) Rising unemployment rate, falling inflation rate.
   - (b) Rising unemployment rate, rising inflation rate.
   - (c) Falling unemployment rate, falling inflation rate.
   - (d) Falling unemployment rate, rising inflation rate.

2. Stagflation is most likely occurring when there is:
   - (a) A movement up along the Phillips curve.
   - (b) A movement down along the Phillips curve.
   - (c) A shift outward of the Phillips curve to a new position.
   - (d) A shift of the Phillips curve to a new position closer to the origin.

Each of the events described in problems 3-9 results in a change involving the Phillips curve. Choose the diagram in Figure 15.4 that most likely represents the change that should occur.

Figure 15.4
Phillips curve

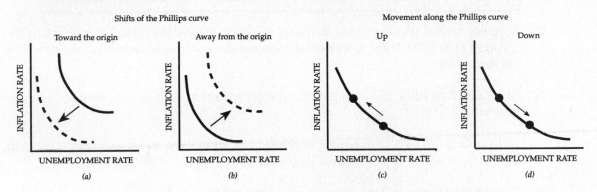

3. Labor unions make wage demands in excess of productivity, forcing businesses to raise prices and even forcing some businesses into bankruptcy.

4. Government safety restrictions cause cost increases to manufacturers, forcing some of them out of business and, consequently, causing prices to rise.

5. The economy is below full employment and prices are stable. The government begins to subsidize businesses that employ and train people who are otherwise hard to employ, *ceteris paribus*.

6. The government increases military spending above previous levels, creating new jobs. Since the economy is close to full employment, inflation worsens.

7. Producers decide to restrict production in order to increase profits by letting market prices rise.

8. The economy enters a recession and businesses try to unload excess inventories by lowering prices. This means fewer people are employed.

9. The government deregulates transportation industries, allowing more firms to enter. The increased competition lowers prices.

Exercise 3

Suppose taxpayers are required to pay a base tax of $400 plus 20 percent on any income over $1,000.

1. Compute the amount of taxes to be paid at the income levels in Table 15.4 by filling in columns 2, 3, and 4.

Table 15.4
Tax calculations

(1) Income ($ per year)	(2) Base Tax ($ per year)	+	(3) Tax on income over $1,000 ($ per year)	=	(4) Total tax ($/year)	(5) Total tax after change In base tax	(6) Total tax after change In marginal tax rate
$ 5,000	_____		_____		_____	_____	_____
$10,000	_____		_____		_____	_____	_____
$15,000	_____		_____		_____	_____	_____

2. Suppose further that the taxing authority wishes to raise taxes by $500 for people with incomes of $10,000. If the marginal tax rates remain unchanged, what will the new base tax have to be?

3. In column 5 of Table 15.4, compute the resulting taxes at each income level with the new base tax.

4. If the base tax of $400 is to remain unchanged, what will the *marginal tax rate* have to be if $500 is to be added to the tax paid by people with incomes of $10,000? _____

5. Use the new marginal tax rate to complete column 6.

6. If taxes are to be increased (columns 5 and 6), a change in the base is:
   (a) More progressive and helpful to work incentives than raising taxes by changing the marginal tax rate.
   (b) More progressive and harmful to work incentives than raising taxes by changing the marginal tax rate.
   (c) More regressive and helpful to work incentives than raising taxes by changing the marginal tax rate.
   (d) More regressive and harmful to work incentives than raising taxes by changing the marginal tax rate.

Exercise 4

The media often provide information about changes in supply-side policies and the effects of such changes. This exercise will use one of the articles in the text to show the kind of information to look for. If your professor makes a newspaper assignment from the *Instructor's Manual*, this exercise will provide an example of how to do it.

Reread the article in Chapter 15 on page 337 entitled "Bust States' Trucking Trusts" from the *Wall Street Journal*. Then answer the following questions.

1. What phrase (not more than a sentence) is the first indication of the government agency or representative that could change the regulations on trucking?

2. What statement (not more than a sentence) reports a policy change that causes a shift in aggregate demand or aggregate supply?

3. What is the statement that indicates the buyers or sellers who are first affected by the policy change?

4. Find evidence of an actual or expected change in quantity or price resulting from the policy change. What is the one phrase that indicates this change?

5. Which diagram in Figure 15.5 best represents the expected shift resulting from deregulation of trucking? (*Hint*: Be sure your choice is consistent with your answers to other questions. Make sure you focus on just one shift.)

Figure 15.5
Possible shifts of aggregate supply and demand

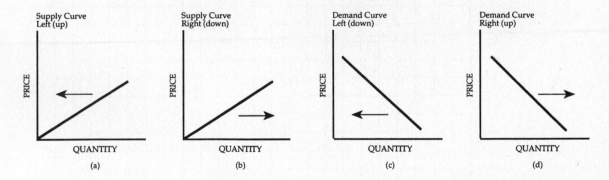

6. What determinant of demand or supply in the trucking services market is changing?

Exercise 5

This exercise shows the relationship between inflation and unemployment and provides practice in using data.

1. On the inside back covers of the text you will find data on the unemployment rate and the consumer price index. In Figure 15.6 graph both of these series and label each.

Figure 15.6
Inflation and unemployment rates

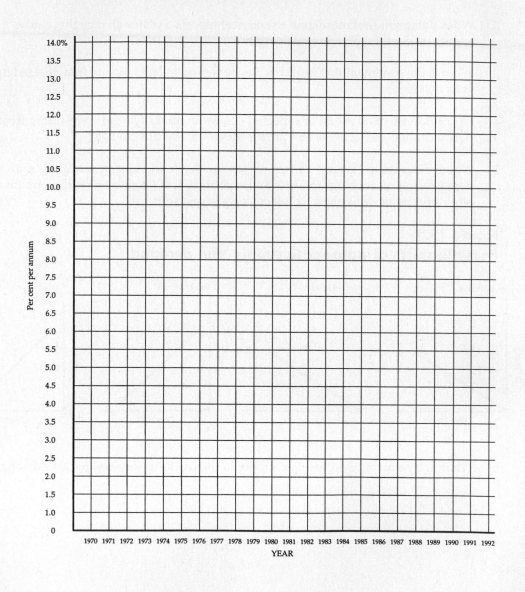

2. The unemployment rate and the inflation rate appear to be (inversely, directly) related.

3. Compare your graph with the Phillips curve in Figure 15.2 on page 322 of text. Does one graph provide information different from that of the other graph? _____

4. Why might the Phillips curve be a better way to provide information than the graph that you have drawn? For example, is it easier to see a change in one type of graph than in the other?

5. Compare your graph in Figure 15.6 above with the misery index graphed on page 325 of the text. What information is lost by looking at the misery index?

6. Which of the following provides the greatest amount of information for each curve that is diagrammed?
    (a)   The Phillips curve.
    (b)   A graph of the unemployment rate and inflation rate through time on the same axes (as you have done in Figure 15.6 above).
    (c)   The misery index.
    (d)   All of the above provide the same information with the same number of curves.

Crossword Puzzle

Select the economic term in the following list that corresponds with each of the definitions and descriptions below. Then fit the term or one of the words within it into the crossword puzzle at the number indicated.

aggregate demand
cyclical unemployment
demand-pull inflation
human capital
inflation rate
investment
labor
labor force
marginal tax rates
market power
market shortage
natural rate of unemployment

nominal income
opportunity cost
Phillips curve
productivity
profit
real income
relative price
saving
stagflation
structural unemployment
tax rebate
unit labor cost
wage–price control

Across

1. The quantity of the next most desirable commodity or service that must be forgone in order to produce a particular good.

4. Often the cornerstone of an incomes policy.

7. Taxes returned by the government.

11. A graph of the relationship between inflation and unemployment.

13. The tax rates applied to increments of income.

16. A measure of the rise in average prices.

17. The dollar value of the goods and services that can be bought in a particular year.

21. People above the age of 16 who are working or are seeking work.

24. The gap between demand and supply of a product, often induced by price controls.

25. Output per unit of labor time.

Down

2. A worsening of both inflation and unemployment.

3. Nominal GNP corrected for inflation.

5. Long-term rate of unemployment determined by structural features of labor and product markets, if government does not interfere.

6. One of the three factors of production; often the source of cost-push inflation.

8. Expenditures on capital.

9. Lack of work because people's skills or locations do not mesh with the needs of the job market.

10. The difference between revenues and costs which rises when a firm has market power.

12. An average increase in prices caused by excess of expenditures above income when the economy is fully employed.

14. Lack of jobs because of inadequate aggregate demand.

15. The unit value of one good in comparison with the unit value of other goods.

18. Often mistaken as being identical to wages, but may be quite different, depending on productivity.

19. Embodiment of skills and education and training that increases productivity.

20. $C + I + G$ + net exports.

22. Disposable income that is not consumed.

23. The ability to alter prices or wages in a market.

Common Errors

The first statement in each "common error" below is incorrect. Each incorrect statement is followed by a corrected version and an explanation.

1. Labor productivity increases when more is produced per dollar of wages. WRONG!

    Labor productivity increases when more units of product are produced per unit of labor. RIGHT!

    Productivity changes are not directly related to wage levels. Wage levels reflect a large number of influences embodied in the demand and supply curves for labor. Productivity, however, is a physical measure of the relation between units of product and the amount of labor needed to produce them.

2. The Phillips curve is simply a demand curve. WRONG!

    Although the Phillips curve is related to supply and demand curves, it is not the same as either a demand or a supply curve. RIGHT!

    Table 15.5 shows some of the major differences separating Phillips curves, market demand curves, and aggregate demand curves. The axes of the three curves are very different.

Table 15.5
Characteristics of three types of demand curve

| | Sources of differences | | |
Type of curve	x-axis	y-axis	Market
Phillips curve	Unemployment	Inflation	Aggregate labor market
Market demand curve	Quantity per time period	Price	Single market
Aggregate demand curve	Output per time period	Price Index	Aggregate product market

3. We can't have full employment with price stability. WRONG!

    Full employment with price stability is possible, although it may be difficult to achieve. RIGHT!

    Look at the definition of full employment again. It is the lowest rate of unemployment with price stability. Although we may be able to increase production above full employment, it will cause inflation.

4. Minimum-wage legislation provides more income to workers. WRONG!

Minimum-wage legislation eliminates low-paying jobs, which may decrease total income received by workers. RIGHT!

A higher wage may mean that businesses cannot afford to hire as many people. The lost wages of those people who are unemployed because of the minimum wages must be weighed against the higher wages received by those who are able to hold onto their jobs.

5. Affirmative-action programs result in higher costs to business and a rightward shift in aggregate supply. WRONG!

Affirmative-action programs can have a wide variety of impacts on aggregate supply. RIGHT!

The crucial criteria to business is to hire the most qualified person for the job that needs to be done at the wage that the business can offer. If discrimination serves as a barrier to hiring the best people, then the ability of affirmative action to eliminate those barriers can result in lower costs to business; businesses can look to a wider group of qualified people. However, if affirmative action is interpreted to give specific individuals or groups a priority to jobs, regardless of qualification, then business costs rise, aggregate supply declines, and prices rise. Finally, aggregate supply reflects more than just the cost to business. It is also necessary to consider the waste of human capital when people are trained but are not employed– a cost society must bear that firms may not have to pay.

•ANSWERS•

Key-Term Review

1.	human capital	6.	aggregate supply	11.	investment
2.	Phillips curve	7.	structural unemployment	12.	equation of exchange
3.	infrastructure	8.	saving	13.	tax elasticity of supply
4.	labor productivity	9.	tax rebate	14.	Laffer curve
5.	stagflation	10.	marginal tax rate	15.	transfer payments

True or False

1.	F	5.	F	9.	T	13.	F	16.	T	19.	F
2.	T	6.	T	10.	T	14.	T	17.	F	20.	T
3.	F	7.	T	11.	F	15.	T	18.	T	21.	T
4.	F	8.	T	12.	F						

Multiple Choice

1.	d	7.	d	12.	c	17.	c	22.	d	27.	d
2.	b	8.	d	13.	d	18.	b	23.	c	28.	c
3.	b	9.	b	14.	d	19.	c	24.	b	29.	d
4.	c	10.	b	15.	c	20.	a	25.	a	30.	c
5.	c	11.	a	16.	b	21.	c	26.	d	31.	b
6.	d										

32. (d) IRAs are savings incentives, not investment incentives. Topics of other groupings are (a) effects of being on the Laffer curve where less taxation provides greater revenue, (b) stagflation; and (c) supply-side levers.

Problems and Applications

Exercise 1

1. D, B, A, C

2. See Table 15.1 Answer.

Table 15.1 Answer

Aggregate demand curve	A	B	C	D
Equilibrium price index	1.1	1.2	1.3	1.8
Equilibrium output	2.0	3.0	4.0	4.0

Table 15.2 Answer

Aggregate demand curve	Unemployment rate (1)	Percentage change in price (2)	Percentage change in output (3)
A	15%	-8.3%	-33.3%
B	8%	0	0
C	5%	8.3%	33.3%
D	5%	50.0%	33.3%

3. See Table 15.2 Answer, column 2.

4. See Table 15.2, column 3.

5. **Table 15.3 Answser**

(Place check mark)	Aggregate Demand Curve			
	1	2	3	4
Depression	X	—	—	—
Deflation	X	—	—	—
Highest unemployment	X	—	—	—
Recession	—	X	—	—
Zero inflation	—	X	—	—
Full employment	—	—	X	—
Price stability	—	X	(8% is not stable)	—
Maximum output	—	—	X	X
Highest inflation	—	—	—	X

6. negative economic growth rate, high unemployment, deflation

7. positive economic growth rate, low unemployment rate, moderate inflation

8. positive economic growth rate, low unemployment rate, hyperinflation

9. *B; C*

10. See Figure 15.3 Answer; Phillips curve.

Figure 15.3 Answer

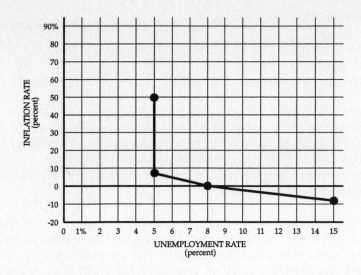

Exercise 2

1. b	3. b	5. a	7. b	8. d	9. a
2. c	4. b	6. c			

Exercise 3

Table 15.4 Answer

(1)	(2)		(3)		(4)	(5)	(6)
			Tax on income		Total	Total tax after change	
Income	Base Tax	+	over $1,000	=	tax		In marginal
($ per year)	($ per year)		($ per year)		($/year)	In base tax	tax rate
$ 5,000	$400		$ 800 (= $ 4,000 x 0.2)		$1,200	$1,700	$1,420
$10,000	400		1,800 (= 9,000 x 0.2)		2,200	2,700	2,700
$15,000	400		2,800 (= 14,000 x 0.2)		3,200	3,700	3,980

1. See Table 15.4 Answer, columns 2-4.

2. $900 (= $400 + $500)

3. See Table 15.4 Answer column 5.

4. 25.6 percent. This is found by solving the following equation, which indicates people with $10,000 in income have a tax of $2,700 (= $2,200 + $500):

$$\$2,700 = \$400 + (\$10,000 - \$1,000)X$$
$$\$2,300 = \$9,000X$$
$$X = 25.6 \text{ percent}$$

5. See Table 15.4 Answer column 6.

6. c

Exercise 4

1. "Congress"

2. "lifting archaic state barriers to competition in the trucking market"

3. Sellers are first affected. "Regulations prompt shippers to choose less efficient modes of transportation, to site warehouses in less advantageous locations, to make longer truckhauls, to run some trucks empty on return trips, and to invest in large, private truck fleets for hauls that specialized truckers could do more cheaply." All of these effects of regulations occur to the providers of trucking services. The lifting of the regulations will therefore affect these providers.

4. Indications of higher cost and higher prices of trucking as a result of regulation: "more diesel fuel consumed, more air pollution, and more wear and tear on the highways." Also, the phrase "that specialized truckers could do more cheaply" indicates prices would be lower with deregulation. Implicitly, price will come down when the regulations are lowered.

5. b

6. price of resources (highways)

Exercise 5

1. **Figure 15.6 Answer**

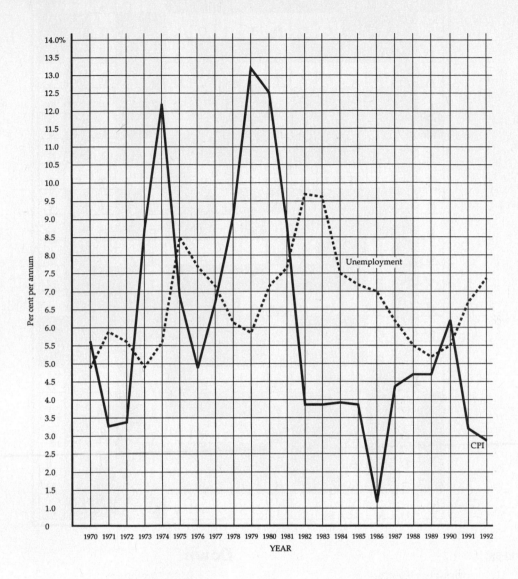

2. inversely

3. no

4. The Phillips curve presents all of the information in one curve, not two separate curves. The negative slope or positive slope of this curve indicates whether the variables are directly or inversely related to each other. If the unemployment and inflation rates are plotted over time, it is more difficult to see the inverse or direct relationship.

5. It's no longer possible to determine whether it is unemployment, inflation, or both which causes the rise in the misery index. The cost of summarizing everything with one simple curve is a substantial loss of information.

6. c

Crossword Puzzle Answer

Across

1. opportunity *cost*
4. wage-price *control*
7. tax *rebate*
11. *Phillips* curve
13. marginal tax *rates*
16. *inflation* rate
17. nominal *income*
21. labor *force*
24. *market* shortage
25. *productivity*

Down

2. *stagflation*
3. *real* income
5. *natural* rate of unemployment
6. *labor*
8. *investment*
9. *structural* unemployment
10. *profit*
12. demand-*pull* inflation
14. cyclical *unemployment*
15. relative *price*
18. *unit* labor cost
19. *human* capital
20. aggregate *demand*
22. *saving*
23. market *power*

CHAPTER 16

Economic Growth: Sources and Limits

Quick Review

Economic growth has been the major source of the ever-rising standard of living of the human race. However, the nature of growth and possible limits to it have long been debated. In this chapter we focus on the following concerns:

- How important is economic growth?
- How does an economy grow?
- Is continued economic growth possible? Is it desirable?

Although short-term growth may be accomplished by moving to the production-possibilities frontier, long-term growth requires an expansion of an economy's productive capacity. For a nation's people to become better off, real GDP must increase at a rate that exceeds the rate of population growth. Growth is a complex process and is not completely understood, but the best sources of increased productivity (increased output per worker) appear to be:

- Improvements in labor quality.
- Greater capital investment.
- Research and development leading to technological advances.
- Improved management.

Given this list, it is obvious that the saving–investment process is a critical ingredient. Government also can do much to influence both saving and investment.

Not everyone feels growth is necessarily good or sustainable. This feeling is best exemplified by the writing of the "doomsday prophets." In this regard, every generation of students rediscovers the work of the eighteenth-century clergyman Thomas R. Malthus. Malthus believed that the means of subsistence could not keep ahead of population growth. Hence, the human race was doomed to starvation unless steps were taken to stave off disaster. Doomsday prophets captured large audiences again in the 1970s. The widespread popularity of *The Limits to Growth*, a study by a group of M.I.T. scientists, and the works of Barry Commoner, Paul Ehrlich, and others, again raised the question, "Is the human race doomed?"

The argument that growth has identifiable limits is founded on two concerns: (1) We are depleting the resources necessary for survival, and (2) we are polluting our environment so badly that further growth may make life increasingly unpleasant or, worse, biologically impossible. The general weakness of these arguments is that they incorporate good arithmetic with a faulty sense of economics and history and a lack of appreciation for the adaptive capacity of our institutions.

Technological advance and adaptive capacity are automatically encouraged by economic forces. As resources become relatively scarce, their prices rise. These higher prices discourage resource use and provide incentives for exploration of new sources of supply and the substitution of alternative resources. From the perspective of resource requirements, growth may be limitless. The pollution problem is perhaps more serious because the market mechanism does not adequately allocate the costs of pollution and thus does not provide the incentives necessary for its correction. Public policy to allocate costs or to set standards is needed to correct for this weakness.

Growth is possible for the foreseeable future. But is it desirable? Most seem to think it is, as long as it means a higher standard of living. On the other hand, an argument can be made that rather than seeking continued growth, we simply need to change the mix of outputs we are producing to bring about an increase in economic well-being. The debate over sustainable growth continues. The "Earth Summit" in Rio de Janeiro in 1992 saw the challenge as twofold; first, as an attack on world poverty; second, as an environmental challenge. Summit participants focused on problem areas—population, pollution, ecological decline, and the like, and advocated a global partnership in pursuing "Agenda 21," which included greater energy efficiency, technology transfers, and so on.

Learning Objectives

After reading Chapter 16 and doing the following exercises, you should:	True or false	Multiple choice	Problems and applications	Common errors	Pages in the text
1. Know the difference between the way output changes in the short run and in the long run.	2-5, 15	1, 19, 20			343-345
2. Know and be able to calculate some indexes of growth.	1, 4, 6, 8, 16	4, 6, 20	2	1	345-349
3. Understand some of the sources of productivity growth.		2-7, 16, 19	3		349-353
4. Understand government's role in the growth process.					
5. Be familiar with the history of the doomsday prophets.	10, 11	8, 12, 14	2	1, 2	354-358
6. Be aware of the shortcomings of the analyses of the doomsday prophets.	9, 12-14	9, 10, 13-16	1, 2	2	358-361
7. Understand the nature of environmental constraints that can limit growth.		11, 17, 18, 22	1	3, 4	361-362
8. Be aware of the concerns and the agenda of the "Earth Summit."		21		4	363-364
9. Recognize what society can do to mitigate the external costs imposed by economic growth.		22	1	3, 4	362

Key-Term Review

Review the following terms; if you are not sure of the meaning of any term, write out the definition and check it against the Glossary in the text.

arithmetic growth   labor force
base period   net investment
crowding out   production possibilities
economic growth   productivity
geometric growth   real GDP
GDP per capita   substitution effect
growth rate

Fill in the blank following each of the statements below with the appropriate term from the list above.

1. The dollar value of an economy's final output divided by total population may be defined as _____ .

   1. _____

2. A series such as 2, 4, 6, 8 represents _____ .

   2. _____

3. A series such as 3, 9, 27, 81 represents _____ .

   3. _____

4. Total output divided by the number of units of input is a measure of that input's _____ .

   4. _____

5. A change in a purchasing pattern as a result of changes in relative prices is called a _____ .

   5. _____

6. An increase in real GDP is referred to as _____ .

   6. _____

7. When nominal GDP is adjusted for price changes, the resulting aggregate is called _____ .

   7. _____

8. In the 1970s, the population as a whole grew much more slowly than the working-age population, which makes up the _____ .

   8. _____

9. Percentage change in real GDP from one period to another is the _____ in real GDP.

   9. _____

10. When an economy's productivity increases, there is an increase in its _____ .

    10. _____

11. To increase an economy's capital stock requires positive _____ .

    11. _____

12. _____ occurs when government borrowing absorbs saving that would otherwise have been used to finance private-sector investment.

    12. _____

13. Real GDP is calculated using the prices of a
_____ to eliminate distortions caused by
inflation.   13. _____

True or False: *Circle your choice.*

T F 1. The United States is among the leading Western countries in improving average yearly productivity.

T F 2. When an economy moves from a point inside its production-possibilities curve to a point on its production-possibilities curve, long-run economic growth takes place.

T F 3. Once an economy is on its production-possibilities curve, further increases in output require an expansion of productive capacity.

T F 4. An increase in nominal GDP means there has been an outward shift in the production-possibilities curve.

T F 5. To achieve long-term economic growth requires an increase in potential GDP.

T F 6. Growth in GDP per capita is achieved when population grows more rapidly than GDP.

T F 7. One result of the post-World War II baby boom was that in the 1970s the population grew more rapidly than the labor force.

T F 8. One of the results of the influx of teenagers and women into the U.S. labor force was a decline in the average productivity of the work force.

T F 9. While the average absolute price of a man's suit has risen over the past thirty years, its cost in terms of "work effort" has fallen.

T F 10. Scarcity of food was viewed by Malthus as a "natural check" on population growth.

T F 11. Malthus believed that population grew arithmetically and that the means of subsistence grew geometrically.

T F 12. Higher food prices will have the beneficial effect of stimulating research on ways to improve agricultural productivity.

T F 13. As some food prices rise, substitution effects in diets can be expected.

T F 14. Substitution effects are an important reason for pessimistic predictions of the doomsday forecasters.

T F 15. Increases in the rate at which we utilize our productive capacity move the economy toward our production-possibilities curve.

T F 16. Increases in the size of the labor force and capital stock have been less important than productivity advances in causing U.S. GDP to grow.

Multiple Choice: *Select the correct answer.*

_____ 1. A major difference between short-run and long-run economic growth is that short-run growth:
   (a) Moves the economy to the production-possibilities curve, while long-run growth shifts that curve outward.
   (b) Increases capacity utilization, while long-run economic growth increases capacity.
   (c) Moves the economy up the aggregate supply curve, while long-run economic growth shifts the aggregate supply curve outward.
   (d) All of the above.

_____ 2. Which of the following would likely contribute to an improvement in the productivity of labor?
   (a) Greater expenditures on training and education.
   (b) Policies to stimulate the saving and investment process.
   (c) Greater expenditures on research and development.
   (d) All of the above.

_____ 3. Which of the following is thought to have been the *greatest* source of advances in productivity?
   (a) Improvement in management.
   (b) Increases in capital per worker.
   (c) Spending on research and development.
   (d) Improvements in the quality of labor.

_____ 4. A sustained net growth in real output of 3.5 percent per year will cause real output to double in about:
   (a) 10 years.
   (b) 20 years.
   (c) 30 years.
   (d) 35 years.

_____ 5. The best measure of productivity could be calculated with data on:
   (a) Real GDP and hours worked by the labor force.
   (b) Real GDP and the population of the United States.
   (c) Nominal GDP and the number of people in the U.S. labor force.
   (d) Nominal GDP and the population of the United States.

_____ 6. Approximately how long would it take for real GDP to double if nominal GDP grew at 5 percent and the price level increased at a rate of 1 percent?
   (a) Approximately 12 years.
   (b) Approximately 14.4 years.
   (c) Approximately 18 years.
   (d) Approximately 72 years.

_____ 7. A process which cumulates by a fixed percentage each year:
   (a) Appears as an accelerating curve through time when graphed.
   (b) Is a geometrically rising process.
   (c) Is the kind of process on which the Rule of 72 can be used.
   (d) All of the above.

_____ 8. Which of the following statements can be attributed to Malthus?
(a) Population grows geometrically and the means of subsistence grow arithmetically.
(b) Starvation serves as a natural check to population growth.
(c) Moral restraint, in the form of delayed marriage and childbearing, is necessary if humankind is to avoid misery.
(d) All of the above are Malthusian statements.

_____ 9. Which of the following would be brought about automatically by changes in relative prices?
(a) Substitution of polluting goods for nonpolluting goods.
(b) Substitution of high-priced resources for low-priced resources in the production process.
(c) Substitution of low-priced foods for high-priced foods.
(d) None of the above.

_____ 10. Which of the following results automatically from the working of the market system?
(a) People do not pollute because all costs of consumption are borne directly by the consumer.
(b) Producers are precluded from polluting because all costs of production are borne directly by the producer.
(c) Neither producers nor consumers are forced to incur all of the costs of their activities.
(d) None of the above results automatically.

_____ 11. Which of the following can help stave off ecological disaster?
(a) Changes in the output mix of GDP.
(b) Government policy to control pollution.
(c) Economic forces that lead to a reduction in population growth.
(d) All of the above.

_____ 12. The description of economics as the "dismal science" refers to the:
(a) Uninteresting subjects of the discipline.
(b) Early predictions of world overpopulation and starvation.
(c) Dull way the subject material is presented.
(d) Absence of humor in the textbooks.

_____ 13. One reason that we can be somewhat more optimistic than the doomsday economists is that:
(a) Land is not in finite supply.
(b) Population is actually decreasing.
(c) Technology continues to advance.
(d) We have less demand for food now than we had years ago.

_____ 14. The doomsday theorists regard technological change as:
(a) A diversion from the fundamental problem of growth in a finite system.
(b) The only salvation from the dire consequences of their calculations.
(c) A cure for the fundamental problem of growth in a finite system.
(d) Unlikely.

_____ 15. An answer to the doomsday theorists is that:
  (a) Past experience and present knowledge support their thesis about productivity and technology.
  (b) We know exactly the limits to technological advancement.
  (c) Past experience and present knowledge suggest that there is hope for increased productivity and substitution.
  (d) We know when and where the technological limits will occur.

_____ 16. The profit incentive tends to:
  (a) Encourage productivity research and pollution abatement.
  (b) Discourage pollution abatement.
  (c) Discourage productivity research and pollution abatement.
  (d) Reduce the need for laws or fines to reduce pollution.

_____ 17. The benefits of pollution abatement:
  (a) Are external to the consumer or firm incurring the abatement costs.
  (b) Are directly experienced by the firm incurring the abatement costs.
  (c) Create the incentive for firms to take action on their own to stop pollution.
  (d) Are minimal and not worth economic consideration.

_____ 18. One probable short-run result of the cost of pollution being reflected in the cost of production is:
  (a) Increased pollution.
  (b) Higher prices for many consumer goods and services.
  (c) More goods produced at lower costs.
  (d) None of the above.

_____ 19. The investment rate can be computed by dividing investment by:
  (a) Real GDP.
  (b) The population.
  (c) The labor force.
  (d) Productivity.

_____ 20. From the longer-run perspective of economic growth, saving:
  (a) Threatens growth because of the paradox of thrift.
  (b) Is a basic source of investment financing.
  (c) Is a leakage which constrains economic growth.
  (d) Shifts the institutional production-possibilities curve inward.

_____ 21. Greater energy efficiency was one plan of action of Agenda 21. The biggest effect of such a plan of action would most likely be:
  (a) Aggregate supply curve shifts to the left.
  (b) Aggregate supply curve shifts to the right.
  (c) Aggregate demand curve shifts to the left.
  (d) Aggregate demand curve shifts to the right.

_____ 22. Environmental restraint was one plan of action of Agenda 21. Such a plan of action would most likely in the short run:
  (a) Be represented as a movement upward along the aggregate supply curve.
  (b) Shift the Phillips curve to the left.
  (c) Shift the production-possibilities curve inward.
  (d) Cause productivity to increase.

Problems and Applications

Exercise 1

This exercise focuses on the supply-and-demand effects of the energy crisis that occurred in the early 1970s.

The volatile energy market should have had an impact on the various markets listed below. Match the letter of the appropriate diagram in Figure 16.1 with each of the markets and events listed below. Then list the determinant of demand or supply that changed. (*Hint:* The nonprice determinants of market demand are income, buyer expectations, the prices of related goods and availability of other goods, and the number of buyers. The nonprice determinants of market supply are technology, the price and availability of resources, expectations, taxes and subsidies, and the number of suppliers.) *Make sure you decide which market is affected before deciding which shift occurs.*

Figure 16.1
Shifts of supply and demand

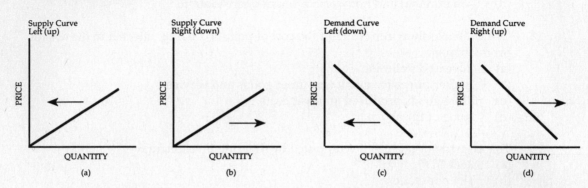

1. Market: Shingles

    Event: OPEC announces it will increase the price of crude oil by 25 percent over the next six months. Crude oil is an input in the production of shingles.

    Shift (Figure 16.1 diagram): _____
    Determinant: _____

2. Market: Drilling rigs

    Event: Government removes price controls on crude oil and the price of crude oil rises.

    Shift (Figure 16.1 diagram): _____
    Determinant: _____

3. Market: Apartments in the suburbs

    Event: Higher commuting costs convince the public it's better to live downtown.

    Shift (Figure 16.1 diagram): _____
    Determinant: _____

4. Market: Gas-run clothes dryers

   Event: Canada and Mexico announce they will no longer sell the United States any natural gas.

   Shift (Figure 16.1 diagram): _____
   Determinant: _____

5. Market: Coal miners

   Event: Government bans the use of crude oil in new electrical generating plants. New plants use coal.

   Shift (Figure 16.1 diagram): _____
   Determinant: _____

6. Market: Home insulation

   Event: The *Farmer's Almanac* forecasts an unusually warm winter and the price of natural gas falls.

   Shift (Figure 16.1 diagram): _____
   Determinant: _____

7. Market: Crude oil

   Event: A huge oil deposit is discovered off the Atlantic coast.

   Shift (Figure 16.1 diagram): _____
   Determinant: _____

8. Market: Natural gas

   Event: New technology improves the probability of hitting natural-gas wells.

   Shift (Figure 16.1 diagram): _____
   Determinant: _____

9. Market: Shrimp

   Event: A Mexican oil well blows out in the Gulf of Mexico and the resulting oil slick damages commercial shrimp beds along the Texas coast.

   Shift (Figure 16.1 diagram): _____
   Determinant: _____

10. Market: Marine insurance

    Event: The world fleet of supertankers expands, increasing the probability of collisions.

    Shift (Figure 16.1 diagram): _____
    Determinant: _____

Exercise 2

The following exercise gives practice in recognizing the difference between arithmetic and geometric growth rates.

Assume that the population of a country is 1 million people in the year 2000 and that it is increasing at the rate of 10 percent per decade. Assume that food production is 1 million tons per year and grows by 100,000 tons every decade.

1.   In Figure 16.2 graph the tons of food per capita over a century.

Figure 16.2
Food production per capita

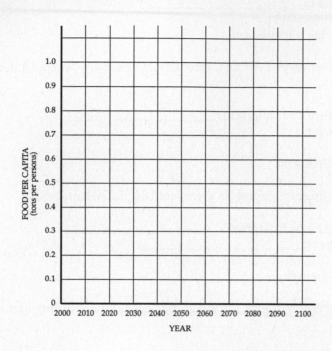

2.   The population growth is:
     (a)   Geometric.
     (b)   Arithmetic.

3.   The increase in food is:
     (a)   Geometric.
     (b)   Arithmetic.

4.   After one century by what percentage has food consumption per capita declined as a result of the population increase? _____

Exercise 3

The media often provide information about events that affect productivity. This excercise will use one of the articles in the text to show the kind of information to look for. If your professor makes a newspaper assignment for this chapter, this exercise will provide an example of how to do it.

Reread the World View article in Chapter 16 entitled "'Investment Gap' Serves as a Rallying Cry" from the *Washington Post* (December 15, 1992, p. 353). Then answer the following questions.

1. What phrase indicates the events that altered productivity and caused a shift in aggregate demand or supply?

2. The productivity growth rate was (better, worse) then expected as a result of the events in problem 1.

3. Which of the four diagrams in Figure 16.1 in the first exercise *best* represents the effect of the event on aggregate supply or demand?

4. What phrase or sentence provides evidence of an actual or expected change in quantity, cost, productivity, or price, as a result of the event?

Common Errors

The first statement in each "common error" below is incorrect. Each incorrect statement is followed by a corrected version and an explanation.

1. Zero economic growth treats everyone equally. WRONG!

   Zero economic growth treats groups unequally. RIGHT!

   Zero economic growth in its simplest dimensions means that GDP would not grow from year to year. Income per capita therefore could not grow unless population declined. Yet we know that U.S. population is growing, although slowly, as a result of new births and increased longevity, and more recently as a result of immigration. If GDP were not to grow, the only way for those at the bottom of the income distribution to have more would be for someone at the top to take less.

2. There is no way to hold off the doomsday prophecy. WRONG!

   Much has been done in the last decade to avoid the cataclysmic predictions of the doomsday prophets. RIGHT!

   It's been over two decades since the deluge of new doomsday literature hit the newsstands. Before that, pollution, the environment, and ecology were issues popularized in the turbulent 1960s. Since then, much has been done by federal, state, and local governments to overcome some of the problems that seemed most acute. The air is cleaner in many areas. So is the water. Even the OPEC actions of the 1970s and early 1980s were of help in this regard. Higher oil prices spurred research into new sources of power and new ways to conserve energy. All of this activity helped us meet the doomsday challenge once again.

3. Zero economic growth will alleviate the pollution problem. WRONG!

   Zero economic growth will maintain the rate of pollution. RIGHT!

   Some people mistakenly think that stifling economic growth is a way to cut down on pollution. It isn't. The best that a zero economic growth policy could do is cut down on the *growth* in pollution. With the same output level and output mix, the rate of pollution would be the same from year to year. To cut pollution would require cutting GDP—that is, a *negative* economic growth policy! The economy has the capability of cleaning up pollution as well as generating pollution as it grows.

4. The world must run out of resources sooner or later. WRONG!

So long as recycling occurs, substitutions are made, and advances in technology take place, we won't run out of resources. RIGHT!

We'll stop relying on most presently used, theoretically exhaustible resources long before they are completely gone. The costs of obtaining them would be too great to deplete them totally. At some point it will be cheaper to recycle, substitute new resources, and devise new technologies than to rely on hard-to-get-at supplies of resources. We won't run out of everything!

•ANSWERS•

Key-Term Review

1.	GDP per capita	6.	economic growth	10.	production possibilities
2.	arithmetic growth	7.	real GDP	11.	net investment
3.	geometric growth	8.	labor force	12.	crowding out
4.	productivity	9.	growth rate	13.	base period
5.	substitution effect				

True or False

1.	F	4.	F	7.	F	10.	T	13.	T	15.	T
2.	F	5.	T	8.	T	11.	F	14.	F	16.	T
3.	T	6.	F	9.	T	12.	T				

Multiple Choice

1.	d	5.	a	9.	c	13.	c	17.	a	20.	b
2.	d	6.	c	10.	c	14.	a	18.	b	21.	b
3.	c	7.	d	11.	d	15.	c	19.	a	22.	c
4.	b	8.	d	12.	b	16.	b				

Problems and Applications

Exercise 1

1.	a	Price of a resource increases
2.	d	number of buyers, income
3.	c	Price of a related good (substitute)
4.	c	Price of a related good (complement)
5.	d	Price of a related good (substitute)
6.	c	Price of a related good (substitute)
7.	b	Number of suppliers
8.	b	Change in technology
9.	a	Prices of resources rise, number of sellers
10.	d	Number of buyers

Exercise 2

1. **Figure 16.2 Answer**

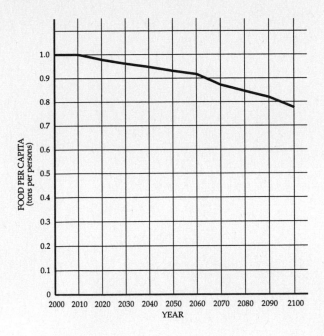

2. a
3. b
4. nearly 25 percent [1 - 0.7711) x 100%]

Exercise 3

1. "reluctance of business to fund research . . . and the failure of government to provide decent public schools and upgrade the country's stock of bridges, roads and water systems"

2. worse

3. a   Because it is the seller who is failing to provide.

4. "Solow calculated that the median family income would be $45,000 today instead of $35,000 if a proper level of investment had been maintained." This indicates the average output per family is much less because of the lack of investment. Since the number of families is closely related to the number of people in the labor force, the measure of output per family is a rough measure of productivity.

CHAPTER 17

Global Macro

Quick Review

Up to this point, we have not paid much attention to economic events in the rest of the world. However, the economies of all nations are becoming increasingly interdependent. We need to consider these questions:

- How does the U.S. economy interact with the economies of the rest of the world?
- How does the rest of the world affect U.S. macro outcomes?
- How does global interdependence limit macro policy options?

One facet of our interaction with other countries is the export and import of goods and services. Exports (X) are an injection and imports (IM) are a leakage. The additional leakage from imports reduces the size of the income multiplier by lowering the amount of *additional* spending on domestic output that results from any increase in our income. In a model of the closed economy, the multiplier is $1/MPS$. However, the multiplier in a model of an open economy must reflect the consumer's desire to spend a little out of every extra dollar for imports, which is called their marginal propensity to import (MPM). The multiplier for the open economy becomes $1/(MPS + MPM)$. The graphic equivalent of this is a reduced slope of the aggregate spending curve in an open economy as compared with a closed economy.

The marginal propensity to import may hinder our application of fiscal policy to achieve domestic goals. Because the multiplier is smaller in an open economy than in a closed economy, any tax or spending change will have to be larger to achieve a given income or employment goal. In an open economy we must also consider exports of our goods. When we import goods, foreigners receive dollars, which they may turn around and spend on goods that we produce. When they decide to buy more goods from us, the aggregate spending curve will shift upward, with a resulting multiplier effect on income. Our exports (determined abroad) are seldom equal to our imports (determined at home). We expect either a trade surplus, $(X - IM) > 0$, or a trade deficit, $(X - IM) < 0$. Although the trade deficit permits us to consume more goods than we produce, it may complicate fiscal policy. A fiscal expansion will increase any trade deficit, *ceteris paribus*.

While we're worrying about our domestic goals and the impact foreign trade has on our potential to achieve them, foreigners are doing the same thing. Our exports are their imports; our imports, their exports. If we have a trade deficit, $(X - IM) < 0$, and consume more than we produce, our trading partners must have an overall trade surplus, $(X - IM) > 0$, and consume less than they produce. Our domestic goals may be incompatible with theirs, or theirs with ours. This may mean that our economy competes with their economies with respect to employment and inflation goals. Policymakers face additional constraints in the open economy.

While trade flows involve the movement of new goods across international boundaries, capital flows involve the purchase of various forms of wealth or of titles to capital across international boundaries. Individuals and corporations purchase securities, bonds, and property in foreign countries or repatriate earnings from abroad. Their actions result in massive dollar flows—capital inflows when foreigners lend to us (e.g., by purchasing a Treasury bond) and outflows when we purchase securities from them (e.g., building up a bank account abroad). Capital flows are seldom in balance. When the outflow of dollars exceeds the inflow of dollars, the U.S. experiences a capital deficit; when the inflow exceeds the outflow, a capital surplus. Capital imbalances can alter macro outcomes too. Inflationary pressures can be fought, *ceteris paribus*, by slowing the growth of the money supply and driving up domestic interest rates. But this action would attract foreigners to our bonds, which they would purchase with accumulated dollars, frustrating the Fed's attempt to reduce the money supply. Domestic goals of various countries are often in conflict.

The critical link between economies in both trade and finance is the exchange rate. The expected imbalance between trade and capital flows implies that the exchange rates fluctuate like other prices determined by supply and demand. For example, if the United States runs persistent trade deficits and foreigners suddenly begin to withdraw their investments from the United States, the value of the dollar in terms of other currencies will go down.

The exchange rate also responds to changes in the specialization and productivity of firms worldwide. Specialization and trade increase world efficiency and output, and stimulate improvements in productivity as producers anywhere must compete with producers everywhere. However, if one country makes dramatically greater improvements in productivity than other countries, then it is likely to run persistent trade surpluses, causing its currency to become more valuable. Significant "swings" in exchange rates sometimes overwhelm productivity changes and reduce the competitiveness of many firms within a country.

Thus, three kinds of rates must be watched very carefully in an open economy: inflation rates, interest rates, and exchange rates. Changes in these rates reflect changes in trade and capital flows. The effectiveness of both fiscal and monetary policy is influenced by changes in these rates.

Learning Objectives

After reading Chapter 17 and doing the following exercises, you should:	True or false	Multiple choice	Problems and applications	Common errors	Pages in the text
1. Understand how international transactions affect U.S. economic performance and the ability to use macroeconomic policy.	20	6, 17, 18			343-345
2. Be able to explain why the open-economy multiplier is smaller than the closed-economy multiplier.	1-5, 7, 10	1, 4, 9, 12, 13, 19	1, 2		345-349
3. Understand why the marginal propensity to import *changes the slope* of the aggregate spending curve.	3-6	2, 5, 12, 13	1, 2, 4		349-353
4. Be able to demonstrate how a change in exports *shifts* the aggregate spending curve.	8, 13	3, 6, 8	2		353-354
5. Be able to show how trade and capital flows counteract normal macro policy initiatives.	9-12, 15-19	7, 10, 11, 14, 16	3		354-358
6. Be aware of the foreign repercussions of U.S. policy initiatives.	10-13, 15-17, 19	11, 16		3	358-361

Learning Objectives, cont.	True or false	Multiple choice	Problems and applications	Common errors	Pages in the text
7. Know the principal vocabulary of the trade and capital accounts.	9, 11-13, 15-19	7, 14-16		3, 4	361-362
8. Be able to relate exchange rate changes to the question of competitiveness in international trade.	21-23	17		1, 2, 4	363-364
9. Know why a common eurocurrency never materialized in 1992.					382-385

Key-Term Review

Review the following terms; if you are not sure of the meaning of any term, write out the definition and check it against the Glossary in the text.

capital deficit   marginal propensity to import (MPM)
capital surplus   marginal propensity to save (*MPS*)
crowding out   multiplier
exchange rate   net exports
exports   productivity
imports   trade deficit
leakage   trade surplus

Fill in the blank following each of the statements below with the appropriate term from the list above.

1. An open economy includes flows of goods and services across borders of different countries. Inflows are called _____ .

    1. _____

2. Outflows of goods and services are called _____ .

    2. _____

3. When _____ are positive, there is a _____, which means that the value of a country's exports exceeds the value of what it imports.

    3. _____
       _____

4. When there is a _____ , the value of a country's imports exceeds the value of its exports.

    4. _____

5. A trade deficit can be financed by a _____, which means that more money for investments and other nontrade purposes is flowing into the country than is being withdrawn.

    5. _____

6. A _____ can result when citizens of a country wish to invest more abroad or when foreigners withdraw funds from the country.

    6. _____

7. Trade deficits and capital deficits both tend to lower the _____ for a country's currency.

7. _____

8. The exchange rate may also fall if a country's _____ in producing goods efficiently deteriorates.

8. _____

9. With a lower-valued currency a country's goods become cheaper and thus more competitive abroad, which leads to increased exports and, through the _____ , increases its income.

9. _____

10. Because imports are a _____ from the income stream, the open-economy multiplier will be smaller, the larger the _____ , *ceteris paribus*.

10. _____

    _____

11. The multiplier will be larger, the smaller the _____ , *ceteris paribus*.

11. _____

12. Budget deficits at home may lead to a _____ of net exports.

12. _____

True or False: *Circle your choice.*

T F 1. Imports are an injection into the circular flow of economic activity.

T F 2. With more imports in an open economy, crowding out is increased, particularly if the economy is fully employed.

T F 3. A larger marginal propensity to import (MPM) means a larger multiplier, *ceteris paribus*.

T F 4. Increases in exports increase the size of the multiplier, *ceteris paribus*.

T F 5. Secondary shifts in aggregate demand resulting from the multiplier will be larger, the larger the marginal propensity to import.

T F 6. The marginal propensity to import is the ratio of the change in imports to a given change in income.

T F 7. If the MPM is 0.1 and the *MPS* is 0.1, the multiplier is 0.2.

T F 8. A reduction in net exports will lower the equilibrium level of income.

T F 9. When the United States has a trade deficit, the value of what the United States produces is more than the value of what it consumes.

T F 10. Import leakages help reduce inflationary pressures, *ceteris paribus*.

T F 11. Fiscal policy to cure unemployment will increase a trade surplus, *ceteris paribus*.

T F 12. Restrictive fiscal policy will simultaneously reduce excess aggregate demand and a trade deficit, *ceteris paribus*.

T F 13. OPEC activities in the 1970s caused both the U.S. aggregate demand curve and the U.S. aggregate supply curve to shift downward.

T F 14. If the United States runs a trade deficit, the rest of the world must have a trade surplus.

T F 15. The purchase of Treasury bonds by foreigners results in a capital outflow.

T F 16. The repatriation of profits on U.S. investments abroad causes a capital inflow.

T F 17. Capital inflows to the U.S. economy finance a U.S. trade deficit.

T F 18. A trade deficit isaccompanied by a capital inflow; a trade surplus, by a capital outflow.

T F 19. When U.S. interest rates rise relative to foreign interest rates, capital flows out of the United States.

T F 20. An exchange rate is the price of a country's currency in terms of another country's currency.

T F 21. A strong dollar makes our exports attractive to foreign buyers.

T F 22. When the dollar gets weaker, the United States becomes less competitive in the world markets.

T F 23. The persistent trade deficits of the U.S. economy are evidence that our producers are less efficient than foreign producers.

Multiple Choice: *Select the correct answer.*

_____ 1. The open-economy multiplier is smaller than the closed-economy multiplier:
  (a) Because imports are a leakage from the circular flow.
  (b) Because the marginal propensity to import is greater than zero.
  (c) Because the denominator is greater for the open-economy multiplier than for the closed-economy multiplier.
  (d) For all of the above reasons.

_____ 2. The marginal propensity to import relates:
  (a) Domestic consumption to the foreign level of income.
  (b) Changes in the domestic level of income to changes in the foreign level of income.
  (c) Changes in the domestic imports with changes in domestic income.
  (d) Changes in domestic consumption with changes in imports.

_____ 3. An increase in U.S. exports:
  (a) Must increase unemployment in the rest of the world.
  (b) Means the rest of the world must be importing more.
  (c) Means the rest of the world must have a trade deficit.
  (d) Means the rest of the world must have a trade surplus.

_____ 4. If the marginal propensity to import is 0.2 and the marginal propensity to save is 0.2, the multiplier is:
  (a) 0.4.
  (b) 2.5.
  (c) 4.0.
  (d) 2.0.

_____ 5. An increase in the marginal propensity to import will:
   (a)   Reduce the size of the open-economy multiplier.
   (b)   Increase the size of the closed-economy multiplier.
   (c)   Shift the aggregate supply curve rightward.
   (d)   Shift the aggregate demand curve rightward.

_____ 6. The relation between total income and domestic spending in an private open economy would be:
   (a) $C + I = Y$
   (b) $C + I + G = Y$
   (c) $C + I + X = Y + IM$
   (d) $C + I + G + X = Y + IM$

_____ 7. A trade surplus implies that the United States is:
   (a)   Consuming more than it produces, and net exports are positive.
   (b)   Consuming more than it produces, and net exports are negative.
   (c)   Consuming less than it produces, and net exports are positive.
   (d)   Consuming less than it produces, and net exports are negative.

_____ 8. If the economy has a shortfall in aggregate demand and a trade surplus, which of the following would be an appropriate policy to follow?
   (a)   A tax cut, with government spending cut by the same amount.
   (b)   A tax cut, accompanied by an increase in government spending.
   (c)   A tax increase, accompanied by a cut in government spending.
   (d)   A tax increase, with no change in government spending.

_____ 9. With an open economy, rather than a closed economy:
   (a)   Smaller tax or spending changes will be required to achieve the same employment goals.
   (b)   Monetary policy will more easily control inflation.
   (c)   The multiplier will be smaller.
   (d)   All of the above are the case.

_____ 10. All nations can run trade surpluses simultaneously when all of their economies are:
   (a)   Below full employment.
   (b)   At full employment.
   (c)   Above full employment.
   (d)   None of the above.

_____ 11. If the U.S. economy has excess aggregate demand and a zero trade balance:
   (a)   A tax increase would reduce aggregate demand and push the trade account into surplus, _ceteris paribus_.
   (b)   A tax increase would reduce aggregate demand and push the trade account into deficit, _ceteris paribus_.
   (c)   An open-market purchase of bonds would worsen excess aggregate demand and would push the trade account into surplus, _ceteris paribus_.
   (d)   An open-market sale of bonds would shift aggregate demand leftward and push the trade account into deficit, _ceteris paribus_.

_____ 12. With more imports in an open economy:
   (a)   Government spending can be raised without cutting back on domestic investment and consumption.
   (b)   Crowding out is reduced, even at full employment.
   (c)   Fiscal stimulus means a greater trade deficit.
   (d)   All of the above.

13. If the government tries to achieve a desired stimulus through demand-side policies, it would be necessary to compensate for a larger marginal propensity to import by using:
    (a) A larger tax increase.
    (b) A larger discount rate.
    (c) Larger government expenditures.
    (d) Larger sales of U.S. bonds by the Fed.

14. A capital inflow occurs when:
    (a) Foreign investors purchase Treasury bonds.
    (b) The Fed increases bank reserves.
    (c) Taxes are increased and/or imports fall.
    (d) All of the above occur.

15. A capital outflow occurs when, *ceteris paribus*:
    (a) Citizens of the United States buy foreign stock.
    (b) U.S. corporations abroad repatriate their profits.
    (c) Foreigners purchase real estate in the United States.
    (d) All of the above occur.

16. The existence of a trade deficit can be financed by:
    (a) A capital surplus.
    (b) A strengthening of the exchange rate for the currency.
    (c) Stimulation of the economy to full employment.
    (d) None of the above.

17. When exchange rates are free to fluctuate, a stronger dollar means:
    (a) Imports become more expensive.
    (b) U.S. producers become more competitive in foreign markets.
    (c) U.S. exports should increase.
    (d) None of the above.

18. The basic argument for trading with other countries is that trade:
    (a) Increases our production possibilities above consumption possibilities.
    (b) Decreases our production possibilities below consumption possibilities.
    (c) Increases our consumption possibilities above production possibilities.
    (d) Decreases our consumption possibilities below production possibilities.

19. Which of the following groupings contains a term that does not belong?
    (a) Imports, exports, trade surplus.
    (b) Imports, taxes, saving.
    (c) Exports, investment, government expenditure.
    (d) Money multiplier, marginal propensity to import, marginal propensity to consume.

Problems and Applications

Exercise 1

Using the consumption function and the import function, it is possible to find the multiplying effect for an open economy. This exercise provides practice.

Assume that an economy is characterized by the consumption function

$$C = 100 + 0.8Y_D$$

where all figures are in billions of dollars.

1. What is the marginal propensity to consume for this closed economy. _____

2. Compute the marginal propensity to save for the closed economy. _____

3. Compute the multiplier for this closed economy. _____

4. If government expenditures were to increase $250 billion, how much would income increase in this closed economy? _____

5. Now suppose the economy has been opened up to imports and has the import function

$$M = 50 + 0.3Y_D$$

where all figures are in billions of dollars. The import function is very much like a consumption function except that it shows how much foreign production is consumed rather than how much domestic output is consumed at any level of income. What is the marginal propensity to import? _____

6. Assuming that the consumption function is the same as in the beginning of this exercise, compute the multiplier for this open economy. _____

7. If government expenditures increase $250 billion, how much does income increase in this open economy? _____

8. T   F   The import sector dampens the effectiveness of fiscal policy. (Compare your answers in problems 4 and 7.)

Exercise 2

This exercise shows why trade deficits get worse as income increases. It uses the import equation from Exercise 1 to illustrate the idea.

Again suppose an economy has imports (M) that can be described by the import function

$$M = 50 + 0.3Y_D$$

where all figures are in billions of dollars. Exports are assumed to be $210 billion per year.

1. In Table 17.1 compute imports, exports, and the balance of trade at the various levels of disposable income indicated in column 1.

Table 17.1
Trade for an open economy
(billions of dollars per year)

(1) Disposable income (Yd)	(2) Exports (X)	(3) Imports (M)	(4) Balance of trade (2) - (3)
$ 0	$_____	$_____	$_____
500	_____	_____	_____
1,000	_____	_____	_____

2. Graph imports against income in Figure 17.1 and label this line *M*.

Figure 17.1

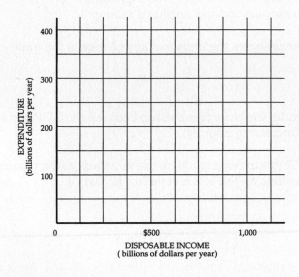

3. Exports are constant at $210 billion. Draw a line in Figure 17.1 that shows exports at each income level at $210 billion and label it X. (*Hint*: The line should be flat.)

4. Show the balance of trade at disposable income levels of $0, $500, and $1,000. Use a bracket to indicate the trade deficit or trade surplus at each income level.

5. Indicate with an arrow where exports equal imports in Figure 17.1.

6. At what disposable income level does the trade balance equal zero? _____

7. T F At disposable income levels below the level at which trade is balanced, there are trade deficits.

8. T F As the government stimulates the economy to higher income levels, the trade deficit will become worse, *ceteris paribus*, because consumer spending on imports increases.

Exercise 3

Trade deficits have become a frequent topic of the U.S. media. This exercise will use one of the articles in the text to show the kind of information to look for. If your professor makes a newspaper assignment from the *Instructor's Manual*, this exercise will provide an example of how to do it.

Reread the World View article on page 368 entitled "Japan Buys Fewer Goods from the U.S." from *The Washington Post*. Then answer the following questions.

1. What phrase names the cause for the change in the U.S. trade deficit?

2. Which sentence indicates that the trade deficit is larger or smaller?

3. Which of the following indicates the direction of change in the trade balance?
   (a) It is in deficit and the deficit is growing.
   (b) It is in deficit and the deficit is falling.
   (c) It is in surplus and the surplus is growing.
   (d) It is in surplus and the surplus is falling.

4. Which sentence shows the impact of any change in the trade deficit?

Exercise 4

This exercise illustrates the close relationship between the GDP and net exports (and, implicitly, the close relationship of income to imports).

1. In Figure 17.2 graph net exports on the same axis as the percentage change in the real GDP (see the data on the inside cover of the text).

Figure 17.2
Net exports and economic growth rates

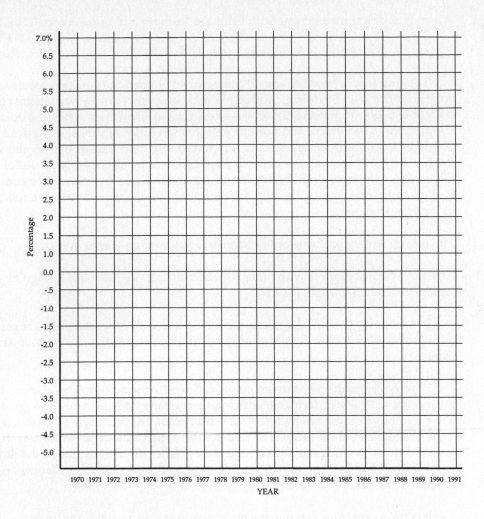

2. The relationship between net exports and the percentage change in the real GDP is best characterized as:
   (a) Direct (positive).
   (b) Inverse (negative).

3. If exports remain relatively constant or do not vary in a systematic way, the relationship between imports and the percentage change in the real GDP is best characterized as:
   (a) Direct (positive).
   (b) Inverse (negative).

T F 4. As U.S. decision-makers make progress against unemployment, they will experience a worsening of the trade deficit.

Common Errors

The first statement in each "common error" below is incorrect. Each incorrect statement is followed by a corrected version and an explanation.

1. A stronger dollar means American firms are stronger and more competitive. WRONG!

   A stronger dollar puts U.S. firms at a competitive disadvantage, *ceteris paribus*. RIGHT!

   The problem is how the word "competitive" is used. It is quite possible that because American firms were strong, productive, and competitive *in the past*, many countries bought U.S. goods and the dollar was strengthened. However, when the dollar strengthens *in the present* and nothing else changes (*ceteris paribus*), American firms are placed at a competitive disadvantage. It may be true that the stronger dollar will force them to be more competitive *in the future*, but they may also simply go out of business. Generally, a stronger dollar today means American firms are less able to compete with foreign companies today, because their output becomes more expensive relative to that of foreign producers.

2. The reason American firms can't compete is that foreign wages are so low. WRONG!

   American firms compete with other American firms, not just with foreign firms, for American dollars abroad. RIGHT!

   In a *given* market, an American firm competes with other American firms as well as with foreign firms. However, the firm is also competing indirectly with *all* American firms.

   When Americans buy foreign goods and send American dollars abroad, they provide the money with which foreigners can buy American goods. If American goods are being bought in large quantities by foreigners and Americans are buying few foreign goods, a trade imbalance will develop. The value of the dollar will rise as foreign exchange markets move to eliminate such an imbalance. This rise in the value of the dollar makes all American goods less competitive internationally—*even if productivity has risen for companies producing those goods.*

   It is not surprising that a manager who makes a firm more productive will become angry when foreign costs seem to be dropping faster than foreign productivity changes. However, the firm may really be experiencing the effects of a strengthening currency. A stronger currency reflects the productivity gains of *all* American firms. The manager's firm is effectively racing with other American firms in all other markets for the dollars held by foreigners.

3. Trade surpluses are good for the economy, and trade deficits are bad for the economy. WRONG!

   Trade surpluses and deficits are neither *inherently* bad nor *inherently* good. RIGHT!

   When we run a trade deficit, we get the benefits of foreign resources *net*. That's good. But persistent deficits can be bad for the economy if they lead to restrictive policies designed to cut down on imports and to a continual depreciation of the exchange rate. Our persistent trade deficits (foreigners' trade surpluses) mean foreigners will eventually accumulate more of our currency than they want to hold. Capital inflows will not be able to stem the glut of the currency. As a result, our currency will depreciate and foreign goods will become more expensive.

4. The U.S. trade deficit means U.S. producers are inefficient. WRONG!

The U.S. trade deficit means U.S. producers are having difficulty competing. RIGHT!

The trade deficit reflects more than our (in)efficiency. As an example, U.S. agricultural producers are extremely efficient, but they have had difficulty exporting because the dollar was so strong for so long. A weaker dollar helps our producers compete. Before we believe the rhetoric concerning competitiveness, we need to know what is happening to exchange rates.

•ANSWERS•

Key-Term Review

1.	imports	5.	capital surplus	10.	leakage
2.	exports	6.	capital deficit		marginal propensity
3.	net exports	7.	exchange rate		to import (MPM)
	trade surplus	8.	productivity	11.	marginal propensity
4.	trade deficit	9.	multiplier		to save (*MPS*)
				12.	crowding out

True or False

1.	F	5.	T	9.	F	13.	F	17.	T	21.	F
2.	F	6.	T	10.	T	14.	T	18.	T	22.	F
3.	F	7.	F	11.	F	15.	F	19.	F	23.	F
4.	F	8.	T	12.	T	16.	T	20.	T		

Multiple Choice

1.	d	4.	b	7.	c	10.	d	13.	c	16.	a
2.	c	5.	a	8.	b	11.	a	14.	a	17.	d
3.	b	6.	c	9.	c	12.	d	15.	a	18.	c

19. d   "Money multiplier" does not fit. Other themes include (a) components of trade balance, (b) leakages, and (c) injections.

Problems and Applications

Exercise 1

1. 0.8. See the consumption function.
2. 0.2 (= 1 - 0.08)
3. 5 (= 1/*MPS*)
4. $1,250 billion (= $250 billion x 5)
5. 0.3
6. 2 [= 1/(MPS + MPM) = 1/(0.2 + 0.3)]
7. $500 billion (= $250 billion x 2)
8. T

Exercise 2

1. **Table 17.1 Answer**

(1) Disposable income (Yd)	(2) Exports (X)	(3) Imports (M)	(4) Balance of trade (2) - (3)
$ 0	$210	$ 50	$160
500	210	200	10
1,000	210	350	-140

2.-5.   See Figure 17.1 answer.

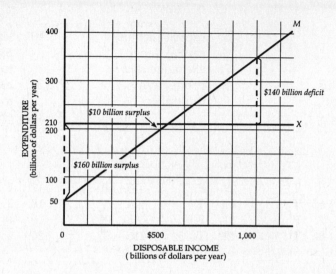

6. $533 billion. In Figure 17.1 the two lines cross at this disposable income level. You can calculate this by setting exports equal to imports as follows: $X = M$; $210 = 50 + 0.3Y_D$. Solve for $Y_D = \$533$ billion.

7. F   For example, at an income level of $500 billion there is a surplus of 10 billion.

8. T   For example, above $533 billion in Figure 17.1 there are only trade deficits.

Exercise 3

1. "The Japanese recession is part of a global economic slowdown that could hamper efforts to boost the U.S. economy."

2. Exports from the United States "dropped 2.6 percent in the first 11 months of 1992"; the article says nothing about United States imports. *Ceteris paribus*, the U.S. trade deficit would worsen as a result.

3. a   Assuming the Japanese recession affects only exports from the United States, then the U.S. trade balance experiences less of a surplus or more of a deficit (the article doesn't say which applies to the United States though we know the United States is in a trade deficit).

340

4. "could hamper efforts to boost the U.S. economy" With fewer exports, the United States loses "jobs, jobs, jobs," as displayed clearly by President Bush.

Exercise 4

1. **Figure 17.2 Answer**

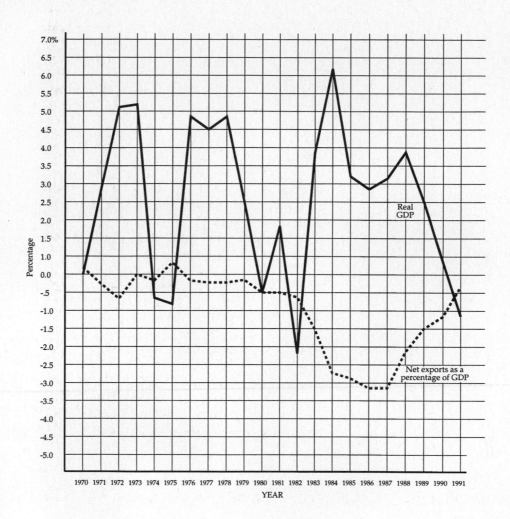

2. b
3. a Remember that imports are *subtracted* from exports in computing net exports.
4. T

CHAPTER 18

Theory and Reality

Quick Review

Designing economic policy for an economy as large and diverse as that of the United States is a very difficult job, and using the many available tools in a complementary fashion to implement the policy adds to the complexity. It is thus appropriate that we consider the following questions:

- What is the ideal "package" of macro policies?
- How well does our macro performance live up to the promises of that package?
- What kinds of obstacles prevent us from doing better?

We begin by noting that the president and Congress are responsible for making economic policy and pursuing economic goals. One goal that is unanimously supported is that of eliminating the business cycle because achieving that goal alone would solve many problems all at once.

There are a number of policy tools or policy levers in the arsenal that can be used to fight upswings and downswings in the economy. Monetary-policy tools (open-market operations, changing reserve requirements, and the like.) and fiscal-policy tools (changing taxes and spending) are the most powerful ones. Supply-side policy (deregulation, retraining, and so on.) is used as well. Economic forecasters, who advise policymakers, follow a variety of indicators and use econometric models to predict problems. Many, many economic resources are devoted to the study and development of economic policy, yet our policies seem often to fail. Why? There are many reasons. One is the lack of unanimity among the economists about how the economy works. Several "groups" of economists can be identified—Keynesians, Monetarists, Supply-siders, Rational Expectationists, and so on—who have somewhat different views about how to achieve economic stability.

Other serious problems plague us, too:

- *Goal conflicts*. Our economy has many macroeconomic goals, including some which have an impact on other economies so conflict seems inevitable. Some would argue that goal conflict has been institutionalized because the Fed is the guardian of the price level and the president and Congress are more concerned with jobs, growth, and the like.
- *Measurement problems*. It's difficult to measure what we want to know, to find current measurements when measurement is possible, or to make accurate forecasts even with current information.
- *Design problems*. We don't know *exactly* how the economy responds to specific policies. Perverse reaction to government policies may actually worsen the problem the policy was intended to solve.

- *Implementation problems.* It takes time for Congress and the president to agree on an appropriate plan of action. Four types of lag seem to prevent policies from being implemented quickly: recognition lag, lag in formulation of a response, lag in the response itself, and lag in the impact of the policy.

For all of these reasons the fine-tuning of economic performance rarely lives up to its theoretical potential. In addition, the continual changes of policy lead to a lack of credibility on the part of policymakers. Because of their rational expectations about the continually changing policies, people are likely to act in ways that defeat policy initiatives of the government.

Presidents Bush and Clinton both confronted the dilemma embodied in both goal conflicts and measurement problems. No matter who is in the White House, the options remain the same.

Learning Objectives

After reading Chapter 18 and doing the following exercises, you should:	True or false	Multiple choice	Problems and applications	Common errors	Pages in the text
1. Know the three basic types of policies and each of the policy levers.	1	2, 4, 6, 7, 9, 10, 13, 14	3	1	386-391
2. Know how the concept of "opportunity cost" defines the basic policy tradeoffs faced in the economy.		8, 12, 18	1, 2, 5	1	391-392
3. Be able to prescribe policies to eliminate an AD shortfall.	2, 3	4, 13, 14	1-3, 5	1	392
4. Be able to design policies to deal with excess AD.	2, 3, 6	4, 6	1-3, 5	1	392-393
5. Be able to suggest policies to control stagflation.	15	9, 11, 17	2, 3, 5	2	393-394
6. Know the general theories of several groups of economists.	11, 12, 16	6, 8, 10			397-398
7. Evaluate how effective policymakers have been in battling inflation and unemployment.	19-23	9, 13	3-5	2, 3	394-396
8. Be able to explain how measurement problems impede the development of effective policies.		25			396-398
9. Understand the concept of a leading indicator.		14-16	1		399-400
10. Understand the design problems encountered in administering policy and the problems of forecasting.		17	4		400-403
11. Know the "rational-expectations" argument about the effectiveness of policy.	7, 18, 22	1, 19, 22-24			407-409
12. Recognize the lags involved in policy implementation.		20, 21			403-407
13. Know the advantages and problems of both rules and discretion in policy.	5				410-411

Key-Term Review

Review the following terms; if you are not sure of the meaning of any term, write out the definition and check it against the Glossary in the text.

AD excess
AD shortfall
automatic stabilizer
business cycle
fine-tuning
fiscal policy
growth recession
GDP gap (real)

monetary policy
multiplier
natural rate of unemployment
rational expectations
stagflation
structural deficit
supply-side policy
velocity of money (V)

Fill in the blank following each of the statements below with the appropriate term from the list above.

1. During a downswing in economic activity, unemployment compensation supports disposable income and is an _____ .

   1. _____

2. A _____ is said to occur when the economy grows at less than 3 percent for two consecutive quarters.

   2. _____

3. When the government adjusts policies to maintain full employment, it is engaging in _____ .

   3. _____

4. Because of the inability of policymakers to eliminate the _____ completely and because of the resulting fluctuations in unemployment, many feel that economic theory is in error.

   4. _____

5. Changes in taxes and expenditures represent changes in _____ .

   5. _____

6. Only if the economy is at full employment will the _____ and the actual deficit be equal.

   6. _____

7. The chairman of the Federal Reserve Board of Governors is the most powerful figure in making _____ .

   7. _____

8. Monetarists argue that the unemployment rate can go below the _____ in the short run only.

   8. _____

9. _____ rests on the assumption that individuals and firms will respond to changes in incentives.

   9. _____

10. The greater the *MPC*, the greater will be the _____ .

   10. _____

11. Monetarists argue that fiscal policy doesn't matter as long as _____ is constant.

11. _____

12. It can be argued that when government policy loses credibility, people act according to their _____ , which counteracts any policy initiatives.

12. _____

13. Keynesian policies are particularly unsuited to fighting _____ .

13. _____

14. The difference between full-employment GDP and equilibrium GDP is the _____ .

14. _____

15. Both the _____ and the _____ are measured at the full-employment level output.

15. _____
_____

True or False: *Circle your choice.*

T   F   1.   Expenditures are automatic stabilizers inversely related to the business cycle.

T   F   2.   Either fiscal policy or monetary policy can be used in attempts to maintain aggregate demand.

T   F   3.   To attain the economy's goals, fiscal and monetary policy should be consistent. For example, when the money supply is increased, fiscal policy should be expansionary.

T   F   4.   Government's tax revenues are inversely related to the business cycle.

T   F   5.   The Gramm-Rudman-Hollings Act of 1985 required a balanced budget by 1991 and authorized new automatic stabilizers to achieve it.

T   F   6.   The Social Security Act Amendments of 1983 increased future retirement benefits and cut payroll taxes to pay for them.

T   F   7.   In defending monetary policy for 1986, during which the money supply grew by 15 percent, the Fed cited an increase in velocity as a justification.

T   F   8.   The structural deficit equals the actual deficit when the economy is at full employment.

T   F   9.   A major change in the personal income tax during the 1980s was the reduction in marginal tax rates.

T   F   10.   The Tax Reform Act of 1986 lowered marginal tax rates which restrained aggregate demand, but broadened the tax base, which stimulated aggregate supply.

T   F   11.   In a recession Monetarists believe that the velocity of money varies in response to fiscal policy.

T   F   12.   Keynesians and Monetarists believe the government should use the money supply as a method to eliminate a positive GDP gap.

T F 13. Government expenditures have a multiplying effect on income measured by PQ/M.

T F 14. Government expenditures have a multiplying effect on income measured by 1 divided by the reserve requirement.

T F 15. When the economy is experiencing stagflation, it is appropriate to ease monetary policy and cut taxes.

T F 16. "Fine-tuning" refers to the ability of policymakers to make slight adjustments to the economy in order to attain economic goals.

T F 17. A growth recession is characterized by an increasing unemployment rate with moderate inflation.

T F 18. Rational expectations about the effect of a government policy may lead to private-sector actions that defeat the policy.

T F 19. The New Classical economists developed a synthesis of conflicting views and feel that they have rescued discretionary economic policy.

T F 20. The Modern Keynesian economists favor steady, predictable policies, such as a constant growth rate in the money supply.

T F 21. Supply-side economists focus on the expansion of capacity through lower marginal tax rates and policies to increase incentives.

T F 22. The New Classical economists favor steady, predictable policies, such as a constant growth rate in the money supply.

T F 23. Marxists believe that the private sector is inherently unstable and likely to stagnate without government stimulus and intervention.

Multiple Choice: *Select the correct answer.*

_____ 1. Which of the following terms does not belong?
  (a) Monetary policy.
  (b) Rational-expectations policy.
  (c) Fiscal policy.
  (d) Supply-side policy.

_____ 2. Major tax cuts of over $250 billion came with the:
  (a) Economic Recovery Tax Act of 1981.
  (b) Social Security Act Amendments of 1983.
  (c) Gramm-Rudman-Hollings Act of 1985.
  (d) Tax Reform Act of 1986.

_____ 3. Which of the following most likely reduced the effect of automatic stabilizers for the economy?
  (a) Economic Recovery Tax Act of 1981.
  (a) The Gramm-Rudman-Hollings Act of 1985.
  (c) Social Security Act Amendments of 1983.
  (d) All of the above.

_____ 4. Monetary policy to eliminate an AD shortfall would include:
(a) A lower reserve requirement.
(b) The Feds selling securities in the open market.
(c) The Monetary Control and Deregulation Act.
(d) A rise in the discount rate.

_____ 5. When Federal Reserve Board chairman Alan Greenspan announced a goal of "zero inflation," which of the following was most consistent with his new goal?
(a) A lower discount rate.
(b) A lower minimum reserve ratio.
(c) Sales of securities in the open market.
(d) None of the above.

_____ 6. Which of the following groups feels that output and employment gravitate to a long-term rate determined by structural forces in the labor and product markets?
(a) Monetarists.
(b) Keynesians.
(c) New Classical economists.
(d) None of the above.

_____ 7. The structural deficit:
(a) Is the deficit that would exist if the economy were at full employment.
(b) Is influenced by discretionary fiscal spending.
(c) Is determined by the U.S. Congress.
(d) All of the above.

_____ 8. A supply-side policy to curb AD excess would include:
(a) Reduced government spending.
(b) Tax incentives to encourage saving.
(c) Open-market operations when the Fed buys securities.
(d) A higher reserve requirement.

_____ 9. Which of the following would most clearly have shifted the aggregate supply curve to the left?
(a) Rebuild American Program of 1993.
(b) Surface Transportation Act of 1991.
(c) Family Leave Act of 1993.
d) Immigration Act of 1990.

_____ 10. Which of the following supply-side efforts did the Clinton administration embrace?
(a) Wage-price controls.
(b) Infrastructure development.
(c) The Budget Enforcement Act.
(d) All of the above.

_____ 11. Stagflation:
(a) Occurs when both the unemployment and the inflation rates are high.
(b) Results in an increase in the misery index.
(c) Shifts the Phillips curve outward.
(d) All of the above.

_____ 12. Which of the following tools can be used to illustrate the inflation-unemployment tradeoff?
   (a)   The production-possibilities curve.
   (b)   The Phillips curve.
   (c)   The Keynesian cross.
   (d)   All of the above.

_____ 13. Which of the following is a reason that many economic policies fail, even if they are properly designed to achieve economic goals?
   (a)   Measurement difficulties prevent policymakers from correctly identifying what is happening in the economy.
   (b)   People often react in ways that may undercut new government policies.
   (c)   There are significant lags in response to policy.
   (d)   All of the above are reasons for the failure of economic policy.

_____ 14. Which of the following is *not* a leading indicator for economic activity?
   (a)   The average workweek.
   (b)   Delivery times.
   (c)   The natural rate of unemployment.
   (d)   The money supply.

_____ 15. The index of leading indicators is an index of eleven indicators that:
   (a)   Are used to predict economic activity three to six months in advance.
   (b)   Are weighted equally together to provide a forecast of the direction of the GDP.
   (c)   Are reported monthly.
   (d)   All of the above.

_____ 16. The leading economic indicator which leads to changes in production and employment in industries which produce consumer goods is:
   (a)   New orders.
   (b)   Equipment orders.
   (c)   Building permits.
   (d)   Inventories.

_____ 17. The reason that economic forecasting of the economy is most important and useful is that:
   (a)   Economists need employment.
   (b)   Business managers need to be able to anticipate government policy changes.
   (c)   Policymakers need to be able to anticipate what needs to be done and take action in time to be effective in achieving the desired result.
   (d)   Consumers can find out when they are going to lose their jobs and income.

_____ 18. Which of the following would a supply-side macro model include to describe the effect of a tax cut?
   (a)   Labor-supply and production responses.
   (b)   Interest rate increases.
   (c)   Multiplier spending responses.
   (d)   A positive relationship between interest rates and investment.

_____ 19. The economic reason that the government must purposely surprise the economy with a new policy is:
(a) To overcome the resistance of malicious bureaucrats.
(b) To avoid perverse behavior that worsens the economic problem that the policy is designed to solve.
(c) To attract attention so people will know there is a new policy.
(d) To allow everyone to get the information in order of their need to know.

_____ 20. Why might Congress or the president hesitate to provide greater income and in-kind transfers?
(a) Voters might become unemployed.
(b) The economy could be pushed into recession.
(c) A greater deficit would result.
(d) All of the above.

_____ 21. The order of policy lags can best be stated as follows:
(a) Formulation, recognition, and implementation lags.
(b) Implementation, formulation, and recognition lags.
(c) Recognition, formulation, and implementation lags.
(d) Formulation, implementation, and recognition lags.

_____ 22. Why might Congress or the president hesitate to apply restrictive fiscal policies?
(a) Monetary policy is always more effective.
(b) Voters might become unemployed.
(c) Fiscal policy is too complex.
(d) Fiscal-year appropriations are not under the authority of Congress.

_____ 23. Because of the theory of rational expectations about government policy changes, some economists recommend that government policy consist of:
(a) Automatic stabilizers like bracket creep.
(b) Discretionary fiscal policy.
(c) Shorter lags in recognition balanced by longer lags in formulation.
(d) Unalterable rules.

_____ 24. Because of rational expectations about government policy changes, New Classical economists recommend that government policy consist of:
(a) Unalterable rules.
(b) Discretion.
(c) Faster measurement.
(d) Surprise policy shocks to the economy.

_____ 25. Which of the following headlines from articles in the text does *not* describe a measurement problem?
(a) "This Just In: Recession Ended 21 Months Ago"
(b) "How They Rate" reports: "A survey . . . finds adults give high grades for accuracy in forecasts to sportswriters, sports announcers and weathermen. Who get low marks? Economists, stockbrokers and people who prepare horoscopes."
(c) "The Politics of Fighting Unemployment and Inflation"
(d) "Whoops . . . . Economists Have a Tough Time Predicting Turnarounds in the Economy"

Problems and Applications

Exercise 1

This exercise shows the relationship between income and various economic aggregates that have presented in Chapters 4-14.

Table 18.1 presents data on interest rates, government expenditures, taxes, exports, imports, investment, consumption, the GDP deflator, unemployment, and pollution for four levels of equilibrium income (GDP). These items appear frequently in newspaper articles about the economy. In the following questions you should be able to explain some of the relationships apparent in Table 18.1.

Table 18.1
Level of key economic indicators, by GDP level
(billions of dollars per year)

Interest rate	30%	20%	10%	0%
Government expenditures	$100	$100	$100	$100
Taxes	$ 25	$ 75	$125	$175
Budget balance	$___	$___	$___	$___
Exports	$300	$300	$300	$300
Imports	$260	$280	$300	$320
Balance of trade	$___	$___	$___	$___
Investment	$ 10	$ 90	$170	$250
Consumption	$750	$790	$830	$870
Nominal GDP	$___	$___	$___	$___
Saving	$___	$___	$___	$___
GDP deflator (index)	1.00	1.00	1.02	1.10
Real GDP (constant dollars)	$___	$___	$___	$___
Unemployment rate	15%	7%	4%	3.5%
Pollution index	1.00	1.80	1.80	1.80

1. Compute the federal budget balance, balance of trade, nominal GDP, saving, and real GDP in Table 18.1, for each level of nominal GDP.
    (*Hint:* Remember the formula $C + I + G + [X - IM] = GDP$; see Chapter 4.)

2. Which of the following policies is the government most likely changing to reach each of the income levels in Table 18.1?
    (a)   Fiscal policy.
    (b)   Monetary policy.
    (c)   Wage and price controls.
    (d)   Labor policy.

3. Which of the following statements best explains why taxes might change with income, as shown in Table 18.1?
    (a)   Taxpayers experience bracket creep.
    (b)   As taxpayer incomes rise, their taxes rise too.
    (c)   The income tax is regressive.
    (d)   Automatic stabilizers link taxes with income.

4. Which of the following statements best explains why imports change as income changes, as shown in Table 18.1?
    (a) Consumers buy more foreign goods as their incomes rise.
    (b) Consumers buy more domestic goods as their incomes rise.
    (c) Government buys fewer domestic goods as income rises.
    (d) Consumers buy fewer domestic goods as their incomes rise.

5. Which of the following statements best explains why exports *do not* change with GDP?
    (a) Exports are determined by the incomes (GDP) of people in other countries.
    (b) Exports increase as GDP rises because firms can afford to produce more.
    (c) Exports decrease as GDP falls because domestic consumers need goods and can pay for them.
    (d) Exports equal imports at all levels of income as the dollar adjusts to bring them into equilibrium.

6. The reason that the price index changes as income changes, as shown in Table 18.1, is most likely that:
    (a) As households receive greater income, they can be more discriminating buyers and find the lowest prices.
    (b) As businesses receive more orders, they make greater profits, which show up in the form of higher prices.
    (c) As households receive greater income, they spend it even when the economy is at full capacity, thus bidding up prices.
    (d) As businesses receive greater income, they are stimulated to expand capacity and must pass the cost of the increased capacity to consumers through higher prices.

7. The reason that unemployment changes as income changes, as shown in Table 18.1, is most likely that:
    (a) As incomes rise, people do not need jobs and therefore leave the labor force.
    (b) As incomes rise, automatic stabilizers provide increased benefits to the unemployed, keeping them out of the labor force.
    (c) As incomes rise, inflation causes both real income and employment to fall.
    (d) As incomes rise, aggregate demand rises, stimulating the demand for labor.

8. As income increases, the balance of trade worsens and lowers the value of the dollar because with higher income:
    (a) Consumers buy more imports.
    (b) Businesses produce more goods for U.S. exports.
    (c) Businesses take goods out of export in order to sell them domestically.
    (d) None of the above is the case.

9. Use the data in Table 18.1 to draw a Phillips curve in Figure 18.1. Compute the inflation rate from the base-year price index (remember the value of the index in the base year is 1.0) for each level of income. (See the first exercise in Chapter 15 for a more detailed description of the way to compute the rate of inflation.)

Figure 18.1

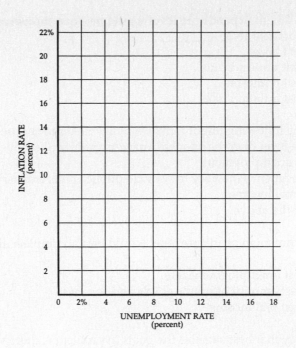

Exercise 2

This exercise shows the difficulties faced by policymakers because of the inevitable tradeoffs in the economy.

Table 18.2 presents data on government expenditure, taxes, exports, imports, GDP deflator, unemployment, and pollution for four levels of equilibrium income (GDP). These items appear frequently in newspaper articles about the economy.

Table 18.2
Level of key economic indicators, by GDP level
(billions of dollars per year)

	Nominal GDP			
Indicator	$120	$160	$200	$240
Government expenditures	$ 0	$ 20	$ 35	$ 50
Taxes	$ 18	$ 24	$ 30	$ 36
Budget balance	$___	$___	$___	$___
Exports	$ 10	$ 10	$ 10	$ 10
Imports	$ 0	$ 10	$ 15	$ 20
Balance of trade	$___	$___	$___	$___
GDP deflator (index)	1.00	1.00	1.02	1.20
Real GDP (constant dollars)	$___	$___	$___	$___
Unemployment rate	15%	7%	4%	3.5%
Pollution index	1.00	1.10	1.80	1.90

1. Compute the federal budget balance, balance of trade, and real GDP in Table 18.2 for each level of nominal GDP.

2. What government expenditure level would best accomplish all of the following goals according to Table 18.2? _____
   - Lowest taxes.
   - Largest trade surplus.
   - Lowest pollution.
   - Lowest inflation rate.

3. Which of the following might induce a policymaker to choose a higher government expenditure level than the one that answers problem 2 (above)?
   (a) High unemployment.
   (b) Government's inability to provide public goods and services.
   (c) Low real income.
   (d) All of the above.

4. What government expenditure level would best accomplish all of the following goals?
   _____
   - Lowest unemployment rate.
   - Highest amount of public goods and services.
   - Highest real income.

5. For the policy that best satisfies the goals in problem 4, there would most likely be:
   (a) A recession.
   (b) Inflation with growth.
   (c) Stagflation.
   (d) None of the above.

6. At what level of government expenditure is the value of the dollar in greatest danger? (*Note:* If there is a large trade deficit, the value of the dollar should fall.) _____

7. Which government expenditure level would best accomplish all of the following goals?
   _____
   - Balancing the federal budget.
   - Balancing the balance of trade.
   - Maintaining pollution at reasonably low levels.
   - Maintaining price stability.

8. At which government expenditure level does full employment occur? (*Hint:* Look at the definition of "full employment." Use 4 percent unemployment as full employment.)
   _____

9. If you were a policymaker faced with the alternatives in Table 18.2, would you be able to say that one of the alternative government expenditure levels was clearly best?

Exercise 3

This exercise checks to see if you can find the appropriate policy action for various undesirable economic conditions.

Choose the policy actions from the list below that would be appropriate to correct the economic conditions at the top of Table 18.3. Mark the letter of each item only once in Table 18.3.

a. Deregulation.
b. Discount rate lowered.
c. Discount rate raised.
d. Free trade
e. Government spending decreases.
f. Government spending increases.
g. Human capital investment
h. Immigration
i. Infrastructure development

j. Open-market operations (the Fed buys government securities).
k. Open-market operations (the Fed sells government securities).
l. Reserve requirement higher.
m. Reserve requirement lower.
n. Tax cuts.
o. Tax incentives to encourage investment.
p. Tax incentives to encourage saving.
q. Tax increases.

Table 18.3
Economic policies

	Recession (AD shortfall)	Inflation (AD excess)	Stagflation
Fiscal policy	1. _____ 2. _____	6. _____ 7. _____	
Monetary policy	3. _____ 4. _____ 5. _____	8. _____ 9. _____ 10. _____	
Supply-side policy		11. _____	12. _____ 13. _____ 14. _____ 15. _____ 16. _____ 17. _____

Exercise 4

The media often provide information about the government's slowness in responding to the economy's needs. This exercise will use one of the articles in the text to show the kind of information to look for. If your professor makes a newspaper assignment for this chapter, this exercise will provide an example of how to do it.

Reread the World View article on page 397 of the text titled "Deficit-Cutting Wilts in Heat from Voters: Entitlements Remain Mostly Off-Limits" from *The Washington Post*. Then answer the following questions.

1. Which *one* of the following obstacles to success is best illustrated by the article.
   (a) Goal conflicts.
   (b) Measurement problems.
   (c) Design problems.
   (d) Implementation problems.

2. What passage specifically mentions the obstacle you have chosen?

3. What passage indicates the decision-maker who is responsible for determining the policy?

4. What passage indicates the situation which requires a policy response?

Exercise 5

The relationship between inflation and unemployment is an important policy problem. Using a graph of the inflation rate and the unemployment rate, you will be able to see what the relationship is.

1. Find data on the percentage change of the Consumer Price Index and the unemployment rate. Graph the two indexes in Figure 18.2 for the period 1970 to 1992.

Figure 18.2
Inflation and unemployment rates

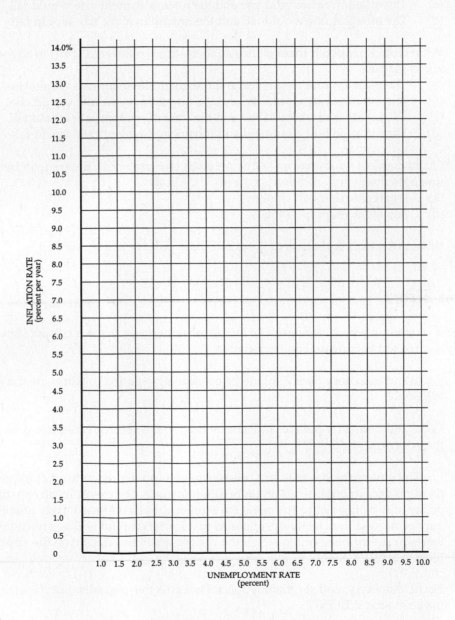

2. The relationship is best characterized as:
   (a) Direct (the slope of the best-fitting line going through the points is positive).
   (b) Inverse (the slope of the best-fitting line going through the points is negative).

3. T F On the basis of your answer to the previous question, a president's success in holding down the inflation rate will result in a higher unemployment rate.

4. T F On the basis of your answer to question #1, a president's success in holding down the unemployment rate will result in a higher inflation rate.

5. What would happen if there were a sudden surge in aggregate demand, *ceteris paribus*?
   (a) The inflation rate would rise and the unemployment rate would rise.
   (b) The inflation rate would fall and the unemployment rate would rise.
   (c) The inflation rate would rise and the unemployment rate would fall.
   (d) The inflation rate would fall and the unemployment rate would fall.

6. What would happen if there were a sudden surge (rightward shift) in aggregate supply, *ceteris paribus*?
   (a) The inflation rate would rise and the unemployment rate would rise.
   (b) The inflation rate would fall and the unemployment rate would rise.
   (c) The inflation rate would rise and the unemployment rate would fall.
   (d) The inflation rate would fall and the unemployment rate would fall.

7. On the basis of your answers to the previous two problems, the tradeoff between unemployment and inflation is a result of cyclical:
   (a) Aggregate demand changes.
   (b) Aggregate supply changes.

8. What is the technical name of the graph that you have just drawn?

Common Errors

The first statement in each "common error" below is incorrect. Each incorrect statement is followed by a corrected version and an explanation.

1. Fiscal and monetary policy should be consistently applied to stimulate the economy. WRONG!

   Fiscal and monetary policies must be tailored to the specific economic problems faced by the government. RIGHT!

   The government sometimes needs to apply apparently contradictory monetary and fiscal policies in order to attain quite different goals. For example, an expansionary fiscal policy may be needed to stimulate the economy, but a contractionary monetary policy may be needed to raise interest rates so that foreign capital will be enticed into the United States. A policymaker must weigh the various goals and decide on the appropriate mix of tools to achieve them.

2. Fiscal, monetary, and stagflation policies are effective regardless of the income level of the economy. WRONG!

   The state of the economy in relation to full employment is important in determining the effectiveness of the various policies. RIGHT!

If the economy is experiencing an excess AD, wage–price controls will prove ineffective in curbing inflation. At relatively low levels of GDP, however, wage–price controls can be effective in holding down inflation. Work-force policies are often more effective in matching people with jobs when many people are looking for work than when unemployment is low. It is easier for the government to increase expenditures to stimulate the economy when there is a recession than to cut them back when there is excess AD.

3. The government has the power to prevent unemployment and inflation, but it just doesn't want to use it. WRONG!

While the government has the power to move the economy closer to any one goal, it faces a tradeoff between different goals that prevents it from achieving all of them. RIGHT!

Remember that the Phillips curve shows that a tradeoff exists between unemployment and inflation. Government policies to lower unemployment may lead to a worsening of inflation. The government must choose between the different goals.

•ANSWERS•

Key-Term Review

1.	automatic stabilizer	9.	supply-side policy
2.	growth recession	10.	multiplier
3.	fine-tuning	11.	velocity of money (V)
4.	business cycle	12.	rational expectations
5.	fiscal policy	13.	stagflation
6.	structural deficit	14.	GDP gap (real)
7.	monetary policy	15.	AD excess
8.	natural rate of unemployment		AD shortfall

True or False

1.	T	5.	F	9.	T	13.	F	17.	F	21.	T
2.	T	6.	F	10.	F	14.	F	18.	T	22.	T
3.	F	7.	F	11.	F	15.	F	19.	F	23.	F
4.	F	8.	T	12.	F	16.	T	20.	F		

Multiple Choice

1.	b	6.	a	10.	b	14.	c	18.	a	22.	b
2.	a	7.	d	11.	d	15.	d	19.	b	23.	d
3.	d	8.	b	12.	d	16.	a	20.	c	24.	a
4.	a	9.	c	13.	d	17.	c	21.	c	25.	c
5.	c										

Problems and Applications

Exercise 1

1. **Table 18.1 Answer**

	30%	20%	10%	0%
Interest rate	30%	20%	10%	0%
Budget balance	- $ 75	- $ 25	$ 25	$ 75
Balance of trade	40	20	0	- 20
Nominal GDP	900	1,000	1,100	1,200
Saving	125	135	145	155
Real GDP (constant dollars)	900	1,000	1,078	1,091

At the 30 percent interest rate, the following calculations (in billions of dollars per year) apply:

Budget balance	= $25 - $100	= -$75
Balance of trade	= $300 - $260	= $40
Nominal GDP	= $750 + $10 + $100 + $40	= $900
Saving	= Disposable income - consumption	
	= (GDP - taxes) - consumption	= $900 - $25 - $750 = $125

2. b   4. a   6. c   7. d   8. a
3. b   5. a

9. See Figure 18.1 Answer.

For example, when income is $1,200, the price index is 1.10. The inflation rate is

$$\left(\frac{1.10}{1.00} - 1.00 \right) \times 100 = 10\%$$

Figure 18.1 Answer

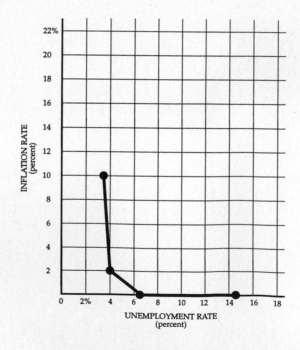

Exercise 2

1. **Table 18.2 Answer**

	Nominal GDP			
Indicator	$120	$160	$200	$240
Budget balance	$ 18	$ 4	$ - 5	$ - 14
Balance of trade	10	0	- 5	- 10
Real GDP (constant dollars)	120	160	196	200

2. $0
3. d
4. $50 billion
5. b
6. $50 billion
7. $20 billion
8. $35 billion
9. no

Exercise 3

1. **Table 18.3 Answer**

	Recessionary gap	Inflationary gap	Stagflation
Fiscal policy	1. n Tax cuts 2. f Government spending increases	6. 8 Tax increases 7. 6 Government spending decreases	
Monetary policy	3. b Discount rate lowered 4. j Open-market operations (Fed buys government securities) 5. m Reserve requirement lower	8. c Discount rate raised 9. k Open-market operations (Fed sells government securities) 10. e Reserve requirement higher	
Supply-side policy		11. p Tax incentives to encouraging saving	12. a Deregulation 13. d Free trade 14. Human capital investment 15. i Infrastructure development 16. o Tax incentives for investment

Exercise 4

1. a   However, there is implicit evidence of design problemsconcerning the best way to cut the deficit.

2. "Even before his proposal [to cut the deficit] took shape, more than 3,000 New Mexico constituents sent him identical postcards opposing any effort to cap entitlement programs." The passage shows the conflict between deficit cutting and the need for inflation-indexed entitlement programs to protect different groups.

3. "Senate, which voted 69 to 28 to reject the proposal"

4. "digging out of the massive federal deficit"

Exercise 5

1. **Figure 18.2 Answer**

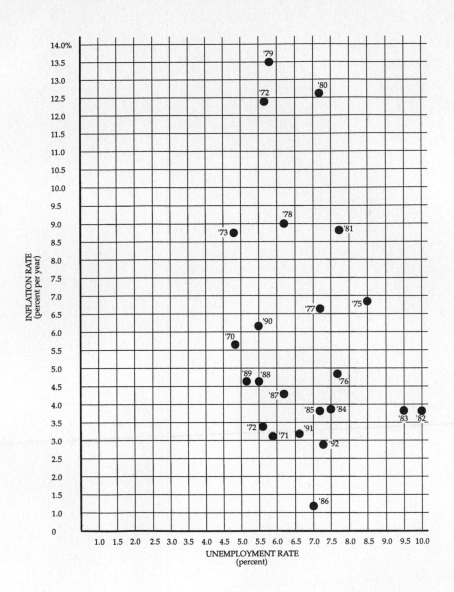

2. b
3. T
4. T
5. c
6. d
7. a
8. Phillips curve

CHAPTER 19

International Trade

Quick Review

Even the most casual observer of economic activity understands that trade between the United States and other nations is very important. Hardly a day goes by without hearing or reading some reference to exports, imports, the "trade deficit," the value of the dollar in foreign-exchange markets, and the like. In this chapter we ask some basic questions about trade, such as:

- What benefit, if any, do we get from international trade?
- How much harm do imports cause, and to whom?
- Should we protect ourselves from "unfair" trade by limiting some or all imports?

In recent decades the United States has become much more dependent on foreign trade than ever before. We export a wide variety of goods, especially agricultural products and capital goods, to many countries, and import from advanced industrial nations such as Japan and Germany, and such poor countries as Bangladesh and Uruguay. Oil has become our most important import. Each nation trades with many others and although overall trade must balance (total exports must equal total imports), exports and imports between pairs of countries seldom balance. Bilateral trade imbalances (surpluses and deficits) are the rule rather than the exception.

Countries are motivated to trade because by doing so they can produce together more total output than they could in the absence of trade. Specialization and trade allow both members of a trading partnership to consume beyond their respective production-possibilities curves. That is, consumption possibilities exceed production possibilities when countries specialize and trade. The economic reason for this situation is rooted in what is called the "law of comparative advantage." This dictum says that as long as the opportunity costs of producing goods in two countries differ, it will always be possible for those countries to specialize and trade to their mutual advantage. Neither the absolute size of the countries nor their absolute costs of production are important. What does count is the relative (comparative) cost of producing alternative goods.

It is obvious that specialization and trade benefit trading nations. While trade increases total world output, it is the terms at which trade takes place which determine how the gains are distributed. In spite of trades overall benefits, special interest groups often exert strong pressure *against* foreign trade. Those who would lose their markets and jobs to imported goods and foreign workers may oppose free trade.

Industries that need raw materials that are being exported may also exert pressure on government to place restrictions on the export of those raw materials. The government may place a tariff or quota on imported goods or provide aid to the affected domestic industry. The government may subsidize industries that are hurt by foreign trade. We have occasionally asked our trading partners to voluntarily limit their exports to us so as to ease the pressure on threatened firms and industries. The government has sometimes made assistance (cash, training, or relocation) available to those whose jobs were lost to foreign competition.

Most of the world's industrialized countries are signatories to the General Agreement on Tariffs and Trade (GATT). This organization, which was created in 1947, commits the world's trading partners to pursue free-trade policies. This includes the dismantling of both tariff and nontariff barriers to trade in goods and services. The organization had significant success in early "rounds," but it has had more difficulty in making important gains recently. The movement toward regional trading groups around the globe is testimony to the power of freer trade. The EEC, NAFTA and other arrangements are all aimed at reducing barriers to trade within the group and capitalizing on specialization along the lines of comparative advantage.

Learning Objectives

After reading Chapter 19 and doing the following exercises, you should:	True or false	Multiple choice	Problems and applications	Common errors	Pages in the text
1. Know some basic facts about U.S. trade patterns.	1	17-19		3	415-418
2. Understand the macroeconomic impact of international trade.	3, 4, 6, 9, 19	11			417-418
3. Understand why specialization and trade increase both production possibilities and consumption possibilities.	2, 10, 11, 14			1, 4	418-423
4. Be able to explain comparative advantage using opportunity costs.	2, 5, 11, 12	1-5, 7, 12-14	1	1, 2	424-425
5. Know how to determine the limits to the terms of trade.	13	15, 16	2		425-427
6. Be able to calculate the gains from specialization and trade at given terms of trade.	2, 14	16, 21	3		425-427
7. Be able to show how trade allows a country to consume beyond its production-possibilities curve.	10		1, 2	4	422, 426
8. Recognize the sources of pressure that result in restricted trade.	7, 15, 16	6, 10, 11, 18	3	2	418-419
9. Know some of the arguments used by those wishing to restrict trade.	7, 17, 18	6, 9	3		429-431
10. Be able to discuss tariff and nontariff barriers to trade.	5, 7, 15-18, 26	8, 9, 20, 21	3		431-438
11. Be able to discuss the reasons for the rise of regional trading arrangements.		22			439-441

Key-Term Review

Review the following terms; if you are not sure of the meaning of any term, write out the definition and check it against the Glossary in the text.

absolute advantage	production possibilities
comparative advantage	quota
consumption possibilities	tariff
embargo	terms of trade
equilibrium price	trade deficit
exports	trade surplus
imports	voluntary restraint agreement (VRA)
opportunity cost	

Fill in the blank following each of the statements below with the appropriate term from the list above.

1. The slope of the production-possibilities curve indicates the quantity of one good that must be given up in order to produce one more unit of another good, or in other words, the _____ .

   1. _____

2. The leakages from the income stream consist of savings, taxes, and _____ .

   2. _____

3. When the opportunity cost of producing a good is lower in one country than in another, the first country is said to have a _____ .

   3. _____

4. A country that can produce more of a good than another country with the same amount of resources is said to have an _____ .

   4. _____

5. U.S. firms manufacture computers and produce agricultural goods and ship them to France. Computers and agricultural goods are U.S. _____ .

   5. _____

6. The various combinations of two goods that a country can produce and consume without trade constitute its _____ .

   6. _____

7. The various combinations of two goods that a country can consume when it engages in trade constitute _____ .

   7. _____

8. An absolute limit imposed by a government on the quantity of a specific item that may be imported is called a _____ .

   8. _____

9. A tax on imported goods is known as a _____ .

   9. _____

10. In 1973 the Arab members of OPEC agreed not to sell oil to the United States. This action was called an _____ .

10. _____

11. Two countries producing two goods must decide how much of one good will trade for a unit of the other good. This ratio indicates the _____ .

11. _____

12. A country that imports more than it exports over a given period of time is said to have a _____ .

12. _____

13. When a country's exports exceed its imports, it is said to have a _____ .

13. _____

14. Under a freely flexible exchange-rate system, the market price will approach the _____ .

14. _____

15. A quota voluntarily placed by a country on its own exports is called a _____ .

15. _____

True or False: *Circle your choice.*

T F 1. Measured in terms of total trade (exports plus imports), Japan is the United States's most important trading partner.

T F 2. The main reason that countries specialize and trade with each other is that by doing so they can get things they cannot produce themselves.

T F 3. The trade balance is calculated by subtracting exports from imports.

T F 4. Any change in exports has a multiplier effect on the aggregate level of income, *ceteris paribus*.

T F 5. A reduction of trade barriers should result in reduced prices and increased consumption, *ceteris paribus*.

T F 6. Net increases in exports tend to lower national income; net increases in imports tend to raise the level of national income.

T F 7. Increased restrictions on trade redistribute income from export industries to import-competing industries.

T F 8. A trade deficit means that imports exceed exports over some relevant time period.

T F 9. Since one country's exports are another country's imports, overall world trade must balance.

T F 10. Specialization and trade allow countries to consume beyond their own respective production-possibilities curves.

T F 11. If the opportunity costs of producing goods in two countries are the same, there is no incentive to trade.

T F 12. If one country has a comparative advantage in producing one of two goods, the other country must have a comparative advantage in the other good.

T F 13. The terms at which countries will trade one good for another will occur between their respective domestic opportunity costs.

T F 14. Since free trade is beneficial to society as a whole, it benefits each individual group in society as well.

T F 15. From the consumer's point of view, quotas have the potential to inflict more damage than do tariffs.

T F 16. The pressure for restrictions on trade tends to increase when the economy is operating near capacity.

T F 17. Tariffs and quotas raise the price of imported goods to consumers.

T F 18. Voluntary restraint agreements are, in reality, "voluntary quotas."

T F 19. Bilateral trade balances refer to trade balances between two countries.

T F 20. Voluntary export restraints by Japanese auto manufacturers resulted in higher prices for automobiles purchased by U.S. consumers.

Multiple Choice: *Select the correct answer.*

_____ 1. Suppose the production of 1 ton of steel in the United States requires the same amount of resources as the production of 100 gallons of oil. In Canada, 2 tons of steel might require the same amount of resources as 200 gallons of oil. This means that:
   (a) The United States has the comparative advantage in steel.
   (b) Canada has the comparative advantage in steel.
   (c) The United States has an absolute advantage in steel.
   (d) None of the statements above is correct.

_____ 2. In Germany, suppose 6 cameras or 4 bicycles can be produced with 1 unit of labor. In Japan, suppose 9 cameras or 5 bicycles can be produced with 1 unit of labor. Therefore:
   (a) Germany has an absolute advantage in the production of both goods.
   (b) Japan has a comparative advantage in the production of both goods.
   (c) Germany has a comparative advantage in the production of bicycles.
   (d) Japan has a comparative advantage in the production of bicycles.

_____ 3. Given the conditions listed in question 2, what is the opportunity cost of producing 1 bicycle?
   (a) In Germany, 1.5 cameras.
   (b) In Germany, 2/3 camera.
   (c) In Japan, 5/9 camera.
   (d) In Japan, 8.1 cameras.

_____ 4. Given the conditions listed in questions 2 and 3, the terms of trade at which these two goods would be traded between Germany and Japan would be 1 bicycle to:
   (a) More than 1.8 cameras.
   (b) More than 1.5 cameras but less than 1.8 cameras.
   (c) Less than 1.5 cameras.
   (d) None of the above, because Japan has an absolute advantage in both goods.

_____ 5. Suppose that France and the United States do not trade and that the competitive price of an ordinary bottle of wine is 20 francs in France and $2 in the United States; the price of wheat per bushel is 40 francs in France and $6 in the United States. This information is sufficient to enable us to state that:
   (a) France has a comparative advantage in the production of wine.
   (b) France has a comparative advantage in the production of wheat.
   (c) Neither country has a comparative advantage in the production of either good.
   (d) The United States has an absolute advantage in the production of both goods.

_____ 6. A person who accepts the arguments for freer trade:
   (a) Will oppose all tariffs, whatever the arguments in their favor.
   (b) Will favor tariffs because they will raise the real income of the countries levying them.
   (c) Could favor tariffs if he or she thought the objectives of policy served by such tariffs were more important than raising real income.
   (d) Will oppose all tariffs but will favor selective quotas.

_____ 7. To say that a country has a comparative advantage in the production of wine is to say that:
   (a) It can produce wine with fewer resources than any other country can.
   (b) Its opportunity cost of producing wine is greater than any other country's.
   (c) Its opportunity cost of producing wine is lower than any other country's.
   (d) The relative price of wine is higher in that country than in any other.

_____ 8. America's tariffs on foreign goods result in:
   (a) Lower domestic prices than those that would prevail in their absence.
   (b) A stimulus to efficient American firms that are not protected.
   (c) Higher employment and output in protected industries than would otherwise be the case.
   (d) A more efficient allocation of resources than would occur in their absence.

_____ 9. A principal objective of GATT is to:
   (a) Protect domestic producers from foreign competition.
   (b) Settle domestic tax disputes internationally.
   (c) Equalize income tax structures in various countries.
   (d) Reduce barriers to trade.

_____ 10. Adjustment assistance is designed to:
   (a) Ease the adjustment problems confronting consumers when a tariff or quota is levied.
   (b) Assist producers and those workers who are adversely affected by a reduction in tariffs or quotas.
   (c) Assist producers and those workers who are adversely affected by an increase in tariffs or quotas.
   (d) Increase the revenues received by the government.

11. A beggar-my-neighbor policy is:
    (a) An attempt by a poor country to get more foreign aid and assistance.
    (b) The imposition of trade barriers for the purpose of expanding exports.
    (c) The imposition of import barriers for the purpose of curbing inflation.
    (d) The imposition of trade barriers to increase domestic demand and employment.

Suppose the productivities of Japanese and U.S. producers are as indicated in Table 19.1. Use Table 19.1 to answer questions 12-16.

Table 19.1
Output per worker day in the United States and Japan

Country	TV sets (per day)	Bicycles (per day)
Japan	2	10
United States	1	8

12. Which of the following statements is true?
    (a) The United States has an absolute advantage in the production of bicycles.
    (b) Japan has an absolute advantage in the production of bicycles only.
    (c) Japan has an absolute advantage in the production of TV sets only.
    (d) Japan has an absolute advantage in the production of both bicycles and TV sets.

13. Which of the following is a true statement?
    (a) The opportunity cost of TV sets is higher in Japan than in the United States.
    (b) The opportunity cost of TV sets is lower in Japan than in the United States.
    (c) It is impossible to tell anything about opportunity cost from the information given.
    (d) The United States has a comparative advantage in the production of TV sets.

14. Which of the following statements is true?
    (a) Japan has an absolute advantage in the production of both products and a comparative advantage in bicycles.
    (b) Japan has a comparative advantage in both products and an absolute advantage in the production of TV sets.
    (c) The United States has an absolute advantage in neither product but a comparative advantage in the production of bicycles.
    (d) The United States has an absolute advantage in neither product but a comparative advantage in TV sets.

15. Suppose the terms of trade are established in such a way that 1 TV set equals 5 bicycles. Which of the following statements would be true?
    (a) These terms of trade provide gains for the United States, but Japan is worse off.
    (b) These terms of trade provide gains for Japan, but the United States is worse off.
    (c) These terms of trade provide gains for the United States, and Japan is no worse off.
    (d) These terms of trade provide gains for Japan, and the United States is no worse off.

16. Which of the following terms of trade would provide gains for both countries?
    (a) 1 TV set equals 5 bicycles.
    (b) 1 TV set equals 8 bicycles.
    (c) 1 TV set equals 6 bicycles.
    (d) None of the above would provide such gains.

371

_____ 17. Which of the following statements is correct?
  (a)   The United States is becoming increasingly dependent on foreign trade.
  (b)   The United States is becoming less dependent on foreign trade.
  (c)   U.S. dependence on trade has remained relatively constant for the past decade.
  (d)   None of the above statements is correct.

_____ 18. When Japan "voluntarily" restrained automobile exports to the United States between 1981 and 1985:
  (a)   U.S. auto producers became more profitable.
  (b)   Firms importing Japanese cars became more profitable.
  (c)   Consumers paid higher prices for both U.S. and Japanese cars.
  (d)   All of the above were true.

_____ 19. Which of the following countries has the *lowest* export-to-GDP ratio?
  (a)   The United States.
  (b)   Japan.
  (c)   Great Britain.
  (d)   Canada.

_____ 20. Nontariff barriers have been used:
  (a)   As a substitute for tariff barriers.
  (b)   By many countries.
  (c)   More frequently since GATT negotiated tariff reductions.
  (d)   In all of the above cases.

_____ 21. Which of the following groupings contains a term that does not belong?
  (a)   Imports, exports, trade balance.
  (b)   Embargoes, tariffs, quotas.
  (c)   Comparative advantage, absolute advantage, protectionism.
  (d)   Infant industries, dumping, national security.

22. Which of the following groupings contains a term that does not belong?
  (a)   Production possibilities, consumption possibilities, terms of trade.
  (b)   Voluntary restraint agreements, bilateral trade agreements, trading blocs.
  (c)   Adjustment assistance, worker assistance, industry subsidies.
  (d)   GATT, ITC, EEC.

Problems and Applications

Exercise 1

This exercise shows how trade leads to gains by all trading partners through specialization and comparative advantage.

Suppose that Japan has 20 laborers in total and that the United States has 40 laborers. Suppose their productivities are as indicated in Table 19.2. (*Be careful:* The table tells you that a worker in Japan can produce 2 TV sets per day *or* 10 bicycles per day, *not* two TV sets *and* 10 bicycles!)

Table 19.2
Output per worker day in the United States and Japan

Country	TV sets (per day)	Bicycles (per day)
Japan	2	10
United States	1	8

1. Draw the production-possibilities curves for each country in Figure 19.1. Assume constant costs of production.

Figure 19.1

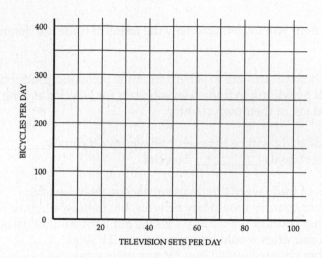

2. Suppose that before trade Japan uses 12 laborers to produce bicycles and 8 laborers to produce television sets; suppose also that in the United States 20 workers produce bicycles and 20 produce television sets. Complete Table 19.3.

Table 19.3
Output produced and consumed without trade

Country	TV sets (per day)	Bicycles (per day)
Japan	_____	_____
United States	_____	_____
Total	_____	_____

3. Before trade, the total output of television sets is _____ ; of bicycles, _____ .

4. What is the opportunity cost of 1 television set in Japan? _____ In the United States? _____

5. What is the opportunity cost of 1 bicycle in Japan? _____ In the United States? _____

373

6. If Japan and the United States specialize according to their respective comparative advantages, Japan will produce _____ and the United States will produce _____ . They will do so because the opportunity cost of bicycles in terms of television sets is (lower, higher) in the United States than in Japan, and the opportunity cost of television sets in terms of bicycles is (lower, higher) in Japan than in the United States.

7. After specialization, the total output of television sets is _____ and the total output of bicycles is _____ . (*Hint:* 20 Japanese produce only TV sets, and 40 Americans produce only bicycles.)

8. This output represents an increase of _____ bicycles and _____ television sets over the prespecialization output. (*Hint:* Compare answers to problems 3 and 7.)

Exercise 2

This exercise will help you understand how the terms of trade are determined. Refer to Exercise 1 for the data.

If Japan and the United States are to benefit from the increased production, trade must take place. The Japanese will be willing to trade television sets for bicycles as long as they get back more bicycles than they could get in their own country.

1. The terms of trade will be between 1 television set equals _____ bicycles and 1 television set equals _____ bicycles.

2. If the terms of trade were 4 bicycles equals one television set:
   (a) Neither country would buy bicycles, but both would buy TV sets.
   (b) Neither country would buy TV sets, but both would buy bicycles.
   (c) Both countries would buy bicycles and TV sets.
   (d) Neither country would buy TV sets or bicycles.

3. Suppose that the two countries agree that the terms of trade will be 6 bicycles equals 1 television set. Let Japan export 20 television sets per day to the United States. Complete Table 19.4. Assume that Japan produces 40 television sets per day and the United States produces 320 bicycles.

Table 19.4
Consumption combination after trade

Country	TV sets (per day)	Bicycles (per day)
Japan	____	____
United States	____	____
Total	40	320

4. As a result of specialization and trade, the United States has the same quantity of television sets and _____ more bicycles per day. (Compare Tables 19.3 and 19.4.)

5. As a result of specialization and trade, Japan has the same number of bicycles and _____ more television sets per day.

Now suppose that at the exchange rate of 6 bicycles to 1 TV set, Japan would like to export 10 TV sets and import 60 bicycles per day. Suppose also that the United States desires to export 90 bicycles and import 15 television sets per day.

6. At these terms of trade there is a (shortage, surplus) of television sets.

7. At these terms of trade there is a (shortage, surplus) of bicycles.

8. Which of the following terms of trade would be more likely to result from this situation?
    (a) 5 bicycles equal 1 television set.
    (b) 6 bicycles equal 1 television set.
    (c) 7 bicycles equal 1 television set.

Exercise 3

As protectionist spirit rises in the United States, the media concentrate more on ways to protect American producers. This exercise will use a newspaper cartoon found in the text to show how to evaluate the effects of such proposals on trade. If your professor makes a newspaper assignment for this chapter from the Instructor's Manual, this exercise will provide an example of how to do it.

Study the cartoon in Chapter 19 from *The Washington Post* about auto protectionism. Then answer the following questions.

1. How does the cartoon on page 436 indicate which product or products are the subject of protectionism?

2. What form of protectionism is changing, according to the cartoon?
    (a) Quotas.
    (b) Tariffs.
    (c) Export subsidies.
    (d) Other (specify: _____).

3. How does the cartoon identify the form of protectionism?

4. How does the cartoon indicate whether protectionism is increasing or decreasing?

5. How does the cartoon indicate the effects of the change in protectionism on quantities or prices of the good, exports or imports of the good, trade relations between countries, or diplomatic relations?

Common Errors

The first statement in each "common error" below is incorrect. Each incorrect statement is followed by a corrected version and an explanation.

1. A country must have an *absolute advantage* in order to gain from trade with another country. WRONG!

    A country must have a *comparative advantage* in order to gain from trade with another country. RIGHT!

    Mutually advantageous trade requires only that the opportunity costs of producing goods differ in the two countries. Another way of stating this is that the production-possibilities curves of the two countries must have different slopes. The two circumstances noted above are indicated in Figure 19.2.

Figure 19.2

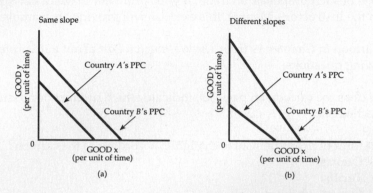

In diagram (a), in which country B has an absolute advantage over country A, the productions possibilities curves have the same slope; thus mutually advantageous trade *is not* possible. In diagram (b), each country has a comparative advantage because the production-possibilities curves of the two countries have different slopes; thus mutually advantageous trade *is* possible.

2. Foreign trade costs a country jobs. WRONG!

    Although jobs may be lost, new ones will be created by the opportunities opened up with trade. RIGHT!

    When countries specialize and trade according to the law of comparative advantage, some particular workers and firms may be hurt by imports, but the economy as a whole gains by trade. More output per resource input will be attainable. Because the economy is able to reach full employment with trade as well as without trade, there is no reason to assume there will be fewer jobs.

3. A country is well off only as long as it exports more than it imports. WRONG!

    Countries may, at times, be well off when they experience a trade surplus, they may also be well off when they have a trade deficit. RIGHT!

    Both trade deficits and trade surpluses can be problems if either situation persists for a long period of time. Trade surpluses mean that a country is giving more of its limited, precious resources in trade than it is acquiring from other countries. The currencies of deficit countries tend to depreciate, which means they will be unable to buy as many foreign goods with a unit of currency.

4. Countries tend to enter into trade to get things they cannot produce themselves. WRONG!

Countries very often trade for things they could produce themselves. RIGHT!

Be careful! Countries often trade for things they could produce themselves because the relative costs of domestic production would be prohibitive. Take baskets as an example. We could certainly produce baskets if we really wanted to. The technique is not difficult to learn and the materials are abundant. But baskets do not lend themselves to machine production, and hand labor is expensive. The cost in terms of goods forgone would be tremendous. (So would the price of the baskets.) We're better off specializing in something like computers, where we have a comparative advantage, and trading for baskets, where we clearly do not have a comparative advantage.

•ANSWERS•

Key-Term Review

1.	opportunity cost	9.	tariff
2.	imports	10.	embargo
3.	comparative advantage	11.	terms of trade
4.	absolute advantage	12.	trade deficit
5.	exports	13.	trade surplus
6.	production possibilities	14.	equilibrium price
7.	consumption possibilities	15.	voluntary restraint agreement (VRA)
8.	quota		

True or False

1.	F	5.	T	9.	T	12.	T	15.	T	18.	T
2.	F	6.	F	10.	T	13.	T	16.	F	19.	T
3.	F	7.	T	11.	T	14.	F	17.	T	20.	T
4.	T	8.	T								

Multiple Choice

1.	d	5.	b	9.	d	12.	d	15.	c	18.	d
2.	c	6.	c	10.	b	13.	b	16.	c	19.	a
3.	a	7.	c	11.	d	14.	c	17.	a	20.	d
4.	b	8.	c								

21. c Protectionism is a form of government intervention. Topics of other groupings are (a) trade balance, (b) forms of government protectionism, and (d) reasons for protectionism.

22. d GATT tries to lower protective barriers, whereas the other groups tend to raise them against outsiders. Topics of other groupings are (a) the curves used to determine optimal trade patterns, (b) forms of protectionism, and (c) methods of protecting groups against the effects of free trade.

Problems and Applications

Exercise 1

1. **Figure 19.1 Answer**

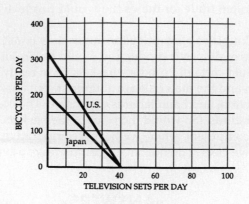

2. **Table 19.3 Answer**

Country	TV sets	Bicycles
Japan	16	120
United States	20	160
Total	36	280

3. 36; 280

4. 5 bicycles; 8 bicycles
5. 1/5 television set; 1/8 television set
6. television sets; bicycles; lower; lower
7. 40; 320
8. 40; 4

Exercise 2

1. 5; 8

2. a

3. **Table 19.4 Answer**

Country	TV sets	Bicycles
Japan	20	120
United States	20	200
Total	40	320

4. 40

5. 4

6. shortage   The Japanese wish to export fewer (10) TV sets than Americans want (15).

7. surplus   The Americans wish to export more (90) bicycles than the Japanese want (60).

8. c

Exercise 3

1. The drawing is of an automobile dealership, and the caption tells us the product is automobiles.

2. a

3. "Tell me again how the quotas . . ." is the caption to the cartoon.

4. The "higher prices" shown in the car windows indicate a recent change upward.

5. The window stickers indicate higher prices for both imported cars and those produced in the United States. The headline on the newspaper suggests trade relations are important.

CHAPTER 20

International Finance

Quick Review

All of the trade between nations discussed in the previous chapter must somehow be financed. And since each country has its own money, we have to ask several critical questions:

- What determines the value of one country's money in terms of other national currencies?
- What causes the international value of currencies to change?
- Can we limit the fluctuations in the value of the dollar? Should we try to do so?

To facilitate trade and to eliminate the need for barter, markets for foreign-exchange have developed. Their function is to determine the exchange rate at which two currencies will trade. The foreign-exchange market is like any other market—it consists of a supply schedule and a demand schedule. Supply and demand mean the same thing here as they do in any other market. The commodity being traded in this case is the money of one country for the money of another. Demand and supply determine the equilibrium price (exchange rate) and quantity of foreign-exchange that is traded.

When the international value of a currency increases, the currency is said to appreciate. When a currency's international value decreases, the currency is said to depreciate. The exchange rate responds to changes in underlying forces, as reflected in shifts of the supply and demand curves. Changes in relative income levels, changes in relative prices, changes in product availability, relative interest-rate changes, and speculative activities are examples of the determinant that cause supply and demand curves to shift, and alter exchange rates.

To keep track of the foreign-exchange flows that accompany the flow of goods and services, each country summarizes its transactions in a statement called the "balance of payments." The balance of payments is based on double-entry bookkeeping and must therefore balance, even though individual accounts may not. The primary accounts are the balance of trade, the current account, and the capital account.

Governments do not always like the way the exchange rates for their currencies fluctuate. Depending on their interests at the moment, they may intervene to support their currencies or those of other countries. In some situations a government may set a fixed price for its currency. Although the world's major currencies are basically free to float, governments still sometimes interfere.

A government enters on the demand side when the price of its currency falls below the level it considers appropriate. It enters on the supply side when the exchange rate rises above the level it considers appropriate. When governments do interfere, we call the resulting situation a managed-rate system, or a "dirty float." In recent years, the U.S. government and the governments of its major trading partners have intervened several times to prevent undesired fluctuations in the value of the dollar.

Trade between nations is difficult in centrally planned economies too, since prices which are set by planners rather than by markets are not accepted internationally. When currencies are not convertible, barter results and countries do not follow the dictates of comparative advantage. These are additional problems to be overcome during the transition from planning to markets.

Learning Objectives

After reading Chapter 20 and doing the following exercises, you should:	True or false	Multiple choice	Problems and applications	Common errors	Pages in the text
1. Understand that an exchange rate is simply a price.		1, 11, 16, 17	1	3	444-445
2. Know the forces that operate on the demand side of the foreign-exchange market.	1, 2, 7	7, 12, 13, 24	1-3	3	445-446
3. Know the forces that operate on the supply side of the foreign-exchange market.	3	24	1-3	3	446-447
4. Understand how supply and demand interact to determine the equilibrium exchange rate.	13	2, 4	1-3		447-448
5. Understand the essentials of balance-of-payments accounting.	15, 17, 18, 20	3, 5, 21-24			449-451
6. Be able to demonstrate graphically the forces that cause a currency to appreciate or depreciate.			1-3	2	451-453
7. Understand why there is resistance to exchange-rate changes.					453-455
8. Be able to describe several exchange-rate systems and their consequences.	4	6, 7, 19, 24			456-462
9. Understand the macroeconomic and microeconomic consequences of exchange-rate movements.	13, 14	9, 10, 14, 15		1	456-457
10. Be able to describe a balance-of-payments problem.		18, 20, 24	3	1, 2	456-457, 460
11. Be aware of the recent history of the international value of the dollar.			2		456-464
12. Be able to discuss the recent problems of the EC.					463-464

Key-Term Review

Review the following terms; if you are not sure of the meaning of any term, write out the definition and check it against the Glossary in the text.

appreciation
balance of payments
balance-of-payments deficit
balance-of-payments surplus
depreciation
equilibrium price
exchange rate
flexible exchange rates

foreign-exchange markets
foreign-exchange reserves
gold reserves
gold standard
managed exchange rates
market shortage
trade deficit

Fill in the blank following each of the statements below with the appropriate term from the list above.

1. Places where foreign currencies are bought and sold are called _____ .

1. _____

2. The price of one country's currency expressed in terms of another country's currency is the _____ .

2. _____

3. The price (exchange rate) at which quantity demanded equals quantity supplied over a given time period is called the _____ .

3. _____

4. A rise in the price of one currency relative to other currencies is referred to as _____ .

4. _____

5. A fall in the price of one currency relative to other currencies is referred to as _____ .

5. _____

6. When the quantity of imports demanded exceeds the quantity supplied at a given exchange rate, there is a _____ .

6. _____

7. The amount by which the value of imports exceeds the value of exports is called the _____ .

7. _____

8. An agreement by countries to fix the prices of their currencies in terms of gold is called the _____ .

8. _____

9. Excess demand by foreigners for domestic currency at current fixed exchange rates causes a _____ .

9. _____

10. Excess demand by domestic residents for foreign currency at fixed exchange rates causes a _____ .

10. _____

11. Holdings of the currencies of other countries by an official government agency, usually the controller, central bank, or treasury, are called _____ .

11. _____

12. Stocks of gold held by a government to purchase foreign-exchange are called _____ .

12. _____

13. When exchange rates are permitted to vary with market supply and demand, they are called _____ .

13. _____

14. Government intervention in foreign-exchange markets to limit but not eliminate exchange-rate fluctuations produces _____ .

14. _____

15. The _____ provides a summary of a country's economic transactions over a given period of time.

15. _____

True or False: *Circle your choice.*

T   F   1.   When a U.S. corporation builds a plant in Germany, it demands foreign currency (marks) to pay for the inputs.

T   F   2.   When Russian gymnasts tour the United States, they create a demand for dollars by supplying rubles.

T   F   3.   The U.S. demand for French francs represents a supply of dollars to the foreign-exchange market.

T   F   4.   The present system of exchange-rate determination is free of government intervention.

T   F   5.   When the supply of dollars increases, *ceteris paribus*, the demand for dollars also increases.

T   F   6.   When the supply of dollars increases, *ceteris paribus*, the quantity of dollars demanded increases.

T   F   7.   Increased foreign travel by Americans tends to cause the dollar to appreciate, *ceteris paribus*.

T   F   8.   When the dollar price of German marks increases, BMW autos become cheaper to U.S. residents.

T   F   9.   When the dollar price of German marks increases, BMW autos become more expensive to Germans relative to U.S. cars.

T   F   10. If the dollar appreciates against the French franc, this change will be favorable to U.S. importers of French wine.

T   F   11. If the dollar appreciates against the franc, this change will be favorable to California vintners.

T F 12.   If income in Japan rises faster than income in the United States, *ceteris paribus,* the yen should appreciate against the dollar.

T F 13.   If the U.S. price level rises more rapidly than the Japanese price level, *ceteris paribus,* U.S. exports to Japan will rise.

T F 14.   A country that experiences a depreciation in the value of its currency over a long period of time will, *ceteris paribus,* be faced with the problem of underemployment in exporting industries.

T F 15.   When the value of exports exceeds the value of imports, a country is said to have a balance-of-payments surplus when exchange rates are fixed.

T F 16.   When the value of exports exceeds the value of imports, a country is said to have a deficit in its balance of trade.

T F 17.   When the value of imports exceeds the value of exports, a country is said to have a trade deficit.

T F 18.   The current account includes both trade and merchandise and services balances.

T F 19.   In the current account, a deficit in the trade balance is necessarily offset by a surplus in the service balance.

T F 20.   If there is a deficit in the capital account, it must be offset by a surplus in the current account.

Multiple Choice: *Select the correct answer.*

_____ 1.   An increase in the dollar price of other currencies will tend to cause:
    (a)   American goods to be cheaper to foreigners.
    (b)   American goods to be more expensive to foreigners.
    (c)   Foreign goods to be cheaper to residents of the United States.
    (d)   Foreign goods to be more expensive to residents of foreign countries.

_____ 2.   Suppose that there exists a flexible exchange rate between the U.S. dollar and the Japanese yen. An increase in the supply of yen (a rightward shift in the supply curve of yen) will tend to:
    (a)   Increase U.S. imports of Japanese goods.
    (b)   Push the U.S. balance of trade in the direction of a surplus.
    (c)   Lower the yen price of the dollar.
    (d)   Raise the dollar price of the yen.

_____ 3.   A U.S. balance-of-payments deficit under fixed-exchange rates suggests that:
    (a)   U.S. imports exceed U.S. exports.
    (b)   U.S. exports exceed U.S. imports.
    (c)   Total payments made by residents of the United States to foreigners exceed total payments made by foreigners to residents of the United States.
    (d)   Total payments made by residents of the United States to foreigners are less than total payments made by foreigners to residents of the United States.

_____ 4. Suppose newsprint sells in the United States for $100 per ton. The cost of shipping newsprint to and from France is $10 per ton. The exchange rate between the French franc and the U.S. dollar is $1:Fr20. Thus the United States will:
- (a) Export newsprint to France if the price of newsprint exceeds Fr2,000 per ton in France.
- (b) Export newsprint to France if the price of newsprint exceeds Fr2,200 per ton in France.
- (c) Import newsprint from France if the price of newsprint exceeds Fr2,000 per ton in France.
- (d) Import newsprint from France if the price of newsprint exceeds Fr2,200 per ton in France.

_____ 5. A country will experience a reduction in its balance-of-payments deficit, _ceteris paribus_, if:
- (a) Its level of GNP rises relative to foreign levels of GNP.
- (b) Its prices fall relative to foreign price levels, _ceteris paribus_.
- (c) The domestic price of the foreign currency falls.
- (d) It lowers its tariffs.

_____ 6. Under a system of fixed exchange rates, if the rate of price increase in the United States exceeds the rate of price increase of its trading partners:
- (a) U.S. exports will tend to rise and imports will tend to fall.
- (b) U.S. exports will tend to fall and imports will tend to rise.
- (c) U.S. foreign-exchange reserves will tend to rise.
- (d) The dollar price of foreign currencies will tend to fall.

_____ 7. Under a system of flexible exchange rates, if the rate of price increase in the United States is less than the rate of price increase of its trading partners:
- (a) The dollar will strengthen against foreign currencies.
- (b) The dollar will weaken against foreign currencies.
- (c) The dollar will maintain its value against foreign currencies.
- (d) The United States will run a balance-of-payments deficit.

_____ 8. Which of the following changes will tend to cause a shift in the domestic demand curve for foreign currencies?
- (a) Changes in domestic incomes, _ceteris paribus_.
- (b) Changes in domestic prices of goods, _ceteris paribus_.
- (c) Changes in consumer taste for foreign goods, _ceteris paribus_.
- (d) All of the above.

_____ 9. Depreciation of the dollar refers to:
- (a) A loss of foreign-exchange reserves.
- (b) An increase in the dollar price of foreign currency.
- (c) Intervention in international money markets.
- (d) A fall in the dollar price of foreign currency.

_____ 10. Import-competing industries in the United States are likely to resist:
- (a) Appreciation of the dollar.
- (b) Depreciation of the dollar.
- (c) Devaluation of the dollar.
- (d) Evaluation of the dollar.

_____ 11. American citizens planning a vacation abroad would welcome:
   (a)   Appreciation of the dollar.
   (b)   Depreciation of the dollar.
   (c)   Devaluation of the dollar.
   (d)   None of the above.

_____ 12. Suppose researchers discover that Scotch whiskey causes cancer when given in large doses to Canadian mice. This finding would be likely to:
   (a)   Increase the demand for British pounds.
   (b)   Decrease the demand for British pounds.
   (c)   Increase the supply of British pounds.
   (d)   Decrease the supply of British pounds.

_____ 13. Suppose that real incomes rise faster in the United States than in Great Britian. In the United States, this situation would likely cause:
   (a)   An increase in the demand for pounds.
   (b)   A decrease in the demand for pounds.
   (c)   A decrease in the supply of pounds.
   (d)   An increase in the supply of pounds.

_____ 14. One World View article reported about the Nobel Prize in 1992: "Sweden's decision last month to let the krona float caused the prizes' value to drop from $1.2 million each when announced in October to $958,000 when King Car XVI Gustaf presents them Thursday." Implicitly, we can conclude that the Nobel Prize is paid in:
   (a)   An appreciating dollar.
   (b)   A depreciating dollar.
   (c)   An appreciating Krona.
   (d)   A depreciating Krona.

_____ 15. Continuing from the previous quotation, we can conclude:
   (a)   There had been a change from a flexible to a fixed exchange-rate system.
   (b)   The Krona had depreciated by 20 percent.
   (c)   There had been a shortage of Krona prior to the decision to let the currency float.
   (d)   All of the above.

_____ 16. Suppose the franc-dollar exchange rate is 5:1. Suppose a Renault automobile costs 20,000 francs in France. If the other costs that might be involved are ignored, what would be the dollar price of the automobile?
   (a) $4,000.
   (b) $10,000.
   (c) $20,000.
   (d) $100,000.

_____ 17. If French speculators believed the yen was going to appreciate against the dollar, they would:
   (a)   Purchase francs.
   (b)   Purchase dollars.
   (c)   Purchase yen.
   (d)   Sell yen.

_____ 18. Suppose that at the prevailing yen-dollar exchange rate, there is an excess demand for yen. To prevent the dollar from depreciating, the United States might:
(a) Raise taxes.
(b) Reduce government spending.
(c) Raise interest rates.
(d) Do all of the above.

_____ 19. Under a fixed exchange rate, a country can avoid a balance-of-payments surplus by:
(a) Decreasing the supply of foreign-exchange.
(b) Using deflationary policies.
(c) Using inflationary policies.
(d) Raising tariff barriers.

_____ 20. Which of the following would be appropriate monetary and fiscal policies for a surplus country to follow under a fixed-exchange-rate system?
(a) Reduce taxes.
(b) Purchase securities in the open market.
(c) Increase government spending.
(d) Do all of the above.

_____ 21. In a floating exchange-rate regime, the overall "balance" of the balance of payments must be:
(a) Equal to zero.
(b) Positive if exports of goods and services exceed imports of goods and services.
(c) Positive if the capital account is in surplus.
(d) Negative if the current account is in deficit.

_____ 22. The current account includes:
(a) Trade in goods.
(b) Trade in services.
(c) Unilateral transfers.
(d) All of the above.

_____ 23. If the balance of trade is positive:
(a) The capital account may be in surplus.
(b) The capital account may be in deficit.
(c) The current account may be in surplus or deficit.
(d) All of the above may be the case.

_____ 24. If the dollar price of a British pound is $2, what would be the pound price of a car that costs $10,000?
(a) 2,500 pounds.
(b) 5,000 pounds.
(c) 10,000 pounds.
(d) None of the above.

_____ 25. As the German mark price of the dollar rises:
(a) The dollar price of the German mark rises, and German goods become more expensive to Americans.
(b) The dollar price of the German mark rises, and German goods become less expensive to Americans.
(c) The dollar price of the German mark falls, and German goods become more expensive to Americans.
(d) The dollar price of the German mark falls, and German goods become less expensive to Americans.

26. One World View article in the text carries the headline "United States Becomes World's No. 1 Debtor." As the investment gap doubles, what should happen to the equilibrium price and quantity in the market for the dollars, *ceteris paribus*, in the short term?
    (a) Equilibrium price and quantity should both go up.
    (b) Equilibrium price should go up, and equilibrium quantity should go down.
    (c) Equilibrium price should go down, and equilibrium quantity should go up.
    (d) Equilibrium price and quantity should both go down.

27. As exchange rates become more volatile, which of the following will be experienced regardless of the direction of the exchange-rate movements?
    (a) Burdens of a greater trade deficit.
    (b) Worsening domestic inflation.
    (c) Costs of uncertainty.
    (d) Greater deficit on the capital account.

28. Suppose a country's currency depreciates. Which of the following could be responsible for the depreciation, *ceteris paribus*?
    (a) The country's interest rate rises relative to those of other countries.
    (b) The country's inflation rate rises relative to the inflation rates of other countries.
    (c) Speculators anticipate that the country's central bank will soon raise interest rates.
    (d) The country's income falls.

29. The major drawback to a system of managed exchange rates is that:
    (a) A country's efforts to manage exchange-rate movements may arouse suspicion and retaliation.
    (b) A country's efforts to effect changes in exchange rates are almost totally ineffective.
    (c) Government efforts to alter exchange rates usually result in violent disruptions of the domestic economy.
    (d) It requires enormous gold reserves.

30. Which of the following groupings contains a term that does not belong?
    (a) Gold standard, fixed exchange rate, foreign-exchange market.
    (b) Relative income changes, relative price changes, relative interest-rate changes.
    (c) Trade account, current account, capital account.
    (d) Trade balance, services balance, unilateral transfers.

Problems and Applications

Exercise 1

This exercise provides practice in determining exchange rates.

1. Table 20.1 depicts the hypothetical demand for and supply of British pounds in terms of U.S. dollars. Use the information in Table 20.1 to plot in Figure 20.1 the demand and supply of British pounds at the exchange rates indicated. Then answer problems 2-4.

Table 20.1
Monthly demand for and supply of British pounds in the United States

Dollars per British pound	Quantity demanded	Quantity supplied
4.50	100	700
4.00	200	600
3.50	300	500
3.00	400	400
2.50	500	300
2.00	600	200
1.50	700	100

Figure 20.1
Demand and supply curves for pounds

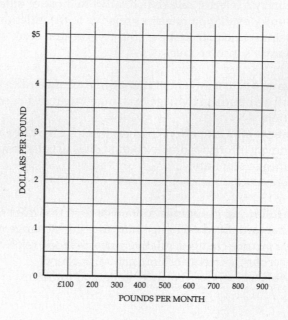

2. What is the equilibrium rate of exchange? _____

3. At a price of $2 per pound there would be excess:
   (a) Demand, and the exchange rate for pounds would rise.
   (b) Demand, and the exchange rate for pounds would fall.
   (c) Supply, and the exchange rate would rise.
   (d) Supply, and the exchange rate would fall.

4. Suppose that Americans suddenly increased their demand for English woolens. The dollar price of pounds would (rise, fall).

5. T   F   Whenever one currency depreciates, another currency must appreciate.

6. As a result of the increased demand for English woolens, the pound price of the dollar would (rise, fall).

Exercise 2

This exercise shows why one currency appreciates when another currency depreciates. It also shows why the demand for $ represents the supply of other currencies, while the supply of dollars represents the demand for other currencies in the foreign-exchange markets. In learning these things, you will get practice in making calculations with exchange rates.

1. Table 20.2 includes the sources of demand and supply of dollars. In the first column check off the items that are the source of the demand for dollars. In the second column check off the items that are the source of the supply of dollars. (*Hint*: There are two kinds of speculators; those who think the dollar will rise and those who think it will fall. You must sort the two types of speculators to determine which type will supply dollars and which will demand dollars).

Table 20.2
Sources of supply and demand for dollars and pounds

	(1) Demand for $	(2) Supply of $	(3) Demand for £	(4) Supply of £
Foreign demand for American exports	___	___	___	___
Foreign demand for American investments	___	___	___	___
Speculation that the dollar will appreciate	___	___	___	___
American demand for imports	___	___	___	___
American demand for investments in foreign countries	___	___	___	___
Speculation that the dollar will depreciate	___	___	___	___

2. If we assume there are just two currencies in the world, the dollar ($) and the pound (£), then the items in Table 20.2 also account for the supply and demand for the pound. Once again place checks in the appropriate blanks of Table 20.2 to indicate which items will constitute the demand for pounds and which items will constitute the supply of pounds.

3. T F In a two country world the sources of demand for dollars are the same as the sources of the supply of the pound and the sources of supply of dollars are the same as the sources of the demand for pounds.

4. T F The sources of demand for dollars are the same as the sources of supply for all other currencies in terms of dollars. The sources of supply of dollars are the same as the sources of demand for all other currencies in terms of dollars.

5. Let's return to our assumption that there are only two countries. Use your observations in the previous two problems and your knowledge of converting values of one currency into another to find the quantities of dollars supplied (column 3) and quantities of dollars demanded (column 6) in Table 20.3. Use the information in Table 20.3, which is the same as the data we used in Exercise 1 above, to compute the supply and demand for pounds.

Table 20.3
Supply and demand for dollars ($) and pounds (£)

(1) Price of a £ ($/£)	(2) Quantity of £ demanded	(3) Quantity of $ supplied	(4) Price of a $ (£/$)	(5) Quantity of £ supplied	(6) Quantity of $ demanded
4.50	100	_____	_____	700	_____
4.00	200	_____	_____	600	_____
3.50	300	_____	_____	500	_____
3.00	400	_____	_____	400	_____
2.50	500	_____	_____	300	_____
2.00	600	_____	_____	200	_____
1.50	700	_____	_____	100	_____

6. Complete column 4 of Table 20.3 by converting the price of pounds (£) in terms of dollars ($) in column 1 to the price of dollars in terms of pounds. (*Hint*: they are reciprocals of each other. Remember that to find the price of any good or currency, that good or currency appears in the denominator!)

7. From the data on the demand for the dollar (columns 4 and 6 of Table 20.3), draw the demand curve for the dollar in Figure 20.2. From the data on the supply of the dollar (columns 4 and 3 of Table 20.3), draw the supply curve for the dollar in Figure 20.2.

Figure 20.2
Demand and Supply of Dollars

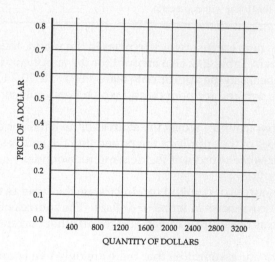

8. The equilibrium value of the dollar is _____ , and the equilibrium quantity of dollars is _____ .

9. When you multiply the equilibrium quantity of dollars by the equilibrium exchange rate for the dollar in terms of pounds (£), you find the quantity of pounds is _____. When you find the reciprocal of the equilibrium exchange rate for the dollar, you find the exchange rate for pounds is _____.

10. T F When you multiply the equilibrium quantity of dollars by the equilibrium exchange rate for the dollar in terms of pounds (£), you have calculated the equilibrium quantity of pounds. (Compare your answer to problem 9 in this exercise with your answer to problem 2, Exercise 1 above.)

11. T F   The equilibrium exchange rate for the dollar equals the equilibrium exchange
            rate for the pound.

Exercise 3

This exercise shows how to analyze the foreign-exchange market using supply and demand
curves. The effects of several historical events in United States–Japanese relations are analyzed.

For each of the events described in problems 1-10, choose the letter of the diagram in Figure 20.3
that best describes the kind of shift that would occur in the foreign-exchange market. The market
should be looked at from the U.S. point of view; that is, the shifts represent changes in the demand
for, and supply of, dollars. Think of the price of a dollar as being measured in yen per dollar.
Remember that exchange rates were fixed until 1971, which prevented them from reflecting supply
and demand changes.

Figure 20.3
Shifts in the demand and supply of a currency

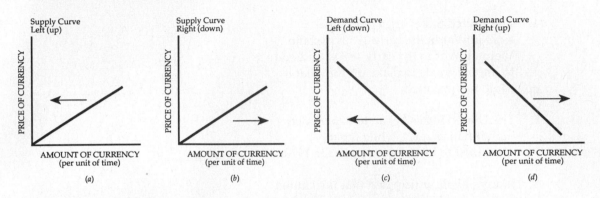

The demand for dollars originates with the Japanese who wish to buy goods and services
produced by U.S. firms or who wish to purchase assets through U.S. markets (e.g., stocks, real estate,
bank deposits). The supply of dollars to the foreign-exchange market originates with U.S. residents
who wish to purchase Japanese goods and services or who wish to purchase Japanese assets.

Indicate whether the shift described in each of the problems below would cause the equilibrium
price of the dollar to appreciate (increase in value) or to depreciate (decrease in value). Also, indicate
with an arrow whether the equilibrium quantity of dollars would increase (⇑) or decrease (⇓). Finally,
indicate in the blanks provided (with the letter of the item) which of the following determinants of
demand and supply had changed:

    a.   Relative income changes and demand for goods and services.
    b.   Relative price changes.
    c.   Changes in product availability.
    d.   Change in relative interest rates.
    e.   Change in speculative activity.

(*Hint:* Do not confuse the demand and supply for imports and exports with the demand and
supply for dollars.)

	Shift (Figure 20.3 diagram)	Change in value	Change in equilibrium quantity	Determinant

1. After World War II the Japanese had little wealth. The U.S. economy had been left intact and experienced strong growth in both income and wealth.

    _____ _____ _____ _____

2. The Japanese replaced capital destroyed in World War II with the most modern production techniques available and began to produce goods for export.

    _____ _____ _____ _____

3. The Japanese protected their emerging industries from foreign (U.S.) competition.

    _____ _____ _____ _____

4. The United States engaged in the Korean War in the early 1950s and the Vietnam War in the early 1970s, and had to import goods to make up for what it could not produce.

    _____ _____ _____ _____

5. The United States began to experience high inflation rates, while Japan continued to have low rates in the 1970s.

    _____ _____ _____ _____

6. Many people anticipated that the United States would go off the gold standard and expected the dollar to float and become much cheaper relative to the yen. In order to make a profit from these anticipated events, they entered the foreign-exchange market.

    _____ _____ _____ _____

7. When the United States went off the gold standard in 1971, commodity prices began to rise rapidly and the United States curtailed exports of scrap steel, soybeans, and logs to Japan. The United States further reneged on commitments to sell grains and oil.

    _____ _____ _____ _____

8. In the mid-1970s Japan and other countries cut their demand for the basic commodities on which the United States had placed restrictions. (This shift showed up after the United States tried once again to sell commodities to Japan.)

    _____ _____ _____ _____

9. In the late 1970s and early 1980s, the United States became concerned about its trade deficit and the competition from Japanese goods in domestic markets. Protectionist sentiment mounted and the United States placed additional restrictions on imports from Japan.   _____ _____ _____ _____

10. In 1988 the United States was successful in getting the Japanese to lift some of the barriers that prevented American goods from entering the Japanese market.   _____ _____ _____ _____

Exercise 4

The media often feature articles about negotiations concerning international financial issues. This exercise will use one of the articles in the text to show how to use supply and demand curves to test the accuracy of reporting on international financial events. If your professor makes a newspaper assignment for this chapter from the *Instructor's Manual*, this exercise will provide an example of how to do it.

Reread the World View article on page 459 in Chapter 20 entitled "Japan's Big Economic Debate" from the *New York Times*. Then answer the following questions.

1. What sentence or sentences describe the effect on the dollar of Japan's stimulation of its own economy?

2. Figure 20.3 (see Exercise 3 above) shows the possible shifts of demand and supply for a nation's currency. Which shift *best* represents the expected shift in the supply or demand for the dollar as a result of the event described in problem 1?

3. The dollar should (rise, fall) in value relative to the yen if exports to Japan increase.

4. Which shift in Figure 20.3 best represents the impact on the supply or demand for yen caused by the event you chose in problem 1?

5. The yen should (rise, fall) in value relative to the dollar if exports to Japan increase.

6. What sentence indicates the direction of the shift in the demand for the dollar?

7. T F The article's prediction that dollar demand would fall contradicts the expected direction for dollar demand in response to Japan's stimulation of its own economy.

Reread the statement that begins, "Although most economists attribute Japan's large and growing trade surpluses to the strong dollar and other macroeconomic factors . . ." Decide the truth of the following statements in problems 8-10.

8. T F If the Japanese stimulate their own economy, the demand for the dollar should become stronger.

9. T F If a stronger dollar causes growing U.S. trade surpluses, as the article suggests, then stimulation of the Japanese economy should increase the U.S. trade surplus.

10. T F As suggested in the article, a more expansionary posture in Japan would help reverse trade and currency imbalances. (*Hint:* Compare this statement with your previous conclusion.)

Common Errors

The first statement in each "common error" below is incorrect. Each incorrect statement is followed by a corrected version and an explanation.

1. The price of a dollar in terms of yen is the number of dollars per yen. WRONG!

    The price of a dollar in terms of yen is the number of yen per dollar. RIGHT!

    This mistake can cost a bundle if you are in a foreign country and don't know how to distinguish the price of a dollar from the price of the other currency. In Japan you don't want to give $100 for a single yen note when you should be receiving 100 yen for $1! Remember that the item for which you want a price must appear in the denominator of the price. For example, the price of tomatoes is the number of dollars divided by the number of tomatoes that are purchased. Similarly, the price of a yen is the number of dollars divided by the number of yen that are purchased. Similarly, the price of a dollars is the number of yen divided by the number of dollars that are purchased.

2. The supply and demand for dollars in the foreign-exchange market is the same thing as the supply and demand for money (dollars) targeted by the Fed. WRONG!

    The supply and demand for dollars in the foreign-exchange market is a totally different concept from the supply and demand for money. RIGHT!

    Remember that the price of money was the interest rate when we were focusing on the supply and demand for money. In the foreign-exchange market the price is the exchange rate, not the interest rate. Furthermore, the supply and demand for money (dollars), which is the focus of the Fed, occurs geographically within the United States. The foreign-exchange market occurs between countries—literally on the phone lines between banks of different countries. We can visualize the foreign-exchange market as an area totally outside of borders in which money temporarily enters for the purpose of being exchanged. While domestic monetary policies may influence the amount of money going into the foreign-exchange market, the link is often indirect. In fact, when the Fed tightens monetary policy to lower the supply of dollars, the foreign-exchange market may see an *increase* in dollars as foreigners seek the higher interest rates from a tighter monetary policy.

3. A country is well off if its currency appreciates steadily over a long period of time. WRONG!

    Both appreciating currencies and depreciating currencies create problems. RIGHT!

Be careful! There are problems associated with steadily appreciating currencies *and* with steadily depreciating currencies. People sometimes view a depreciating currency as a source of national shame and dislike the higher cost (and inflation) associated with higher prices of foreign goods. However, depreciation may make a country's exports more competitive, may set up more jobs, and may help correct trade deficits. By contrast, the country with an appreciating currency sets up employment problems and loss of competitiveness with other countries, even if it has more buying power as a result.

4. When countries have trade deficits, money really flows out. When they have surpluses, money really flows in. WRONG!

   Money is not physically sent in most transactions, but the claim to ownership is. RIGHT!

   Most foreign trade is transacted by check and is just a "flow" of bookkeeping entries. Even when gold is sold, it seldom *physically* flows anywhere. In the case of the United States, under a fixed-exchange-rate system, it stays in Fort Knox even though someone else owns it. Thus, it is the claim to ownership that flows, not the money. When countries run trade deficits, their trading partners add to their claims against them. For countries with a trade surplus, the reverse is true.

5. There are balance-of-payments surpluses and deficits under floating exchange rates. WRONG!

   The balance of payments is always zero under floating exchange rates. RIGHT!

   Under fixed exchange rates, the government must balance surpluses and deficits on the balance of payments with changes in a reserve currency. Under floating exchange rates, there is no reserve currency and any transfers abroad by the government are simply classified as unilateral transfers that are included within the current account. By definition, the current account and the capital account balance each other under a floating exchange-rate system.

•ANSWERS•

Key-Term Review

1. foreign-exchange markets
2. exchange rate
3. equilibrium price
4. appreciation
5. depreciation
6. market shortage
7. trade deficit
8. gold standard
9. balance-of-payments surplus
10. balance-of-payments deficit
11. foreign-exchange reserves
12. gold reserves
13. flexible exchange rates
14. managed exchange rates
15. balance of payments

True or False

1. T	5. F	9. T	12. F	15. F	18. T
2. T	6. T	10. T	13. F	16. F	19. F
3. T	7. F	11. F	14. F	17. T	20. T
4. F	8. F				

Multiple Choice

1. a	6. b	11. a	16. a	21. a	26. c
2. a	7. a	12. b	17. c	22. d	27. c
3. c	8. d	13. a	18. d	23. d	28. b
4. b	9. b	14. d	19. c	24. b	29. a
5. b	10. a	15. b	20. d	25. d	

30. a   With fixed exchange rates, foreign-exchange markets are not needed. Topics of other groupings include (b) differences in price and growth rate changes, (c) international accounts, and (d) account balances.

Problems and Applications

Exercise 1

1. **Figure 20.1 Answer**

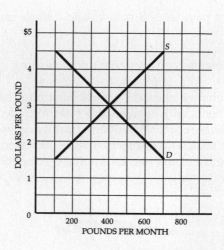

2. $3 per British pound   3. a   4. rise   5. T   6. fall

Exercise 2

5. and 6.   **Table 20.2 Answer**

	(1) Demand for $	(2) Supply of $	(3) Demand for £	(4) Supply of £
Foreign demand for American exports	X	—	—	X
Foreign demand for American investments	X	—	—	X
Speculation that the dollar will appreciate	X	—	—	X
American demand for imports	—	X	X	—
American demand for investments in foreign countries	—	X	X	—
Speculation that the dollar will depreciate	—	X	X	—

3. T
4. T
5. and 6. **Table 20.3 Answer**

Price of a £ ($/£) (1)		Quantity of £ demanded (2)		Quantity of $ supplied (3)	Price of a $ (£/$) (4)	Quantity of £ supplied (5)	Quantity of $ demanded (6)
4.50	x	100	=	450	0.222 = 1/4.50	700	3,150
4.00	x	200	=	800	0.25 = 1/4	600	2,400
3.50	x	300	=	1,050	0.29 = 1/3.50	500	1,750
3.00	x	400	=	1,200	0.33 = 1/3	400	1,200
2.50	x	500	=	1,250	0.40 = 1/2.50	300	750
2.00	x	600	=	1,200	0.50 = 1/2	200	400
1.50	x	700	=	1,050	0.67 = 1/1.50	100	150

7. **Figure 20.2 Answer**

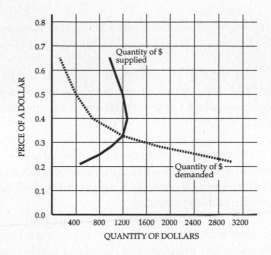

8. 1/3 £ per dollar; $1,200

9. 400 (= 1,200 x 1/3); $3 per pound [= 1/(1/3)]

10. T

11. F   The equilibrium exchange rate for the dollar equals the *reciprocal* of the equilibrium exchange rate for the pound.

Exercise 3

	Shift (Figure 20.3 diagram)	Change in value	Change in equilibrium quantity	Determinant
1.	b	depreciate	⇑	a

With higher incomes, Americans could buy more Japanese goods and assets. They therefore supplied more dollars to the foreign-exchange market.

2.	b	depreciate	⇑	c

With more Japanese goods to purchase, Americans were willing to supply more dollars to the foreign-exchange market.

3.	c	depreciate	⇓	c

With fewer sales to Japan, there was less need for U.S. dollars from the foreign-exchange market.

4.	b	depreciate	⇑	a

To buy more Japanese goods, the United States had to supply more dollars to the foreign-exchange market.

5.	c or b	depreciate	uncertain	b and e

Not wishing to hold dollars that would purchase less because of inflation, speculators would supply these dollars to the foreign-exchange market to buy more stable currencies, such as the yen.

6.	b or c	depreciate	uncertain	b and e

Not willing to hold dollars that would purchase less because of the expectations of the depreciating dollar, speculators would supply these dollars to the foreign-exchange market to buy more stable currencies.

7.	c	depreciate	⇓	c and b

As the Japanese curtailed purchases of American goods, they did not need to buy as many American dollars in the foreign-exchange market.

8.	c	depreciate	⇓	a or c

As the Japanese curtailed purchases of American goods, they did not need to buy as many American dollars in the foreign-exchange market.

9.	a	appreciate	⇓	a or c

The United States submitted fewer dollars to the foreign-exchange market, since there was less product to purchase from Japan.

10.	d	appreciate	⇑	a or c

The Japanese could buy more American goods and therefore needed more dollars from the foreign-exchange market with which to buy the goods.

Exercise 4

1. "United States officials . . . have suggested that a more expansionary posture domestically would help to reverse trade and currency imbalances." More specifically, "If Japan took steps to stimulate its domestic economy . . . [Japanese] consumers would have more money to spend on imports."

2. d   The Japanese need to buy more dollars to buy more American imports.

3. rise

4. b   The Japanese buy dollars in the foreign-exchange market by supplying more yen.

5. fall

6. "Less demand for the dollar might also spur its fall against the yen, making American products less expensive in Japan, and Japanese products more expensive in the United States." This sentence comes right after the statement "If Japan took steps to stimulate its domestic economy, . . . consumers would have more money to spend on imports." This statement suggests the two concepts are related to each other when, *in fact, they involve contradictory shifts.*

7. T   See the answer to problem 6.

8. T   This is consistent with our analysis that demand for the dollar will shift to the right as the Japanese import more from the United States.

9. T   The logic of this statement is impeccable, but the article's statement about the existence of a strong dollar is misleading and is the source of the problem. The dollar may become even stronger as a result of Japanese stimulation of its economy. Perhaps the dollar is not strong enough. The key is that the Japanese will be able to import more, despite a strong dollar, if they stimulate their economy.

10. T   The imbalances will be redressed but not by a weaker dollar. The trade balances will be redressed because of greater Japanese income. The article has confused a shift in demand for dollars because of growing Japanese incomes with a movement along the demand curve because of a change in the value of the dollar.

CHAPTER 21

International Development

Quick Review

This chapter is about poverty and despair on a worldwide scale. The questions that drive the description and analysis are:

- Why has the Third World stayed so poor?
- How did some countries manage to grow so quickly?
- What policies would promote still faster growth?

To begin with, we find commonality among the less developed, or Third World, countries because they have extremely low per capita incomes and slow GNP growth rates. These two characteristics are more often than not combined with low life expectancy and illiteracy—all are symptoms of extreme poverty. What's more, these countries' prospects for improvement are poor because there are many barriers to development.

Some of the barriers have to do with domestic resources—land, labor, and capital. Sometimes, but not always, the country does not have fertile land or mineral resources. Less developed countries (LDCs) frequently have populations that are young, large, and growing more rapidly than the labor force. Thus, it is very difficult for them to produce a surplus that can be saved and invested to form capital.

The need for additional resources and the reallocation of existing ones permeate development policy. Both require saving by some group so that resources somewhere are released from current uses to more productive long-term uses. Financing is thus a key ingredient.

External financing, both public and private, has been made available to such countries for a long time. The amounts provided have usually been very small relative to the global problem. The debts owed to multilateral public agencies or to private lenders must be paid back. Very often this requires hard-currency earnings, which can be acquired only by exporting or by incurring more debt.

Many LDCs tried to develop through export-led growth, but even here there are barriers. The markets they enter may grow very slowly, have price inelastic demand, or be characterized by such barriers as quotas and tariffs.

Advances in technology are also very difficult to achieve. Sometimes ingrained attitudes prevent the adoption of new techniques; sometimes the required infrastructure is not in place. Nevertheless, the desire for development is strong, and many countries have adopted strategies and made difficult choices in an attempt to move forward.

Some argue that the traditional approach to development has placed too much emphasis on government and too little on people, markets, and entrepreneurship. The move toward reliance on markets worldwide will help us assess this conjecture.

Learning Objectives

After reading Chapter 21 and doing the following exercises, you should:	True or false	Multiple choice	Problems and applications	Common errors	Pages in the text
1. Know some of the economic characteristics of poor countries.	1	1-3			467-471
2. Understand some of the barriers to economic growth in poor countries.	2-4, 6-7	10-14	2		471-472
3. Be able to discuss and describe some of the difficulties encountered with various types of private external financing.	5	4-6, 12-14			
4. Know some of the sources for public external financing.	8-11	14	1		475-480
5. Understand the constraints that inhibit the introduction of new technology in poor countries.	12, 13	7			480-481
6. Be able to discuss the debt crisis.		11	1		476-479
7. Be able to describe some of the strategic questions that must be answered before choosing a growth strategy.	14	8			482-487
8. Know some of the issues relating to reliance on foreign and domestic markets.	15	9, 12		1	484-486

Key-Term Review

Review the following terms; if you are not sure of the meaning of any term, write out the definition and check it against the Glossary in the text.

barter	market mechanism
capital flight	market shortage
comparative advantage	price elasticity of demand
debt servicing	production possibilities
disguised unemployment	productivity
GDP per capita	quota
hard currency	

Fill in the blank following each of the statements below with the appropriate term from the list above.

1. Individuals who are working but producing little or nothing are an example of _____ .

1. _____

2. When output per unit of input declines, it is correct to say there is falling _____ .

2. _____

3. The savings-investment process is made difficult in economies that rely on _____ .

   3. _____

4. LDCs, as well as other countries, must allocate resources by tradition, command, or the _____ .

   4. _____

5. In economies using the market mechanism as an allocating device, the signal for greater production is a _____ .

   5. _____

6. Governments have sometimes responded to increased competition from imports by imposing a _____ .

   6. _____

7. Quotas and other impediments to trade have sometimes prevented LDCs from developing production in products in which they have a _____ .

   7. _____

8. One impediment to export-led development is that LDC products may face a low _____ .

   8. _____

9. Long-term growth of an LDC requires an expansion of the country's _____ .

   9. _____

10. Countries are classified from rich to extremely poor on the basis of their _____ .

    10. _____

11. One of the difficulties faced by Third World countries is that their _____ requirements are in hard currencies.

    11. _____

12. Political instability and graft are a frequent cause of _____ from poor countries.

    12. _____

13. The best source of _____ for poor countries is the export market.

    13. _____

True or False: *Circle your choice.*

T F 1. Developing countries are those with high growth rates.

T F 2. Disguised unemployment in poor countries is synonymous with discouraged workers in developed countries.

T F 3. The WHAT question is determined largely by the requirements for subsistence in poor countries.

T F 4. In poor countries the inefficiency of a money economy is overcome by barter.

T F 5. Although barter is less efficient than money exchange, it does speed up the savings-investment process.

T F 6. The republics of the former Soviet Union and the People's Republic of China have very high voluntary savings ratios, as evidenced by their high savings rates.

T F 7. Inflation is a way to "force" saving on the economy.

T F 8. The term "hard currency" refers to money that is based on precious metals.

T F 9. The World Bank provides poor countries with general balance-of-payments assistance.
T F 10. A soft loan can be made with hard currency.

T F 11. Because loans must often be repaid in hard currency, export-producing projects will often be favored over domestic projects.

T F 12. Lack of infrastructure is an impediment to foreign investment.

T F 13. Emphasis on the agricultural sector can be justified because the balance of trade may improve if imports of food decline.

T F 14. Balanced growth is a viable approach to development in poor countries.

T F 15. The "infant industry" argument has led to inefficient industrial development in LDCs.

Multiple Choice: *Select the correct answer.*

_____ 1. Which of the following problems plagues less developed countries?
   (a) Low per capita incomes and high GDP growth rates.
   (b) Low population growth and low per capita income.
   (c) Low per capita incomes and slow GDP growth rates.
   (d) Low per capita incomes and high saving rates.

_____ 2. Poor countries are characterized by:
   (a) A low caloric intake.
   (b) A low ratio of doctors to population.
   (c) A low energy consumption per capita.
   (d) All of the above.

_____ 3. Which of the following would be classified as a "low-income country"?
   (a) Singapore.
   (b) Brazil.
   (c) India.
   (d) All of the above.

_____ 4. Which of the following would be likely to make a hard-currency loan for a specific project?
   (a) IBRD.
   (b) IDA.
   (c) IFC.
   (d) Exim Bank.

_____ 5. Which of the following agencies would be most likely to participate in equity financing for a specific project?
   (a) IBRD.
   (b) IDA.
   (c) IFC.
   (d) The Asian Development Bank.

_____ 6. Which of the following would most likely be classified as a hard-currency loan?
   (a) A loan repayable in the borrower's own currency over a twenty-year period.
   (b) A loan repayable in dollars over a twenty-year term.
   (c) Cofinancing of an equity investment project through the IFC.
   (d) None of the above.

_____ 7. In which of Walter W. Rostow's stages is the savings-investment process alleged to increase?
   (a) Preconditions to takeoff.
   (b) Takeoff into sustained growth.
   (c) Drive to maturity.
   (d) High mass consumption.

_____ 8. LDCs that attempt to enter export markets often face which of the following challenges?
   (a) Competition from other LDCs.
   (b) Competition from developed countries.
   (c) Restricted access to developed-country markets.
   (d) All of the above.

_____ 9. The demand for food tends to be:
   (a) Price elastic.
   (b) Price inelastic.
   (c) Income elastic.
   (d) None of the above.

_____ 10. Capital formation is difficult in LDCs because:
   (a) The savings rate is low.
   (b) If a barter system exists, saving often takes illiquid forms.
   (c) Borrowing abroad at reasonable terms is very difficult.
   (d) All of the above are the case.

_____ 11. A hard currency is one that is:
   (a) Backed by a precious metal.
   (b) Made up of coin, as opposed to cash.
   (c) Traded internationally.
   (d) Hard to come by, that is, a collector's item.

_____ 12. Multilateral loans are:
   (a) Preferred to bilateral loans by poor countries.
   (b) Made only by the IBRD.
   (c) No-strings-attached loans.
   (d) All of the above.

_____ 13. Which of the following projects would be a suitable candidate for a loan to a poor country to be repaid in U.S. dollars?
   (a)   A loan to build a new school.
   (b)   A loan to install a new sewer system.
   (c)   A loan to purchase equipment to produce textiles for sale abroad.
   (d)   A loan to purchase emergency medical supplies.

_____ 14. Which of the following contains a term that does not belong?
   (a)   Low internal savings, capital flight, low external financing.
   (b)   Human capital, production possibilities, hard currency.
   (c)   IBRD, IDA, LDC.
   (d)   Population, GDP, GDP per capita.

Problems and Applications

Exercise 1

This exercise will show how the debt of underdeveloped countries can get out of hand because of high interest payments. Many Latin American countries have problems meeting even the interest payments on their foreign debt, not to mention paying anything on the amount borrowed (the principal). They must be able to make payments on their foreign debt using foreign currencies that they earn by exporting goods and services.

1. Table 21.1 shows estimated data on key economic statistics compiled by international organizations for four Latin American countries for 1983. Compute (to the nearest tenth of a billion dollars) the interest that must be paid on this debt at an interest rate of 10 percent per year, and place your answers in row 2 of the table.

Table 21.1
Burden of the debt

	Mexico	Venezuela	Brazil	Argentina
Total debt (billions of dollars)	$ 89	$ 34	$ 93	$ 48
Interest (billions of dollars per year)	$____	$____	$____	$____
Export earnings (billions of dollars per year)	$ 21.0	$ 13.7	$ 21.4	$ 8.3
Growth rates in gross domestic product (per year)	-4 %	-2 %	-5 %	+2 %
Inflation rate (per year)	91.9%	6.4%	21.1%	401.6%

Of course, a country cannot spend all of its export earnings on debt repayment. It must also import goods and services. This means that the country can use only the surplus of exports over imports to service the debt. If it cannot run such surpluses, it must borrow again just to make interest payments. Let's see what happens to the debt of Argentina if it borrows simply to make yearly interest payments.

2. In Table 21.2, column 1 shows the year, column 2 shows the debt existing at the beginning of that year, column 3 shows the interest payment on that debt, and column 4 shows what the new debt will be if Argentina borrows in order to pay off the interest. In the years following 1983, assume that the interest rate on the total debt is 10 percent. The first row has been done for you. Complete the other rows. (Round to the nearest tenth of a billion dollars.)

Table 21.2

(1) Year	(2) Debt (see col. 4 of previous year) (billions of dollars)	(3) Interest on debt (10% of col. 2) (billions of dollars per year)	(4) Total debt after borrowing to pay interest [(2) + (3)] (billions of dollars)
1983	$48.0	$4.8 (0.10 x 48)	$52.8
1984	52.8	_____	_____
1985	_____	_____	_____
1986	_____	_____	_____
1987	_____	_____	_____
1988	_____	_____	_____
1989	_____	_____	_____
1990	_____	_____	_____
1991	_____	_____	_____
1992	_____	_____	_____

3. By what percentage will the debt at the end of 1992 (see the last number in column 4 for 1992 in Table 21.2) exceed the debt at the beginning of 1983 (see column 2 for 1983 in Table 21.2)? _____

4. If Argentina is able to sustain a real growth rate in gross domestic product (GDP) of 2 percent per year, by what percentage will the real GDP of 1992 exceed the GDP of 1983? _____

5. Between 1983 and 1992, the ratio of the external debt will grow relative to GDP by:
   (a)   10 to 30 percent.
   (b)   30 to 50 percent.
   (c)   50 to 80 percent.
   (d)   More than 80 percent.

The situation in Argentina deteriorated in 1985 as the following *Business Week* article (July 1, 1985, p. 34) recounts:

> On June 14, Argentine President Raul Alfonsin . . . decreed . . . a series of draconian economic measures to throttle the country's 1,010% rate of inflation . . . While dramatic, the introduction of australes (a new currency) and a wage and price freeze may turn out to be the least important reforms. They do little to get at the root of the problem: government printing of money to finance an $8.4 billion budget deficit . . .
> Economy Minister Sorrouille insists that from now on state agencies will be funded only from their own tariffs and foreign borrowing. "The printing machine will cease to function," vows Sorrouille.

6. From this article it can be concluded that Alfonsin's new austerity program will:
   (a)   Increase the debt/GDP ratio.
   (b)   Decrease the debt/GDP ratio.
   (c)   Leave the debt/GDP ratio unchanged.

7. Suppose the interest rate is 15 percent per year, not 10 percent. Fill in Table 21.3 in the same way you completed Table 21.2, using an interest rate of 15 percent.

Table 21.3
Debt, interest and growth in debt

(1) Year	(2) Debt (see col. 4 of previous year) (billions of dollars)	(3) Interest on debt (15% of col. 2) (billions of dollars per year)	(4) Total debt after borrowing to pay interest [(2) + (3)] (billions of dollars)
1983	$48.0	$_____	$_____
1984	_____	_____	_____
1985	_____	_____	_____
1986	_____	_____	_____
1987	_____	_____	_____
1988	_____	_____	_____
1989	_____	_____	_____
1990	_____	_____	_____
1991	_____	_____	_____
1992	_____	_____	_____

8. If the interest rate rises from 10 percent per year to 15 percent per year, by 1992 the debt will also rise. By what percentage would the debt at the higher interest rate (Table 21.3) exceed the debt at the lower interest rate (Table 21.2) by the end of 1992? _____

9. Table 21.1 shows the inflation rates and the rate of growth in GDP for four Latin American countries. Which of the following statements is *false*?
    (a) Because of the negative growth rates, these countries have a difficult time preventing the debt/GDP ratio from expanding and placing even greater burdens on the economy.
    (b) Because these countries are unable to use the debt-repayment funds for internal growth, the growth rate in GDP suffers.
    (c) Because internal needs cannot be met with foreign funds, the government issues more money, which stimulates inflation.
    (d) The high inflation rate means that the value of the debt in real terms is becoming smaller.

10. What, in fact, has happened to prevent these Latin American countries from being destroyed by their debt? _____

Exercise 2

Except for a few key newspapers, the media do a very shallow job of reporting on less developed countries. However, careful reading of those articles that are found can provide a wealth of information on the barriers to a country's economic growth. By using one of the articles in the text, this exercise will show the kind of information that can be found by careful reading of an article about a less developed country. If your professor makes a newspaper assignment for this chapter, this exercise will provide an example of how to do it.

Reread the World View article on page 826 in Chapter 21 entitled "China Lowers Birth Rate to Levels in West" from *The Washington Post*. Then answer the following questions:

1. What sentence indicates a barrier to the country's growth?

2. What sentence indicates actions designed to overcome the barrier to growth?

Common Errors

The first statement in each "common error" below is incorrect. Each incorrect statement is followed by a corrected version and an explanation.

1. Foreign aid has been a huge giveaway program for poor countries. WRONG!

    Foreign aid has not been large relative to the development problem, and much of this aid is in the form of loans, not "gifts." RIGHT!

    Foreign aid has sometimes been large in absolute dollars, but it has never reached the magnitude envisioned by its early proponents. It has really been quite small relative to the global problem it is designed to alleviate. Moreover, much of it is not "given," but takes the form of loans, sometimes on onerous terms and with many strings attached. The "strings" may take the form of requirements that purchases must be made in the donor country, shipped in donor-country ships, and the like. Often these requirements result in inefficiency and high prices. For these and many other reasons, one can say foreign aid is not large and much is not a gift.

2. Macroeconomic models that apply to developed economies apply equally as well to developing economies. WRONG!

    The assumptions behind macroeconomic models must be examined carefully before those models are applied to developing economies. RIGHT!

    Strong cultural differences exist between countries. Because macroeconomic theory relies heavily on the notion of the relationship between investment and saving, the theory may be difficult to apply in developing countries, where there is little trust of financial institutions and financial institutions cannot trust people to pay off loans. In economies undergoing serious hyperinflation, it no longer is appropriate to use Keynesian theory that presumes constant prices when the economy is below full employment. When we assume that there is no burden of debt from redistributing from taxpayers to internal bondholders, we must revise that conclusion when debt is so large in an economy that a significant portion of the GDP must be taxed in order to service the debt; there is a political limit to taxation and serious disincentives set in when people feel they will be taxed most of what they earn. If a macro model assumes an economy is a closed economy, it will miss some of the most important aspects of the underground economy, international financial flows, and the terms of trade which decide the fate of many developing countries.

•ANSWERS•

Key-Term Review

1.	disguised employment	8.	price elasticity of demand
2.	productivity	9.	production possibilities
3.	barter	10.	GDP per capita
4.	market mechanism	11.	debt-servicing
5.	market shortage	12.	capital flight
6.	quota	13.	hard currency
7.	comparative advantage		

True or False

1. F	4. F	7. T	10. T	12. T	14. F
2. F	5. F	8. F	11. T	13. T	15. T
3. T	6. F	9. F			

Multiple Choice

1. c	4. a	6. b	8. d	10. d	12. a
2. d	5. c	7. b	9. b	11. c	13. c
3. b					

14.　c　LDCs are not international financial institutions. Topics of other groupings are (a) causes of underdeveloped capital markets, (b) barriers to growth, and (d) the components of the GDP per capita.

Problems and Applications

Exercise 1

1. **Table 21.1 Answer**

	Mexico	Venezuela	Brazil	Argentina
Interest (billions of dollars per year)	$8.9	$3.4	$9.3	$4.8

2. **Table 21.2 Answer**

Year	Debt	Interest on debt	Total debt
1983	$ 48.0	$ 4.8	$ 52.8
1984	52.8	5.3	58.1
1985	58.1	5.8	63.9
1986	63.9	6.4	70.3
1987	70.3	7.0	77.3
1988	77.3	7.7	85.0
1989	85.0	8.5	93.5
1990	93.5	9.4	102.9
1991	102.9	10.3	113.2
1992	113.2	11.3	124.5

3.　2.59 percent $\left[= \dfrac{(124.5 \text{ billion}) \ 1992}{(48.0 \text{ billion}) \ 1983} \right]$

In other words, the debt has increased by 159 percentage points.

4.　1.219　[= (1.02) x (1.02) x (1.02) x (1.02) x (1.02) x (1.02) x (1.02) x (1.02) x (1.02) x (1.02)]
　　　　　　1983　1984　1985　1986　1987　1988　1989　1990　1991　1992

In other words, GDP has increased by 21.9 percentage points.

CHAPTER 22

The Collapse of Communism

Quick Review

The collapse of communism accelerated to its climax in 1989. The collapse was most remarkable in the Soviet Union, where General Secretary Mikhail Gorbachev followed his earlier pronouncements concerning *glasnost* and *perestroika* with a call for restructuring of the entire Soviet economy. The problems that brought the Soviet Union to its knees were the mirror image of the problems that plagued other economies dominated by the Soviet monolith; Poland, East Germany, Hungary, and others all moved in the direction of freedom and of markets as an allocating mechanism. After some seventy years of communist rule and unfulfilled promises, the creaking machinery of central planning ground to a halt.

In this chapter we look back at the communist ideology and the central planning which was used to implement it. Then we investigate the inherent problems of attempting to plan a large, diverse, and complex economy. Finally, we look at "transitional problems" as the formerly planned economies move toward market-based systems of resource allocation. Specifically, we attempt to answer the following questions:

- What is the appeal of central planning?
- What are the basic problems of central planning?
- What impedes the transition to market economies?

Every economy has to answer the WHAT, HOW, and FOR WHOM questions. In the United States these questions are answered when consumers attempt to maximize satisfaction with limited incomes, business people attempt to maximize profits, and voters express their preferences about the way they are governed. In planned economies, the big decisions, such as the division of output between capital goods and consumer goods, are made by a central authority.

The central authority (i.e., the planners) attempts to allocate resources to achieve specific objectives. Very often these objectives include a particular income distribution and a strong military establishment. Planners use such techniques as input-output analysis to allocate their scarce resources; in contrast, in a market economy prices automatically signal where resources are to move. Prices are used in planned economies to perform a rationing function, but not the allocation function that they perform in a market economy.

Trade between nations is difficult in centrally planned economies too, since prices which are set by planners rather than by markets are not accepted internationally. Currencies are not convertible, barter results, and countries do not follow the dictates of comparative advantage. These are additional problems to be overcome during the transition from planning to markets.

The movement to market-based systems of resource allocation is not an easy task. Setting prices free brings about wild price gyrations in an economy as unbalanced as that of, say, Poland or the Soviet Union. It takes time for new equilibrium prices to be established and for markets to work. This assumes, of course, the successful conversion of attitudes and institutions, and this is perhaps the most difficult change of all. Should the transitions to markets be fast or slow? Shock therapy brings the benefits earlier. The costs are borne earlier too.

Learning Objectives

After reading Chapter 22 and doing the following exercises, you should:	True or false	Multiple choice	Problems and applications	Common errors	Pages in the text
1. Know the historical background of communism and the appeal of central planning.	1	1, 2, 10, 17, 19, 22	3	3	491-493
2. Recognize that every economy is restricted by its production-possibilities curve and the choices that result.	6, 9, 20, 22	4	1	2	493
3. Recognize the very serious difficulties encountered in "planning" for large economies.	5, 8, 11, 13, 15, 21	3-6, 8, 9, 11, 13, 21	1		494-499
4. Recognize that every economy, no matter how it's organized, must answer the WHAT, HOW, and FOR WHOM questions.	9, 11, 13, 15	3, 9, 11, 13, 14, 20, 21, 24	1	2	494-499
5. Understand the roles that prices play in market and planned economies.	2-4, 8, 10, 14	7, 11, 12, 14, 16, 24	1, 3	1	496-499
6. Know what input-output analysis is and how it is used by planners.	12		2		496
7. Know the relative strengths and weaknesses of market and planned economies.	5, 7	11	2, 3		494-496
8. Understand that suppressed inflation is the symptom of even more serious underlying problems of planned economies.	16, 17, 19, 20	12, 23	1		503
9. Know that inconvertible currencies lead to inefficiency in the allocation of resources both domestically and internationally.	16, 18, 22, 23	18, 19			503-505
10. Understand that moving from centralized planning to markets as an allocating mechanism requires changes in both attitudes and institutions.	2, 3, 10, 18	15, 18	2, 3	3	507-510

Key-Term Review

Review the following terms; if you are not sure of the meaning of any term, write out the definition and check it against the Glossary in the text.

barter
capitalism
communism
comparative advantage
economic growth
hard currency
investment
involuntary saving

market economy
market mechanism
market shortage
production possibilities
profit
socialism
suppressed inflation

Fill in the blank following each of the statements below with the appropriate term from the list above.

1. An outward shift of the production-possibilities curve indicates that an economy can experience _____ .

   1. _____

2. To use markets to allocate resources requires a reliance on the _____ motive.

   2. _____

3. To _____ means to trade without using money as a medium of exchange.

   3. _____

4. The stage of the Marxist revolution in which resources are allocated by the state is called _____ .

   4. _____

5. The system of organization that relies on the market mechanism to allocate resources is called _____ .

   5. _____

6. Those economies that desire to grow more rapidly must devote substantial amounts of resources to _____ .

   6. _____

7. The final stage of the Marxist revolution is called _____ .

   7. _____

8. _____ occurs when consumers earn incomes but goods are not available for them to purchase.

   8. _____

9. The alternative combinations of final goods and services that could be produced in a given time period within the limits imposed by available resources and technology are called _____ .

   9. _____

10. In a _____ resources are largely allocated by the _____ .

   10. _____
   _____

11. A _____ of many goods and services at fixed prices is evidence of underlying _____ .

11. _____
    _____

12. A _____ is one which is generally acceptable as a means of payment in international trade.

12. _____

13. If resources are not allocated according to _____ , consumers are denied increased consumption possibilities.

13. _____

True or False: *Circle your choice.*

T F 1. The historical order of Marx's stages is (from first to last) . . . capitalism, socialism, communism.

T F 2. In planned economies, black-market prices are a better guide to the real cost of goods and services than are official prices.

T F 3. When the official price for goods and services is below the equilibrium price in a market, prices no longer perform their rationing function efficiently.

T F 4. The nonprice determinants of demand in planned economies are different from the nonprice determinants in market economies.

T F 5. In the planned economies of Eastern Europe unemployment was understated because a significant amount of underemployment existed.

T F 6. Both planned economies and market economies have limited production possibilities.

T F 7   Planned economies tend to experience low underemployment and high unemployment.

T F 8. The supply side of the market is not as responsive in planned economies as it is in market economies.

T F 9. In a fully employed economy, the oppurtunity cost of greater output of investment goods is measured in terms of output of other goods forgone.

T F 10. The basic function of prices in a centrally planned economy is to signal to producers that some products are relatively scarce and others are relatively plentiful.

T F 11. The efficiency of a market economy might be considered undesirable because of distributional effects when the markets determine prices.

T F 12. If the coal sector which is listed along the side of an input-output table has an input-output coefficient of 0.00216 in the column entitled "Automobiles," then the coefficient means that 0.216% of the value of a car is needed to produce a unit of coal.

T F 13. Income equality is greater in the United States than in the planned economies.

T F 14. In a planned economy prices can signal where resources should move, but they do not serve to ration consumer goods.

T F 15. In the former Soviet Union, the productivity of "worker-owned" land was significantly greater than the productivity of "state-owned" land.

T F 16. When suppressed inflation exists, the official rate of exchange undervalues the currency in foreign exchange markets.

T F 17. Because they were successful in suppressing inflation, the East Germans achieved high living standards.

T F 18. When currencies are not convertible, they cease to perform their medium-of-exchange function in the domestic economy.

T F 19. When limited availability of goods leads to involuntary saving, workers are encouraged to work harder.

T F 20. Shortages can be alleviated with imports, but importing requires that inflation be suppressed.

T F 21. Countries in transition from central planning to markets have been able to avoid inflation when controls on prices were removed.

T F 22. The ability of the Soviet Union to maintain living standards in the 1980s was damaged when prices for its exports fell.

T F 23. The abandonment of the official value of the zloty was an example of price reform.

Multiple Choice: *Select the correct answer.*

_____ 1. The motivating principle of the communism Marx envisioned would be:
 (a) Protection for the capitalist class because they are the ones who do the saving.
 (b) Private ownership of factors of production because this would provide an incentive to accumulate.
 (c) "From each according to his ability, to each according to his need."
 (d) Freedom in the pursuit of private economic gain.

_____ 2. The socialist state envisioned by Marx was similar to the mixed capitalism of today's developed countries:
 (a) In the existence of a guiding state.
 (b) In the ownership of the means of production.
 (c) In reliance on profit accumulation.
 (d) In distribution of goods according to each person's need.

_____ 3. It is likely that output per worker in the United States exceeds that in China because:
 (a) Chinese workers are lazy and American workers are not.
 (b) Chinese workers participate in a centralized economic system.
 (c) American workers have more capital to work with than do Chinese workers.
 (d) Chinese workers are not unionized.

_____ 4. Which of the following accounts for the decentralization observed in the Chinese planning process?
(a) The successful experience during the period of guerrilla warfare.
(b) The sheer size of the Chinese economy.
(c) The effectiveness of decentralization in helping workers identify with communal goals.
(d) All of the above.

_____ 5. Planned economies typically suffer from:
(a) Underemployment but not unemployment.
(b) Both unemployment and underemployment.
(c) Neither unemployment nor underemployment.
(d) Unemployment but not underemployment.

_____ 6. In both planned and market economies, increased capital formation requires:
(a) Lower interest rates.
(b) Increased saving.
(c) Increased consumption.
(d) Reduced business taxes.

_____ 7. Which of the following statements *best* describes the role(s) played by prices in a planned economy?
(a) Prices are used to ration final goods and services but not to allocate resources.
(b) Prices play the same role as in a market economy.
(c) Prices are used to allocate resources but not to ration final goods and services.
(d) None of the above statements is descriptive.

_____ 8. Which of the following economies was the most centralized during the twentieth century?
(a) The United States.
(b) The Soviet Union.
(c) The People's Republic of China.
(d) Yugoslavia.

_____ 9. Which of the following is *most* responsible for revolutions that lead to planned economies?
(a) The answer to the WHAT question.
(b) The answer to the HOW question.
(c) The answer to the FOR WHOM question.
(d) All of the above.

_____ 10. Historically, which of the following results in massive unemployment?
(a) The transition from capitalism to communism.
(b) The transition from socialism to capitalism.
(c) The transition from communism to capitalism.
(d) All of the above.

_____ 11. Which of the following statements justifies the rejection of the market mechanism by planned economies?
(a) If prices were used to allocate resources, planning goals would be jeopardized.
(b) If prices were used to allocate resources, capital-goods production would be reduced.
(c) If prices were used to allocate resources, income-distribution goals would be impaired.
(d) All of the above justify such a rejection.

_____ 12. Because of their pricing policies, socialist planners are likely to cause:
  (a) Involuntary saving.
  (b) Market surpluses because the prices of necessities are set below equilibrium.
  (c) Market shortages because prices of consumer goods are set above equilibrium.
  (d) Galloping inflation marked by rapidly rising prices.

_____ 13. When socialist central planning and the market mechanism are used side-by-side:
  (a) Material incentives cause resources to migrate toward the private sector away from the public sector.
  (b) Material incentives cause resources to migrate toward the public sector away from the private sector.
  (c) The systems are consistent and complementary to each other.
  (d) The system evolves into communism.

_____ 14. When a government sets an effective minimum price for a commodity:
  (a) Quantity supplied will be greater than the equilibrium quantity, price will be greater than the equilibrium price, and surpluses result.
  (b) Quantity supplied will be greater than the equilibrium quantity, price will be less than the equilibrium price, and shortages result.
  (c) Quantity supplied will be less than the equilibrium quantity, price will be greater than the equilibrium price, and surpluses result.
  (d) Quantity supplied will be less than the equilibrium quantity, price will be less than the equilibrium price, and shortages result.

_____ 15. Which of the following has been used as an incentive to increase worker productivity under the former Soviet Union?
  (a) Terror.
  (b) Income bonuses.
  (c) "Ownership" of small plots of land.
  (d) All of the above.

_____ 16. In the planned economies of Eastern Europe, prices of goods:
  (a) Were low relative to income, and living standards were low.
  (b) Were high relative to income, and living standards were high.
  (c) Were high relative to income, and living standards were low.
  (d) Were low relative to income, and living standards were high.

_____ 17. Which of the following groupings contains a term that does not belong?
  (a) Communism, capitalism, socialism.
  (b) Underemployment, unemployment, shortages.
  (c) *Perestroika*, deregulation, privatization.
  (d) Equity vs. efficiency, security vs. uncertainty, politics vs. economics.

_____ 18. When currencies are nonconvertible:
  (a) The official rate is determined in the black market.
  (b) The currency is not useful for trade in the domestic market.
  (c) Foreign suppliers often require hard currencies in payment for goods.
  (d) The official rate is determined by negotiations between governments.

_____ 19. Countries that use barter instead of currencies in international trade will:
  (a) Not be able to specialize in production to the extent they would if currencies were used.
  (b) Not be able to consume on their true consumption-possibilities curve.
  (c) Be forced to devote more resources to the arrangement of trade than if currencies were used.
  (d) All of the above.

_____ 20. A historical comparison of developed capitalist and communist economies would most likely indicate that the capitalist economy would experience:
  (a) Greater equality in income distribution and a higher standard of living.
  (b) Greater equality in income distribution and a lower standard of living.
  (c) Less equality in income distribution and a higher standard of living.
  (d) Less equality in income distribution and a lower standard of living.

_____ 21. In many transition economies, there is widespread unemployment because:
  (a) Shortages of resources are caused by price controls.
  (b) Inefficient factories would not be profitable.
  (c) With newly convertible currencies, barter eliminates consumption possibilities.
  (d) A shortage of workers is induced by underemployment.

_____ 22. Which of the following would violate the intent of _perestroika_?
  (a) Wage rates based on performance.
  (b) Factories, retaining "profit" to be used for bonuses.
  (c) A requirement that factories sell their output to the state.
  (d) None of the above.

_____ 23. At the time of German unification:
  (a) East Germans had significant amounts of personal savings.
  (b) East Germans feared unemployment and loss of security in the future.
  (c) East Germans were concerned that the West German currency was overvalued relative to their own.
  (d) All of the above.

_____ 24. One World View article in the text reports: "If one has the right item to trade, he can bypass some of the other exasperating and ubiquitous lines and the frequently empty shop shelves." On the basis of the quotation we may conclude that the FOR WHOM question is being solved by:
  (a) Barter.
  (b) Long lines.
  (c) Involuntary saving.
  (d) All of the above.

Problems and Applications

Exercise 1

The production-possibilities curve for a planned economy is shown in Figure 22.1. Assume that the economy is operating at point A. Suppose the planners decide that the society must increase its production of defense goods from the amount indicated by D_1 to the amount indicated by D_2.

Figure 22.1
Production possibilities

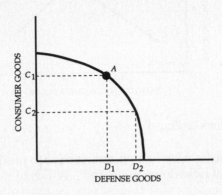

Production possibilities and opportunities

1. The opportunity cost of increasing the output of defense goods from D_1 to D_2 is:
   (a) Zero, since there are unemployed resources in the economy.
   (b) $0C_2$ of consumer goods.
   (c) $0C_1$ of consumer goods.
   (d) C_1C_2 of consumer goods.

2. To get the workers to switch from the production of consumer goods to the production of defense goods, the planners will be most surely successful if they:
   (a) Raise the wages of workers who produce defense goods.
   (b) Lower the wages of workers who produce consumer goods.
   (c) Raise the wages of workers who produce defense goods relative to those of workers who produce consumer goods.
   (d) Raise the wages of workers who produce consumer goods relative to those of workers who produce defense goods.

3. If more defense goods are to be produced, resources will have to be taken away from consumer goods, and consumers will have fewer consumer goods to purchase. Suppose the demand and supply of consumer goods are as indicated in Figure 22.2. The equilibrium price-quantity combination is:
   (a) P_2, C_1.
   (b) P_1, C_1.
   (c) P_2, C_2.
   (d) P_3, C_2.

Figure 22.2
Supply and demand for consumer goods

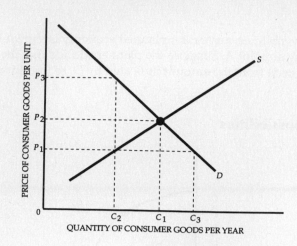

Taxes and price limitations (ceilings)

4. To prevent producers from having an incentive to produce too many consumer goods, the planners might hold down prices to P_3. Which of the following results would you expect?
   (a) Excess inventories.
   (b) Excess profits.
   (c) Long queues of people waiting to buy.
   (d) All of the above.

5. When the planners cut production from C_1 to C_2, the result is a:
   (a) Surplus at prices below P_1.
   (b) Shortage at prices below P_2.
   (c) New equilibrium at P_3, C_2.
   (d) None of the above.

6. To get consumers to restrain their consumption to output C_2, the planners could levy a tax equal to the distance:
   (a) $0P_3$.
   (b) $0P_1$.
   (c) P_2, P_3.
   (d) P_1, P_2.

Subsidies, price supports, and floors

7. Suppose the government wishes to control diseases by making more medical services available. Figure 22.3 shows the demand and supply curves for medical services. The equilibrium price-quantity is:
   (a) P_1, M_1.
   (b) P_2, M_2.
   (c) P_3, M_3.
   (d) P_1, M_3.

424

Figure 22.3
Supply and demand of medical services

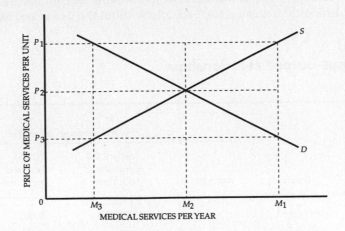

8. Suppose the government wants M_1 of medical services produced. If the government sets a price like P_1 so that the desired quantity of medical services would be supplied, you would expect:
   (a) Underemployment of medical personnel.
   (b) Shortages of medical services.
   (c) Improvements in health to the degree that the government targets.
   (d) All of the above.

9. In order to encourage fuller use of the services available at M_1, the government could introduce a subsidy per unit of medical service of:
   (a) P_1, P_3.
   (b) M_3, M_1.
   (c) P_2, P_3.
   (d) P_1, P_2.

10. If the government wanted M_1 of medical services to be offered, wanted to subsidize no one, and wanted to keep the price at P_3, it would have to build medical facilities to provide:
    (a) M_3, M_1 of medical services.
    (b) $0M_1$ of medical services.
    (c) $0M_2$ of medical services.
    (d) $0M_3$ of medical services.

11. At the price of P_3, private medical practices would provide:
    (a) M_3, M_1 of medical services.
    (b) $0M_1$ of medical services.
    (c) $0M_2$ of medical services.
    (d) $0M_3$ of medical services.

    (*Hint:* The supply curve reflects what would be provided in the private market.)

Exercise 2

This exercise should give you an idea of how to use input-output analysis. It should also give you an idea of how difficult it is to allocate resources without the use of prices.

Table 22.1
Soviet input-output relationships

(1)	(2)	(3)	(4)	(5)	(6)
			Input requirement per unit of:		
Sector number	*Inputs*	*Automobiles*	*Tractors and agricultural machinery*	*Bread, flour, and confections*	*Electric and thermal power*
1	Specialized M & E	0	0.00004	0.00054	0
2	Fish products	0	0	0.00040	0
3	Sugar	0.00000	0.00006	0.05334	0.00000

Source: U.S. Congress, *Soviet Economic Prospects for the Seventies: A Compendium of Papers Submitted to the Joint Economic Committee, June 27, 1973* (Washington, D.C.: U.S. Government Printing Office, 1973)

1. You are a planner faced with the Soviet input-output relationships shown in Table 22.1 on page 497 in the text and Table 22.1 above. You are responsible for ensuring that the bread, flour, and confections industry (column 5 in Table 22.1) has all of the required inputs needed to produce 100,000 rubles of bread, flour, and confections. You succeed in obtaining all of the necessary requirements except those produced by three industries. Table 22.2 shows the amounts (column 2) of the various requirements in these three industries that you are able to obtain. In column 3 of Table 22.2 write the input-output coefficients for each of these sectors (use Table 22.1 above).

2. You should be able to calculate the amounts of the three requirements in Table 22.2 that you would need to produce 100,000 rubles of bread, flour, and confectionery goods. Place these amounts in column 4 of Table 22.2. (*Hint:* The coefficients in column 3 tell the fraction of the total cost of bread, flour, and confectionery goods that goes into each input.)

Table 22.2
Shortfall for requirements in three industries to produce bread, flour, and confections

(1)	(2)	(3)	(4)	(5)	(6)
Industry	*Amount obtained (rubles)*	*Input-output coefficient*	*Amount (rubles) needed to produce 100,000 rubles of output 100,000 x (3)*	*Fraction of target that can be met (2) ÷ (4)*	*Maximum production possible given input available 100,000 x (5)*
Specialized M & E (sector 1)	45.0	_____	_____	_____	_____
Fish products (sector 2)	30.0	_____	_____	_____	_____
Sugar (sector 3)	533.4	_____	_____	_____	_____

3. You are now ready to find the percentage of bread, flour, and confectionery goods you can make with the available inputs that you have. In column 5 of Table 22.2 you can compute the ratio of what you have available of each input to the amount needed to reach your target of 100,000 rubles of bread, flour, and confection output. This same ratio tells the fraction of your 100,000-ruble production target that you will be able to produce. Compute this maximum production in column 6, Table 22.2.

4. Which input causes the production of bread, flour, and confectionery goods to be the lowest?
   (a) Specialized M & E.
   (b) Fish products.
   (c) Sugar.

5. Assuming that production can be increased only if you have enough of each input and that production can be expanded only in proportion to the available inputs, the maximum output of bread, flour, and confectionery goods that can be produced with available inputs is:
   (a) 1,000 rubles.
   (b) 10,000 rubles.
   (c) 100,000 rubles.
   (d) 90,000 rubles.
   (e) 83,333 rubles.
   (f) 75,000 rubles.

6. Since you are able to meet only one-tenth of your target for bread, flour, and confectionery products, you will have (surpluses, shortages) of all of the inputs to these products except sugar.

7. For each of the commodities in Table 22.3, compute the amount of surplus you have of each of the listed inputs as a result of your inability to use them. The input-output coefficients are from Table 22.1 on page 497 in the text. Since you had enough of each of these inputs to produce 100,000 rubles of bread, flour, and confectionery goods, you can assume that column 3 in Table 22.3 represents the amount of each input you were allocated. (*Hint:* Find the input coefficient and then compute the amount of factor needed as you did in Table 22.2.) Since you can use only 10 percent of the factors you were allocated, because of the sugar shortages, your surplus will be 90 percent (column 4) of what you were allocated (column 3).

Table 22.3
Excess inputs as a result of sugar shortage

(1) Input	(2) Input-output coefficient for bread, flour, and confections. (See Table 22.1 in the text.)	(3) Amount (rubles) needed to produce 100,000 rubles of output	(4) Amount unused 0.9 x (3)
Coal (sector 5)	_____	_____	_____
Electric and thermal power (sector 9)	_____	_____	_____

8. You are also the planner for automobile production. You have to produce 1 million rubles of output of automobiles. If you fail you will go to Siberia. You receive the allocation that you need from all sectors except for the two shown in Table 22.4. Complete Table 22.4 as you did Table 22.2 of this study guide, this time using the automobile column (column 1) in Table 22.1 on page 497 of the text to find the input-output coefficients.

Table 22.4
Shortfall of requirements to produce one million rubles of automobiles

(1) Input	(2) Amount obtained (rubles)	(3) Input-output coefficient	(4) Amount (rubles) needed to produce 1 million rubles of output 1,000,000 x (3)	(5) Fraction of target that can be met (2) ÷ (4)	(6) Maximum production possible given available inputs 1,000,000 x (5)
Coal (sector 5)	1,945.8	_____	_____	_____	_____
Electric and thermal power (sector 9)	11,592.9	_____	_____	_____	_____

9. How would you be able to reach your automobile target?
   (a) Transfer bread, flour, and confectionery products to the automobile industry.
   (b) Transfer cars to the bread, flour, and confectionery industry.
   (c) Transfer sugar, fish products, and specialized M & E to the automobile industry.
   (d) Transfer coal and electric and thermal power from the automobile industry to the bread, flour, and confectionery industry.
   (e) Transfer coal and electric and thermal power from the bread, flour, and confectionery industry to the automobile industry.

10. How much more coal (in rubles) does the automobile industry need from the bread, flour, and confectionery industry in order to reach its target without any waste?
    (a) 1,171 rubles.
    (b) 214.2 rubles.
    (c) 117.1 rubles.
    (d) 2,160 rubles.

11. Are there still surpluses of inputs for some industry after the automobile target is reached? _____

Exercise 3

This exercise will use one of the articles in the text to show the kind of information to look for to identify the type of economic system used in another country. If your professor makes a newspaper assignment for this chapter from the *Instructor's Manual*, this exercise will provide an example of how to do it.

Reread the World View article "China Striving to Rebuild Socialist Ideals" on page 472 in Chapter 22 from the *Washington Post*.

1. What country is involved?

2. Where is the country first mentioned in the article?

3. How would you classify the way the economy of this country has been organized in the past? (circle one)

   Communism   Socialism   Mixed economy   Free market

4. What passage is consistent with the way you have classified the past economy?

5. What passage indicates an example of the way the economy is changing to a new economic structure (for example, from communism to capitalism)?

6. How would you classify the direction toward which the economy of this country is moving? (circle one)

   | Toward communism | Toward socialism | Toward a mixed economy | Toward a free market |

7. What passage is consistent with the way you have classified the direction toward which the economy is moving?

Common Errors

The first statement in each "common error" below is incorrect. Each incorrect statement is followed by a corrected version and an explanation.

1. Prices serve no function in a planned economy. WRONG!

   Prices are used to allocate resources and goods in accordance with central plans. RIGHT!

   In planned economies prices are not allowed to perform the same functions as in a market economy. Prices do not generally provide the signal for resources to move (their allocation function), but they do perform the rationing function. Luxury goods have high prices, and necessities carry lower price tags.

2. The average city dweller in China subsists on an income of approximately $340 per year. WRONG!

   The average Chinese city dweller is at about the U.S. poverty line. RIGHT!

   This "common error" points up the difficulty of making comparisons of living standards across international boundaries. Simple dollar comparisons gloss over the radical differences in economic organization. Some of the things that carry high price tags in the United States, such as medical services, carry low price tags in China. Housing is another example. Many services that are provided without charge by the state in China must be paid for by the consumer in the United States. Such differences create significant distortions, so simple comparisons are very misleading. After adjustments, it appears that the average Chinese city dweller has an income roughly equivalent to that at the U.S. poverty line.

3. Capitalism is a system characterized by democracy. WRONG!

   Capitalism is an economic system in which individuals own the factors of production and use the market mechanism. RIGHT!

Do not confuse the classification of political systems with the classification of economic systems. It is conceivable—even if not historically common—for tyrannies to practice capitalism and democracies to practice communism. An economic system focuses on the ownership of the means of production and the mechanism by which goods are exchanged. A political system focuses on the issue of collective decision making.

•ANSWERS•

Key-Term Review

1. economic growth
2. profit
3. barter
4. socialism
5. capitalism
6. investment
7. communism
8. involuntary saving
9. production possibilities
10. market economy
    market mechanism
11. market shortage
    suppressed inflation
12. hard currency
13. comparative advantage

True or False

1. T	5. T	9. T	13. F	17. F	21. F
2. T	6. T	10. F	14. F	18. F	22. T
3. T	7. F	11. T	15. T	19. F	23. F
4. F	8. T	12. F	16. F	20. F	

Multiple Choice

1. c	4. d	7. a	10. d	13. a	15. d
2. a	5. a	8. b	11. d	14. a	16. c
3. c	6. b	9. c	12. a		

17. b Shortages are not a form of surplus labor. Topics of other groupings are (a) methods of owning, organizing, and controlling resources, (c) factors involved in retreating from a command structure for the economy, and (d) major tradeoffs faced in an economic system.

18. c	20. c	21. b	22. c	23. d	24. d
19. d					

Problems and Applications

Exercise 1

1. d   3. b   5. b   7. b   9. a   11. d
2. c   4. c   6. c   8. a   10. a

Exercise 2

1.-3. **Table 22.2 Answer**

(1) Industry	(2) Amount obtained	(3) Input-output coefficient	(4) Amount needed	(5) Fraction of target	(6) Maximum production
Specialized M & E	45.0	0.00054	54	5/6	83,333
Fish products	30.0	0.00040	40	3/4	75,000
Sugar	533.4	0.05334	5,334	1/10	10,000

4. c

5. b

6. surpluses

7. **Table 22.3 Answer**

(1) Input	(2) Input-output coefficient	(3) Amount needed	(4) Amount unused
Coal	0.00238	238	214.2
Electric and thermal power	0.00284	284	255.6

8. **Table 22.4 Answer**

(1) Input	(2) Amount obtained	(3) Input-output coefficient	(4) Amount needed	(5) Fraction of target	(6) Maximum production
Coal	1,945.8	0.00216	2,160	0.9008	900,800
Electric and thermal power	11,592.9	0.01171	11,710	0.9900	990,000

9. e   10. b   11. yes

Exercise 3

1. China

2. first word of the title

3. Communism or socialism would be appropriate. Neither of the other two would be characterized by a centralized economy.

4. "with reforms designed to free up part of China's centralized economy." Centralized decision making is typical of communist systems of organizing an economy.

5. The passage "where a money-first mentality has burgeoned along with reforms designed to free up part of China's centralized economy" indicates there is rapid change toward decentralizing the economy and increasing material incentives, which is more typical in a capitalist economy.

6. Toward a mixed economy. The article shows there is backlash against some of the manifestations of capitalism. A mixed economy is a good guess about where the economy is headed.

7. "People in China these days are looking too much to money" indicates a characteristic of capitalist economies or mixed economies with a substantial capitalist sector.